EGO AND SELF
IN WEEKLY PSYCHOTHERAPY

EGO AND SELF
IN
WEEKLY
PSYCHOTHERAPY

Gene Bocknek

INTERNATIONAL UNIVERSITIES PRESS, INC.
Madison   Connecticut

Library of Congress Cataloging in Publication Data

Bocknek. Gene.
  Ego and self in weekly psychotherapy / Gene Bocknek.
    p. cm
  Includes bibliographical references.
  Includes index.
  ISBN 0-8236-1545-6
  1. Ego (Psychology) 2. Self. 3. Objects relations
(Psychoanalysis) 4. Psychotherapy. I. Title.
  [DNLM: 1. Ego. 2. Objective Attachment. 3. Psychoanalytic
Therapy. 4. Self. WM 460.5.E3 B665e]
RC489.E35B63 1991
616.89′ 14—dc20
DNLM/DLC
for Library of Congress   90-4923
                                                                    CIP

Manufactured in the United States of America

TABLE OF CONTENTS

PREFACE

Despite the predominance of therapists who loosely identify themselves as "dynamically oriented," and even though once-a-week therapy is the most usual form of practice, very little of the literature addresses those factors which are distinctive about weekly contact. Yet, because so much of psychoanalytically oriented technique is based on the psychodynamics inherent in an intensive contact therapy situation, the implications for weekly contact need clarification.

How does one discuss psychoanalytic psychotherapy without laying primary emphasis on transference, interpretation, resistance, and other traditional ingredients of the process? What happens to these dynamic issues when the patient is seen only once a week? As every therapist discovers, except for the most labile and the most psychologically sophisticated patients, weekly contact grossly attenuates the emergence of significant psychogenetic material. The spontaneous flow of associations and fantasies is inhibited, and resistances magnified, by the long interval between sessions. For many patients, the abstinent silence of traditional therapists is irksome and unacceptable without the support of frequent meetings to bring to the surface the unconscious significance of the issues being raised. Small wonder that weekly therapy conducted from a psychoanalytic perspective has been short term, supportive, or difficult to sustain with many populations.

I am one of the myriad therapists who has grappled with this practical problem. Like most of my colleagues I have found practical ways of contending with the difficulties encountered, developing my version of a "less-than-the-best" accommodation to the inevitable reality of patients who could not or would not come for therapy more frequently than once a week. But I may have had a particular advantage by reason of my other role, that of training graduate students in professional psychology. The probing questions of my students continually confronted me with the discrepancies between theoretical nicety and clinical reality. I was forced to examine the inconsistencies, and to ask myself what I was actually doing with patients. For a time I assumed I had simply forsaken the psychoanalytic orientation I had been trained in, in favor of some nonspecific psychodynamic eclecticism. Colleagues with whom I spoke were equally vague. We readily concurred that seeing patients even twice weekly helped the therapy, but rarely did we venture into how we modified our practice to accommodate to the reality that over the years more and more patients demanded weekly therapy.

With the introduction of developmental and relational theory into psychoanalysis I became clearer on some of my own thinking. But until I recognized that the requirements of weekly contact also structured my therapy, the central insight continued to elude me. When I came to that last point I also realized that there was, indeed, room for another book on psychotherapy.

My generation of practitioners has benefited from witnessing the virtual birth and development of psychotherapy. We inherited the writings of the first psychoanalysts, and were in training ourselves when people like Alexander and French, Deutsch and Murphy, Edward Bibring and Dewald, were systematically extending psychoanalysis into psychotherapy. We matured into an increasingly diverse professional world of mental health, confounded with a polarity of competing theories such as those of Carl Rogers, Fritz Perls, and the behaviorist group. While these approaches had glaring theoretical limitations, their differing techniques were bound to challenge young professionals eager to meet the urgent needs of emotionally troubled people. An important feature of these competing approaches was their origin outside the medical hegemony. It would be of interest to trace the effect of world events upon the evolution of psychotherapy as a discipline. On a more individual level, however, it was clear to me and to my professional peers that psychotherapy was an imperfectly understood process, despite whatever successes we achieved.

With more time and experience, similarities as well as differences between therapies have surfaced. Most importantly, as psychoanalysis has matured, its explanatory power has increased. The clinical utility of specific techniques in other therapies can often be better accounted for by constructs in drive theory, object relations theory, self psychology, or ego psychology. As the conceptual umbrella which most parsimoniously incorporates the widest array of normal and clinical findings, psychoanalysis is without peer. And as we continue to explore our own divergencies, compatibility and synthesis become more feasible.

In the course of reaching an understanding of how weekly psychotherapy works in a psychoanalytic framework, it seems evident that there are genuine lines of convergence which, at least for me, override the areas of disagreement among the several psychoanalytic splinter groups. Indeed, I suspect that only by adopting an integrated perspective was it possible to forge a psychoanalytically derived approach to once-a-week therapy. In turn, I hope that this book will advance one more step those efforts to create a comprehensive theory of therapy which is congruent with an equally comprehensive theory of personality growth and development.

A number of colleagues and students have helped me to clarify the issues I was grappling with in the early stages of this work. Doris Held was a compassionate but firm critic. Steve Davidson and Earl Ireland had the dubious pleasure of reversing the advisory role with me. Numerous others challenged me with their questions and observations, in my doctoral proseminar at Boston University. The critical feedback and encouragement from Judy Pierson, Joe Rabinovitz, Aurelie Goodwin, Jack Darbyshire, Monica Roizner, Jan Park, Roxy Van De Water, Cary Gearhart, and Elizabeth Hubert were valued. Other professional friends contributed. Arnold Miller was supportive and specific with useful suggestions. Jon Ehrenworth and Max Schleiffer read substantial sections of the manuscript and offered their comments. At later stages of the manuscript I received invaluable feedback from Chris Schlauch and Jim Barberia. Access to Chester Pearlman's private library saved me large amounts of time. And it would be impossible to write a book on psychotherapy without the tacit contribution of so many patients—both mine and those of other practitioners—whose pain and perseverance are the ultimate arbiters of innovation. Respect for their integrity mandated that I take great care to insure the anonymity of those patients. While I have preserved the clinical essence of their case material in the book, I have freely changed their names, locations, occupations, and the identity of their therapists. I have also condensed interview material, in the interest of space economy. As a result, some of the illustrative material may be more focused, or intense, than might naturally have occurred in the ordinary course of a therapy session.

The encouragement of family and friends is something I would like to acknowledge. My wife, Judy, is my intellectual partner as well as an inestimable source of emotional support. Her contribution is unique and enduring. The editorial staff at International Universities Press blended keen eyes with professional sensitivity to sharpen and shape the basic manuscript into its final form. And thanks to my redoubtable word processor, which has converted the labors of writing into a special pleasure.

The sabbatical tradition and general support of research in academia were absolutely essential to the completion of this work. Reflective thought cannot be scheduled into an appointment book, between patients or classes. It must have a larger realm of flow, be recognized, accommodated, and supported as a necessary component of one's workload. That sort of thinking does not always register well in an environment where the bottom line is preeminent. But the advancement of a profession depends upon an appreciation that teaching and research unaccompanied by ongoing practice is devoid of its most essential ingredients. As with therapy, if learning is not imbued with experience one may legitimately question whether it has occurred in any real sense.

CHAPTER 1

AN OVERVIEW OF WEEKLY PSYCHOTHERAPY

The majority of psychotherapeutic practice today is conducted on a weekly basis. Most people cannot afford, or will not invest, the time, effort, and money required by intensive psychoanalytically oriented psychotherapy. Other factors also complicate the situation. The proliferation of therapists and therapies in contemporary life, most of whom willingly offer weekly psychotherapy, and the spreading influence of cost-driven third-party carriers further limit the opportunity to institute intensive psychotherapy. Finally, the public has been disabused of the idyllic fantasies that psychoanalysis once evoked, of "permanent cure" and "total personality reorganization." Do these events presage the demise of reconstructive psychotherapy? Will the insights of modern psychoanalytic theory become inaccessible to all but a tiny fraction of emotionally disordered people? For many psychoanalytically oriented practitioners the canons of sound therapeutic practice and the exigencies of the marketplace pose a serious conflict.

At the same time, recent advances in psychoanalytic theory are providing opportunities for development in therapeutic technique that could resolve the apparent conflict. The emerging synthesis of object relations theory and self psychology with ego psychology opens a doorway to intervention strategies that expand the role of weekly psychotherapy. It is no longer necessary to restrict individual therapy to time-limited, expressive (usually intensive), or supportive (usually weekly) activities. By

1

selectively addressing the organization and function of intra-psychic processes, weekly psychotherapy can yield structural change by enhancing ego operations, repairing pathological formations, and recruiting newly available resources.

If we recall that Freud (1949) expected psychoanalysis to be a research technique rather than a prominent treatment approach, few of us need be surprised by the primacy of psychotherapy in clinical practice. Nevertheless, orienting oneself to a weekly psychotherapy practice is no simple matter. Weekly therapy does more than dilute the frequency of therapy; it affects some of the foremost elements of the treatment. Compared with three to five weekly sessions of psychoanalysis, once-a-week contact does not have an impact on daily life of nearly the same intensity, so that the realistic demands of everyday life impede psychoanalytic focus on fantasies and associations. The leisure to interpret a dream over successive sessions evaporates when seven days intervene between sessions. Conversely, events of present-day life assume greater importance in what the patient brings to therapy. Similarly, transference occupies a different place in weekly therapy. Instead of being the primary affective experience, other affective experiences must also be mobilized for therapeutic intervention. Weekly face-to-face contact elicits other kinds of relationship in addition to transference material. Reliance on therapy, and the amount of regression encouraged, are also markedly affected. Put in another perspective, patients' higher levels of function, their developmental attainments, must be monitored and mobilized more systematically on behalf of the therapeutic effort.

If it seems paradoxical to speak of a psychoanalytic approach to once-a-week therapy, having already acknowledged the severe constraints this imposes on the role of certain procedures, it is essential to distinguish between that body of knowledge which is a theory of personality operations, that which is a theory of therapy, and that which refers explicitly to clinical technique. So deeply immersed are some practitioners in all three areas that the boundaries can sometimes be blurred. While interpretation, free association, genetic reconstruction, transference, and countertransference are useful clinical constructs, they are not inherently essential elements of a psychoanalytic theory of personality or therapy. As clinical events, however, they are probably essential elements of a successful psychoanalysis. By contrast, the objectives of reorganizing personality structure and enhancing personality function are fundamental tenets of a psychoanalytic therapy, as are theory and technique. A vital concern for intrapsychic process and development is fundamental to psychoanalysis as a personality theory as well as a therapy technique.

This book offers a conceptual synthesis of modern psychoanalytic thought, emphasizing the contributions of ego, self, and object relations theories. The product of this synthesis is referred to as egoself theory. Its clinical utility can be measured by its value in building a psychoanalytically oriented weekly psychotherapy. Egoself theory and therapy speaks to the task of restructuring personality operations in the context of weekly therapy sessions. More specifically, egoself therapy addresses goals such as restructuring of self and object representations, enhancing differentiation and utilization of ego operations, and promoting integration of the autonomous functions with other intrapsychic processes.

Egoself therapy has evolved as a useful approach in my own practice over the past dozen years. On the theoretical plane this synthesis works toward resolving some of the fractious disputes concerning the relationship between ego, self, and object relations. It also accords well with independent findings in developmental and personality psychology, thus bringing modern psychoanalytic thought into closer harmony with other scientific data. As the name *egoself* suggests, the evolution and operation of personality is viewed organismically. Ego and self describe aspects of intrapsychic structure and function, different facets of an interactive whole. Object relations theory accounts for the selective, unique manner in which each person creates pattern and meaning, beginning with its earliest experience. This conceptual base of egoself theory is found in chapter 8.

By emphasizing structural processes, egoself therapy can suggest intervention strategies that yield structural personality change with weekly psychotherapy. At times these changes can occur when least expected.

Mr. A was a burly construction foreman, white, in his early forties. His abusive outbursts toward women threatened to destroy his most recent relationship. He was referred by his closest friend, who had been treated by the same therapist. Nevertheless, on entering the office Mr. A was overtly suspicious, belligerent, and defensive. He asked if there were recording devices hidden and expressed his doubts about coming to see "a head doctor." The oldest child of an alcoholic father and clingingly dependent mother, Mr. A's earliest memories were of shopping for his mother, taking care of his younger sister and brother, and being chased and beaten by other boys in the neighborhood. A period of rapid physical growth prior to puberty enabled him to dominate his peers physically. Prowess in fighting bolstered his shaky self structure and gave him a sense of manliness. He quit school and went to work, where his size and strength won him respect and financial security. At nineteen he impregnated and married the first woman he slept with. The life pattern that evolved consisted of excessive drinking and smoking, barroom fights, sexual promiscuity, and verbal and physical abuse of his wife. At work he was shrewd, tough, and resourceful, proving himself to be an effective worker and foreman. Three years earlier he had met and fallen in love with his neighbor's wife. She left her husband, he divorced his wife, and they began a clandestine affair. As the relationship intensified he found himself becoming uncontrollably angry with his new love, cursing and threatening her. Unwilling to accept this abuse, the woman insisted he get therapy or she would refuse to see him. During the first interviews Mr. A presented as agitated and irritable, speaking of fears of being alone, feeling depressed, and sucking his thumb to ease his emotional pain. He had fantasies of cutting off his tongue as a way of stopping his abusive outbursts. Suicidal ideation was denied. Mr. A's primitivity, early history, and fragile defensive structure were indicative of severe borderline pathology, complicated by alcoholism and autistic thought processes.

Mr. A reluctantly agreed to regular weekly meetings and angrily rejected the recommendation that he be seen twice weekly. After a few months, Mr. A terminated treatment. In a belated letter accompanying his last payment, Mr. A said he no longer needed treatment. One of the later therapy sessions had explored in close detail the intrapsychic events surrounding an explosive episode, locating the time at which Mr. A first became aware of angry affect. At that time he suppressed his feelings, telling himself it was too trivial to bother with. The therapist pointed out that Mr. A was still in control of his feelings at the time, and that "saying something to let off steam" could avert an angry episode later on.

In a follow-up telephone interview three years later Mr. A revealed he had married his woman friend. He reported that his drinking had moderated, brawling ceased, and the abusive outbursts were extremely rare, statements confirmed by his wife. Mr. A attributed the changes to a lack of external pressures on him, "Now I've got nothing to get upset about"; but a few sentences later said, "I get things out before they build up." Apparently the progress he has made was disassociated from any understanding that timely verbalization of affect could promote impulse management. In evaluating that progress it would be naive to assume that extensive ego restructuring occurred in so few weekly therapy sessions. But the nature and duration of the reported change—recognizing and intercepting his incipient rage, converting the impulse into signal anxiety, and then mobilizing ego functions for verbalization and catharsis—indicate that in a limited area of ego operation, intervention had resulted in structural change.

The details of weekly therapeutic procedure will be described in a later chapter. In the present context it is notable that the therapeutic strategy was a direct application of recruiting or building ego functions on behalf of the patient's self structure and ego operations. Despite the patient's overall primitivity, and evidence of dysfunctional early enmeshment with mother, weekly therapy helped him to differentiate early and current object cathexes, activating latent ego competencies in that effort.

In deference to the pragmatic needs of practicing therapists, this book is organized to present clinical aspects first, followed by their theoretical underpinning. Psychoanalytically oriented readers need no reminder of the vital role of theory to inform practice, but also know that theory must always be responsive to the mandates of experience. The history of psychoanalytic psychotherapy, reviewed in chapter 2, reveals two trends: in one, psychotherapy is practiced as a modified form of psychoanalysis; in the other, there is more acknowledgment of the differences between analysis and therapy. This volume takes the second path, building upon the initiatives already created for a weekly psychotherapy firmly rooted in psychoanalytic theory. By contrast, the first path imposes several preconditions—intensive transference, observing ego, psychological mindedness, and the capacity for insight (Paolino, 1981)—which are not required in this approach.

An overall clinical sense of weekly egoself therapy can be gained from chapter 3, which is devoted to the therapeutic management of a number of issues, such as medication, lateness, fee contracting, termination, and the assumptions and attitudes underlying these strategies. Chapter 4 probes the therapeutic process itself, laying out in considerable detail techniques and procedures in egoself intervention strategy. Chapter 5 covers an essential feature of weekly psychotherapy: the forms of therapeutic relationship that evolve, and their differential impact on the ongoing work, particularly in the context of weekly contact. The concept of a therapeutic partnership clarifies the experiential and developmental aspects of egoself therapy as these are arrayed with other forms of encounter between therapist and patient.

Assessment plays a major role in weekly egoself therapy. Along with the familiar assessment of pathology is an examination of healthy ego and self operations. In addition, developmental assessment often yields clues to prepotent resources which may be available for therapeutic recruitment and mobilization. What constitutes average expectable development of a young adult? When does the capacity for insight develop? Skilled clinicians intuitively adapt their approach to the life stage of the patient. But making explicit the expectable features of each life stage brings those clinical resources and risks into more systematic therapeutic access.

The post-Freudian period began with the advent of ego psychology, and now incorporates the findings of object relations theory and self psychology. These three units are often described and studied in relative isolation from one another, each having acquired its own adherents. As they are assimilated into modern psychoanalytic literature, it becomes more apparent that object relations, ego, and self are functionally interrelated aspects of intrapsychic structure. Each construct extends further the general understanding of psychodynamic operations and directs us toward more precise applications of therapeutic technique. Chapter 8 describes the interconnection between ego, self, and object relations. It examines the implications of ego psychology for an understanding of basic functions and their organization. Object relations theory establishes psychoanalysis in a developmental framework and accounts for processes of growth and pathology found in self and ego. Self psychology fills a conceptual gap in psychoanalytic personality theory by describing its experiential aspects, and connecting that to the role of narcissism. While theory development in psychoanalysis is far from complete, these worthy additions have powerful implications for therapeutic application, particularly with reference to ego building and self structuring.

Chapter 9 introduces an area with which there is less familiarity, the contribution of developmental psychology. Object relations theory teaches that structure and meaning are products of developmental experience. Basic tenets underlying developmental assessment are reviewed, and constructs such as resistance are reexamined in the light of contemporary findings. The book concludes with a chapter reflecting on egoself theory and therapy: the premises underlying its usage and the understanding that has evolved regarding the nature of therapeutic change.

The egoself approach views object relations as the key to understanding the evolution of growth and pathology. Ego and self are fundamental aspects of personality, systems which are qualitatively different from each other yet functionally and structurally interrelated. Both serve organismic needs for organization and growth; ego is the system of functions which organizes processes, patterns, and competencies; self is concerned with cohesion, self-esteem, making meaning out of experience. Their operation is complementary and mutually interdependent. Both are rooted in object relations, in the evolving patterns of self and object representations, the means by which experience is internalized to build intrapsychic structure (McDevitt, 1979). Thus, therapeutic interventions directed at self and object representations also augment self structuring, help clarify the patient's beliefs, and, often, strengthen certain ego functions. Conversely, interventions which strengthen ego operations can have a beneficial impact on narcissistic investment. By virtue of operating from a coherent theoretical base the psychoanalytic psychotherapist gains an effective, comprehensive means of assessing, intervening, and evaluating the therapeutic work.

Weekly egoself psychotherapy is designed to redress structural pathology encountered in ego, self, and object relations. Although it has also been applied to intensive psychoanalytic psychotherapy, this approach is specifically appropriate to the demands of weekly contact. Throughout the therapy, an awareness of the parameters of weekly contact exerts a continuing influence on how psychoanalytic theory is translated into technique. In the handling of transference material, for example, readers will see the influence of Malan (1980) or Strupp and Binder (1984) more than that of, say, Mann (1973) or Dewald (1964). Helping clients restructure self and object representations experientially may be similar to Kohut's "transmuting internalizations" compared to more classically derived concepts of therapeutic abstinence or neutrality. Recent literature on transference (Blanck and Blanck, 1974, 1979, 1986; Paolino, 1981; Gill and Hoffman, 1982; Strupp and Binder, 1984) reflects a more inclusive definition of that process, with corresponding changes in how it is used in therapy.

For some psychoanalytic practitioners, psychotherapy not predicated upon transference analysis is not psychoanalytic therapy. When such transgressions are compounded with less attention to classical psychodynamic conflicts and a readiness to treat clients weekly, these practitioners perceive a cherished tradition being stripped of its most familiar features, and reject the change as a distortion of psychoanalytic therapy. But what "remains" is not an eviscerated psychoanalysis. Rather, it is a therapy which acknowledges that while the *practice* of psychoanalysis is greatly limited in weekly contact, psychoanalytic *theory* continues to have powerful application. Weekly egoself therapy is solidly based in modern psychoanalytic theory, consistent with the historical evolution of psychoanalytic therapy, and applies techniques utilized by outstanding psychoanalytic practitioners. If certain aspects seem unfamiliar, it is the necessary result of adapting technique to the clinical realities of weekly frequency. At the heart of this approach is a recognition of what experience permits and the times require: a spectrum of psychotherapeutic modalities that can be provided by the community of modern psychoanalytically oriented practitioners.

Significant progress inevitably entails a transitional period of skepticism and resistance. The history of the psychoanalytic movement overflows with such examples, dating back to its earliest period. But the ongoing viability of the psychoanalytic tradition is also due to that same willingness to undergo reexamination and appropriate modification. The alternative, dogmatism reified, is the enemy of scientific advance.

EGO AND SELF

The interaction between ego, self, and experience is fundamental to contemporary psychoanalytic theory and practice. From the first dyadic contacts onward, personal experience is transformed into structure and meaning. Object relations, the intrapsychic processing of experience, is among the earliest ego functions, and ego structure develops from the pacing of object relations with other emerging functions (Spitz, 1959). Simultaneously these experiences provide a basis for the organization and content of the self. The developing organization of ego and self give rise to the patterns that respectively define structural properties and create meaning for the evolving human being. Self and ego, therefore, are complementary systems for organizing experience. These systems, and their developmental history, determine structural health and pathology. Thus, both pathology and health are considered as functions of the human being's evolving capability to organize experience, utilizing the limitations and potentialities operative at a particular point in its development.

By contrast with cultural or behavioral therapists who emphasize environmental factors, or existential therapists who are exclusively concerned with inner meanings, modern psychoanalytic thought is attuned to the interaction between experience and the intrapsychic processes which govern its impact. Experience—inner and outer, past and current—is the raw data from which structural pattern and dynamic meaning is continuously derived. But the multiple roles of experience: as real events, as the stimulant for intrapsychic organization, as the subject of meaning making, and as the medium of organism–environment interchange, is of secondary importance to the therapist. Our first priority is the systems of psychological process which organize experience: object relations, ego, self. Here, within the intrapsychic structure, is where the dysfunction occurs and where our efforts at remediation are directed. The egoself approach to weekly psychotherapy exemplifies this principle.

WEEKLY EGOSELF PSYCHOTHERAPY

Within the context of the therapeutic relationship, intervention strategy is geared to restructuring pathological distortions and malformations of those processes and meanings which affect ego operations and self structure. As Malin (Panel, 1980) reports, the target of reconstruction is not an event or fact but pathological "emotion-laden quasi memory," which structures both child and adult behavior in distorted and restrictive ways. By contrast with intensive psychotherapy, which adheres to traditional techniques of retrieving early derivatives of the core conflict (Deutsch and Murphy, 1955; Dewald, 1964; Paolino, 1981), weekly therapy stays closer to present time, focusing on contemporary derivatives of the patient's pathology. This orientation is as true for Strupp and Binder (1984) as it is in egoself psychotherapy. In addition, the egoself approach shares with Blanck and Blanck (1986) a focus on restructuring object relations. Therapy is based on a careful assessment of ego operations and self structure. The intervention strategy emphasizes locating the consequences of pathogenic experience in current ego functions, object relations, selfobject and self identity structuring. In addition, the therapist helps recruit appropriate ego resources from the patient's available developmental competencies. Specific interventions assist patients to mobilize resources, building structure and enhancing function. Meanwhile, the countervailing influences of resistance, secondary gain, ego syntonic pathology, chronicity, and acting out are handled as expectable aspects of therapeutic management. Since the weekly frequency of appointments mitigates against rapid intensification of transference material, alternative foci of intervention are commonly employed. But the essential element of the transference, as the arena for significant emotional learning (Strupp and Binder, 1984), is retained by continuously focusing on derivative affective experiences and their consequences for the structuring of ego and self organization.

Using this approach permits an extended range of clientele to be seen for restructuring therapy on a weekly basis. Selected borderline and narcissistic disorders can also be treated weekly, preferably when therapy can be extended over a number of years. By contrast with brief and supportive psychotherapy, the techniques described here are not limited to sustaining existing ego resources but to building new ones, reorganizing self and object representations, and restructuring the narcissistic investment of self.

PRECEPT AND PRACTICE

The conditions imposed by weekly contact affect all aspects of therapy. Above all other considerations, the place of therapy in patients' lives is significantly diluted by weekly contact. This elemental fact affects the perception of therapy, the therapist, the relationship, and the balance between therapy and the rest of the patient's life. Inevitably, the everyday experiential world takes on greater prominence; the character of therapeutic activity is affected; management assumes different meaning in view of the reduced frequency of contact. In order to optimize the greater influence of everyday events, more of the patient's daily life is brought into the therapy; conversely, therapy issues are selectively applied to facets of everyday life, converting it into a living laboratory.

For these reasons it is important to make explicit the flow from psychoanalytic precepts to therapeutic practices in weekly egoself psychotherapy. Lacking that theoretical linkage therapeutic intervention may seem disconnected from the objective of permanent intrapsychic restructuring. The theoretic origins of the precepts and their application to clinical situations are both necessary components of a coherent system. Weekly psychotherapy veers from standard psychoanalytic technique at significant points. But, because it derives from psychoanalytic theory, it is consistent in its application of modern concepts and insights about the nature of personality, pathology, and development. Throughout the book clinical material is used to illustrate conceptual and technical issues.

PARADOX AND PROMISE

It is ironic in the extreme that at a time when psychoanalytic theory is expanding rapidly, and psychoanalytic precepts are being applied with greater frequency to the interpretation of history, art, and literature, the practice of psychoanalytic therapies should be under such massive assault. Clearly the depth and persuasiveness of psychoanalytic insights have had an impact on significant segments of the thinking community. Somehow the therapeutic application of psychoanalytic theory must recapture the trust and hope that it has enjoyed in earlier periods. Amid the current wave of professional literature that is extending psychoanalytic applications to psychotherapy it is hoped that the egoself approach will make a legitimate contribution.

We live in a time of rapidly expanding information, a time of ferment and change when traditional beliefs are challenged on every side. As humans our inherent proclivity is twofold: to defend and adhere to that which is familiar, but to develop, also, in concert with the reality principle. Thus, while a reliance on dogma may enhance a sense of security, the demands of realistic adaptation underscore the advantages of open-mindedness. The structural approach to psychoanalytic therapy is still relatively new, and many of us have been trained along more traditional lines of thought. I believe that close and critical examination of self psychology and object relations theory, and the technical variations that they imply, is necessary to the health and growth of the psychoanalytic movement. But fragmentation into opposing factions benefits no one, and certainly not our patients. I often remind my students that these skilled and experienced therapists belonging to different groups are not fools, however much their approaches may seem different. They are sharing the results of their clinical discoveries, and we are the fools if we ignore what they have found. Faced with the limitations of traditional technique when applied in the context of current practice, it seems prudent to extend fundamental psychoanalytic concepts to fit emerging knowledge. It is an encouraging sign that some of our most distinguished colleagues, such as Schafer (1980), Pine (1987b), and Singer (1987), have already chosen to do so.

When colleagues probe beyond the nomenclature of ego building and self structuring and into the therapeutic activities they denote, the observations and techniques often seem familiar. It is as though egoself theory provides a conceptual umbrella which accounts for how their interventions have evolved. At other points the theory suggests a possible extension or modification toward which their experience has been leading them. I am impressed and encouraged by that clinical consonance. I trust the cumulative wisdom of my peers, and take it as evidence that my writings have not wandered far from the dictates of sound practice. However, I harbor no illusion that these pages offer more than another step in the continuing elaboration of that venture to which we are all committed —providing more useful services to people's intrapsychic dysfunction.

To those who see the emergence of ego psychology, object relations, and self theory as signs of revitalized energy, psychoanalysis is not languishing but surging ahead, and leading to a deepening of our understanding of human nature and pathology. Contemporary theory and practice forges ever closer connection with colleagues in affiliated disciplines: psychology, anthropology, education, and neurology. Counterbalancing the internal resistance to revising one's professional role is the excitement of finding new and wider applications of the basic insights of psychoanalysis, as a basis for understanding human nature and as a means of ameliorating human distress. Proponents of object relations, ego, and self theories can each mount a credible stance for their position, on heuristic, theoretical, and clinical grounds. These theories are the product of careful study by highly skilled, gifted investigators. My view is that each theory provides distinctive insights, vital contributions to our understanding of human function, psychopathology, and its treatment. The egoself approach tries to incorporate these insights into a framework applicable to weekly psychotherapy.

CHAPTER 2

THE EVOLUTION OF PSYCHOANALYTIC PSYCHOTHERAPY

The history of psychoanalytic psychotherapy reenacts the classical developmental pattern of conservation and change. True to Freud's own methodological insistence on revising that which continuing experience could not justify, modern psychoanalytic workers revise theory and practice as new discoveries or changing times affect their clinical activities. While some writers may feel that the validation of psychoanalytic thinking and practice rests on retaining its orthodoxy, others take the view that the field must continue to grow.

A brief review of the evolution of psychoanalytic psychotherapy will make it easier to reflect on the directional flow of these changes. Seeming innovations or departures from the classical tradition often turn out to be reasonable evolutionary steps, once they are viewed in their appropriate psychohistorical context. Other variations are little more than extensions of fundamental precepts, updated in the light of contemporary findings. This review will underline the evolutionary changes which have occurred in the theory and practice of psychoanalytically oriented psychotherapy. As a result, there are psychoanalytic writers who do not receive the sort of attention that their contributions might merit in a more comprehensive historical review. It is my hope that readers will tolerate my focus on the broad sweep of evolution, leaving for others the precise detailing that a more complete history would require.

15

A century after its inception, psychoanalysis remains preeminent in the thinking and practice of those who use an intrapsychic approach to psychotherapy. Beneath this general rubric, a variety of therapeutic emphases can be observed. However, the fundamental ingredients of classical psychoanalysis, described by Fenichel (1941), Wolberg (1968, 1977) and others, are well recognized by most psychoanalytic practitioners. These ingredients include free association, analysis of resistance, induction of the transference neurosis, reconstructive interpretation, and the analyst's dual functions as blank screen/catalyst and interpreter. From its earliest periods psychoanalysis has been a generic, modified somewhat by each of its practitioners. Still, these basic ingredients form the prototype for defining the psychoanalytic approach; in addition, they provide the baseline from which subsequent modifications have evolved.

The free association method was devised as a means of eliciting unconscious fantasies and repressed drives and impulses. Along with dream analysis, free association serves numerous functions: uncovering of repressed material; catharsis; inducing and revealing controlled regression; and facilitating the emergence of the transference neurosis. A second cornerstone of classical psychoanalytic method is the analysis of resistance. This procedure focuses on the elucidation of defenses, acting out, and certain transferential reactions. Analysis of resistance is intended to clarify the layering of defenses, necessary for a genetic retracing of the development of the patient's core conflict. Inducing and analyzing the transference neurosis lies at the heart of classical psychoanalytic theory and practice. The analysand's perceptual distortions, fantasies, wishes, and fears—displaced onto the analyst—make it possible to reconstruct and reenact the earliest pathogenic experiences in order to resolve them.

The classical psychoanalytic role has two predominant features, as catalytic blank screen and as interpreter. By abstaining from giving advice and suggestions, or intervening in patients' everyday life activities, free associations and dreams are kept in focus. Answering questions and giving information can encourage infantile dependence, feed resistance, and interfere with autonomous growth. Most important, the analyst's silence creates a climate catalytic to controlled regression. It is in this context that the role of interpreter assumes its deepest meaning. Interpretation provides the dynamic connections between genetic reconstruction of patients' early pathogenic conflict and the pathological symptoms of their present lives. Interpretation is the means for achieving insight, which is the essence of all psychoanalytic treatment.

The early literature on psychoanalysis suffered from a paucity of attention to technique (Fenichel [1961] cited in Menninger [1958]). Formal training in psychoanalysis was inaugurated at the Berlin Psychoanalytic Institute in 1920; the first American Institute was founded in 1929. Several decades passed before there was any consensus on the practice of psychoanalysis or on the definition of such primary concepts as transference, interpretation, resistance, and the like.

Although psychoanalytic discoveries opened a new door to the treatment of emotional disorders, Freud soon realized that psychoanalysis was not suitable for a number of these problems. "Thus we learn that we must renounce the idea of trying our plan of cure [i.e., psychoanalysis] upon psychotics—renounce it for ever, perhaps . . ." (Freud, 1940, p. 37). Severely disturbed people could not tolerate the regressive demands of free association and dream analysis. For others their tenuous hold on reality precluded participation in the intensity of affects aroused by the transference. For still others the intellectual, financial, or time requirements of psychoanalysis were too draining. By midcentury various applications to psychotherapy were being attempted by mainstream psychoanalytic workers. Foremost among these efforts was the work organized by Alexander and French (1946), with the staff of the Chicago Institute for Psychoanalysis, including Therese Benedek, Roy Grinker, and Martin Grotjahn.

ALEXANDER AND FRENCH

In at least two fundamental respects the Chicago group was representative of traditional psychoanalytic thought of the time. They held the view that core conflict lay at the root of every

neurosis, and that the transference was the most powerful therapeutic tool for treating neurosis. In addition, Alexander and
French emphasized the point that: *"Every neurosis and every psychosis represents a failure of the ego in performing its function of
securing adequate gratification for subjective needs under the existing
external conditions"* (1946, p. viii). Alexander and French took
the position that traditional psychoanalytic technique was only
one way of applying psychoanalytic theory, and that specific
therapeutic procedures should be modified for each patient
and each phase of therapy. They were among the first psychoanalytic writers to distinguish between therapeutic strategies
of uncovering, support, and environmental manipulation, ad-
vocating active modification of the standard therapeutic technique.

> Among the modifications of the standard technique are: using
> not only the method of free association but interviews of a more
> direct character, manipulating the frequency of the interviews,
> giving directives to the patient concerning his daily life, em-
> ploying interruptions of long or short duration in preparation
> for ending the treatment, regulating the transference relation-
> ship to meet the specific needs of the case, and making use of
> real-life experiences as an integral part of the therapy [1946,
> p. 6].

These extensions of psychoanalytic technique in psychotherapy
also broadened its scope of application from chronic neuroses
to mild and acute forms, as well as to "incipient cases of emotional disturbance." In view of the current widespread use of
psychotherapy, particularly weekly psychotherapy, Alexander
and French's advocacy of flexibility of technique and specificity
of treatment plan seems particularly prophetic. Regarding the
etiology of disturbance, they argue for a more "relativistic concept," that only the most severe cases are traceable to infantile
experience, while other neuroses are due to experiences and
ego failures in later life. In support of this assertion Alexander
and French cite Freud's position on the etiology of neurosis,
bolstered by their own evidence from the treatment of traumatic
war neuroses.
     At the heart of Alexander and French's approach to psy-

choanalytic psychotherapy is their insistence upon a "corrective emotional experience" as the primary therapeutic ingredient.

> The patient, in order to be helped, must undergo a corrective emotional experience suitable to repair the traumatic influence of previous experiences. It is of secondary importance whether this corrective experience takes place during treatment in the transference relationship, or parallel with the treatment in the daily life of the patient [1946, p. 66].

While it may appear from the above quotation that Alexander and French minimize or dilute the power of transference in their therapeutic approach, quite the opposite is true. They define transference in classical terms as a stereotypic displacement from the past. They encourage the utilization of transference reactions in insight therapy, consistent with their view that these reactions provide significant material for a corrective emotional experience. However, they discourage patients' tendency to develop a transference neurosis in psychotherapy, on the grounds that its management is more appropriately handled in psychoanalysis. Consequently, they recommended that therapists not adopt the neutrally impersonal blank screen of the standard psychoanalytic role.

> In other words, we not only behave in such a way as to correspond to the patient's normal expectations, but we also tentatively treat the patient as a normal and rational human being and we continue to do so except when the patient himself proves the contrary . . . thus we lay the groundwork for the cooperation of the patient's ego in the task of understanding the motives for his less rational behavior . . . the very fact that our behavior does not encourage the patient's irrational tendencies makes them all the more conspicuous when they do occur [1946, p. 87].

Thus, the discrepancy between the patient's irrational reactions and the everyday normalcy of the therapist's behavior may provide a therapeutically corrective emotional experience. For Alexander and French the therapeutic goal is always "the increased capacity of the ego to deal with emotional constellations which were unbearable in the past" (p. 153). Insight, like transference interpretation, is instrumental but not fundamental to the achievement of this purpose. Transference reactions, in particular, are monitored very closely in the psychotherapy in order to modulate their intensity and avoid the build-up of hostile feelings, unless the dynamic formulation of the patient's conflict indicates they are necessary.

The work of Alexander and French elucidates the close connection of their approach to psychoanalytic theory, and yet the technical departures necessary in distinguishing between psychotherapy and psychoanalysis as treatment methods. Their view of psychotherapy as an educative experience as well as an ego-building process anticipates the fundamental premises underlying some contemporary psychotherapeutic approaches.

AMERICAN PSYCHOANALYTIC ASSOCIATION PANEL MEETING, 1953

The emerging importance of psychotherapy was heralded by a series of panel meetings sponsored by the American Psychoanalytic Association in 1953 and 1954. Panelists' reactions varied from those who felt that psychotherapy was a diluted form of psychoanalysis to those who considered it to be a procedure for which a separate set of conceptions, apart from those of psychoanalysis, would be necessary.

Chassel suggested that psychoanalytic psychotherapy relied more heavily "on a newer knowledge of 'ego psychology' " (Panel, 1953, p. 551). Other panelists, such as Gill and Steele, emphasized the more conscious, reality-based character of psychotherapy.

> [I]n so many instances, the rapid pace in psychotherapy, the need for immediate decisions on the part of the therapist and the lack of data and time, require greater intuition and a more automatically available insight and judgment than is ever required in a case of formal analysis where the pace is slower . . . [Panel, 1953, p. 554].

The report of the 1953 proceedings underscores the degree of novelty attached to psychotherapy at that time by psychoanalysts. Many of the panelists took issue with Alexander and French's position on the need for preplanning of treatment and the value of the corrective emotional experience, emphasizing instead the spontaneous flow of the classic psychoanalytic process and the central role of transference neurosis. As Gill observed, for many of the participants there was little or no distinction between psychotherapy and psychoanalysis as technical procedures. The panel seemed to be an accurate reflection of the times. It was a common practice for psychoanalytically oriented psychotherapists to prefer working intensively with patients, adopting a role of affective neutrality, observing transference reactions closely for interpretable material, and generally applying basic working principles of psychoanalysis to the therapy situation. Weekly contact with patients was commonly felt to have little value beyond that of support and maintenance.

AMERICAN PSYCHOANALYTIC ASSOCIATION PANEL MEETING, 1954

The following year a second panel was convened to examine similarities and differences between psychoanalysis and dynamic psychotherapy. Alexander reported that transference is the major tool in both procedures but that the analyst is more of a detached observer whereas the therapist interacts more with the patient's ongoing life. Stone's position was similar, noting that psychotherapy is more focused on the patient's life situation and behavior, and less on the core conflict. A "more selective" transference emerges in psychotherapy, but there is less opportunity for new discoveries about the patient's personality. Grotjahn affirmed that in therapy insight remains the main goal and transference reactions the preferred environment for these to emerge.

Previewing a book to be published later that year, E. Bibring (1954) said that all forms of treatment use five techniques, each of which is associated with particular curative effects. The first, suggestion, induces certain beliefs in the patient. Abreaction provides a relief from tension. Manipulation, of the patient or his environment, creates the opportunity to learn from new experiences. Clarification and interpretation, the fourth and fifth techniques, have the common curative value of offering the patient insight into his problems. Bibring described interpretation as an intervention referring to unconscious, repressed material and its derivatives. In psychoanalysis the insight derived from interpretation is paramount. This results in ego change, which consequently affects changes in the id and superego. Any modifications of this approach may accelerate change, and effect long-range curative results and have important implications. Bibring felt that a therapeutic approach based on other than interpretation would have implications for the underlying theory of neurosis. In addition to reaffirming the unique place of psychoanalysis, Bibring may have been anticipating future discoveries on the origins of psychopathology.

For the most part, then, psychoanalytic psychotherapy was seen by analysts of the time as a modified application of psychoanalysis. Psychotherapy was tacitly believed to be a diluted form, offering less pervasive and less permanent curative effects, but using the techniques and precepts of psychoanalysis to whatever extent the existing conditions would permit. Perhaps the most dissident voice at the 1954 panel was that of Sperling, who suggested that the choice between analysis and therapy was a function of different values. In psychoanalysis the greatest value is to know what one is doing, the profound understandings of insight. In psychotherapy the greatest value is to achieve therapeutic gain, a better functioning ego in Stone's words. Sperling's comments are a reaffirmation of Freud's original contention that analysis is a premier instrument for research and exploration of mental processes, an objective much broader than that of psychotherapy.

Viewed in a historical context, Alexander and French asserted that the goal of therapy is ego strengthening, achieved primarily by a change in emotional experience which might or might not include insight. Sperling suggested that insight and therapeutic gain may be viewed as separate objectives. But neither of these views fell within the mainstream of psychoanalytic theories of change, which envisioned permanent cure as a feasible goal.

DEUTSCH AND MURPHY'S SECTOR ANALYSIS

Future historians of psychotherapy will undoubtedly record the decade following World War II as a uniquely fertile period of growth in the field. In addition to psychoanalysis, three of the most influential schools of psychotherapy were founded during this period: the client centered approach (Rogers, 1951, 1954); behavior therapy (Dollard and Miller, 1950; Skinner, 1953; Wolpe, 1958), and Gestalt therapy (Perls, Hefferline, and Goodman, 1951).

Faced with increasing mental health awareness, and the limited applicability of traditional psychoanalysis, analytically oriented practitioners sought ways of applying psychodynamic understanding to therapeutic processes. In 1954 Wolberg observed, "It was soon apparent that a special kind of training was necessary before the therapist could effectively handle, on a once- or twice-a-week basis, the kinds of cases that were being referred to the [Postgraduate] Center [for Psychotherapy] . . ." (p. vi).

In 1955 Deutsch and Murphy published the results of their work in designing a psychotherapeutic approach suitable for training and application. Called sector analysis, their approach was clearly an adaptation of psychoanalysis but limited in time and scope. The foundational principles for sector analysis reflected both a traditional psychoanalytic position on the role of insight, and contemporary understanding of the prime role of the ego in healthy functioning. "The most important goal in psychotherapy is . . . insight which . . . may be a measurement of the degree of the cure" (1955a, p. 15). "Material concerning the function of the ego and its defensive and integrative system in everyday living is now felt to be more basic and useful in psychotherapy than complex genetic formulations" (1955a, p. 14).

Therapists were trained to relax their detached, emotionally neutral role, modifying it by repeatedly echoing key emotionally toned words and by encouraging a positive identification with the therapist as a benign parental figure. Sector analysis was designed to trace the genetic origins of presenting problems in a circumscribed area, using an associative approach (Deutsch and Murphy, 1955a,b). Therapeutic gain is based on insight, the relationship of present behavior to the past. When the patient achieves this sector-limited insight, "he becomes able to see and exercise a measure of control over the childlike part of him that at times threatens to overwhelm the adult part of his ego" (1955b, p. 12).

Insight serves the purpose of enhancing control functions, one of the primary activities of the ego. Murphy later went on to elaborate on the therapeutic role as one entailing "educational retraining," "guidance," and "manipulation" on behalf of the patient (Murphy, 1965). But these interventions are directed at the patient's fantasies and not at reality problems of everyday life. Therapeutic activity is for the purpose of helping the patient "revise his own history and see it more objectively" (1965, p. ix), consistent with exposing past conflicts to the ego's reality testing.

A number of evolutionary developments are evident in Deutsch and Murphy's sector analysis. The increasing influence of ego psychology in psychoanalytic theory is reflected in the emphasis placed on affecting specific ego functions, such as synthesis, control, and reality testing. Recognition of the need for greater interaction and intervention on the part of the therapist is a significant departure from the classical role of the analyst. Concomitant with this greater activity is a subtle deemphasis of the place of transference as the critical element in successful psychotherapy. Instead, Deutsch and Murphy introduce the concept of ego splitting as an intervention technique. The therapist is instructed to differentiate the patient's adult ego from the child ego. An alliance between therapist and adult ego is forged, using anamnestic material from the clinical interviews. Therapist and adult ego join forces to uncover and correct distortions of the child ego. Finally, within the psychoanalytic family of therapies, what Wolberg (1954) called "insight therapy with reeducative goals" joined the ranks of supportive and insight therapy. Of these three forms, only pure insight therapy was considered to be reconstructive; that is, capable of restructuring the personality so as to produce permanent change.

Over the next few years the assimilation and practice of

psychoanalytically oriented psychotherapy seemingly went through a latency period, characterized by the consolidation of the rapid changes it had undergone. This period also coincided with further discoveries into the nature of psychopathology, a greater awareness of characterological problems, and other early but nonpsychotic disorders. The next reference point is Dewald's (1964) volume on psychotherapy.

DEWALD

The acquisitions and experience of nearly a decade of practice with psychoanalytic psychotherapy is evident in Dewald's (1964) book on psychotherapy. He describes a therapeutic "spectrum," continuing from supportive to insight oriented. In its purest form supportive therapy aims at symptomatic relief and overt behavior change, with no attempt to resolve early unconscious conflicts or modify basic personality. The degree of supportive emphasis is a function of the severity of the person's disturbance and tolerance for personality change. At the other extreme, insight therapy aims at self-awareness and personality change, achieved by uncovering, resolving, and working through unconscious conflicts. Insight addresses not only unconscious psychic conflict but "patient awareness of [his or her] own mental processes . . . include[s] not only the drives and drive derivatives, but also the unconscious and preconscious ego and superego functions" (1964, p. 100).

The traditional definition of insight is thus extended to include proportionately more of the mental processes, relative to the earlier emphasis on conflicts and dynamics. Clinical skills in evaluating defenses and other aspects of ego structure become increasingly important in the therapeutic work. In supportive therapy the therapist must selectively fortify existing defenses and introduce new ones which are compatible with the rest of the patient's ego structure. Insight therapy utilizes interpretation to help the patient relinquish defenses in order to become aware of the underlying conflict. Dewald's description of insight therapy is in most other respects only quantitatively different from classical psychoanalysis. The major distinctions are his recognition and advocacy of a therapeutic alliance which stands apart from transference reactions; his recognition that an important source of resistance is attributable to fear of change; that one must utilize the patient's adult ego resources as the alternative to the early defenses which were all that was available to the child.

At the same time, Dewald describes the patient's use of identification in insight therapy as a resistance, a defense against developing an independent identity. As in analysis, growth toward autonomy through understanding is considered to be the ultimate goal of therapy. But where analysis explores early conflicts back to childhood, insight therapy stops with their derivatives, rarely earlier than adolescence or latency. Where analysis encourages temporary regressions to primary process levels, insight therapy limits regression to secondary process material.

An important evolutionary step, evident by the midsixties, was the freedom accorded the patient's volitional ego processes. In sector analysis the patient's associative processes were cued by the therapist's interventions. By contrast, Dewald avoids reference to associations and fantasies, preferring to assist patients in producing material with a minimum amount of inhibition. Other ways of activating volitional ego processes are also described by Dewald. Patients' self-observations are encouraged and solicited. Rather than provide reinforcement by approving of patients' self-initiated changes, the preferred method is to ask patients to evaluate consequences for themselves. Dewald sees this approach as encouraging the independence of his patients. Later therapists will describe this procedure as ego building. In supportive therapy, recommended almost exclusively for severely disturbed people, suggestions, prohibitions, and rewards are more commonly used to compensate for the patient's limited ego resources.

The preferred content of the insight therapy interview is drive derivatives, expressed as everyday experiences. The therapist does not probe for associations and fantasies generally. Instead there is frequent use of interpretation to elucidate the connection between current conflicts and their earlier sources.

[I]n psychotherapy the therapist looks for generalized patterns and reconstructions of reactions, and may offer these to the patient as an explanation of the origins of his behavior, but he focuses most of his attention on the manifestations of the current derivative conflicts. *A significant degree of structural personality change can frequently be obtained with such a more limited focus* [1964, p. 209; emphasis added].

In other words, structural change can be achieved without recreating the patient's earliest conflicts. Change of this depth can apparently be achieved through more contemporary insights which emphasize personality reactions rather than core etiology. In this respect Dewald's conclusions are similar to those of Alexander and French, which had been received skeptically some twenty years earlier.

Dewald recommends seeing clients once or twice weekly, even for insight therapy. Consistent with this frequency, transference material is utilized sparingly. While he acknowledges the ubiquity of transference reactions in therapy, "a significant component [of the therapy relationship] occurs at the level of a reality agreement and interaction" (1964, p. 192), and transference material is only "one means" of bringing the patient's unconscious conflicts into consciousness. The therapist avoids behavior which would intensify transferential content in either supportive or insight work. While the therapist actively monitors transference materials as a way of understanding the patient's problems, assessment rather than intervention seems to be the rule. In this respect Dewald has extended a notch further the evolutionary contributions of Deutsch and Murphy (1955a,b), whose work deemphasized the role of transferential material in sector therapy. Deutsch and Murphy address the need for a positive relationship, confronting transference material only when necessary. Dewald speaks of establishing a therapeutic alliance, closely akin to the sector analysis approach of affiliating with the adult ego, referred to earlier.

Continuing to look for evolutionary continuity, Dewald's discussion of working through seems like a more sophisticated version of the corrective emotional experience (Alexander and French, 1946). Both versions are continuous with earlier concepts of working through (Fenichel, 1945). However, Dewald provides the most explicit description of the process. Where Alexander and French suggest that a single instance may suffice for a cure, Dewald emphasizes the more common need for repeated activation, mobilizing the conflict and its attendant anxiety as they appear in a variety of circumstances. Dewald emphasizes the importance of integrating warded-off material, gradually eroding it, under differing affective and content conditions. He points out that variety of approach and exploration are essential for the patient to experience and relearn how to cope with the problem in its several manifestations. Therapy assists and supports the patient's efforts to experiment with new solutions. Even in supportive psychotherapy a form of working through can occur, despite the absence of insight. Repeating various forms of derivative gratification, abreaction, and defense can help shore up these alternatives to anxiety-laden repetition compulsion.

Dewald considers termination to be "analogous to the normal developmental stage of adolescence" (p. 274) in that it activates a conflict between dependence and independence. In this allusion to a postchildhood developmental stage Dewald may have been anticipating the increasing emphasis that would be given to life-span development in the psychotherapeutic writings of the 1970s and 1980s.

BLANCK AND BLANCK

As the theory and practice of psychoanalytic psychotherapy entered the 1970s, certain principles were well documented: it was possible to describe and conduct effective therapy which was based on nonintensive contact, once or twice weekly. This kind of therapeutic approach departed from standard psychoanalytic practice in a number of significant respects: it could be used with a much wider array of people seeking help; it deemphasized the place of transference analysis, dreams, associations, and fantasies in favor of a focus upon derivatives of early conflicts and the ego processes they activate. While transference reactions were monitored for greater clinical understanding, therapists strove to create a therapeutic alliance with their patients, an affiliation with the patient's ego strengths as resources in grappling with his or her problems. Insight and interpretation were more actively extended to examining structural aspects of ego reactions, and not confined to explaining key relationships and core conflicts. Therapeutic emphasis subtly shifted from psychosexual development to ego psychology. Concomitantly, there began to emerge a belief that significant personality restructuring could be accomplished within the scope of weekly psychotherapy.

While these ideas were taking hold, other discoveries were also making their impact on the field. Chief among these was the evolution of psychoanalytic theory from a drive psychology to a developmental psychology. The reasons for this change are so complex that they are not yet entirely understood. Still, some of the factors seem to be well recognized. Clinical practitioners found that their neurotic clients were diminishing, and being replaced instead with more primitively organized people. Ego dystonic symptoms and classical psychosexual conflicts gave way to ego defects, narcissistic personalities, and borderline structures. Further modifications of therapeutic procedure were needed, as there was general consensus that these disorders were generally not amenable to psychoanalysis (Kernberg, 1967). These problems had often been considered refractory or untreatable by psychoanalytic methods, since exploratory and uncovering techniques commonly used in therapy could precipitate severe regression, acting out, or psychosis in these clients. As psychoanalytic caseloads declined and more people were seen in psychotherapy, it became evident that relatively little attention had been given to the study of technique in psychoanalytic psychotherapy.

Fortunately, the surfacing of these issues coincided with a fruitful period of research in infantile development, culminating in the work of Margaret Mahler on separation–individuation. The effects of early interactions on the formation of mental representations, and consequently on the structuring of ego development, laid the groundwork for a new understanding of the role of object relations. Studies of early ego development focused on the role of experience in structuring object relations and less on the transmutation of drives. Ego organization superseded core conflict in considerations of the etiology of primitive psychopathology. This shift in emphasis was reflected in writings that referred to ego lacunae and developmental defects (Glover, 1958; Jacobson, 1964), while regression and pregenital fixations assumed relatively lesser roles in these discussions. In turn, explorations of therapeutic technique would benefit from adapting a perspective that was grounded in developmental theory. Repair and reconstruction would require ego building, and the relationship between object relations and ego structure would assume a new prominence in the design of intervention strategy (Holt, 1971).

Fueled by the separation–individuation paradigm, from the 1970s onward psychoanalytic psychotherapy has received an attention unparalleled in its entire history. The impact of this intensified interest cannot yet be fully assessed. Changes that may appear to be revolutionary in short-term focus often turn out to be evolutionary when viewed in a historical perspective. Not unlike other developmental phenomena, it is not always clear which changes represent qualitative departures from previous operations and which are really extensions of an ongoing process. This is particularly true of weekly psychotherapy, which has evolved as an expediency more often than as a specifically preplanned procedure. Even in the 1980s it can be authoritatively stated that: "Training in the practice of psychotherapy is less well organized and less well conceptualized than is training in psychoanalysis" (Joseph and Wallerstein, 1982, p. xv). Among psychoanalytically oriented clinicians in particular, the differentiation of psychotherapy from modified psychoanalysis has been chronically blurred. In part this has been due to the conscious preference of those practitioners who view psychoanalysis as the ultimate treatment, and try to retain as much of that theory and procedure as possible in their psychotherapeutic applications. In part it is due to less systematic training in psychotherapy, since most therapy supervisors received their own training when psychotherapy was in its childhood. Until relatively recently, distinctions have been clearest on what psychotherapy is not. Zimmerman reflects that consensus succinctly: "It is the interpretation and analytic resolution of the transference that the psychoanalyst is trained to accomplish . . . on the other hand . . . one or two sessions per week, for example—preclude his accomplishing it" (1982, p. 52).

As we know, insight—usually achieved through interpretations of transference material—has been the backbone of psychoanalytic treatment, whether on the couch or in face-to-face psychotherapy. At the same time, this historical review indicates the long-standing recognition that ego restructuring as a therapeutic goal has superseded methodology of technique as the top priority of some practitioners and theoreticians.

Among those whose writings most explicitly address the application of object relations theory to the practice of psychotherapy are Blanck and Blanck (1974, 1979, 1986). Faithful to psychoanalytic traditions, they have labored to reconcile classical theory and technique with the exigencies of current knowledge and practice. Their contributions can be enumerated under several headings. First, they make the point that object relations theory is the latest step in the evolution of a normal developmental psychology, emerging from psychoanalytic theory. As a consequence of this evolution, therapeutic intervention can be modified to achieve a better fit with each patient's own level of development. Guided by Mahler's separation– individuation model, they describe a developmental "fulcrum." On one side of the fulcrum is impaired ego organization, incompletely developed during some phase of separation–individuation; on the other side is the organizing process (ego) subsequent to its "psychological birth." From this fundamental developmental diagnosis issues a basic distinction in choice of treatment. For those people who have achieved the level of separation–individuation, Blanck and Blanck recommend the standard forms of psychoanalytic treatment, either therapy or analysis. But those people whose development is prefulcrum, and who are still grappling with aspects of separation–individuation, require more structured intervention suitable to their severe ego vulnerabilities.

Second, Blanck and Blanck describe five forms of faulty ego development: premature (uneven) development; ego distortion (faulty self and object representations); ego deviation (faulty developmental sequencing); ego regression (loss of one or more functions already attained); and ego defects (untreatable constitutional limitations). Third, Blanck and Blanck describe procedures for working with prefulcrum problems in ego development. These procedures involve techniques of ego building and the character of the therapeutic relationship. Until basic ego operations are established, the ego's function as the organizing process of the personality is incomplete and the person is at psychological risk. Ego building is, therefore, of paramount importance in the therapy of borderline and pathologically narcissistic structures. Among the ego-building techniques they describe are neutralizing affect, anxiety tolerance, regulation, support, exercise of ego functions, and building internalizations (object relations). In practice, this means that the thrust of therapeutic intervention is structural, directed at the development of the basic "organizing processes"—which is how Blanck and Blanck define ego.

Finally, the nature of the therapeutic relationship advocated in working with primitive disorders is that the therapist should assume the role of "real object" (Blanck and Blanck, 1979, chapter 7). In its simplest form, being a real object means that therapists relinquish their role as neutral, dispassionate observers. Blanck and Blanck identify several ways in which real object functioning contributes to the therapeutic process. By demonstrating warmth, empathy, and acceptance a climate is created which fosters the "quickening" of ego functions; by seeming more human, the therapist provides a more ready identification figure, for building and internalizing newer and healthier object relations; and by facilitating ego growth:

> [W]here capacity for self and object relations is deficient, [it] sometimes has to be provided by the patient with considerable help from the therapist in arranging for it. One accomplishes this by helping the patient acquire capacities for self empathy and self soothing . . . actively encouraging the patients to look back at the children they were and to provide empathy for themselves [1979, p. 118].

Stated most concisely, as a real object, "the therapist usefully and deliberately allows himself to be experienced as a nontransference object" (1979, p. 121).

Blanck and Blanck are careful to note that the real object role is a therapeutic stance, and not to be confused with "being oneself" in a personal relationship with patients. By not getting drawn into patients' usual modes of relating to others, the therapist avoids their affective distortions of object images. Instead, an alternative is provided. From these "reparative experiences" patients can build new object images and thus, new self and object representations can be internalized. The object world expands, permitting ego reorganization of object relations and consequent growth. Thus, the therapeutic role includes that of "leader into the object world." This description of real object locates its function in a way which is different from that which is commonly prescribed in supportive therapy. Despite certain apparent similarities, it is clear that Blanck and Blanck are describing ego reconstruction, based upon systematic restructuring of object relations.

In their exploration of other standard therapeutic issues, Blanck and Blanck suggest additional modifications, utilizing their developmental approach. Resistance may sometimes be in the service of individuation, rather than a defense against uncovering anxiety-laden repressions. In these instances, it may be preferable to defer or avoid standard interpretations. Regarding transference, Blanck and Blanck offer the clinical guide that interpretation should be restricted to those instances in which regression will be reversed by the intervention. In addition, they emphasize that the primitive nature of many disorders precludes frequent use of interpretation, since it risks further disorganization of already fragile ego integration. Instead, they recommend a form of confrontation in which patients are helped to look at their experience. This form of intervention "is in and of itself therapeutic because it promotes the ego's capacity *via exercise of function*" (1974, p. 353). This view of confrontation represents a sharpened focus of application, in contrast to the diversity of opinions found by Adler and Myerson (1973). In their compendium, Adler and Myerson describe therapists' emphasis upon patients' hostile or immoral behavior. With this content, the kind most commonly described by the various chapter authors, confrontation was employed as a way of managing difficult behavior rather than as an exploration of psychological processes.

The Blanck and Blanck approach to psychotherapy, applying a developmental perspective to object relations theory and ego psychology, constitutes another evolutionary step in the field. They interpret object relations theory as a meta-theoretical extension of psychoanalytic theory into life-span developmental theory. Their thinking is grounded in Hartmann's contributions to ego psychology and Mahler's research on separation–individuation. They have constructed a theory of therapy which extends psychoanalytically oriented practice and confirms the view of earlier workers (Alexander and French, 1946; Deutsch and Murphy, 1955a,b; Dewald, 1964) that psychotherapy can restructure as well as support and reeducate. Their emphasis on ego operations and object relations continues to be the trend of more recent discoveries, which emphasize personality structuring in a developmental context.

While it would be presumptuous to attempt a full description of the entirety of the Blanck and Blanck approach, for present purposes certain of their ideas do require further elaboration here. It is important to clarify how they conceptualize the impact of psychological development, the real object role, and the meanings of resistance and experience as these contribute to our perspective on the evolution of psychotherapy.

On the subject of psychological development, Blanck and Blanck list several points: that development is "ceaseless," continuously affecting organismic changes, "and may even repair the damage of an earlier process" (1979, p. 134). They identify the structural changes during the rapprochement subphase as the critical fulcrum of early ego development. They describe development as an interactive process to which the organism is a contributing party rather than a passive recipient.

Their views on development, especially in the prefulcrum period, lead them to reconsider transference, resistance, and how they are managed in psychotherapy. Depending upon the "development and structuralization" of the ego, they consider certain therapeutic material to be a "search for replication of experience" (1974, p. 13) rather than a displacement, as in transference. In these situations they call for therapists to adopt a real object role.

The purpose of real object activities is to provide "corrective experiences," not just kindness or a sharing of personal material, but providing "wider object choices than were available in childhood" (p. 123). It does not seem unreasonable to characterize the real object role as one of facilitating ego development by providing selective learning experiences. They cite the example of a patient who felt that anything said in the therapy session would be done for the sake of the therapist. The therapist's reply was, "if it is for me, do not do it," thus emphasizing the patient's autonomy and the importance of her volitional choice—both of which are ego activities.

On the subject of resistance, Blanck and Blanck state that "resistance and like phenomena, especially in borderline and narcissistic pathologies, more usually represent unsuccessful attempts at separation–individuation than opposition to the treatment" (1979, p. 151). That is, oppositional comments and behavior can be interpreted as activity on behalf of growth rather than as a defensive or pathological manifestation. This view is in keeping with their emphasis on the power of the developmental thrust, and with their commitment to building ego structure as the first priority in psychotherapy. In support of their position, and to show the continuity of their thought with mainstream psychoanalytic theory, they cite the rule of addressing defense (i.e., structure) before content (i.e., psychodynamics): "support of the developmental thrust before interpretation of conflict-bound resistances" (1979, p. 148).

Blanck and Blanck direct their energies toward those disorders which they identify as "prefulcrum," which derive from incomplete or unsatisfactory maturation of the organizing process, which, as already noted, is their definition of ego. These disorders—psychotic, narcissistic, and borderline—are due to developmental difficulties occurring during separation– individuation. The nature of ego operations in these primitive, distorted, or regressed states necessitates modifications in traditional technique, modifications which facilitate the basic therapeutic task of ego building. Their approach can be summarized in terms of several distinctive features. First, it is explicitly developmental in that it is grounded in separation– individuation theory and specifies the need for developmental diagnosis as a justification for employing particular concepts and methods. Second, it is properly considered a structural rather than psychodynamic approach, since it deals with interventions directed at ego organization rather than core conflicts. Third, it calls for the reconceptualization of drives, resistances, and transference as relates to their use with people who have not reached the developmental fulcrum of the rapprochement subphase in separation–individuation. Next, it defines a therapeutic role of the "real object"—a position which is qualitatively different from the traditional postures of neutrality or support. Finally, they acknowledge the need for future technical and theoretical modifications as the effect of ongoing development transforms ego functioning. Some of these modifications were soon forthcoming.

COLARUSSO AND NEMIROFF

Further evidence of the consonance of the developmental approach with mainstream psychoanalytic thought is provided by the work of Colarusso and Nemiroff (1981). "A developmental orientation can change the therapist's understanding of the purpose, process, and results of his work with patients, leading to a broader and more complex conceptualization of psychotherapy" (p. 225). Colarusso and Nemiroff cite the 1974 report of the Conference on Psychoanalytic Education and Research, which describes development as "a continuous and life-long process." Following up on this position, Colarusso and Nemiroff proceed to apply modern psychoanalysis to adult development and psychotherapy. Their approach specifies a number of clinical hypotheses, generating from a core framework:

> [S]ince development is considered to be a lifelong process, the patient *of any age* is understood to be in the midst of dynamic change. Since he is still developing, *diagnosis and treatment focus on the current, phase-specific, adult-developmental tasks* as well as the residue from earlier experiences and conflicts. . . . Because the developmental orientation focuses on the potential for *healthy*

development, *it brings the* whole person *into focus as the primary interest of the therapist* [1981, p. 217; emphasis added].

The clinical hypotheses emphasize that adult developmental processes help shape psychopathology, and alter the form in which issues continued from childhood are manifested. Adult development is concerned with the evolution and use of existing psychic structure. Colarusso and Nemiroff further suggest that there are phase-specific issues of adulthood, just as there are in childhood. Among these issues, they identify coming to terms with the finiteness of time and the inevitability of personal death. While their writing highlights the issues of middle age, it is clear that their comments are intended to include the entire adult life span.

Colarusso and Nemiroff discuss the clinical application of their approach to such traditional therapeutic issues as resistance, transference, and defense. On the subject of resistance, they caution therapists "to distinguish between resistance and unavoidable developmental tasks." They encourage recognition of patients' life-stage circumstances, and urge therapists to exercise greater flexibility in responding to their patients' own developmental pressures as these may affect frequency and timing of appointments. It is important to differentiate between genuine defensive resistance to therapy and impediments to customary procedure which result from healthy developmental requirements in peoples' lives which impinge on the therapy. Since facilitation of growth is the ultimate therapeutic task, it may be counterproductive to insist that patients put a higher priority on therapeutic procedure than they do on the realistic imperatives of their constructive lives. Routinely interpreting patients' fidelity to family or career demands as resistance may be experienced as a lack of empathy or rigid insensitivity, putting at risk the entire therapeutic enterprise.

The traditional consensus asserts that resistances and defenses are selectively interpreted in exploratory, insight-oriented therapy and circumvented whenever possible in supportive therapy. A developmental perspective informs that intervention, according to Colarusso and Nemiroff. They utilize Vaillant's (1971) developmental hierarchy of primitive, neurotic,

and mature defenses, suggesting that phase-appropriate defenses be less often interpreted than primitive and maladaptive
ones. Colarusso and Nemiroff feel that the more mature defenses are likely to be employed in handling phase-appropriate
developmental issues. Therapists are cautioned to avoid inter-
fering with normally progressing developmental processes. Empathic regressions and selective identifications of parenthood
exemplify such normal adult developmental phenomena.

In the management of transference, the application of
principles of adult development augments "both the complexity
and the potential for deeper understanding" (p. 232).

> Consider again the idea of transference as a new edition of the
> past. From a developmental standpoint, that new edition does
> not emanate solely from the childhood past but results from a
> complex, multidimensional past (i.e., the life cycle—infancy,
> childhood, adolescence, young adulthood). Furthermore, the
> new edition is constructed by the mind of the present. *What is
> presented to us is the past as interpreted by the patient's mind in the
> present* [1981, p. 232; emphasis added].

Consequently, transference reactions may be complicated by
adult patients' experiences with aging parents, or by the impact
of becoming parents themselves. In situations where patients
are significantly older than their therapists, "a son or daughter
transference may be central to the therapeutic alliance and to
an understanding of the patient" (p. 233). The multidimensional past can evoke multiple transference images, therefore:
of an infant's mother, an adolescent's mother, a young adult's
mother, a dying mother—images which fuse and interact as
they are expressed in the therapy. Colarusso and Nemiroff
describe therapeutic interactions in which therapists are alter-
nately invoking active participation in the therapeutic alliance
or eliciting transferential material through therapeutic neutrality; acting as adult consultant and being perceived as a caring
adult child.

As they describe it, the adult developmental perspective
enriches both the transference and the therapeutic alliance. On
the part of therapists, the task is one of ongoing assessment,
evaluating the material being produced within a context of the

whole person and his range of locations on the life span—its implications for a more precise delineation of resistance, defenses, and kinds of transference material. Another aspect of this developmental awareness is for therapists to recognize how it affects their empathic understanding of patients. This "developmental resonance" extends to realizing what it means for patients to be experiencing life from whatever point they are at on the life span, what it means to be a late-blooming adolescent or a retired adult. With their explicit commitment to treating the whole person, they redefine the goal of therapy: "Again, the goal of treatment is not the elimination of symptoms, but the removal of blocks to development and the integration of phase-specific developmental themes" (p. 222). This statement of purpose concurs with the American Psychoanalytic Association's 1974 position in rejecting the medical model of disease in favor of one which pictures a continuously evolving person contending with developmental impediments.

In other respects, Colarusso and Nemiroff hold pretty much to the traditional structuring of psychotherapy. While they acknowledge the relevance of both supportive and insight-oriented (exploratory) therapy, their attentions are largely given to the implications of adult development for an insight-oriented mode of intervention. Their recommendations for modifications in therapy are concerned with expanding the breadth of therapists' understanding, and less with revisions in technique. They advocate greater flexibility in the therapist's role, permitting nonverbal communications, discussing third-party contacts, but remain committed to an associative, insight-oriented approach based on standard psychoanalytic principles. Their contributions to the evolution of psychotherapy weigh most influentially in the incorporation of a true life-span psychology with the practice of psychoanalytic psychotherapy.

From an evolutionary vantage point, Colarusso and Nemiroff have contributed significantly to the expansion of psychoanalytic psychotherapy. Perhaps their most distinctive contribution is in underlining the impact of adult development in shaping psychological experience and intrapsychic structure. This assertion, bold as it may appear in psychoanalytic literature, is well supported by the longitudinal data of several independent studies, which are described in chapter 9. What emerges from these findings is the importance of developmental assessment, a conclusion reached by Blanck and Blanck (1974, 1979, 1986), Masterson (1972), and others. Colarusso and Nemiroff concur, but also extend the depth and breadth of that recommendation to cover the whole person, over the entire life span. They emphasize that assessment of pathology occurs in the context of an evaluation of the entirety of the person's developmental status.

Both sets of authors stress the shaping influence of ongoing development, as it affects early pathology. The unconscious may be timeless, but development is unceasing and ever-changing. As Colarusso and Nemiroff note, much of the specificity of adult personality derives from adult identifications such as mentoring. These postinfancy identifications are different from parent–child identifications (Levinson, Darrow, Klein, Levinson, and McKee, 1979), and may be an instance of the more general phenomenon of social learning (Bandura, 1971). The role of object relations in shaping early ego development may well describe a process which continues throughout life. That process is experiential learning, an ego function which is as powerful an influence in adults as it is in the childhood years. Thus, extending the therapeutic role to include intervention with adult ego operations makes good sense clinically as well as logically. The clinical illustrations presented by Colarusso and Nemiroff, some of which are cited above, demonstrate the unique therapeutic insights created by that approach.

From the beginning of this review, the place of transference in psychotherapy has been the subject of much attention. By general consensus, induction and analysis of the transference neurosis is more properly lodged in psychoanalysis. Beyond that consensus, the developmental paradigm of conservation–change seems to characterize the history of transference usage. While the occurrence of transferential material in therapy is inevitable, the nontransferential aspects of the therapeutic relationship are now being accorded increasing attention. Colarusso and Nemiroff faithfully represent that evolutionary pattern in their consideration of transference and therapeutic alliance issues. They point out that transferential material of adults is permeated by the developmental character of parent–child relations, as well as patients' own experiences with becoming parents themselves. While the definition of transference as displaced images from the past remains essentially unchanged, it is clear that the past can no longer be exclusively located in the first months of life. The past also follows developmental laws of ongoingness and change, as adult experience reshapes the meaning of early experiences.

STRUPP AND BINDER

The place of transference in the therapeutic relationship is being reshaped developmentally in yet another way. Several writers, of whom Strupp and Binder (1984) are the most explicit, suggest that the relationship includes significant elements beyond the transference and the therapeutic alliance. "[T]here are always features of the therapist's behavior that lend themselves to being assimilated into the patient's transference ideas and fantasies" (Gill and Hoffman, 1982, p. 140). Paolino (1981) identifies at least four components of the psychoanalytic relationship: transference, working alliance, real relationship, and narcissistic alliance. Strupp and Binder (1984) comment that therapists make inevitable impact with their "personal style" which can be "positive or negative." In sum, there is concordance that nontransferential elements compound the complexity of the relationship and infuse it with interpersonal tones that derive from sources other than early objects.

Strupp and Binder present their findings as part of a research project on time-limited dynamic psychotherapy (TLDP), a version of weekly psychoanalytic psychotherapy limited to twenty-five to thirty sessions. Their work exemplifies the recent interest in clarifying and updating the nature of theory and practice in psychoanalytic psychotherapy. "The principle [sic] technical strategy of TLDP is the careful, systematic elaboration of the interpersonal transactions between patient and therapist" (1984, p. 142).

Their focus is on working with "human relatedness" problems, in which classical transference material plays one part.

Like Blanck and Blanck, they also prefer to have patients arrive at their own interpretations within a context of experiential learning.

> The essence of psychotherapeutic change, however, . . . is the result of a human *experience* in which he or she [the patient] feels understood and in which this understanding is given new meanings. Therefore, what the therapist clarifies or interprets is far less important than what the patient experiences in the context of the interaction [1984, p. 45].

Flexibility on the therapist's part is also emphasized by Strupp and Binder. A more accepting, less distant or confrontational style seems to be suggested. Material which in traditional treatment might call for interpretation or some other direct intervention, is noted silently by therapists using the more flexible approach. But it is also true that Strupp and Binder describe a much more limited role for their therapeutic approach. In particular they prefer to deal with explicit interpersonal problems rather than with the more intricate issues of intrapsychic organization and operation. To that extent the therapy is not only time-limited but goal limited as well. Time-limited dynamic therapy has, as its stated objective, "a more adaptive view of adult reality" (1984, p. 43). Furthermore, it requires that the patient be able to establish a "collaborative relationship," a precondition which may exclude many people with severe pathology. Insight into contemporary problems of living, rather than structural change, is the more realistic expectation of this focused approach. In assessing the contribution of time-limited dynamic therapy one notes that it extends the period of contact beyond really short-term work. More important, it recognizes the limitations of a transference model of treatment in weekly therapy. In its place Strupp and Binder utilize an explicit partnership relationship, whose role is to create "a laboratory *in vivo*" (p. xiv).

CURRENT TRENDS

Concomitant with these changes in the conceptualization of transference material, modified requirements of a therapeutic alliance have been advanced. Sharing an increasingly common view, Colarusso and Nemiroff also recommend that therapists exercise flexibility, judiciously adapting their schedules to the legitimate imperatives in their patients' lives. While they advocate teaching patients to use free association, they also permit selective use of nonverbal demonstrations, and will integrate real world events into the therapy—such as accepting phone calls from interested third parties. These modifications are intended to strengthen the therapeutic alliance by reflecting sensitivity and empathic awareness of powerful and developmentally relevant factors in patients' lives. They counter the infantilizing risks of seeming to disregard the vital nature of patients' everyday problems. At the same time, these alterations of role take the therapy further away from the detached neutrality which enhances the emergence of transference material. Blanck and Blanck indicate that among primitively organized patients much of the material directed at therapists is pretransferential, the repetition of early experience which is developmentally prior to the evolution of defenses such as displacement. For this reason they suggest that very early material be handled in a real object context. Colarusso and Nemiroff seem to adopt a similar position, that certain materials are more suitable for intervention within the therapeutic alliance when they are developmentally phase-appropriate—a position consonant with that of Gedo (1979). In their analysis of resistance, Colarusso and Nemiroff concur with Blanck and Blanck's view that content which suggests resistance may be serving developmental needs instead. Thus the developmental perspective has necessitated certain revisions in the conceptualization of therapy content and procedure. In part this is so because object relations are increasingly to be understood as lifelong in their evolution. As a result, this deeper understanding of manifest material leads to certain alterations in intervention technique. Attuning more sensitively to developmental issues focuses attention more closely on ego operations and self representations, and hence on the structural aspects of therapeutic material. Nowhere is this more true than in weekly psychotherapy.

Summarizing the historical lines we have been tracing, the identity of psychoanalytically oriented psychotherapy seems to derive from two sets of roots. One of these root systems is the study of intrapsychic processes and their vicissitudes. The second studies technique in the amelioration of psychopathology, utilizing an interlocking combination of insight and the therapy relationship. The study of intrapsychic processes and their vicissitudes has shifted over time from an emphasis on basic drives and their development to structural organizaton (ego, object relations, self) and its development. While clinical training over most of this time frame emphasized the content of patients' histories rather than the structure of their development, it was generally assumed that history was development spelled backwards. More precisely, history has long been the standard method for assessing the impact of development.

As noted earlier, the emergence of ego psychology and developmental theory provided access to a large scientific literature. The current saliency of object relations theory and self psychology is rapidly being synthesized into modern psychoanalytic theory and practice. The integration of these data permits contemporary clinicians to conduct better informed and more extensive assessment of intrapsychic processes than was possible in the past. At the same time, the evidence supporting the feasibility of structural change through psychotherapy has increased interest in strategies of intervention which focus on structural features of patients' psychopathology. The natural outcome of these trends is an explicit recognition that modern psychoanalytic practice, particularly as it is reflected in weekly psychotherapy, is oriented toward an approach which addresses pathological structure from a more complex appreciation of the therapeutic relationship. Contemporary practitioners now attempt to incorporate teachings from ego psychology, self psychology, and object relations theory.

IN CONTINUATION

A serendipitous consequence of reviewing almost a half-century of the history of psychoanalytic psychotherapy is an appreciation for the progress that has been achieved in that relatively short period of time. Changes in society, and in psychopathology, have made an important difference. Also, the democratization of access to therapeutic services has meant that many more people are requesting services. In turn, this has broadened the spectrum of need and opportunity, challenging clinical practitioners to create therapeutic modalities suitable to these diverse needs. From management strategy to technical intervention, from therapeutic goals to conceptualizing the relationship, weekly egoself therapy is responsive to these ongoing imperatives. Just as important, egoself therapy continues the developmental line of contemporary psychoanalytic thought. Consonant with that tradition, I believe it is feasible to conduct restructuring therapy on a weekly basis. Attentive to the many forms that relationship takes, attuned to recruitable resources as well as pathology, using the therapy hour as a living laboratory, the interweaving threads of intrapsychic structure can be applied to the patient's functioning much like the surgeon uses the latest techniques of microsurgery to restore and aid in regeneration.

CHAPTER 3

MANAGEMENT ISSUES

The maturation of psychotherapy as a professional practice has been accompanied by closer attention to its component parts: assessment, intervention, technique, management. The decision to see a patient weekly carries with it inherent implications concerning the management of therapy. Prior to the advent of ego psychology it was commonly assumed that the goals of weekly psychotherapy were largely restricted to supportive maintenance, education, guidance, and environmental adjustment. Permanent restructuring was believed to require intensive uncovering work, a procedure which entails the application of techniques derived from psychoanalysis. Now it is recognized that restructuring can be accomplished in weekly contact (Strupp and Binder, 1984) and/or by directly addressing the structural processes of ego and self (Wolberg, 1977; Blanck and Blanck, 1986).

Other therapy policies—handling of lateness, medications, resistance—require reexamination and modification within the constraints imposed by weekly contact, but also due to an approach which targets structure as the focus of intervention. In the material which follows it will soon be evident that adapting modern psychoanalytic theory to a weekly context demands a recasting of therapeutic principles which can be quite dramatic. These changes are necessitated because of the qualitative difference between psychoanalysis and weekly therapy. They are independent of other discussions concerning theory and technique in psychoanalytic practice.

47

FEATURES OF WEEKLY PSYCHOTHERAPY

Comparing weekly psychotherapy with more intensive contact brings into focus one of its most essential aspects: its place in the patient's everyday life. Seeing the therapist once a week inevitably dilutes the impact of intrapsychic experience, since so much of the patient's life is engaged by everyday events. Of necessity therapy is less focal. Indeed, the unique advantages of psychoanalysis as a vehicle for uncovering unconscious fantasies, conflicts, and dynamics, are specifically handicapped in weekly psychotherapy. Face-to-face contact once a week is a radically different experience from multiple sessions on the couch. The conditions underlying assessment for weekly psychotherapy are in significant ways different from those encountered in psychoanalysis or intensive psychotherapy. Relevant information emerges more gradually, and is often more censored, due to the limited contact. Pressures and perceptions, motivations and resistances, are more tentative, more ambiguous than is the case when the therapeutic partners are planning for multiple weekly meetings for a period of years. Weekly therapy patients are likely to have a more circumscribed view of their problems, and of what therapy will require of them. They are less likely to view therapy as the focus of their lives. While weekly therapy can come to dominate the person's experience, more often it is something to be fitted into one's life. Thus the level of involvement, need, and commitment is likely to be more diluted than in analysis. Weekly therapy is often thought of as valuable rather than essential.

To be most effective in weekly contacts, therapists trained in psychoanalytic methods have to modify or relinquish deeply ingrained intervention preferences. Weekly therapy mitigates against transference neurosis, deep uncovering, and exhaustive exploration of associations and fantasies. These techniques are predicated upon assumptions that do not obtain in weekly contact: extended screening of candidates; ongoing monitoring by the therapist; regular, repeated stimulation of associations, dreams, and fantasies; the protection and safety of frequent meetings; the saliency of therapy created by building one's daily schedule around it. Weekly psychotherapy capitalizes instead upon its own distinctive features: the imminence of everyday life and the more periodic face-to-face contact with a concerned, caring professional partner. Consistent with this format, weekly therapy targets those intrapsychic processes which oversee the interface between the person and everyday life, the ego and self systems. In weekly psychotherapy the strategy is not to maximize self understanding but to enhance psychological effectiveness. While genetic insight is neither a goal nor a requisite, it may be a consequence of the therapeutic work.

In keeping with this focus, weekly egoself therapy is specifically designed for the task of restructuring self and ego processes. As students of psychoanalytic psychotherapy have long noted (Dewald, 1964), early derivatives are rarely accessible to face-to-face therapy. An insight-oriented approach is further constrained by the limitation of weekly contact. Conversely, there is an enormous practical advantage to a weekly format, one which is further highlighted by the egoself orientation. The emphasis on restructuring intrapsychic processes by focusing on everyday experience makes therapy functionally accessible to a wider base of clientele. By recasting intricate processes in everyday experience a broader spectrum of people can understand how therapy relates to their lives.

Much of the essence of a psychotherapeutic approach is revealed in the way universal issues are managed. Over the course of therapy, the specific techniques used—probing, persuasion—may be of lesser importance than the tacit rules which govern the handling of issues which arise predictably in working with patients. Sabetti (1976) compared the Gestalt, psychoanalytic, and behavior modification schools on the dimension of attention focusing—those aspects of the session which were emphasized by the therapist. Using both the writings and therapy transcripts of major authors from each school, he demonstrated consistent differences in the emphasis placed, using parameters such as central versus peripheral awareness, and present versus past time focusing. Thus, apart from whether the therapist asked questions or gave directions, Sabetti found consistently different patterns of focusing the patient's attention in the three schools of therapy.

I have selected from the plethora of psychodynamic issues

those which seem to recur most typically. Some of these issues, such as assessment, are so large that they have been discussed as special topics elsewhere in the book. Others, such as the relationship in psychotherapy, are so pervasive that different facets are also treated in different sections of the book. What remains is a list that is still too long, considering the attention each issue merits. But, by discussing the rationale for managing these issues from an egoself perspective, comparison with other approaches will be clearer. More important, the cohesion of theory and practice for weekly psychotherapy will become more evident.

MANAGEMENT ISSUES

Frequency of Sessions

If it seems ironic to discuss frequency of sessions in a book on weekly psychotherapy, enjoy the humor while acknowledging that therapy is not a Procrustean bed to which each patient is forcibly adjusted. Although weekly contact is the basic frame of reference, flexible response to therapeutic imperatives will always take precedence over policy.

It is a clinical truism that frequency of contact significantly affects the psychotherapeutic process. Frequency has a regulative impact on the intensity and role of therapy in the person's life. Thus, even while weekly psychotherapy is the central focus, frequency of sessions must be monitored to match the therapeutic requirements of the ongoing process. This includes maintaining the character of the relationship as a working partnership. In addition, the balance between therapy as a corrective experience laboratory and the everyday world as the arena of experience is sensitive to the frequency of sessions. Also, the financial capacity of clients (and their third-party supports) is a factor in the equation. An approach designed for weekly contact cannot ignore conditions (trauma, crisis, acute regressive episode) which may mandate temporary modifications of the regular pattern.

The principle of regularity is important to egoself psychotherapy, since it underlies the working character of the re-lationship. Regularity of sessions establishes a working rhythm, especially for the patient. At all levels of awareness, knowing one has therapy on Tuesdays at 10:30 becomes part of the organizational process of ego activity. Memories are stored, feelings mobilized, activities planned—consciously and uncon-sciously—with the regularly scheduled therapy session as an anchoring point. Dependable rhythms seem to catalyze work efficiency. Weekly regularity leaves time for the pacing and internalization of therapeutic material. The nature of egoself psychotherapy—incorporating experience into structure—is better suited to temporally separated, meaningful segments of contact than to intensive exposure.

Unfortunately, present knowledge does not permit psy-chotherapists to pinpoint consistently which specific issues re-spond best to particular time intervals. As that knowledge develops, the regularity demands for dealing with therapy is-sues may take precedence over other frequency considerations. Regularity is therefore not a dictum but a principle. Its value is in direct proportion to its validity as a rationale. Thus, if there are sound psychological reasons for altering the rhythm of weekly sessions, a change in frequency may be therapeutically beneficial. The management of frequency is, therefore, geared to function. Wolberg (1968) offers the following indicators:

1. One or two sessions weekly:
   a. in supportive or reeducative therapy
   b. in many forms of psychoanalytic psychotherapy
   c. to prevent a hostile, dependent relationship
   d. to avoid transference neurosis developing
   e. in people who substitute transference for real-life ex-periences
   f. in people who are not too disturbed.
2. Three to five sessions weekly:
   a. in psychoanalysis, especially for transference evocation
   b. with threatened ego collapse, needing constant support
   c. where concentrated attack on defenses is essential
   d. in people with poor motivation for therapy
   e. with people who are intensely hostile

    f.   with people who need an external check on their acting-out impulses.

    In egoself practice, weekly sessions of fifty minutes provide a useful frequency and duration until or unless there are specific indications, such as those suggested by Wolberg, for more frequent meetings. But even an increase to twice weekly causes a major alteration of therapeutic intensity. During particularly stressful periods of therapy—or life events—it can be helpful to increase frequency beyond weekly sessions. When therapy calls for more active, anxiety-arousing work, and/or when patients are encountering periods of severe disturbance and vulnerability, two or more sessions per week may be necessary for a period of time. While intensive contact can be supportive, and energize exploratory efforts in focal areas, it also encourages regressive dependency or a defensive reaction against those regressive urgings. Measured against those time and expense costs, the egoself therapist exercises judicious caution in recommending long periods of intensive contact.

    At the other end of the frequency continuum, reducing sessions to less than weekly contact is a procedure usually reserved for patients whose need for therapy is reducing. Even biweekly sessions radically dilute the impact of psychotherapy in the person's life. Consequently, reducing frequency is usually a way of beginning to terminate therapy. Patients sometimes cite financial reasons for wanting to cut back on sessions, just as they may cite the need for "more depth" or a more rapid "cure" when requesting greater frequency. Further exploration may reveal other, less "practical" reasons for the requested change, often connected to transference issues. But even when transference reactions are not prominent, modifying frequency for financial reasons is rarely in the best interests of the patient's psychotherapy. Since it can be harmful to have either partner assume a large financial or emotional debt in order for the therapy to continue, it is sometimes useful to consider stopping therapy for a while rather than letting the costs undermine progress. Addressing the issue from this perspective can be helpful in eliciting whatever underlying issues may be operative. While weekly sessions are preferred, the principal criterion remains that of adapting frequency to the ongoing monitoring of patient need, with the patient participating actively in that assessment. Experience suggests that weekly contact is an effective response to the therapeutic and real-life demands of most Americans.

Initial Inquiry

Therapy begins with the very first contacts. In our society the initial inquiry is likely to be tentative and cautious, conveying interest but not commitment. It is common for this inquiry to be less personal than face-to-face contact, and usually made by telephone. The initiating party's identity is therefore partially obscured, retaining anonymity. While the ostensible reason for the contact is fact-finding (Do you offer such a service? Are you available? What are your charges?) its underlying purpose is often more fundamental: can I place my trust and confidence in this person?

During the initial contact, the practitioner has the complex task of simultaneously assessing, responding, and initiating a relationship. From these earliest moments of contact are sewn the seeds of the work that is to come. The response lets the caller know how he or she is going to be treated, what a relationship with this professional person is likely to be. For that response to be most effective the clinician needs to address who the caller is, in terms of developmental status, ego strength, distress level. At the same time, the manifest content of the interaction must be responsive to the caller's words of inquiry. The task would be overwhelming if it was not a unified reaction, to which the component parts are mutually contributory. Nevertheless, the initial contact is a busy, difficult time. Who is the caller, and what is he seeking? Is it an older person seeking evidence of maturity and experience or a younger person concerned about a generation gap? What is the degree of distress, and how is the caller handling it? What is the person asking for, and what can I provide? Is the inquiry on the caller's own behalf, or for someone else? Is the inquiry voluntary or pressured? As is so often the case in psychotherapy, what therapists hear is more important than what they say. One brings to that first brief contact all the knowledge and skill that can be mustered. Weekly therapy, and the theory which guides it, begins with the first contact made by the patient. The theoretical anlage attunes the therapist to pick up clues to assess and synthesize the incoming data, which inform the way one addresses these first contacts.

The initial inquiry bears a certain resemblance to crisis intervention, in that the clinician is called upon to act quickly with little information available. Certain principles of crisis intervention are applicable here: buy time, establish continuity, build trust. As applied to an egoself approach, trust and continuity are served by estimating the developmental and ego assets of the inquirer. In a telephone call, vocal features of tone and speech provide numerous clues to gender and life stage. Severity of pathology and distress level are more readily masked. Since the caller has chosen a mode and topic of inquiry, one responds directly while leaving room for a clearer formulation of the nature of the inquiry, gearing one's words to an emerging image of the caller. From the outset I attempt to establish a tone of parity, speaking to the most adult level manifested, but remaining vigilant for clues that the person may require immediate support. Reassurance is not offered reflexively, nor is it routinely withheld. Optimally, the caller will hear a response which offers concerned professional service—no sweeping promises, no unconditional love, no superiority.

Caller: I'd like to speak to Dr. X.
Therapist: This is she.
C: Do you work with, uh, uh, marriage problems?
Th: Yes, I do.
C: What if . . . they're not married?
Th: How do you mean?
C: I mean, like if they fight but they're not married . . . at least, not yet.
Th: How can I help you?
C: It's not me! I'm calling for a friend of mine. Her and her boyfriend are always fighting, and she doesn't know if she should marry him.
Th: She'd like to talk to someone about her relationship with her boyfriend?
C: Yeah, or maybe you could talk to her boyfriend. . . .
Th: It sounds like you're not exactly sure what she wants, like maybe you're in the middle.

C: Yeah. She was too nervous to call you herself. She didn't know what to do.

Th: How did you get my name?

C: You saw another friend of mine, Andrea, a couple of years ago.

Th: Oh, yes, I remember Andrea. How is she doing?

C: Pretty good.

Th: Look, why don't you tell your friend that she or her boyfriend can call me if they want to, and I'll be glad to do what I can. Okay?

The therapist responded to the first question affirmatively, structuring a basis for further inquiry on both sides. The caller's next comments indicated confusion and uncertainty. The therapist provided further structure by focusing on an offer of help. The caller sounded young, inexperienced in the situation, perhaps immature. By exploring for the source of the call, the therapist was able to establish an affective linkage with the caller. This approach was more valuable than trying to elicit more information about the presenting problem from someone who is an apparent third party. The offer of services is refocused to the troubled couple, the caller has established a network connection, and the contact can be concluded.

The initial inquiry is over. The inquirer has made a professional contact, established a communication link, has an offer of continued contact, and has been presented with a recommendation consonant with the initial inquiry. It is unclear whether further contact will be forthcoming. The caller did not seem positioned to make that decision. The inquiry was appropriately brief, touching on the relevant issues without attempting to elaborate upon them within the confines of a telephone call or letter. Thus, the initial inquiry sets the stage for an evaluation interview.

The toning of the interaction was consistent with egoself precepts: respecting the overt request by responding directly to it, handling the caller's uncertainty by providing structure, staying in present time, offering professional assistance. Despite its brevity and the uncertainty of outcome, the initial inquiry has a useful role. In its optimum form it tests the feasibility of further working together by inaugurating a tone and character for a future relationship, and identifying the style and expectations of the participants. At the descriptive level, it may appear that the surest measure of a successful initial inquiry is the setting of an appointment for an interview. If the caller agrees to a second contact, some needs must have been satisfied. But overt behavior is not always a reliable indicator of intention. Unless the inquirer requests an appointment, it is possible that the practitioner has exerted a subtle pressure which the inquirer found awkward to resist. In these instances the person may fail to keep the appointment; or, the relationship may start with a set of expectations that will create problems later on. Since the caller has initiated the contact, and the practitioner has indicated a willingness to explore the issue further, the option for entering the professional relationship rests with the inquirer.

Implicit in every initial inquiry is the caller's question, Can you help me? The reflexive urge of the psychotherapist, whose professional raison d'etre is helping, is to respond affirmatively, to encourage hope. But that intention must be tempered by the commitment to engage in a relationship of parity between partners. At the inquiry point the caller is expressing need. The brevity of the situation requires a simple response, but one that neither distorts the work nor overcommits either party:

C: Can you help me?
Th: I do work with this sort of problem (person); but I'd need to know more about your specific situation.

Or, to emphasize the value of an assessment,

Th: If we could discuss this situation, I'd be able to tell you what I could offer and you'd be in a position to know if this is what you're looking for.

However, even these simple exchanges must be moderated by whatever has been discerned about the caller's level of egoself function. In the two vignettes above one sees the therapist's commitment to parity: disclaiming prescient powers in the first instance, and empowering the caller in the second. The efficacy of the initial inquiry is therefore gauged by a response which reflects professional interest, by indicating whether the referral is within the practitioner's competencies, and, if so, by suggesting the utility of further discussion—usually in a face-to-face interview. Patients' readiness to schedule an appointment after this interaction signals a further step toward genuine involvement. Sometimes, particularly when there may be a delay before an appointment can be arranged, one can estimate urgency by asking what precipitated the inquiry.

Therapeutic Contracting

The purpose of contracting is to establish the tone and conditions for the work that is to follow. Sometime before or during the first interview, depending on the impressions garnered during the first contact, it is usual practice to recommend a period of mutual assessment of three or four sessions. This is, in effect, a preliminary contract, even though it is not labeled as such. The person who comes with a pressing problem has more urgent concerns than the formal structuring of a relationship which may never develop. Patients are not usually attuned or prepared to think in those terms at the outset. However, the suggestion to meet three or four times is often heard as a promise, a commitment of time to the person. During this preliminary period it is not uncommon to mention the confidentiality of the meetings and the expectation of punctuality, particularly if the therapist has a sense of the immediacy of these issues for the patient. In this way some of the structural features of the relationship are set in place in a natural fashion.

As the therapeutically relevant issues emerge during this assessment period, both parties get a sense of what it would be like to work together. By the third or fourth interview the time is propitious for discussing whether the parties will continue to work together, and with what expectations. Therapists will have had time to assess patients and their presenting problems in egoself terms (chapters 6 and 7), and to evaluate their own ability and readiness to work with them. Patients will have been exposed to the therapist and the therapeutic process sufficiently to form opinions and questions. At that point it is customary for therapists to summarize their assessment in everyday language, incorporating the patient's own contributions to that understanding. The patient's assessment is also solicited, if it has not already been offered, so that both parties can compare perceptions. A mutual discussion is then encouraged, to explore views on what seems to be indicated as the next step. When continued psychotherapy is indicated, if I am available and willing, I offer to work with the person, at a recommended frequency. This places the decision in the individual's hands, an important gesture of psychopolitical empowerment. With people who are ambivalent, tentative, or obsessional, I may urge them to take a day or more rather than feel pressured to make the decision in my presence, in my office. Egalitarian relationships are created; they are not inherent in the structure of psychotherapy. Because of all these preliminary activities, the final negotiation for therapy does not occur until both parties have agreed to work together.

A number of considerations govern an egoself approach to contract management. The first is to cast the process in a way that models the separate but equal nature of the relationship. The second is to assure that essential elements are identified, understood, and agreed upon. A certain tension often intrudes here between the two points. People rarely have perspective or experience in psychotherapy contracting; thus they are disadvantaged by not seeing possible implications or realizing their right to negotiate. At the same time, the therapist wants to be fair, yet not get caught up in legalistic detailing of all the possible meanings. My resolution of the issue is to reduce, simplify, and keep flexible my expectations. I do not use the word *contract*, because of its legalistic and impersonal connotations. Certain elements are fundamental: I emphasize the patient's rights of confidentiality; the therapeutic importance of regularity and punctuality (and the mutual expectations for prior notification of lateness or absence); the day(s) and time(s) of appointments; the mutual obligation to make up canceled sessions, except for prearranged vacations; my right to charge for missed appointments; and the mutual right to ask for a discussion and renegotiation of these points.

The right to renegotiate is particularly important. Younger patients may have never had this opportunity, particularly with an older adult. Impulsive people may leap to agree now, and have second thoughts later. But all patients need this right as leverage against agreements which they may have earlier misunderstood, and as emblematic of their capacity to engage with their world constructively. For example, I assert my right to charge for missed appointments even when they have been canceled in advance. This can seem arbitrary and one-sided, and especially irksome to people with authority problems. By opening the option to discuss and negotiate that decision the stage is set for later encounters with rational authority. For patients in the adolescent–young adult transition period, many of whom are caught up in separation–individuation issues, this becomes an opportunity to differentiate early and current self boundaries within an ongoing relationship. Therapists can also use the right to renegotiate as leverage in confronting passivity or inhibition ("you really wanted to go to that concert, yet you didn't try to change our appointment"); suspicious distrust ("you feel I tricked you into that agreement; but we also agreed we could talk about changing the agreement"); or manipulation ("I'd like to talk about how we use the confidentiality of our meetings").

By contrast, contracting to effect therapeutic changes is counter to the ethos of psychoanalytic psychotherapy. At best, it risks putting a premium on manifest behavior change, which may not be the most important area for therapeutic intervention. Or, by implying that the outcome can be known at the outset, it may seem to endow the process or the therapist with magical qualities. Since egoself psychotherapy attempts to help people potentiate their own capabilities, neither fixed outcomes nor the therapist's prescience reflect that mission. However, one can tailor an agreement to the needs of a particular case. I said to a person with a long history of changing therapists, "I would like to be your last therapist," and the patient heartily concurred. For the patient it was a promise of stability, and of protection against his seductive manipulations. For the therapist it was a statement of durability and a base for later confronting the patient's anticipated flight reactions.

In practice, the word *contract* fails to describe accurately the sort of mutual understanding engaged in during egoself psychotherapy. That essence is one of an ongoing process, based on current understanding, and subject to renegotiation as conditions warrant. In contrast to other schools of thought, which use contracting to define objectives or to establish fixed limits, the egoself approach is designed to minimize points of potential abrasion and to augment patients' sense of participatory power.

Diagnosis and Assessment

Diagnosis is an increasingly controversial subject among theorists of psychotherapy. In medical practice the standard components of a diagnosis are symptoms, etiology, prognosis, and treatment. Medical practice is founded upon accurate and precise diagnosis. Accurate diagnosis pinpoints the clinical pathology and its symptomatology, specifies therapeutic options, and prognosticates outcome. It is a procedure which isolates the disease from its host and ministers to it with observably distinct methods and predictably consistent outcome expectations.

In psychotherapy it is the exception, not the rule, that diagnosis accurately describes symptoms, etiology, prognosis, and treatment. Unlike medical practice, inconsistency of diagnosis is the rule in psychopathology. Diagnostic criteria for the same syndrome vary from clinic to clinic and within and between professional groups (Smith and Kraft, 1983). In some areas of severe psychopathology, particularly those where there is evidence of genetic or constitutional predisposition, accurate differential diagnosis can be of considerable value. Endogenous depression is one such instance. On the other hand, acute anxiety, despite varying symptoms and etiology, is nevertheless prescriptive of specific intervention procedures. In egoself therapy assessment rather than diagnosis is emphasized. I share with others (Blanck and Blanck, 1979; Strupp and Binder, 1984) the view that personality organization overshadows symptomatology as the prime consideration in designing a strategy for therapy.

Symptom clusters alone have limited value in prognosis and treatment. Schizophrenia is a severe thought and language disorder, yet people with schizophrenia complete college, conduct medical research, parent children. Rarely is schizophrenia cured, but it has been successfully controlled with psychotherapy, electroconvulsive therapy, chemotherapy, psychosurgery. Hysterical neurosis has been treated, successfully and unsuccessfully, with hypnosis, bed rest, psychoanalysis, and most forms of psychotherapy. Yet, despite the demonstrated lack of consensus on specific diagnosis, the practice of psychotherapy grows and empirical data point to its increasing effectiveness. Another challenge to the utility of diagnosis is its impact in structuring psychotherapeutic intervention strategy. Unlike medical practice, psychotherapeutic specialization is virtually unknown. Who are the therapists who specialize in obsessional neurosis, in reactive depression, in school phobia? Rosenbaum and Muroff's (1984) reconsideration of the famous case of Anna O. illustrates my point compellingly. This young woman, with a seemingly classical hysterical paralysis, was unsuccessfully treated by Breuer. Her disabling "illness" did not stop her from achieving international prominence as a writer, politician, and feminist. More important for this discussion, the fourteen contributors to the Rosenbaum and Muroff volume find little agreement among themselves, relative to contemporary therapeutic intervention. It is fair to say that most psychological problems are treated by most psychotherapists. Until diagnosis demonstrates greater utility for psychotherapeutic practice, the time and energy it demands may be more effectively expended in psychological assessment.

There are sharp differences between assessment and diagnosis, differences which may ultimately be incorporated into future diagnostic procedures. The multiaxial format adopted in *The Diagnostic and Statistical Manual of Mental Disorders* (DSM-III) (APA, 1980) which includes "psychosocial stressors" and "highest adaptive functioning," may be a forerunner of significant eventual reconceptualization of diagnosis in psychotherapy (Millon, 1983). But whereas assessment is a necessary component of contemporary practice, diagnosis can be an impediment. In egoself practice, assessment targets intrapsychic organizational processes. Assessment focuses on the person's functioning in these core areas in order to translate the presenting problem into the psychotherapeutically workable language of assets and vulnerabilities. Developmental assessment establishes the parameters which describe object relations, and locate the person in life span terms as well as teleological style. The assessment of ego functions describes the factors affecting the organization of the person's functioning. Monitoring self functions and structure, and transferential material, clarifies the affective toning of the interaction. The assessment process incorporates patients' active participation, as contributors of experience and perspective which is uniquely their own. Social supports, competencies, and life situation are part of every assessment. Since these processes are described in other chapters I will not recapitulate them here. But assessment, not diagnosis, is the groundwork upon which are laid the specific concerns of the patient.

One must understand the patient's pathology, but also how those pathological processes impact on the rest of the person. Borderline conditions are likely to affect young adults differently than middle-aged adults, men differently than women, the economically privileged differently than those who are indigent, and Hispanics differently than Scandinavians. The management of an emotionally labile, adult member of an affluent, stoic family is vastly different from the adolescent who belongs to an emotionally volatile family of limited means. Intimacy and emotion will be quite different experiences in either situation.

In a related matter, the chronicity of a problem may be as important as its severity in designing therapeutic strategy. Reactive depression to a spouse's death poses different issues, depending upon whether the death occurred ten weeks or ten years earlier. The impact of trauma in the acute case, and secondary gain in the chronic case, will selectively shape the treatment of each reactive depression. To the extent that terms such as *neurotic process, psychotic reaction,* or *narcissistic disorder* convey a consistent understanding of some aspect of psychological structure and function, they are used in that general descriptive sense.

One of the most important features of egoself assessment is its emphasis on identification of strengths and recruitable assets in the patient. Alleviating pathology does not assure that healthy and appropriate operations will automatically replace them. Only as patients discover more useful ways of experiencing and functioning, are pathological malformations and their secondary gains likely to erode.

Resistance

In traditional psychoanalytic literature, resistance is symptomatic of heightened anxiety, manifested by the activation of defense mechanisms, and often accompanied by quantitative or qualitative changes in the transference. Technically, it indicates that the therapist is "getting warm" in approaching the client's core conflict area. Other sources of resistance derive from patients' weak motivation, hostile or dependent needs, character problems, or the spontaneous eruption of strong transference feelings toward the analyst. For the classical analyst, resistance is an essential ingredient of the therapeutic process, central to revealing defenses and uncovering the basic neurotic conflict.

The egoself view of resistance differs not so much in conceptualization as in application. The interpretation of resistance must also allow for alternative explanations: the client's reaction may be in defense of cherished values which the therapist seemed to deprecate or ignore; the reaction may also be due to erroneous interpretation, or countertransference. In weekly egoself therapy resistance is typically viewed as an impediment to the partnership, and approached in that light. Management of resistance incorporates a developmental perspective. In that sense resistance can be seen as conservation, a holding to sameness, constancy. In this construction of personality dynamics, resistive patients may be struggling to retain a sense of stability, to protect their identity, or moving toward greater intrapsychic autonomy. The content of the resistance is subordinate to the need to enhance or conserve the integrity of the self. It is no accident that adolescents, for whom identity crisis is stage-specific, are among the most resistant of clients. Consequently, the analysis of resistance is subordinate to helping the patient sustain an identity that will permit further growth. Resistance often dissipates spontaneously when egoself growth occurs in related areas.

Persistent lateness is a classic example of resistance (Wolberg, 1968). James, a young adult, was invariably late for therapy. From earlier information, his tardiness seemed to have two functions: it reflected his anxiety about being in therapy, that he would be found "mentally ill"; it also repeated transferentially his passive aggressive way of provoking his father's anger. Addressing the roots of his lateness in weekly therapy would have dug James deeper into his self-denigration as mentally ill and further strengthened his negative identity. Instead, the therapist chose to focus on supportive confrontation, uncovering abilities and assets which James minimized or repressed. As he became able to acknowledge a healthy side of his identity, the tardiness dissipated spontaneously. The traditional approach might have arrived at the same result, but the egoself approach also promoted a concomitant growth in self-esteem.

In egoself terms genuine resistance, like transference, is a temporal displacement—an instance of the past operating in the present. Evidence of resistance therefore informs the weekly psychotherapist the way sonar informs marine navigators, to beware of lurking obstacles, not to confront them. While resistance cannot be ignored if it has a corrosive effect on the working partnership of weekly psychotherapy, the time restrictions of weekly contact impede the delicate detailing necessary for proper elicitation of the patient's insight. Instead, an effective response is modeled on the basic premise of aikido. Although it is a martial art, aikido is often conducted like a dance, in which the contestants are partners. Unlike other martial arts, in aikido the participants do not block the partner's thrusts. Instead, they recruit the energy of the thrust by pivoting away from the target area and then, following alongside the energy flow, guide it to other uses. In egoself psychotherapy potential resources are sought, mobilized, and recruited wherever they are found. The clients' resistive manifestations represent commitments of energy which define the direction of effort at that time. Psychological aikido informs therapists to recognize those energies and to find constructive uses for them. As good partners, therapists join their patients and contribute their own efforts, thereby exercising a positive influence on the direction they are taking.

Th: (noticing patient's continuous fidgeting) You seem kind of restless today.

P: Who, me? No, I'm not nervous or anything.

Th: You seem to be fidgeting more today.

P: Naw, nothing special today; I'm always like this.

Th: Like what?

P: What do you mean?

Th: You said you're always like this, and I was trying to get clear on what "like this" is.

After her two resistive comments, I joined the patient's energy flow with "like what?" Her response, "What do you mean?" is almost a role reversal, taking the therapist position of asking for clarification. We are now moving together in the same direction, with one difference: now she is explaining herself to me on her terms instead of defending against my perceived attack. I continue to explore her current feelings, advancing the therapy in a way more consonant with her own direction, no longer on a collision course with her.

Another important component in the management of resistance is compassion. The irritable, rejecting, or withdrawn behavior of resisting patients masks their sense of threat. Therapists have little problem with expressing compassion for patients who are in obvious pain. But reflecting compassion toward an attacking, rejecting person does not come naturally. Just as important is helping patients to be compassionate toward themselves, particularly as they become aware that their resistive feelings toward the therapist originate in themselves. Professional objectivity may not sufficiently help patients who have been vituperatively resistive. Unemotional therapist reactions may be tantamount to retaliatory emotional withdrawal, and perceived as punitive, even as deserved punishment. Patients who have been defending their vulnerability by resisting invasive exploration can attack themselves as harshly as they do their therapists. Boldly supportive confrontation, especially when the patient seems depressed or remorseful, validates the legitimacy of protecting one's identity even as those representations are changing. Moreover, it urges the need for accepting oneself with compassion, healthy adult narcissism. Some patients are able to understand their resistance as a voice from the past, the child in them clinging to its ways. The adult patient with an observing ego can, perhaps, understand that the child needs love and respect for its feelings in order to grow up. Primitively organized patients may be able to utilize the intervention for self-soothing, by identifying with and internalizing the therapist's compassion.

While resistive episodes are unavoidable in psychotherapy, their potential for corroding the therapeutic relationship necessitates effective management. In weekly therapy, using psychological aikido and urging a compassionate attitude on both participants can significantly reduce the adverse impact of resistance.

Anxiety Dynamics

Anxiety, and its intrapsychic management, are at the core of psychotherapy. Anxiety is incremental, so that it must be dissipated or it eventually becomes intolerable. Anxiety is also a universal, inevitable, part of human experience. Its ubiquity ranges from severe psychopathology into the tensions of everyday life. Consequently, the management of anxiety is an ongoing imperative for people whether or not they require therapy. Thus, while anxious suffering is a primary reason for people to enter psychotherapy, its effective management can have salutory repercussions throughout the life span.

Weekly therapy targets the patient's current methods of anxiety management. Since the effects of anxiety are pernicious whatever its origin, therapeutic strategy is based on the necessity for identifying and mediating its pathological impact. While mild quanta of anxiety may stimulate ego functioning, its incremental effect is progressively disruptive and disorganizing to ego operations. Signal anxiety serves to mobilize egoself resources toward adaptation and actualization—meeting and mastering challenges, and fulfilling potentialities. Pathogenic anxiety magnetizes ego functioning toward survival, activating processes aimed at dissipating or eliminating its noxious impact. While all ego functioning is geared to maintaining the integrity of personality organization (Hartmann, 1958), it is the coping processes (Haan, 1977) which are the most effective. Ego coping processes address the issues which precipitate anxiety, rather than the anxiety itself. These dynamics involve egoself mediation of affective intensity so that adaptive resources can be activated. The management strategy is twofold: identifying the immediate source of pathology in anxiety, and then helping patients to mobilize whatever intrapsychic resources are available to them. There are five processes evoked by anxiety: coping, defense, fragmentation, motor discharge, and somatic discharge. All are employed, individually and in combination, in the continuing task of managing anxiety. Developmentally, the earliest are the motor and somatic discharge pathways. Both of these reactions obviate the affective experience, by dissipating the tension in muscle activity (motor) or through physiological activation (somatic). Motor discharge ranges from postural change to exercise to fight-or-flight reactions, including the acting out use of intoxicating substances. Anxiety experienced as physical discomfort is usually relieved by activity designed to relax the muscle system. Muscle activity, fighting, drinking, and other forms of impulse discharge are the common manifestations—obliterating anxiety by acting out. Somatic discharge utilizes somatization processes to transfer anxiety to organs or physiological systems. Transient episodes of somatic hyperactivity produce familiar symptoms as "affect equivalents" (Fenichel, 1945)—rapid heartbeat, blushing. Chronic hyperactivation can result in physical illness and tissue damage. In its chronic forms, somatization is rarely accompanied by conscious experience of anxiety.

Coping and defending processes are organized responses to anxiety, whereas fragmentation represents a breakdown during which ego operations are overwhelmed. While Haan (1977) insists that all three processes are normally expectable, they are clearly not equivalent. Fragmentation disrupts reality contact and results in autism, pathological debilitation, whether its duration is measured in seconds or years. Defense processes preserve ego or self integrity by reducing or avoiding anxiety, thus bringing it within tolerable limits. But the price of chronic defense is the constriction of thought and action which characterizes pathology. As Haan (1977) points out, defense processes are grounded in magical thought and secondary gain. Instead of addressing the source of the anxiety, defenses are palliative measures which, when activated successfully, become chronic. Defenses thus have limited adaptation value, and inhibit growth. Only coping processes focus on the source of the anxiety, attempting to resolve the precipitating problem, rather than the noxious affect it generates. Consequently, only coping provides a means for resolving sources of anxiety in a way which promotes growth. While coping is the modal, everyday method for handling distress, its application to therapeutic intervention is necessarily more complex.

The egoself approach to anxiety management involves both standard and nontraditional procedures. The usual methods of "talking treatment" are applied—catharsis, objectification, differentiation, clarification. These help patients reduce anxiety, or raise tolerances, to sustainable levels. In severe, primitive, and chronic problems, to help clients recruit and mobilize ego assets to address the anxiety, preferably at its source, prescriptive use of specific techniques for reducing severe anxiety is encouraged. These include focused exercises for ego-mediated motor discharge, cautiously combining these with clarification and support for fragmentation reactions; and adding confrontation, differentiation, and other exploratory techniques with defense processes. Patients appreciate and readily participate in these more tangible efforts to reduce their misery. These techniques, which involve the patient actively, are often a preferable alternative to medication. Some people prove to be remarkably adept partners in this enterprise. Honing and shaping egoself resources to the task of anxiety management can be a uniquely satisfying part of weekly psychotherapy for both partners. Beyond the immediate palliative effects it is a useful example of applying one's own resources to the problems one encounters.

> After four years of marriage, Dave's second wife was leaving him. Dave was distraught, and enraged. He threatened to kill her; he begged her to reconsider; he wept; he couldn't eat or sleep. Assessment revealed an extremely primitive level of egoself organization, with a lifelong pattern of failed interpersonal relationships and assaultive incidents. Dave described the loss of his wife as intolerable. Both he and she seemed at great risk. She called the police, who said they were powerless to intervene.

Dave refused medication or hospitalization, but agreed to see me twice weekly. One morning, during the second month of therapy, I received a telephone call from Dave's mother. He was in her living room, incoherent, tearing at the walls with his fingers, crying and calling for help. At my suggestion, his mother carried the phone over to Dave and held it so that I could talk to him. He recognized me. In between incoherent rambling and cries for help, he described somatic delusions of his flesh bubbling and crawling, and visual hallucinations of demons on the walls. His agitation did not permit him to sit or stand still. He could not control his hands enough to hold the phone. I asked his mother to bring him a kitchen chair and asked him to sit on it, then grab the seat in each hand and try to lift it up. Several moments of this activity brought some relief, but then he could no longer tolerate sitting. His arms and back were alive with tension. I suggested an exercise, a form of vertical pushups against the wall. His crying and desperation subsided into a mumbling, then into a rhythmic repetition of words I didn't understand. Finally, he explained: he had converted my exercise into a T'ai chi movement he had learned. In another half-hour the psychotic panic had responded to the T'ai chi activity, completely remitted, and did not return.

Recruiting the patient's propensity for motor discharge led to rechanneling his overwhelming anxiety from autistic fragmentation to ego-mediated discharge. When the patient later idealized me as "the one who saved my life," I could help him see that his innovative use of his old T'ai chi skills had been equally important. My supportive statement confronted Dave with his own contribution to his recovery. This intervention may have allowed him to share the glow of the idealizing transference (Kohut and Wolf, 1978), encouraging self structure as an alternative to his symbiotic attachment to me.

The same principles of anxiety management apply across the life span, whenever anxiety overwhelms healthy functioning. First, to introduce ego mediation, using the pathways most familiar to the client. Then, to recruit the highest levels of function available to the person. According to Haan's data, coping is the "normative" process, the way people function when psychological conditions are relatively quiescent. Helping patients moderate their anxiety facilitates coping. Analyzing patients' history of using ego processes, therapists can help mobilize their most effective coping methods.

> Mr. H, a middle aged man in his fifties, was depressed and drinking to excess. He was hurt and disappointed by how his children were "turning out": one was "a pothead," one was in trouble with the law, another a runaway. A widower, he was overwhelmed by parenting four children. He came home from work at night and turned off their demands by turning on the TV and opening a six-pack of beer. His silence contrasted with his perilously high blood pressure and facial scowling. He was unaware of feeling anger or guilt concerning his children. Therapy contained many long silences, during which his mood seemed to alternate between truculence and withdrawal. Eventually he could exhibit fleeting outbursts of rage at the ingratitude of his kids who let him down by their problem behavior. Meanwhile, his repressive defenses against anger and depression endangered his health and his family.

Intervention strategy began with supporting the legitimacy of his right to feel angry and depressed and to let his children know how upset he was. Mr. H rejected any connection between his emotional woodenness and his high blood pressure. In his emotionally depleted state he was quite receptive to having his feelings justified, however. Gradually, he became able to growl and yell at his children, even demanding that they help out around the house. No longer emotionally cut off from their father, the children became more responsive. Mr. H's repressive defense was becoming suppression, a coping process, as he learned to express himself selectively. Whenever he could function this way, his depression lifted and his drinking moderated.

This therapeutic technique is hardly original. Experienced therapists tend to develop similar techniques. The power of the egoself approach lies in its theoretical consistency—being grounded in modern psychoanalytic theory—and thus providing a parsimonious basis for diverse therapeutic strategies.

Medication Management

In weekly psychotherapy with very anxious or depressed people the ancillary use of psychopharmaceutical agents can facilitate the therapy. In some schizophrenic and depressive reactions, medication may be the treatment of choice, a more effective means of symptom reduction. When the psychopathological reaction is incapacitating, prudent management may indicate that the physical and psychological side effects of medication are warranted by the risks facing the patient. By the same reasoning, prudent management militates against the use of medication in the absence of specific indications for its prescription. Any agent that blunts or alters patients' ability to participate actively in therapy is to be viewed with great caution.

Pharmaceuticals, legal and illicit, pervade American life. The complex problem of monitoring people's medications has become a matter of concern to consumers, pharmacists, and most health care professionals. Because physicians often prescribe tranquilizing medication in treating medical complaints, independent of whether the person is in psychotherapy, it is useful to inquire about clients' use of medication, both legal and otherwise. Where it seems appropriate, I inquire about the need, and/or request permission to contact the client's physician. At a minimum, my purpose is to question what is so often assumed, that drugs are an expectable part of everyday life. This attitude is antithetical to basic egoself precepts and therefore must be brought to the surface and confronted. While moralizing on the subject is counterproductive to the partnership, so also is ignoring it. The purpose of discussing medication is to make my position known to the patient, who is free to disagree—as long as we both recognize it as a disagreement.

I have never refused to work with people because of their possible abuse of medicines, illegal drugs, alcohol, or other intoxicants or addictive substances. But I insist on my right to discuss that use if and when it seems to put either the patient or the therapy at risk. A distinction is necessary here between abusive use of intoxicants and acting out. Patients who have been taking medication regularly, including the days they come for therapy, are not necessarily acting out—even though the anxiety-mollifying effects may interfere with optimal therapeutic work. Patients may not feel able to discontinue their reliance on medication, but they can be helped to see what it costs them in their lives. One measure of the impact of psychotherapy is reduced reliance on psychoactive medications. In genuine acting out, when patients' drug use is linked to stressful life events (including therapy), a selective abstinence agreement can be suggested: "Can you agree not to smoke dope on the day we have our meeting?"; or "Will you agree to tell me if you've smoked dope on the day of our meeting? I think it would be helpful to take a look at what you're feeling that makes it necessary for you to smoke then."

In the more standard use of medication, there are times when patients' suffering indicates the need for medical intervention. Patients vary in their willingness to accept medication, and their reluctance may increase if they sense their therapists' disapproval. Part of therapeutic learning is the discovery of one's thresholds for pain, humor, sorrow. Thus, referral for medical assistance occurs in a context with exploration of the feelings and meanings associated with suffering and seeking its relief. By this method, medication is actively incorporated within the developmental work of therapy rather than allowed a role external to the process.

In life-span developmental terms, the use of medication tends to have selective meanings. Children take medicine when they are sick; youthful people are supposed to be healthy, immune from illness or incapacity; with aging, the need for medication is associated with progressive infirmity. People in the middle third of the life span—whose identity often contains elements of physical invincibility—are more likely to feel threatened by the need for medical attention. As people age and acclimatize to their years, medication may seem a right to which they are entitled. Third World, blue collar, and less verbal people are more likely to interpret psychogenic problems in somatic terms and are accustomed to seek cures from medication. These varying perspectives on medication mandate selective therapeutic management.

In object relations terms, attitudes and expectations toward medication can reveal much about self and object representations, reinacted in the patient's covert expectations of treatment: how realistic are they, how hopeful? Anxiety about being vulnerable, needing help, and the fantasies it generates, can be useful in other aspects of the therapeutic work. These unconscious self–world interactions affect everyday behavior. Patients' reactions to stress may mirror reaction patterns—coping processes, defensive maneuvers—to other stress-inducing situations. In sum, it is important for patients to utilize medication in a manner consistent with egoself precepts: to restructure passive overreliance on medication into an ego mediated assessment and management of this event in their lives. The effect of medication on cognitive processes, affective thresholds, and general awareness is enormously variable and often unknown. While side effects are commonplace with virtually all medicines, their more subtle impact is not always recognized.

An alternative approach to medication, much more consonant with the egoself orientation, is embodied by the holistic health movement. With its philosophic roots in self-healing and optimizing human growth resources, it has obvious kinship with the egoself emphasis on personal empowerment and growth. Holistic health integrates diet, exercise, and consciousness as a way of confronting stress. Inherent to this thinking is a belief in providing people with natural skills of self-care, based on a conception of human functioning as unitary, holistic. While life-threatening illnesses may require traditional medical attention, the holistic approach accords well with the structure of weekly egoself therapy. Since more of everyday life is automatically brought into the weekly session therapists find it necessary to be attuned to patients' current life situation. The egoself orientation makes a virtue of this necessity by helping patients adapt life to meet their therapeutic needs.

Lateness and Missed Sessions

Separate but interlocking issues come into play in therapeutic strategy regarding tardiness and absence. The issues are therapeutic and professional. The professional issues have to do with the time and money involved, since psychotherapy is usually a fee-for-service business arrangement. Therapeutic concern is naturally directed at the meaning of the behavior; at the same time, egoself emphasis on an egalitarian partnership necessitates the construction of policies which are rational and fair to both partners.

My standard policy is announced at the outset of therapy. We meet every week at the agreed day and time. Sessions begin and end on time. Both parties are expected to notify the other in case of lateness or absence. I reserve the right to charge for late or canceled sessions, pending discussion of the underlying circumstances.

It is essential that the management of late and missed sessions recognizes differences in patient and therapist positions, to minimize arbitrary decisions and policies. Even policies which were previously agreed on can seem arbitrary in the context of later experience. Whenever patients feel treated as less than equal, there are likely to be cost consequences for the therapeutic work. Put another way, sometimes patient complaints of inequity are legitimate, rather than reflections of narcissistic entitlement. Since the psychopolitical structure of the relationship favors psychotherapists—we are the experts, sitting in our offices, using our language and techniques—we are readily perceived as authorities who possess special (superior, magical) qualities. These attributes are likely to enhance client passivity and regression, even though the purpose of our work is to foster initiative and growth. Therapists cannot effectively confront dependent helplessness in patients when the structure within which they work subtly reinforces patients' perception of their subordinate status.

The egoself perspective incorporates both reality and intrapsychic considerations in implementing absence–lateness policy. People outside the urban middle-class world have much less contact with precise time schedules, and a much less specific perception of the passage of time. To set strict schedule policies with such patients may make a difficult situation worse. These considerations must inevitably influence the carrying out of an absence–lateness policy, although they do not obviate the need for such a policy. Patients with impaired ego functioning are also likely to have difficulty with regularly scheduled appointments. Some ambulatory schizophrenics lack sufficient reality contact, and special arrangements have to be made if they are to be seen regularly on an outpatient basis. On the other hand, people with impulse control problems may benefit therapeutically by exposure to a system of self-regulation which is tied to predictable, tangible consequences: regular, scheduled, timed appointments; set fees; firm policies on lateness and cancellations.

In weeky psychotherapy unscheduled breaks in the regular patterning are assumed to be counterproductive. It is reasonable policy to require of both parties prior notification of impending absence or lateness. Patients can be expected to schedule ample time for travel to the therapist's office. Therapists can be expected to schedule ample time between appointments so that they can remain punctual through the day. Sometimes patients appear to bear a disproportionate share of the burden for missed or abbreviated sessions. They are more subject to traffic snarls and transit system breakdowns, causes of lateness which may exceed reasonable time allowances for travel. Tardy therapists are penalized by adding extra time to their working day; tardy patients are penalized by paying for an abbreviated session. Meeting only once a week, that lost time is a significant impediment to therapy. Countertransference resentment toward tardy patients can further complicate management. Certain arrangements made at the outset of therapy are at variance with everyday customs, in ways that set therapists apart as "special people." These agreements, casually accepted by patients at the start of therapy, may not become significant until months later, when they suddenly feel trapped by them. One such arrangement is that the only appointments which can be canceled without charge are those which fall during the therapist's announced vacation(s). Patients who cannot arrange their vacations to coincide with the therapist's must choose between forfeiting their vacation times or forfeiting sessions, for which they are charged. Less extreme, but more complex, are the conditions for which a canceled session is charged. While it is common practice to charge for uncanceled sessions, some therapists require twenty-four hours notification, some require medical verification of illness also, and some insist on making up the canceled session(s) within the options of the therapist's schedule.

There are usually legitimate reasons undergirding these policies. The principle of regularity of meetings has been discussed earlier, emphasizing the importance of dependable, rhythmic, ongoing sessions. Another reason is the clinically valid concern that lateness and absence may reflect resistive acting out. Still another reason is to discourage arbitrariness on the part of clients who feel that they can judge beforehand whether sessions will be fruitful. A fourth reason is that therapists have the right and need to charge for scheduled sessions in order to assure themselves of a dependable income. Unfortunately, the social service ethic which is presumed to motivate most psychotherapists sometimes makes them uncomfortable with openly acknowledging that they also have economic motives for their work. But failure to acknowledge this legitimate motive can lead to policy rationalizations which later complicate the professional relationship.

The disadvantage of fixed, prearranged, policies is that they may not serve these legitimate purposes. Canceling a day or a week in advance does not insure that there will be adequate clarification of the reasons underlying the action, nor does it obviate avoidant acting out as the clinical determinant of the cancellation. Similarly, requiring a medical document does not prevent patients from manipulating their family physician, or from developing psychophysiological reactions which are valid medical illnesses. Finally, despite the importance of regularity, there are legitimate reasons why patients need to cancel sessions (Colarusso and Nemiroff, 1981). More urban jobs today require distant travel, day-long meetings, overtime hours, and other intrusions on a predictable schedule. Life-style issues and other personal values may be just as important as weekly therapy to many of our patients.

Other reasons are more dynamically familiar, but are complicated by the tenuous character of weekly contact. One such instance derives from having been in therapy for a period of time. Initial progress is often followed by a plateau, during which patients may be consolidating the new experience, resting from their efforts, or resisting further exploration. A request to cancel a session, or atypical lateness, may presage such an occurrence. Insistence on consistency must be weighed against what the patient is able or willing to absorb, risking that intellectual understanding, affective withdrawal, or feelings of inadequacy and resentment may result. A second possibility is that patients may have come to a point where life experience, or autonomy from the therapy (Blanck and Blanck, 1974), serves individuation more efficiently than would further exploration at that point.

> Sandra had begun to understand how her clinging to men was causing them to move away from her. She felt ready to try another relationship, with the active monitoring and support of therapy as a basic component of the experience. Unfortunately, there were no other men, current or impending, in her life. It was decided to cancel a few sessions until some new opportunities for meeting men developed. "Instead of seeing you on Wednesday evenings, I'd rather put in time at that folk dancing class."

This anecdote also highlights a third consideration, which is financial. Many people, especially those who have been in therapy for a while, have limited expendable income. The gains of psychotherapy, although still incomplete, may encourage them to experiment with unfamiliar freedoms. Sometimes those freedoms are purchased by choosing between financial expenditures, one of which is psychotherapy. The situation with Sandra, above, was precipitated when she abruptly canceled a session in order to enroll in the dance class. At the next meeting she explained what she had done. The therapist, in turn, explained that she would have to be charged for the session, but that they could explore what she would like to do about other Wednesday evening sessions. When acting out replaces communication, a fundamental basis of therapeutic engagement is jeopardized and must be confronted. But the ultimate measure of therapeutic effectiveness is its impact on patients' lives. When life activities have to be experienced at the cost of therapy, sometimes that is the preferable path.

Given the variety of circumstances that can affect attendance at sessions, I am unable to set fixed rules about prior notification. My approach is to discuss the principles of regularity and punctuality with clients, and to indicate the priority of reason in determining when charges will be levied. We begin by agreeing that sessions will begin on time, we will meet as scheduled, and the patient will be charged accordingly. When sessions must be delayed or canceled, it is our joint responsibility to try to arrange an alternative time. But I cannot justify penalizing patients in time or money for external events which frustrate their best efforts to meet with me. I cannot justify setting the priority of my schedule or financial needs over theirs without tacitly encouraging a perception of me as an implacable, irrational authority. I prefer to establish our mutual right to discuss and negotiate when there are legitimate charges for missed sessions, whether or not they have been formally canceled by the patient. By the same token, a phone call canceling a session does not preclude the patient being charged for the meeting; nor does a medical note; nor do pleas of poverty. That decision, and negotiating its terms, resides within the partnership. Through negotiation patients can discover the psychological connection between their medical symptoms and precipitating events. Negotiation provides therapists with an opportunity to adjust their schedule or fees temporarily, if the circumstances warrant. Strict adherence to the principle of an egalitarian relationship is, in my experience, a therapeutically valuable opportunity. As that principle affects late and canceled sessions, what we agree on is upheld until we change it. And changing it is a bilateral decision. Holding the relationship to adult standards of interaction, inherent in weekly egoself therapy, requires a flexibility different from that which is practiced in psychoanalysis.

There are times when it seems therapeutically important for patients to act unilaterally, when separation–individuation issues are focal or when other concerns affecting intimacy or identity are involved. As Blanck and Blanck (1974) suggest, unannounced incidents of lateness or absence may reflect a patient's efforts to risk separating from the relationship in the service of increased autonomy. While it would be an error to interpret such occurrences as resistance or acting out, because they are unilateral acts it is appropriate that the patient be charged for the session. In egoself strategy, part of the benefit derives from the patient's expectation of being charged, the predictable cost of the unilateral decision. By contrast, insisting that patients take vacations when I do or be charged for missed sessions devalues the relative importance of their own lives. Due to the variety of underlying reasons for late or missed sessions, each set of incidents should be evaluated developmentally as well as for its dynamic meaning in the therapy. In practice, it soon becomes clear when behavior derives from countertherapeutic origins, and must be confronted. If the therapist has been reasonable in previous instances, the task of therapeutic exploration is eased. Unlike intensive therapy, where one instance can be examined several times in the same week, a lateness issue can quickly seem distant and picayune if it has to be carried forward for weeks on end. Many of the same concerns affect the way fees are managed.

Fee Management

Traditional discussions of fee management in psychotherapy literature attend closely to the psychological significance of money and paying a fee. While many of those principles remain pertinent today, current financial practices may vitiate their impact. The tradition of setting and paying fees used to be part of the therapeutic agreement, and was an ongoing component of the interaction between patients and therapists. The involvement of other financial sources, such as insurance carriers, families, and subsidized clinics, has widely broadened access to therapeutic services, but has significantly dislodged patients and therapists from their financial interactions. The conditions of fee payment—amounts, regularity, duration—frequently have less to do with patient and therapist than with procedures external to the therapeutic process. The enormous social gain, in the numbers of people who can receive psychotherapy due to third-party payment, has not been achieved without cost.

In a monied society financial transactions assume disproportionate significance, more so when the relationship extends over months or years. Since egoself psychotherapy is attuned to real world impact, fee payment strategy must be psychologically managed within real world constraints. The first hazard of third-party payment is in augmenting whatever tendency patients may have to dilute the professional, fee-for-service, nature of the relationship. For some people, "it doesn't cost anything, so why not try it?" is a convenient rationalization for dipping only one's toes into the unknown waters of psychotherapy. For others, the magical insurance payments may augur other magical processes, rather than personal effort, as the vital ingredients of therapy. For both parties, the Big Brother quality of third-party involvement can detract from the primacy of the patient–therapist relationship. Therapists' annoyance with third-party bureaucracy: extra paperwork, delayed cash flow, discounted fees, lack of patient accountability, may contribute to a subtle annoyance which can be displaced to patients as the nearest target. While third-party payments are rapidly dissipated in intensive treatment, in weekly therapy that intrusion continues for months.

Since the egoself perspective mandates the active partnership of patients, it is useful to clarify what meaning third-party payment may have for the therapy. In cases where psychotherapy seems likely to extend beyond the period covered by carriers, it is important for patients and therapists to resolve future financial arrangements in advance. Engaging these issues directly from the outset of the relationship sets the tone and expectation of a working partnership.

Whatever may be their own philosophy of fee setting, therapists do well to be aware of currently prevalent rates. In a society where monetary value is commonly associated with worth, fees convey a message that should be consistent with other therapist communications. This is particularly true when dealing with middle-class patients, those most likely to interpret fees in terms of worth, prestige, and fairness. But the seeming equity of charging everyone the same amount may be viewed quite differently by rich patients, for whom a twenty-dollar difference may be negligible, and poor people, for whom twenty dollars is more than is affordable. Ideally, fees and payments should be designed to reflect the realities of each relationship, with patients bearing prime responsibility for their own costs since they are to be the prime beneficiaries. In practice, the system is far less rational, and it is vulnerable to forces which are not always accessible to therapeutic use. Relatively few patients are financially independent of others where therapy is concerned. Thus, fees and payments usually involve other people's financial and emotional support of the considerable costs of therapy. As a further complication, some of the other people involved may be intimately connected, and caught up in the patient's emotional problems. Thus, payment of fees can get enmeshed with the changing currents of the client's other personal relationships.

> Sylvia was a full-time graduate student. Her father, a wealthy corporate lawyer, reluctantly agreed to pay for her therapy. As the therapy went on, Sylvia revealed her doubts of her father's love. She distrusted him, and was convinced that he would desert her by reneging on therapy payments. She was encouraged to discuss her concerns with her father, who responded with ambiguity to her anxious queries. A major reason for the therapy was Sylvia's distrust of men. When she badgered her father about his habitual tardiness in paying her bills, he became even more irregular. The therapist used this interaction to help Sylvia connect her expectations with her actions, and the reaction this evoked in others. Closer examination of her father's general behavior helped Sylvia to acknowledge that he seemed to be a man of integrity and, consequently, someone who would make good on the responsibilities he shouldered. The therapeutic work was aided, and the therapist's anxieties assuaged, when father finally began regular, if belated, payments. It may not be coincidental that payments resumed after Sylvia was able to relate to her father in ways more consistent with her adult status.

In traditional practice fee payments are expected punctually. While most psychotherapists would undoubtedly prefer such an arrangement, my experience is that the timing of weekly therapy fees paid directly by patients is quite variable. For some patients, the longer therapy continues the less regular the payment pattern. At any given time, a full-time private practitioner can accumulate a significant backlog of payments. The monies owed therapists are usually proportionate to their tolerance for client indebtedness, and their own inner conflicts over charging fees, confronting patients, personal worth, and so on. Patients can come to regard therapy bills with the same equanimity accorded numerous other monthly payments. Sometimes there is an unspoken realization that therapy bills do not carry the heavy interest charges of other monthly billings. For many people, the special place of therapy in their lives becomes routine over time, the therapeutic relationship notwithstanding. Contemporary American life contains a number of personal and financial commitments for patients; learning how to juggle them successfully entails keeping a balanced perspective on the lot. Those who assign the greatest weight to psychotherapy are not necessarily those who are psychologically or financially in the best position to pay promptly. Young and established adults, the two cohorts who constitute the major clientele of psychotherapists, also carry the heaviest financial burdens relative to income. Weekly psychotherapists who insist that therapy fees exist in a special domain of priority risk being seen as archaic or arbitrary. In either case, the relationship will suffer unnecessary strain, and more so if therapists see the issue in an exclusively psychodynamic context. Therapists accustomed to intensive therapy contact may be particularly vulnerable to this perception.

These comments are made to remind therapists that their fees may not command priority attention in the way the literature has traditionally described. However, it would be equally erroneous to ignore the significant psychological meanings inherent in fees and payments. Thus, to be worthy of a large fee, or of no more value than a substandard fee, can have great meaning for either partner. Any time a payable service is provided, there can be significant implications connected to the giving or receiving: being special, being loved; feeling obligated, feeling cheated. While important transference and countertransference material may surface as a result, many of these money issues also derive from postchildhood experience. For therapists as well as patients the power of money is deeply ingrained in our cultural traditions. "You get what you pay for" is a middle-class truism. Consistent with the precepts of egalitarianism and psychoeconomics, fees for extended psychotherapy need to be discussed within an awareness of what the patient can afford, what the fee is likely to mean, what therapists are willing to charge, and what they usually charge.

> Mr. V, partner in a small business, gave no evidence of financial hardship. Negotiating for "the best deal on price" was very much part of his ethos, however. Unwilling to be caught up in a haggling game, the therapist stated her fees in a way that foreclosed negotiation on price. At the same time, she indicated willingness to adapt the appointment time to Mr. V's limited availability.

Mrs. L, an indigent mother, was referred by a former client the therapist had seen at a community agency. Desperately hurting, yet intimidated by the trappings of the private office, Mrs. L asked, "What do you charge for this?" The therapist responded, "I adjust the charge to people's income; is that okay with you?" Mrs. L silently nodded. The urgency of her emotional pain was the first priority; failing to charge anything in a private practice could appear suspect. Fee adjusments, if needed, could be discussed at a later date.

Having discussed the problems of rigidly insisting on prompt payment of fees, it should be acknowledged that the alternatives present their share of practical and psychological difficulties too (Banta and Saxe, 1983).

One patient, a psychiatric casework student, nurtured the fantasy that he was such a fascinating patient that the therapist was not pressing for back payments because he did not want to risk losing him. This disclosure allowed the partners to confront the actual alternatives: "But here we are now, taking that risk; let's look at that."

Ms. P moved out of state after terminating therapy, still owing $250. She wrote to her therapist periodically, and eventually returned for another session. Discussion of the $250 debt led to the realization that it, the continued billing, and her own letter-writing were ways of remaining connected to the therapy relationship. She felt bad about not paying, but insisted she needed the contact. Her therapist interpreted this as a way of clinging to the past, which was impeding her successful entry into her new world. The therapist assured her of his psychological availability during the transition period, a more helpful contact than unpaid bills. It was suggested that, if she was really unready to cope alone with her new situation, transferring to a therapist near her current address would be more useful to her. Using back fees as a security blanket could only sustain her connection to an unfulfilled past, while she really needed to begin enjoying what she had created in moving to a new environment.

The exchange of money for service is, after all, a marketplace tradition and not a natural law. Any form of ongoing transaction will evoke psychological issues in the participants. Egoself therapy considers the meaning of fees and payments in the light of its impact on the patient's self structuring, relative to self and object representations, grandiosity versus self-esteem, and the kinds of demands money management places on ego operations, such as planning, deferring gratification, making commitments. Protecting the reasonableness of fees in the therapeutic relationship retains it as a model for patients' other relationships, as a process that can foster the ingredients vital to continued growth. Fee payments are therefore discussed in ways that encourage the development of personal competence, worth, and realistic self-appraisal within the cultural context. In clinics, by contrast with private practice, fee setting and collection tend to be less enmeshed in the therapeutic relationship. Proportionately more of the patients come from ethnic and racial minorities, are either indigent or working poor groups where fee-for-service traditions are not as strong. Policies consonant with the ethos of mainstream society may be less pertinent to the milieu of a community clinic. And useful therapeutic work is regularly performed without the benefit of having fees become an integral part of the therapeutic process. My own preference here, as with other issues, is to retain the flexibility of adapting the procedure to the specific client: depersonalizing fee setting and collecting when it is intrusive, structuring it within the therapy when it can or must be implemented that way. Countertransferential aspects of fee management are equally complex. For the therapist therapy rates are rarely a simple matter of marketplace equity. Personal values and philosophy, and one's livelihood needs and expectations, compete with earlier meanings of money in one's life experience: as lovable, esteemed, accomplished. In our materialistic world, dollar values impinge as much upon us as upon our patients.

Acting Out

The usefulness of the term *acting out* has been significantly impaired by the tendency to apply it to any behavior which is disapproved, socially or therapeutically (Adler and Myerson, 1973). As defined in the present context, acting out refers to behavior intended to obliterate the impact of anxiety (Bellak, Hurvich, and Gediman, 1973). Acting out is therefore couched in intrapsychic terms, and not in terms of socially disapproved behavior. Impulsive action often occurs without regard for the social or personal consequences of the action beyond the blotting out of anxiety. At times, those consequences create more pain for the person than does the anxiety the behavior is designed to obliterate.

> Jane was late in submitting an outline for a graduate school paper. The professor had high standards and Jane was eager to win his respect. She was determined to do an exceptional job, but each topic she chose seemed no better than ordinary. The professor pointed out that the specific topic was less imporant than the quality of her research. Feeling desperate, she made an appointment with him "to finalize a topic." The morning that the meeting was scheduled, she overslept the appointed time. Mortified, she avoided the professor thereafter, and did not complete the course. So great were her narcissistic fears that she acted out by oversleeping. Then, she could not bring herself to face her professor or complete the paper, jeopardizing her career rather than risk further narcissistic insult.

People who act out have been traditionally regarded as difficult to work with in psychotherapy. Unlike symptom formation, the immediate consequences of acting out are tension reducing and/or pleasurable. The ego dystonic components are usually externalized, and may not be connected with the acting out behavior. In addition, acting out, conscious or unconscious, is ubiquitously accompanied by rationalization or magical thought: "I have no choice; the pain is intolerable and this is my only way out." In some patients, neither pain nor responsibility is consciously acknowledged: "I just sat down to have a beer; next thing I know, they're carrying me out." Among some addictive and assaultive people, the acting out may be perceived as volitional choice: "I don't have to get high; I want to. It's the greatest experience"; "The sonofabitch kept bugging me, so I just unloaded on him." Underlying these manifestations is the gratification of an ego syntonic reaction; in place of distress there is catharsis.

The egoself approach is particularly well suited to addressing acting out. Those precepts dealing with cost–benefit analysis, connecting intentions and consequences, and feeling empowerment are particularly relevant in these cases. Management strategy centers on three points: ascertaining how the acting out, or its consequences, is ultimately experienced as ego dystonic; this enables patients to confront the cost their behavior exacts from them. Then, locating the point at which ego controls are still functional confronts patients with volitional opportunity. Finally, isolating and tracing the options and their relative consequences helps patients experience the ego dystonic outcomes of acting out. Most important, the exploration of alternatives which use existing egoself resources helps patients achieve an acceptable objective.

> Mr. P, a forty-six-year-old plumber, has become abusive with his second wife. He had also abused his first wife, "but she deserved it." His second wife indicates she will leave him if he continues being abusive, and he fears losing her. A large, gruff, aggressive man, Mr. P is respected by his peers and earns a good income. He drinks and smokes to excess, has received medical warnings about hypertension and emphysema. His reflexive response to any warning, from anyone, is an angry, "I can take care of myself."

In the third interview Mr. P says, "It don't pay to worry about anything" and then goes on to reveal that sometimes when he is alone and sad he sits in a corner of his room and sucks on his thumb. He also talks of his resentment at people making demands of him—to borrow money, do free work, use his car. He finds it difficult to refuse, since these requests come from friends, family, wife. Gradually it becomes clear that Mr. P is struggling to retain an identity as an invulnerable man, while concealing his unconscious wish to be a protected child, and being assailed by deteriorative signs of aging—further clues of his real vulnerability. So much of his attention has gone into warding off childhood that he was unprepared for middle age. Abusive acting out makes him feel strong and helps him deny his need for a mothering wife.

  Introspection disturbs Mr. P. Consequently, the therapist uses a minimum amount of exploration to arrive at a supportive confrontation, noting that Mr. P feels put upon by the demands of others—the dystonic component. He is aware of burgeoning resentment, and can see that that awareness is his last choice point before hostile acting out takes over. What are his options?

Th: If you don't tell her when you're getting irked, by the time your "bullshit" it's too late—you're out of control.

P: She always says if I'm upset about something we should talk about it. I'll give her credit—she doesn't sulk or get nasty like my first wife did. . . . The other thing is, she's gotta stop bugging me about Thursday nights. That's bowling night, boys' night out, and she's not gonna see me 'til I crawl into bed.

Empowering the patient to acknowledge his ego dystonic hurt and vulnerability permitted the location of options— expressing his upset, insisting on Thursday night out—that would provide gratification without abusiveness. Later, Mr. P was able to generalize his new ability to other social situations, so that he could limit the demands on him without feeling like a weakling or triggering abusive rage.

Even when acting out reflects pathological malformations of ego structure, contemporary processes outweigh etiological considerations in designing therapeutic strategy. Egoself therapy remains focused on location of ego dystonic components and creating options:

After repeated arrests for being drunk and disorderly, the judge assigned John to the psychiatric court clinic for evaluation and treatment. John was a twenty-one-year-old college junior. His father was a lifelong alcoholic, and John's early years were rife with behavior problems. Bright and attractive, he became adept at enlisting aid on his behalf. He received scholarships to prep school and college, where he took pride in eluding and bending regulations. In college he took courses in which the same exams were used annually, located copies, used them, and then sold them for reuse. Off-campus he lived with an older woman who supported him. Much of his time was spent in drinking and gambling.

John resented being ordered into therapy. He found nothing wrong with his life, and insisted that the police were picking on him. The therapist unsuccessfully tried to confront him with his manipulative life-style that was so much to his liking. Yet he would take no credit for his life, saying that things "just fell into place" that way. The ego dystonic element in his life turned out to be his gambling. He enjoyed poker, but could rarely afford to play. If his luck was bad, losing became expensive.

Th: How do you play when you're winning?
P: No special way. If the cards are running my way I win; if not, I lose.
Th: Then you're a loser.
P: What are you talking about?
Th: You're a loser. Anyone who thinks poker is just luck is going to lose a lot of money. Tell the truth, don't you lose most of the time?

Reluctantly admitting he usually did lose, John was willing to look at his card play. He bet on streaks of luck, not the cards in his hand. Losing challenged his underlying omnipotence needs, and got him depressed. With this access to his dystonia, and also to his characterological style and thema: "Everything just happens; I am not responsible for anything"—the stage was set. As he began to confront his poker style his awareness spread. The alternative, that he was an agent of his successes and failures, could then be applied to other facets of his life: how he selected courses and professors; how, and how much, he "happened" to be drinking on a particular night. John's drinking abated significantly. As an ironic epilogue, he later graduated from college and gained admission to law school.

Consistent with the precept of cost–benefit analysis, effective strategy with acting out requires that the partners find a better ratio of pleasure and pain than that which is operative. Sometimes, "better" entails a more accurate awareness of how costly is the operative pattern. Sometimes, alteration of the life situation—such as leaving a destructive marriage or job—will obviate the pressure to act out. The methods may seem behavioral, but the management strategy is rooted in intrapsychic operations. A great advantage of the psychoanalytic orientation is in providing insight into what underlies manifest behavior. Acting out is not defined by behavior alone, as we have seen. Ego operations and intention are essential ingredients.

Acting out in the therapeutic relationship jeopardizes the treatment itself. The most common manifestations are being late or missing sessions and/or payments. Less frequent, but more serious, are actions to assault or seduce one of the partners. At the same time, interpretation of acting out must take prior account of differing social customs according to generational cohort, cultural subgroup, etc. Among younger patients forms of dress and manner may seem more flagrantly sexual or aggressive than actually intended in the context of therapy.

Among rich and/or Third World clients custom favors tardiness rather than punctuality in attendance or payment. It can be counterproductive to label these social patterns as acting out without other supportive data. While it is quite legitimate to explore these behaviors as part of the therapy, at the same time it is important to differentiate between acting out and other actions which impinge on therapy.

> Alice, an adolescent, is late or absent for 40 percent of her sessions. Payments arrive thirty to sixty-five days after billing. Alice is habitually late or absent from work or school at the same or greater frequency, and for the same collection of reasons: oversleeping, illness, accidents. Her bills are paid by her legal trustee, but she has lost telephone and electric service, and overdraws her checking account, because of her own derelictions. She works seriously in therapy, and the relationship is one of the sustaining influences in her life. Alice's ego functioning is tenuous, compounded by long-standing problems with judgment and impulse control. As a result, her ability to comply with the therapeutic agreement is impaired. To address the problem as one of acting out against therapy or therapist would seriously jeopardize one of the few solid structures in her life, and put her at further psychological risk. But using her therapy behavior as yet another instance of her organizational difficulties may provide a strategic opportunity for therapeutic intervention.

> Lou owed $300 prior to his therapist going overseas for six months. He promised to render payment before his therapist returned, and before any further appointments would be scheduled. Seven months later, less than half the money had been paid. Yet, he was a responsible adult who managed his money capably. The therapist billed Lou, and enclosed a note suggesting he call for an apointment to discuss the situation. In the session which followed, Lou apologized and described his financial difficulties. But further exploration uncovered his resentment over his therapist's departure, and the discovery that he had always believed he was a special person in the therapist's life. Withholding payment acted out his resentment, and also reestablished his fantasy as favored person, one who got therapy without paying for it.

No discussion of acting out can ignore the recurrent, vexing issue of physical contact between patients and therapists. If sexual contact is no more frequent than previously believed, it is at least more readily acknowledged. Instances of assault are also more often reported, sometimes described as inherent to certain forms of therapy. Child psychotherapists have generally been accustomed to physical interaction with their patients, hugging or restraining them as conditions warranted. With the advent of expressive therapies such as Gestalt, primal scream, and bioenergetics, affective and behavioral release of feelings complements or displaces the traditional "talking treatment." Weekend workshops and intensive residential therapeutic programs provide further opportunity for aroused feelings to be directly played out. Prior to this time, seductive or threatening behavior—"incipient physical contact"—was also considered to be acting out. In addition, contact between the participants outside the therapy session was generally disapproved. How does a contemporary psychoanalytic psychotherapy view these issues?

In contrast to those therapeutic forms which advocate the primacy of the existential moment, most psychoanalytic aproaches assert the primacy of therapists' professionalism. The fundamental premise upon which the egoself partnership is based is that patients have come for professional help with psychological problems. That consideration governs psychotherapeutic behavior, not the urgencies of the existential moment. Irrespective of a therapist's talents as a gifted lover, or the patient's need for a gratifying sexual experience, and conceding all the virtues of a meaningful sexual encounter, sexual expertise is not the professional expertise of a psychotherapist. Similarly, the patient's real need for angry expression or social contact do not replace the therapist's primary commitment as therapist.

But the line can seem finely drawn in the therapy hour. When certain interactions risk serious diminution of patients' integrity, or encourage irrational expectations, there is good reason to suspect acting out (or manipulation, as a variant of acting out). There is no better guide for these determinations than careful assessment.

Len, twenty-three, was cognitively and vocationally a young adult but hovered between dependent infantilism and clumsy juvenility in many other respects. After a year of unrewarding therapy, Len announced at the conclusion of a session that he felt very weak, almost unable to move.

Th: (waits for Len to rise; when he doesn't, therapist gets up) Our time is up; see you next week.

P: (gradually struggles to his feet, staggers toward the door, eyes half closed) I feel very weak, like I can't stand up. Can I stay here?

Th: Why don't you have a seat in the waiting room, and see how you feel. I think you'll soon feel better.

P: (suddenly slumps against the wall, knees buckling) I'm very weak; I don't know if I can even stand up.

Th: (feeling alarm, then annoyance, at this first-of-a-kind behavior, suspecting it to be uconscious manipulation) Len, you're feeling weak but you're okay. This is something we can talk about next week. If you find you can't wait that long, call me and we'll get together sooner.

P: (in a weak, whiny voice) Don't you understand? I can't even stand up (starts to slide down slowly, eyes half closed and mouth slack).

Th: LEN!! (sharply)

P: (jerks upright in shock, then wobbles as though drunk)

Th: (opens office door) See you next week.

Len staggered and stumbled out the door. The following week he arrived as usual. Therapist was able to use Len's ability to get safely home, despite his feelings, to contrast his adult capabilities with his helpless feelings. The fine line between the therapist acting out his countertransference annoyance or acting on behalf of the patient's therapeutic need was hinged on the ongoing assessment of Len's strengths and problems. The results appeared to justify the assessment.

Rosa, a shy inhibited woman of thirty-two, came from a strict Roman Catholic background. At first, she complained of depression and a lack of friends. After several sessions she tearfully "confessed" to being lesbian, a mortal sin. During college she had several brief sexual experiences, initiated by her dormitory director. She had always been too shy to go out with boys. Eighty sessions of weekly therapy yielded minimal gains. Rosa was more verbal in therapy, but reclusive outside her job. During this period, her therapist's recent marriage was breaking up. He found himself progressively more attracted to Rosa, at the same time that he knew she still clung to the fear she was a lesbian. As Rosa was leaving at the end of a session, he embraced her. She offered no resistance, and he suggested they go to her apartment. This marked the beginning of a mutually gratifying affair that lasted several years. Rosa soon became orgasmic and was able to dispel her fears of being homosexual. It also marked the end of Rosa's psychotherapy, a choice denied her by the circumstances.

The fine line between acting out and acting on behalf of the patient was breached by the therapist's awareness of his life circumstances and personal needs. He reassured himself that he understood Rosa and had acted on her behalf as well. He felt that the outcome had been beneficial to her, whereas the therapy had been of minimum value. Outcome notwithstanding, impulse-dominated behavior is acting out; as such it runs counter to the structure and purpose of psychotherapy. Acting out risks jeopardy to the ego boundaries of the participants and, secondarily, to the viability of the therapy. When either is at risk, due to acting out or for whatever cause, it is imperative that the issue(s) be confronted and jointly resolved.

TERMINATION

The longer I practice, the more convinced I become that I was not effectively trained in the management of termination. In the 1950s termination was treated as a final ending, invariably recapitulating earlier experiences with loss, grief, mourning. It was the therapeutic task to work through these experiences, as the last phase of therapy. I was trained to plan for termination months ahead, to raise the issue, set a date with the patient, and progressively cut back on frequency of sessions. I carefully monitored the patient's behavior and material for content relative to my leaving, or other losses. As a fledgling therapist my frequent inability to elicit "termination reactions" was living proof of my inexperience. But my patients in a Veterans Administration facility were also habituated to an endless parade of trainee therapists, and often seemed more concerned with determining who they would next go to for ward privileges than with producing associations to significant early losses, precipitated by my impending departure. My next patient population, students at a university counseling center, were often appreciative and cheerful about impending termination, satisfied with the resolution of their problems. They were sometimes perplexed by my relentless pursuit of less felicitous meanings to the conclusion of our meetings. As I saw people longer and more intensively I could begin probing earlier and deeper. In some cases significant issues did surface, tied to early losses; other patients feared being alone and unready to deal with the world, enabling us to work on their anaclytic needs and regressive longings. But often what emerged—as successful therapy drew to a close—was the mixed reaction of sadness at parting, but also gratification, recognized and shared by two people who had done special work together.

Eventually I came to realize that a formal termination date has variable meaning. Many patients terminate and are not heard from again. From others—weeks, months, or years later—there are further contacts: referring someone else, requesting a statement for tax purposes, new problems or recurrences of the old. I have seen one patient for about four years, spread out over twenty-two years: prior to the birth of his youngest child, when he was on the brink of psychosis; seven years later because of a work crisis; a dozen years after that, when he ended his marriage and warded off alcoholism; for periodic consultations thereafter. Whither termination? When a patient in long-term weekly psychotherapy is ready to terminate, it is likely that a planned ending will evoke residual anxieties related to a number of sources, including fear of loss or desertion. Some very important therapeutic work gets accomplished at these times, and I will stay with those issues rather than hold rigidly to a fixed final meeting date when the situation so warrants. But since no problems are ever completely resolved, or early wounds cured, the therapeutic work of termination must help patients accommodate these inevitable disappointments. At the same time, we review areas of growth and highlight continuing sources of vulnerability, recognizing that working through is an endless learning process. As these matters are addressed and sessions attenuated over time, a reasonably smooth transition to termination is accomplished.

But at another level termination is an anomaly, implying an end when the essence of the life span is its ongoingness. Termination is beginning as much as ending, part of the continuous life process. While egoself therapy is sensitive to the power of the therapeutic relationship and all that it can evoke, the orientation favors incorporating the future and relinquishing the past. A critical weakness of many therapies is to assume that resolving a problem from the past is sufficient, that growth and healing tendencies will somehow "know" how to proceed beneficially once the psychopathological impediments are removed. In egoself psychotherapy the seeds of termination are planted early, with the recruitment, mobilization, and implementation of growth processes, to help the person to move into the future. As patients gain increasing capacity to apply their ego and developmental assets to their problems, and self restructuring joins this awareness, there is less felt need for psychotherapy.

Terminations in weekly psychotherapy rarely manifest the affective intensity which is evoked in intensive therapy or analysis. The powerful impact of the transference—so much a part of long-term, intensive work—is diluted by the other forms of relationship described in chapter 4. As a result, the therapist rarely becomes as focal, either in reality or as a projective screen. Instead there comes to both patient and therapist, often at about the same time, the realization that it is timely to wind down. This mutual confirmation is one of the surest indications of its accuracy. A period of discussion and review ensues, in which the partners reexamine the processes and situations which had been troublesome. Instances of current functioning and meaning making are explored, attending to reported experiences and their relevance to the problem area, the patient's handling of its consequences, its impact on the patient's self-image, and its implications for the patient's ability to utilize psychological skills without further professional intervention. During this time the therapist is especially alert to the patient's reaction to impending termination. As these matters are dealt with arrangements are made for attenuating the sessions. Both parties participate in these arrangements; patients are encouraged to suggest a schedule they prefer, while therapists monitor the process in the light of their assessment of the patient's current egoself and developmental operations. Patients are thus given the opportunity to take the initiative in directing their lives, consistent with the self-directing mode they will need after terminating. Therapists are free to suggest modifications, and a plan emerges from this discussion. Sometimes, several weeks or a month without meeting is agreed upon, effective immediately. More commonly, an indefinite period of biweekly meetings is put into effect. Occasionally the patient wishes to terminate quickly. Except for when there is clear risk, the therapist will accede to the patient's preference even when there is a margin of doubt. Once the therapist has concluded that termination is appropriate, the patient's expertise must be respected. The partners agree that the plan is tentative, not binding. Sometimes the agreement is no more formal than "Let's go for a couple of weeks and see how I feel." Usually, a future appointment is made, but sometimes not. As a result, it may be impossible to know at the time which session is the "last" session. It may not even be important. As long as therapists can say, or know, "I'll be here," patients have a safe harbor if it is needed. Prior to separation–individuation a practicing subphase is developmentally useful. Perhaps because it is internalized, it is rarely needed. The therapeutic work has been completed (for now), but a special relationship of trust and intimate understanding will remain. Depending on the vagaries of life circumstance, there may be future meetings. As Rutan (1978) comments, "The right termination, like the right interpretation, can be right for only the specific patient under consideration at the time."

Even in absentia and posttherapy, the therapist is retained in object constancy, and continues to play a role: as transitional object to other relationships; as an internalized selfobject; or to provide the psychological "nutrient" for other internalizations.

Optimally, termination is a time of tempered celebration: significant work has been done and the client (usually) is aware of therapeutic gains that have been tested successfully in the everyday world. In egoself perspective, termination occurs when clients are engaging their world, better equipped than they were, knowing and trusting their potential for continued growth, aware of their vulnerabilities, understanding and respecting their human limitations. This last attitude is one of the major outcome criteria for successful termination. One element

I routinely try to introduce during the terminal segment of therapy is to relate the patient's current status to impending developmental prepotencies.

> Ms. D, 42, a former nun, had married a widower with eight children a dozen years earlier. Although she had a master's degree and extensive career experience, she had felt it her responsibility to provide the parenting her husband's children had lacked. However, her best efforts were resisted and sabotaged, throwing her into depression and jeopardizing her marriage. Therapy successfully helped her to recognize the connection between her identity as idealistic perfectionist, her perceived failure as a parent, and her depression. With the humanizing of her identity her depression lifted and Ms. D felt ready to conclude our work.
>
> Recognizing that Ms. D was moving into middle age, it seemed probable that she would encounter a period of extensive self-confrontation, threatening to reactivate the issues she had managed to address in therapy. This was likely to include a review of the acute disappointments of her parenting efforts, arrayed against her lifelong commitment to human service. Guided by these expectations, we talked about her future plans, and how they related to the continuation of her human service work, now that her parenting tasks were ending. In addition, I recommended a book on the experience of stepparenting and suggested that she might explore setting up a support group for stepparents. These suggestions opened opportunities for Ms. D to reorganize her experience in ways that might provide some continuity as she prepared to move on with her life.

Events can overwhelm anyone, and could necessitate further consultation at some future time. But the gains of psychotherapy are, like development itself, built upon continuity, sequence, and change.

Therapeutic Failures

One form of termination that merits separate exposition is therapeutic failure. The topic is complicated by the variety of criteria utilized in measuring therapeutic outcome. Unlike medical practice, where symptoms and pathogens are more specific and treatment goals more focused, psychotherapy outcomes may be most important in their least demonstrable manifestations. The old saw about the man who hated spinach is clinically valid: when he told a friend that he had successfully completed therapy, the friend asked if he now enjoyed spinach. "No," was the reply, "but it doesn't matter to me any more."

In the converse form, relief from the presenting symptoms may not augur therapeutic success. The married couple who no longer fight may have settled on alcoholism. Therapeutic failures tend to fit into one of the following categories: the patient's suffering has worsened; the patient terminates therapy in frustration or disappointment, with other indices of effect indeterminate; the patient's originally stated objectives were not achieved; major therapeutic objectives were not achieved, but there was behavior or attitude change in the desired direction. Even this classification is troublesome, however. Experienced psychotherapists can pull cases from their files in each of those categories and cite evidence of therapeutic gain. Even so, the following instances would seem indicative of therapeutic failure:

Arnold, a college student of superior measured intelligence, was seen for two years because of an emotionally based reading problem. His grades worsened, however, and the Dean advised him to withdraw from school. Arnold and his parents thought that hypnotherapy might be more effective, and he decided to move to a city where that would be available.

Mr. R, acutely depressed, overdosed on sleeping pills two weeks after beginning therapy. Accidental discovery prevented his death. He was hospitalized, and the therapist resumed seeing him, working with him as an inpatient and subsequent to his discharge. Therapy was discontinued twenty months later, when Mr. R again attempted suicide and his family decided to try orthomolecular vitamin therapy with him.

Ms. F came for therapy because of her inability to sustain relationships with men. Therapy was seemingly successful in addressing her need to control and her fear of intimacy, with behavior and attitude change evident in both areas. Other aspects of her life also improved. But after three years of therapy, and another three years posttherapy, another relationship had ended and no new ones had ensued.

Mr. Y was referred by a colleague because of his impotency

problem in his marriage. Actually, the problem was chronic, premature ejaculation, and covered his entire sexual history. Mr. Y's adolescent sexual experiences had been furtive and "dirty." After meeting his wife his durability improved for a brief period, but then relapsed. The marital relationship was tenuous, and its future was in doubt for several years. Even after significant improvement, however, the sexual problems remained. The wife, supported by her own therapist, refused to participate in any sexual activity—prescribed or not—other than "no hands" coitus. Therapy concluded after three years with no improvement in sexual functioning.

Further follow-up of these cases proved interesting, but did not reveal any consistent pattern. Arnold returned after two years of unsuccessful hypnotherapy, convinced me to try again, and within ten months was a Dean's List student. His "reading and study" problems were, as I had always maintained, manifestations of his passive aggressive reactions to authority. The difference was that this time around he was able and willing to work with this explanation. Arnold's newfound readiness seemed to correspond with his evolution from adolescence into young adulthood.

Mr. R sent a Christmas card several years later. He was living and working on the grounds of a state mental hospital, alive but still actively disturbed.

Ms. F was an attractive, confident, capable public communications professional. Her personal and psychosexual maturity were evident. But the opportunities for meeting marriageable men were few, and she was not sanguine about her prospects for the future. Otherwise, her life was full and satisfying.

Four years after termination, Mr. Y had had two years of intensive psychoanalytic psychotherapy, was still married, still had made no improvement with his premature ejaculation, and his wife still refused to touch him sexually or try behavioral approaches.

In my own assessment, each case was a therapeutic failure at the point of termination. Arnold and I had been stalemated; Mr. R's pathology was so profound, and the attraction of death so strong, that I did not expect him to survive. Mr. Y's problem seemed inextricably tied up with his wife's and she was obdurately opposed to any involvement. I felt Ms. F had achieved maximum benefit from psychotherapy, but it seemed to have made no difference in the life issue which brought her into therapy.

These were my assessments at that point of termination. Yet, only Arnold was disappointed with the experience of psychotherapy. The others all felt that they had experienced significant gains. Then, and subsequently, those reactions remained positive. Evidently, the impact of psychotherapy is only partly that of treatment. Repeated studies indicate a 30 to 40 percent rate of improvement, but satisfaction rates are well over 50 percent. It may be that the education in personal development derived from psychotherapy is of equal or greater importance, seen from the consumer perspective. An explanation consistent with egoself theory is readily available. When people suffer from their reactions to anxiety, they seek and require relief. Psychotherapeutic intervention is minimally effective to the extent that anxiety and its consequences are made tolerable, in the context of organismic functioning. My original work with Arnold "failed" because he was unwilling to relinquish his passive aggressive reaction to authority. Instead, he hoped to be passively hypnotized out of his problem. Only after that illusion was burst, and he met a woman who was a college graduate, was he ready to let go of his passive aggressive defensive style. Mr. R, who was more schizophrenic than borderline, seemed to find the sensual attraction of suicide less frightening than the terrors he anticipated prior to intimacy or separation. Ms. F could chronicle her personal growth during and after therapy, including the quality of her relationships with men. Mr. Y had come to realize he had to choose between his marriage with its restrictive sexual conditions or strive for further growth but risk the loss of his wife. Satisfied with the overall quality of his life, he seemed willing to settle for the status quo. Her sexual frustration was part of the cost of the compromise.

Phenomenological reports from patients would suggest that therapeutic failure is not always synonymous with failure to eradicate presenting symptoms. Conversely, therapeutic success may be measured by patients' improved capacity to manage anxiety. Gains in enhanced ego operation and developmental potentiation can lead to improved self-acceptance, identity clarification, greater tolerance, and better ability to cope with life. For the egoself psychotherapist, these may be truer measures of therapy's impact.

There are, of course, other sources of therapeutic failure. I agree with Wolberg (1968) that many of these instances result from therapists overestimating their own or their patients' capacities for inducing change. But equally important is the insistence that patients adapt to abstract, verbally oriented therapeutic forms when alternative approaches would be more compatible with patient experience. Strict adherence to the egoself precept to work with patient assets implies a readiness to accept and adapt—to concrete thought patterns, flagrant emotionality, or predispositions to action. Too often these expressions are treated as symptomatic of pathology rather than cohort, class, culture, or stylistic differences. Close attention to ego operations can differentiate emotionality from impulsivity, or a volitional action orientation from uncontrolled acting out. The relation between intention and outcome, carefully monitored, provides one of the surest guides to past preconceptions about cohort group, class, and subculture.

Some therapists feel they are "unprofessional" or "seducing" their patients if they modify their usual behavior in response to that patient's style: allowing more emotion in their comments, offering a hug or pat on the back, communicating genuine acceptance of the client's style on the client's terms. If thirty-five-year-old Mr. S likes to be called "Al" in the rest of his world, it does not infantilize him to be called Al in the office. In fact, to insist on referring to him as Mr. S may elicit a response of, "this guy doesn't understand me and my world." It does not pander to patients when therapists recruit their natural modes of expression in behalf of enhanced ego functioning. As long as there is ego mediation, expression can take many forms.

Th: How does the kid know when you're pissed off at him?
P: He knows.
Th: I know he does; but I don't know how you show it.
P: I give him a look . . . if he still don't move I'll whack him.
Th: How does he know when everything is okay?

P: He can tell when I'm not ticked off.
Th: Ever give him a wink, or a friendly nudge?
P: What for?
Th: (smiling) Fair is fair.

The therapist's language is simple and direct. A specific suggestion is offered, utilizing the patient's style of motor expression. The patient's question is answered, not reflected back. There is an implied confrontation, that the client's behavior is not fair. The interaction is less likely to become a verbal exercise when the affective toning is consonant with the patient's inner flow of experience, when the words and images evoked are in forms that are familiar. Interventions must be technically appropriate, but also stylistically relevant to the person's development.

In egoself terms, therapeutic failure occurs when patients' healing and growthful assets have not been effectively applied to the problems. More specifically, the risk of failure increases when ego operations and developmental processes are not effectively mobilized, or are inadequate to the task. Since optimum resource utilization depends upon a thorough egoself assessment and an optimal working partnership, psychotherapists can contribute most to reduce failure by prioritizing these considerations.

Reconciling the demands of weekly psychotherapy with traditional psychoanalytic precepts has been, I suspect, a catch-as-one-can experience for most therapists trained in the 'fifties and 'sixties. The theory of psychotherapy was only just then being formulated. For the most part weekly therapy grew from the progressive dilution of the "true ore" of psychoanalysis. What we are finding instead, after a generation of experience and new information, is that weekly therapy is a qualitatively different form of treatment in many respects. These chapters synthesize the distillate of that thirty-year process.

CHAPTER 4

PROCEDURE AND TECHNIQUE

The intention here is to distill theory and strategy into practice. In the effort to clarify weekly egoself therapy I have divided the chapter into discrete units. If a side effect is to make therapy seem like a mechanized process it may be useful to recall how the written composition of a musical score compares with its actual presentation. My purpose is to elucidate the specific methods of treatment.

Many of these methods are familiar, and other methods may be equally applicable. My determining consideration in selecting therapeutic techniques and procedures here relates to their serviceability in a weekly psychotherapy practice consistent with the structural orientation of egoself therapy. As previously noted, much of the earlier writings in psychoanalytic psychotherapy were predicated upon extrapolations from classical psychoanalysis, which necessarily operates from a different set of principles (Dewald, 1964). This chapter addresses the techniques and procedures of psychotherapy based on weekly contact. By studying procedure and technique in microcosm, as it were, their specific applications will become more explicit. Restructuring—involving the assessment, recruitment, and mobilization of resources—is a central feature of this approach.

STRUCTURAL EMPHASIS

One of the key precepts in egoself psychotherapy is the preeminent importance of structural components. The central work of psychotherapy is dedicated to strengthening the efficacy and organization of the patient's personality structure. Therapeutic *procedure* is, literally, constructive, mobilizing patients' representations of experience to help them differentiate intrapsychic resources applicable to their problems. Therapeutic *technique* focuses specifically on those functions and representations which constitute the systems of ego, self, and object relations. Consequently, the thrust of intervention strategy is tripartite: to evaluate existing structural operations, notably egoself organization and function; to array these data against an assessment of patients' current developmental status; and to synthesize these findings, intervening at points of structural vulnerability by applying the person's strengths and capacities. Patients' ongoing history of egoself functioning provides the baseline data for current strengths and vulnerabilities. The developmental status evaluation, described in chapter 6, provides an estimate of which resources may be available for recruitment and mobilization.

Thus, while manifest communication between patient and therapist may emphasize the content of the patient's fears, wishes, and difficulties, therapeutic handling of interview material emphasizes its structural implications. Blanck and Blanck (1974, 1979) have taken the view that ego building is the treatment of choice for people whose problems they diagnose as originating "prefulcrum," in the first three years of life. They also recommend that psychotherapy aim at structural reorganization: "An apparent paradox is that structural change can be greater in psychotherapy than in psychoanalysis. This is because, in psychotherapy, structure building is the very purpose of treatment" (1974, p. 122).

Since restructuring inevitably involves egoself operations, Blanck and Blanck's view can be extended to include most patients who are treated with egoself psychotherapy.

The usual work of therapists—maintaining empathic contact and communication with patients while simultaneously analyzing interview material and planning and timing interventions—is probably no greater when using an egoself approach. Compared to many other therapeutic orientations, the greatest difference is likely to be found in the emphasis placed on analysis of structural components of patients' experience:

P: I don't feel any emotions, like there's a wall around me.
Th: (Patient presents an awareness of affective inhibition. How does it operate?) Can you think of an example of that?
P: With my wife (eyes moisten briefly). I moved out a year ago, but I agreed to see her every day. I spend a couple of hours with her in the evening, but then I don't want to be there anymore. I get restless and I leave.
Th: (Dysphoria and anxiety aroused by proximity to wife. Inhibited affect with wife is close to surface: due to intensity of affect, permeable ego defenses, or both? Explore further.) How do you feel about your wife?

The therapist's attention is directed at how the problem affects current operations. The first intervention attempts to elicit specific experiences, for a closer analysis of those operations in vivo. The discrepancy between the patient's physical reactions and reported experience provides early cues to egoself function. The dynamic content of his marital relationship is secondary to the structural analysis. The therapist's second question acknowledges the wife's importance, provides for continuity of inquiry, and makes contact with the patient in an area of sensitivity that he has chosen to speak about. In keeping with the therapist's purpose, it should reveal further details about the interaction of affective intensity with defenses, boundary issues, and the developmental status of intimacy–closeness. While depressive affect is noted, its impact on egoself operations is the focus.

THERAPEUTIC PROCEDURE

As the term *procedure* is used here it refers to a purposeful set of activities, organized around a strategy for intervention. These activities tend to be initiated in sequence, but the sequence can be varied to fit ongoing conditions. Procedure is not rigidly prescribed ritual, but a directional pattern to be adapted to ongoing therapist–patient interaction. As such, it gives shape and purpose to the therapy. Without it, the application of technique would be professional gesturing: mechanistic and sterile or intuitive groping. Conversely, the deliberate utilization of techniques and procedures is what distinguishes a professional psychotherapeutic relationship from well-intentioned friendship. In addition, the egoself approach considers how the inner meaning of patients' experiences and intentions informs procedure. Thus, statements such as, "I depend too much on my older sister," are considered in light of their impact on ego organization (evidence of an observing ego, severity of impairment) and also as meaning making functions (implications of "depending" for self-image representation, self–other differentiation). Therapeutic procedure can be analyzed best by its content and process components. But both components are monitored against a background of the patient's history, developed during the previous assessment.

THERAPEUTIC CONTENT

One of the important functions of psychotherapists is to reorganize patients' material into coherent patterns. By following and shaping the flow of content, patients are helped to discover purposes and consequences of their behavior which have been obscure. In the process, therapists learn how to modulate interventions to blend in with each client's unique readiness and style.

Experience

As therapists monitor patients' flow of material in the interview, certain areas of content emerge as salient. In its most usual form patients describe an experience, which they are encouraged to elaborate as to context and details. Content thus hones in on particular experiences, which are then connected to specific (and, preferably, recent) life situations.

Context

Lodging the problem in a recent life situation engages patients in the immediacy of their difficulties. As a result, it provides therapists with direct access to the patient's perceptions and inner experience so that there can be a shared frame of reference. Recency also evokes more vivid affective involvement. Framing the experience in an event helps establish whatever psychological distance the patients may be capable of. This can protect certain patients from being overwhelmed by the reexperiencing of painful affects as they work toward assimilating them. If the patient resists by trivializing the event, the usual "has this ever happened before?" can help link it to earlier patterns of experience.

Intentions

Together the partners explore the patients' intentions in the situation, relative to what actually happened. For some people this is their first confrontation with the role they play in the enactment of their life dilemmas. In addition, concentrating on patients' intentions underlines the mission of the inquiry as a quest on their behalf. Rarely will therapists explore the merits of the intention at this point. The toning of the inquiry is a businesslike examination of strategy and results. That baldly functional tone, with its apparent distance from personal and moral considerations, has some of the advantages associated with the use of paradoxical intent (Frankl, 1963). To a degree, patients are temporarily freed from the humiliations or secondary gratifications of their intentions, reducing the pressure to defend or disguise its purposes. Recasting the issue this way augments participation of mature ego functions. Instead of defensively protecting their motives and fears, patients are tacitly encouraged to see themselves as agents of their own action. This facilitates the mobilization of an observing ego perspective. At the same time, it provides an opportunity for therapists to assess that capacity.

Happenings

The partners then explore what happened in the situation, including inner experiences as much as actual events. Impulses, fears, perceptions, plans, and judgments are arrayed against descriptions of who said what, how, and when. Putting life events under this microanalysis elucidates the intrapsychic processes at work, while further involving patients as expert witnesses actively participating in a reconstruction of the scenario. At the same time, this provides rich opportunities for therapists to draw inferences about the patients' reactive processes, and the conditions under which they are evoked. Closely monitored recapitulation of the happenings involves the partners in an experiential inquiry into what took place from the patient's perspective. Patients' abilities to report, as well as their mode of reporting, provide a wealth of data on which of those egoself operations are pathogenic and which are healthy.

Consequences

Consequences are reviewed affectively as well as operationally, since exploring these outcomes often elicits the irrational expectations which shaped patients' participation in the situation. This consideration of consequences leads to an appraisal of the event relative to meeting the patient's needs. If the outcome was dystonic for the patient, this appraisal can consider possible alternatives: of intention, action, persons, places. Sometimes the situation serendipitously reveals patient assets, which can be explored by supportive confrontation.

Either way, patients' response to this appraisal work indicates much about their developmental status, at its most primitive and most advanced levels: what can be tolerated, what relinquished, what does frustration evoke, what happens when expectation and reality clash? The therapeutic role here is to assist in appraisal, not to insist on growth. Helping patients to acknowledge their unattained wishes can be one of the most poignant and powerful of therapeutic experiences. Moreover it can take time, especially when relinquishing certain wishes represents accepting the loss of an internalized object. In those instances where the pathology produces ego syntonic action, linking the dystonic consequences to the person's behavior may be the most effective leverage available.

In the case described earlier, of the man spending time with his wife, the specific happening had occurred the previous night. When further attempts to elicit feelings were ineffective, going into the past revealed a pattern of being a dutiful son and good boy to a disabled mother who depended upon him for company and assistance. Repressed rage and frustration lay beneath his inhibited sadness. His conscious thoughts were of his obligation to put aside his own wishes in order to take care of his needy mother. The parallel with his promise to visit his wife even though he had moved out was striking, but no surprise to the patient. Precisely because of his earlier history, it seemed the reasonable thing to do: the overt behavior was ego syntonic.

Alternatives

The next part of the sequence is absolutely crucial to an optimal psychotherapeutic outcome—the examination of alternatives. For some patients consideration of alternatives is their first encounter with objectifying infantile wishes. These people must first confront the emotional impact of recognizing that deeply invested fantasies or expectations may never be realized. But, even here, the dim awareness that there may be alternatives provides at least a modicum of hope. Patients' reaction to the issue of alternatives reveals a great deal about the interplay between structural capacity and narcissistic investment. The beginnings of therapeutic change often originate subtly at this point.

The patient mentioned above was so deeply invested in his lifelong pattern of hostile dependency and a good boy self-image, that inquiry into an alternative way of relating was a revelation. It proved to be the first step toward an amicable divorce.

In another case, Alex had a seventeen-year history of involving himself in intense relationships which either he or his partner could not sustain. This pattern seemed to replicate his lifelong relationship with his father, a doting parent who was too depressed and remote to tolerate closeness. While the origin of his pattern had long been apparent to Alex, that knowledge was of little value in affecting his compulsive and ambivalent involvements, either with women or with men. As therapy challenged

Alex's fantasy that perfect relationships magically "happened," he experienced a classic grieving reaction: denial, fury, and then despondency. Alex came out of his depression by considering an alternative—he would attempt to build an adult relationship with his father.

Unfortunately, he discovered that his father was incapable of the closeness Alex sought. While his disappointment was great, Alex could eventually learn from the experience about ego boundaries, human limitations, and, ultimately, his own ability to engage an intimate relationship.

Consideration of alternatives offers patients option and power, varying with the level at which they are ready to engage these opportunities. In actuality, when patients can examine alternatives egoself growth has already begun. The entire procedure of content analysis involves the therapeutic ingredients of participatory exploration, catharsis, differentiation, synthesis, and confrontation. The exercise of option and power within the limits of one's competence, as called for in the consideration of alternatives, is itself an ego-building, self-differentiating action. By itself, the task of differentiating alternatives invokes reality in place of magical fantasy—no small developmental achievement for some patients. For that reason, careful assessment is necessary to distinguish between patients' expressions of readiness and evidence of developmental capability. The way patients approach alternatives provides clues to their readiness, and the level of engagement for which they are prepared. Are the alternatives constructive or retributional, fantastic or realistic, hopeful or despairing? What do they reflect of the patient's egoself functioning?

While Alex was discovering his capabilities: learning to trust his competencies instead of relying on magical solutions, differentiating and experiencing degrees of closeness, he remained unsuccessful in his quest for an enduring love relationship. When his father developed a fatal illness Alex desperately tried to extend his life. His pattern of resentful distancing from his depressed, remote parent gave way to the urgent need to reconnect with an idealized father, a paragon who would not withdraw and disappear. The therapist's question, "Why don't you let him go?" was met with outrage, then truculence. But within six months of his father's death, Alex entered a relationship and now has been living harmoniously with his lover for several years.

The finality of his father's death, and Alex's previous work on his magical needs, enabled him to put to rest his anaclytic fantasy of perfect union with a perfect father. The result freed Alex to pursue an adult love relationship. Despite his resistance to it, the suggestion to "let go" of his father laid the groundwork for Alex to relinquish the idealized representation of his father or, more precisely, to enrich the infantile image with more appropriate contemporary representations. "Letting go" suggested there was some option in managing the inevitability of his father's death. The option was psychologically accessible when he was ready to use it.

There are many reasons for viewing alternatives as a crucial step in psychotherapeutic procedure. To consider an alternative is to acknowledge that deeply invested methods or wishes have not worked out. Encountering that narcissistic blow, and then discovering that one has survived the blow, can be profound experiences. So often people are unaware of the difference between their wishes and their methods of achieving them. Giving up on either means losing everything. It's the only way they have ever known, the only chance they ever had. For many people, the idea of an alternative is equivalent to accepting a very poor second choice, or worse. At another level, it is often the distinction between relinquishing a childhood derivative and coming to terms with the reality of adult possibilities. Yet, part of the power of the alternative is to confront patients once again with their wishes, this time in a context of asking, "How can we make it work—here and now?" From another perspective, exploring options has the explicit role of broadening therapy to include healthy resources as well as pathology. Through this procedure the therapist gains further insight into the patient's capacity and readiness to apply those resources.

Broaching the possibility of an alternative is the egoself way of suggesting that basic gratifications are possible by means that are realistically feasible. In its most fundamental form, the alternative is the contemporary version of Freud's injunction, "where id was, ego shall be." By staying with patients' intentions, wishes, and goals, therapists communicate their readiness to continue the work of the partnership. For patients the wish describes that work, because the wish is as much self structure as content. The image is an internalized representation, not a reality. For therapists the procedure of helping restructure the image in acceptable contemporary terms defines the work. Each party is correct, for each makes his own contribution to the therapy. In psychotherapeutic procedure, structuring alternatives is a major step toward bringing gratification within the scope of healthy egoself functioning.

Planning

The next step after considering alternatives is planning how to implement them. Therapy, having overcome the psychological hurdles to this point, now encounters the challenge of helping patients to create new options. Planning mobilizes numerous egoself operations, including some of the most recently acquired functions. How are the grandiose fantasies of primitively functioning patients to be reconciled with the sophisticated skills required in designing and carrying out complex plans? In a fine treatment of this subject, Glasser and Zunin (1979) recommend that plans be simple, flexible, closely monitored, and geared to achieve success. In other words, therapists play an active part in the design and implementation of plans. Planning is shaped to conform to patients' wishes, but it is informed by therapists' assessment of ego tolerances and capacities. Therapists' function in this role approximates that of "real object" (Blanck and Blanck, 1979), by encouraging reality testing and helping to "correct affective distortions of the object world" (p. 123). Patients thus engage in an ego-strengthening activity, designed in the partnership, and structured to utilize existing and prepotent egoself resources, with a strong likelihood of satisfying significant client needs. But while the partnership may seem conducive to this mutual planning, it is vital that the underlying relationship also be suitable. Patients can feel overwhelmed, or their fragile esteem threatened. If their narcissistic needs for mirroring require unconditional acceptance, any implied pressure to perform can be interpreted as rejection, criticism, or unreasonable demand.

> Alex, the patient described earlier, returned again and again to memories of his unresponsive father, recalling innumerable incidents with a man who was physically present but emotionally inaccessible. Each recounting would reactivate his rage and despair at his father.

> *P*: I just can't let it remain this way, the way it's always been. I have to do something to get through to him.
> *Th*: What would you like to have happen?
> *P*: Once, just once, I would like him to look at me, really see me, and ask me what my life is like. Or what it was like, having a father who was always depressed, whom we had to cover up for all the time.
> *Th*: Is there any way you could go about doing that?
> *P*: I've been thinking about going home for a visit. Maybe I could sit down and talk with him then.
> *Th*: About what? (sensing the need to concretize, to circumvent yet another failed fantasy)
> *P*: I don't care about what. I just want a real contact, just once.
> *Th*: But we've seen that just wanting it doesn't work. That's how you end up getting hurt.
> *P*: Okay. Suppose instead I . . . (describes a plan for a day trip with his father).
> *Th*: That sounds like it might be nice to do, but what will it get you, in terms of what you want from him?
> *P*: Maybe if we had a fun time together, shared a few laughs, maybe then I'd feel we had something genuine, even if it was just one time that it happened.
> *Th*: And if it doesn't work out?
> *P*: Ah, hell! What's the use?
> *Th*: And if you don't try?
> *P*: Either way, I lose.
> *Th*: No, not really. That part is up to you. If you tried, and could be really satisfied that you tried, no matter how it works out, then it might be worth your while to know you did everything you could.

Instead of passively allowing Alex to take what seemed like a desperate long-shot risk, the therapist intervened to modify the planning of the trip. If Alex could experience it as worthwhile irrespective of his father's behavior, the plan might contribute to egoself growth, perhaps by affecting his self-image of helpless frustration in his relations with his father. If not, he might be better advised against taking the trip. In the latter event, further consideration of alternatives would be called for.

The imperative to try something was too strong to be ignored. As an established adult, with stage-appropriate needs for tangible effectuation (see chapter 7), any effort whose consequences Alex could tolerate would be preferable to not trying at all. The plan that emerged from this interaction was one which directly addressed Alex's felt needs and minimized the psychological risks. By involving Alex in the use of specific ego functions, therapy simultaneously addressed structural and experiential features. But this venture would have been compromised if Alex had not been transferentially amenable to such a procedure.

In contrast, Randolph, an enormously talented man, lived a marginal life in which he backed into jobs or relationships because he could never express or act on a commitment. Any attempt at deliberate planning would trigger immobilizing panic or depression. He was convinced that his wants were insatiable, and therefore doomed to fail. Over years of therapy his narcissistic disorder prevented him from tolerating any intervention beyond mirroring.

Implementation

The final step with regard to the content of therapeutic procedure is implementation. Descriptively, implementation may seem like behavior modification. But implementation differs sharply from behavior modification in its focus upon intrapsychic processes. Behavioral and cognitive approaches, by contrast, focus on altering manifest behavior to meet explicit objectives, irrespective of the unconscious motives or structural capacity of the person.

In carrying out the plan it is vital that intrapsychic function be kept in the foreground. Implementation is a reworking of experiences which reflect the patient's chronic problems. Anxiety, distortion, resistance, and defense are, therefore, expectable concomitants to any real-life encounter with these issues, despite whatever enthusiasm patients show. Narcissistically invested self representations may become more accessible as the patient confronts the inability to move in a consciously valued direction. Implementation provides an experience carefully designed to mobilize patients' resources for functional effectiveness in an area of psychopathological dysfunction. Thus, strict adherence to the original plan is unnecessary if, in the proving ground of the real world, options arise which can improve its therapeutic utility. The partners can exercise flexibility in determining how the plan is carried out, since the first priority at all times is its role in the therapy. Patients need to adapt the general objectives of the plan to their own style, circumstances, and readiness. Successful completion of the plan is less important than successful activation of patients' egoself resources. By contrast, rigid adherence to a plan which falls short of its therapeutic purpose is contrary to the spirit of developmental growth which implementation serves.

The design and implementation of ego-mobilizing experiences are part of the therapy, and not a replacement for it. While both partners participate in its design, the manifest plan reflects client desires, negotiated to achieve outcomes compatible with the imperatives of intrapsychic growth. Thus each of the therapy partners contributes from their own area of expertise. Patients' encounter with this guided experience provides rich, focally relevant material for exploration in therapy sessions. Because of their vulnerability during these trial efforts, patients are specially susceptible to misinterpreting the experience. Regular therapy sessions, supplemented with telephone contact if needed, are essential for realistically appraising and supporting the value of the experience. Even more fundamental is a solidly established working partnership. In the absence of such conditions the entire procedure may backfire.

> Mr. E was terminating therapy, apparently having worked through a pernicious self-defeating tendency. While he and his therapist were on their respective vacations, Mr. E planned to go on his first solitary trip. Upon returning, the partners would review the experience. A reasonable amount of therapy time went into discussing Mr. E's preparation for his vacation, a five-hundred-mile trip on his motorcycle. Routes, maps, road conditions, equipment, and contingency plans were all considered. The trip was to be a psychological voyage, in which Mr. E could try out his readiness to be his own best friend.

> Mr. E did not appear for his scheduled postvacation ap-

pointment, an unusual occurrence. Two weeks went by without contact. Into the third week Mr. E called for an appointment. He arrived looking humiliated, defeated, and depressed. The vacation had been a disaster for him. It began with mechanical trouble to his motorcycle, which he repaired before starting out. His original destination was flooded, so he had to fall back on his alternate plans. On his return trip his rear tire blew just as he was passing a car on the expressway. Somehow, he managed to steer the cycle over to the right and off the traffic lane before overturning. His helmet and leather jacket protected him from serious injury when he landed on the pavement. Convinced that he had once again sabotaged himself, Mr. E was too ashamed to come for therapy. Finally, his increasing depression forced him to return.

Close scrutiny of the events revealed that quite the opposite of self-sabotage had occurred. At every point where planning and precautions were possible—from delaying his trip in order to check out his motorcycle, to the expert driving that had saved his life when his tire blew—Mr. E had used sound judgment and realistic care. His long history of self-directed rage and failure left him vulnerable to harsh self-criticism when his plans did not pan out as intended. But detailed examination of what occurred, intrapsychic and environmental, led to the supportive confrontation that he had never before been as capable as he had been on this vacation. On the transferential level, the therapist's reaction contrasted with Mr. E's ingrained expectation of criticism from a rejecting father. Termination followed soon afterward; four years later, Mr. E was continuing to function effectively.

Implementation therefore serves as the laboratory and testing ground in which the psychotherapeutic work is put to practical experience, honed, and verified. The historic conception of working through finds its contemporary application in this methodology. The instance just described also illustrates the important role of follow-up review, a component of therapeutic process.

THERAPEUTIC PROCESS

The structural analysis of process occurs concomitantly, and interactively, with the analysis of content. Content and process analysis together comprise therapeutic procedure. Where content analysis explores patient phenomenology as part of its data base, process is concerned with resources utilized, their appropriateness and coherence, and recruiting and mobilizing other resources. It is a more conceptual approach, but equally functional and equally necessary. Where content draws most heavily on utilizing patients' expert familiarity with their own experience, process depends more on therapists' knowledge and experience of egoself processes.

Assessment of Experience

Beginning with the same sort of in vivo issue which was presented as content, therapeutic process analysis lodges the experience in situational context in order to assess the kinds of resources used, and the developmental level(s) they denote. The results of patients' psychological activity are examined relative to such ego functions as reality testing, capacity for delay, use of foresight and judgment, and in the light of its efficacy.

> *P*: (facial muscles tense, manner pugnacious) I just quit my job. Fuck 'em, nobody treats me like that. Fuck them!
> *Th*: You're really smoking.
> *P*: You better believe it . . . sonsabitches.
> *Th*: What happened?
> *P*: No foreman's gonna put me on another job. Fuck 'em.

The patient's rage activates all discharge modes: somatic, affective, verbal, motor. Developmental primitivity is indicated by the diffuse reaction and its continuing intensity despite the intervening time since the incident. Ego assessment suggests impulse permeability and a readiness to externalize blame. The low frustration tolerance and outpouring of affect is indicative of primary process function. This is supported by an apparent unconcern for the consequences of suddenly quitting a job. How, and under what conditions, does she reconstitute adult functioning? Will she be able to gain ego distance during this session, evaluate what happened, consider the consequences for her, make some plans? In this vignette, the patient evinces little defensive operation and no coping process. But this is only a brief segment, a cross section taken during a period of stress.

A longer time context is needed. It would be helpful to know more details about the antecedent conditions leading to the incident, and how she responds now that these events have occurred. The curtain has dropped on one scene, but the drama continues. In particular, process analysis will look closely for whatever resources the patient marshals to resume higher levels of functioning. This information will inform therapeutic procedure significantly, by indicating patient's recruitable assets and providing clues to their eventual mobilization.

Patient spent the remainder of the session in morose silence. The following week she returned, appearing calm.

> *P*: Well, I got my job back.
> *Th*: Oh?
> *P*: Yeah. I told the foreman I couldn't go to work in that other department. My ex-boyfriend's new girlfriend works there, and I'd never want to be anywhere near her. The foreman understood, and he knows I'm a good worker so he didn't want me to quit.
> *Th*: I'm in shock. Last week when you were in here you were so ripping mad and upset you stopped talking entirely. Now you come in and tell me you talked to your foreman and got your job back. What happened?
> *P*: When I get upset like that there's no talking to me. It just takes me a while to simmer down and then I'm okay. I got a lot of shit out here last week and the next day I went in and spoke to him.

Resources Used

The patient's ego functioning is permeable, volatile, labile, yet she demonstrates significant resiliency, including the adult ability to see herself in perspective. Self-knowledge, and the ability to articulate it, is also consistent with at least young adult ego development. The wide developmental range she spans and the naive quality of her self-disclosure suggest a hysterical personality style. How does this relate to her presenting problems? The other side of the coin of her apparent self-acceptance is that this style may be ego syntonic and thus resistive to change. Can she see it as dysfuntional? How does she go about "simmering down" and getting "okay"? She seems to be using the support and catharsis of last week's session effectively.

The session continues,

Th: What is it like for you when you're as mad as you were last week?

P: I just need to be left alone, and then I'm all right.

Th: What does it feel like inside, when you're feeling that way?

P: It's okay; I don't mind it. Sometimes I just need to get mad, and then I get over it.

Th: How do you get over it?

P: I don't know; I just do. It's no big deal.

Th: What does it cost you to get that way, when you blow up at people, quit your job?

P: Hey, that's the way I am. If people don't like it, that's their tough luck.

The patient's ego fluidity is ego syntonic, at least in regard to angry self-assertion. She defends it as part of her identity, and is thus far unaware or unwilling to acknowledge any disadvantage to maintaining that way of functioning. In actuality, she needs to see that it is not simply a style, but that she often loses control. Her last comment betrayed a belligerent defensiveness that emerges under minimal provocation. In part, she feels safety in anger, and it erupts reflexively when she feels threatened; in part she does not use more adult means of self-assertion, resorting to emotional storms (and manipulation?) when negotiation might be more effective in the long run. To achieve a full cost–gain analysis of her emotional storming will require closer, repeated examination. Since her ego functioning is young adult in other ways, adult functions in this realm should be recruitable when the timing is right for it. But first it must be determined whether the present costs are greater than she realizes.

Several weeks later, another emotional flareup occurs, this time with her family. During the intervening time, the therapist had tried to explore earlier incidents with the client. Each time she explained away any connection between them.

P: My mother is such a bitch! She called the other day, and all of a sudden she's on my case, jumping all over me. I told her to fuck off, and hung up on her.

Th: What did that get you?

P: It got her off my back. I don't have to take that shit from her.

Th: You don't? You told me she's the one person you can count on, the one who's closest to you.

P: It's okay. She'll come around, eventually.

Th: And meanwhile? What happens to you until she comes around? Who do you go to with your needs, your feelings?

P: What am I supposed to do, take all that shit?
Th: I don't know; it costs you either way. Which way is worse for you?
P: SHIT!!! (Lapses into morose silence.)

This is a classic example of a patient being confronted with the psychological cost of maintaining an ego syntonic defensive posture. It is now up to her to evaluate its worth, and decide if she is willing to engage the hard work of trying to change. Patients vary enormously, of course, in their readiness to acknowledge their need to change or to undertake the work of changing. People with primitive structures tend to be more tenacious, and invest more rigidly in a constant self-image. More sophisticated, developmentally more mature people are often more ready to commit themselves to change. This is not surprising, since the threat to ego integrity is less severe in those who have reached higher levels of ego development. However, the determining factors in a successful outcome are more complex. Sometimes the more primitively structured patients are able to leap ahead, if they trust the therapist and the threat posed by their problems is clear. Paradoxically, some patients who seem developmentally well organized encounter great difficulty in changing. They are clear on the utility and feasibility of change, it would appear, but the other gratifications in their lives seem to drain off the energy that a greater sense of urgency might provide. Chronicity and primitivity do not, by themselves, prognosticate as poorly as I once believed. When they coexist with other areas of mature ego organization, the prognosis may be less guarded. The same can be said of working with older adults. On the other hand, developmental and/or egoself maturity does not by itself prognosticate favorably. The gratifications in patients' life circumstances, the centrality of the problem to their core values, and the tenacity with which they hold to the identity they have structured seem to bear heavily on therapeutic outcome.

Returning to therapeutic process analysis, the assessment of patient experiences in situational context helps the therapist to locate the egoself resources and developmental level that may be available for mobilization. Efficacy assessment then explores the accessibility of real or potential resources. Therapists often begin this sort of inquiry during routine exploration of the patient's history. But the inquiry tends to focus on psychopathology, with less explicit attention given to ego resources. The assessment process needs to consider which functions are effective, as well as those which are impaired. And the evaluation of developmental level can indicate whether functional deficits are due to impairment, disuse, or sheer unawareness. This appraisal of deficits and resources provides the therapist with a survey of areas in which the patient is at risk, and where he or she may be ready to engage therapeutic work.

Efficacy Assessment

In this segment, patients' functioning is explored in a situation which demonstrates the psychopathology. It is useful here to stay with the same kind of cost–gain perspective described earlier. The situation is explored and the therapist is careful to include the consequences of patients' functioning. Where these results create great pain there is no reason to underscore them. But when patients are only attuned to ego syntonic elements it is important for them to be confronted with the full consequences of what their activities yield them. Returning to the last case,

> *P*: Look, I can't help it when I blow up. It just happens.
> *Th*: That's right, a lot of the time you can't help blowing up. But if we understand what's happening, maybe you can prevent it before it happens.
> *P*: (looks blankly, unconvinced; patient was saying "I'm not responsible for blowing up" and therapist is saying "You're out of control")
> *Th*: Why don't we take a look at one of the times you blew, something recent.
> *P*: (describes a recent incident at a supermarket checkout counter) . . . so I said, "keep your fucking groceries" and I walked out of the store.
> *Th*: Okay, now what was going on with you just before that?
> *P*: I was getting ripped! Two times I asked her what she was ringing up on the cash register and she never answered me.
> *Th*: But it was more than that. You told me you only had a certain amount of money and you'd be embarrassed if she rang up more than you could pay for (content she had provided earlier).
> *P*: So what am I supposed to do, stand there and let her make a fool out of me?

Th: I don't think that's it. I think you were embarrassed to tell her that you didn't want to spend more than $15.

P: It's none of her business how much I want to spend.

Th: It's her business to ring up what you put on the counter. You're blaming her for your embarrassment. It sounds to me like you were embarrassed that you only had $15 to buy food with.

P: Don't you think I feel bad enough about it, without letting the whole world know? Fifteen dollars doesn't buy anything today.

Th: That's right, and you knew that even before you went into the store. Do you remember how you felt when you were thinking about going shopping?

P: Yeah, like I had lead in my stomach. I was thinking, "Why the hell do I even bother going to the store, if that's all I've got?"

Th: There's your clue—that lead feeling in your stomach. Can you remember other times when you've had that feeling?

P: (verifies, with other instances, that the leaden feeling is a precursor to her rage reactions)

Th: Okay. At the point that you get that leaden feeling, you're still in control. And you know you're heading for an explosion you don't want to have.

The partnership has now identified the dynamic process: perceived threat elicits a somatic reaction (leaden feeling in stomach), presumably an anxiety equivalent; this generates a readiness for a rage reaction, which is justified by projecting blame upon the most suitable environmental figure. The patient's capacity for perspective may permit her to recognize that this is a pattern which she creates, which gets her into trouble, and which she may be able to affect. The therapist feels that the patient's developmental mode (see chapter 7) here is adaptational, in that it is oriented to mastery and challenge. This mode may be recruitable for the therapeutic tasks ahead, particularly since it also can be linked up with her (presumed) young adult prepotency for getting actively involved in new tasks.

Survey of Needs, Resources, Readiness

Confronting the patient with an option is no guarantee that she will be ready to experiment with alternatives. This was particularly true of Janet, whose reliance on projection and the secondary gain of acting out did not dispose her to try other methods.

P: Look, I don't get what you're talking about. Are you telling me it's my fault?

Th: I'm not talking about anybody's fault. I'm saying it doesn't do you a lot of good to walk off the job you want to keep, or get into fights with your mother, or blast the checkout girl. How do you feel after those things happen?

P: Look, that's just the way I am, that's all.

Th: I know, but how do you feel at those times?

P: It depends. Sometimes they deserve to be put in their place. Sometimes I feel like a jerk afterwards.

The therapist steers clear of imputation of blame, even responsibility, regarding the patient's actions, knowing that she is ready to flare up at him if those feelings are aroused. Instead, he hopes to recruit her adaptational mode of striving to master, by challenging her to confront what she can be. Avoiding a resistive reaction, focusing on a growth task, and invoking recruitable resources describe a process consistent with egoself principles. Identifying an ego dystonic element—"I feel like a jerk"—may provide therapeutic leverage. If the patient is willing, reorganization will begin, working toward the goal of helping her create ego options to replace her current reflexive reactions.

Reorganization

Reorganization occupies the same central role in the therapeutic process that the alternatives do in therapeutic content. Functionally, they are the identical activities. This is the point at which the therapist's understanding of the patient's resources are applied to the restructuring of egoself operations. While therapists may function more prescriptively than usual during this period, the dominant style remains one of partnership with patients. Now the partners must agree to try out alternatives within the client's recruitable potential. Reorganization efforts within and outside the therapy will provide the data to assess their adequacy for the job to be done. Like the traditional process of working through, from which this derives, reorganization entails experiential relearning. Reorganization shapes and informs these experiences with more specific information generated from assessing patients' egoself and developmental resources, balanced against pathological vulnerabilities. Specific ego operations and situational tactics are suggested, deriving from the assessment data. The process differs from standard psychoanalytic therapy technique in several respects: by concentrating on the present, future, and recent past rather than invoking early memories and relationships; by not responding to transference cues unless they intrude on the other work; by emphasizing the implementation of change using newly recruited egoself resources.

It is inappropriate to conceptualize the past as though mental representations are fixed in place. Egoself development is ongoing, and past experience is constantly being reworked (see chapter 6). By working with patients' contemporary lives one deals with those ongoing transformations of the past as they are functioning actively in the present.

Returning to the reorganization process, therapists' entire array of skills are often tested at this juncture. Patients are given the opportunity to grapple tangibly with their problem, but only by relinquishing the familiar, partially gratifying psychopathological functions they have been using. Sometimes the therapeutic work entails fundamental ego building, such as the ability to differentiate kinds and amounts of affect. Sometimes pathological structuring of self, object relations, or ego operations must be addressed first. More often, reorganization entails the extension of ego competencies from practiced areas of application to areas of function in which they have not been used. In either circumstance, therapists can contribute actively and significantly to a beneficial outcome. This can be exemplified by returning to the same case illustration we have been using, that of the primitively aggressive Janet:

After indicating that her angry outbursts could become an option, the therapist suggested some experimentation, to empower the client by recruiting available ego resources. The prior assessment of egoself and developmental resources now assumes major importance in locating what is recruitable.

> *Th*: Sometimes you feel like a jerk. It might be really nice if you could put people in their place when they deserve it, but not feel like a jerk when they don't.
> *P*: Yeah, that's easy to say, but you can't change who you are.

Th: Maybe you don't have to change, just use it better. Like, when do you feel like a jerk?

P: Well take that time at Purity Market. I called the cashier an asshole. She got real upset, and I thought she was gonna cry. I said to myself, "Geez, you really clobbered her." I felt real stupid, I didn't mean to hurt her like that; I was just mad.

Th: You didn't realize you could hurt someone so easily?

P: No, I was just mad because she. . . .

Th: You didn't realize how strong you are (focusing on patient's power, rather than her guilt).

P: She was just a kid, about my age.

Th: About the same age you are, yet you could overpower her (a supportive confrontation, in this context). What does that say about you?

P: What are you talking about?

Th: It sounds like you don't realize your own strength.

P: (pause) You might be right about that.

A discussion followed, in which Janet recalled other instances in which people acknowledged her forcefulness and strength. Then she could admit to feeling weak and undeserving when she wanted something, especially wanting something from others.

Th: I have a hunch that many times when you get angry, it's because you want something and you're afraid no one will listen to you.

P: Sure I get that idea. Nobody cares what you want. If you don't take care of yourself, nobody else will.

Th: But maybe, if you realized how strong you are, you could take care of yourself better (this is designed to recruit her adaptational mode of challenge and mastery).

P: How?

Th: By using your strength by not using it.

Having planted the seeds for affirming her self-image as a strong person (and leaving tacit her notion that strong equals good) the partners discussed how Janet could experiment with asking, rather than demanding, when she wanted something. It was agreed they would review what happened in these efforts. The following week, Janet returned for her scheduled session:

Th: What's been happening?

P: Well, I tried out what we talked about. My sister had a baby and I want to visit her for a long weekend. So I went to my boss and asked him for a day off, and he said he'd let me know.

Th: How does that sit with you?

P: I don't like it. What am I supposed to do now? I can't make plans or anything.
Th: What happened when you asked him? Can you describe it to me?
P: I decided not to push him, just ask. So I said, "Charlie, can I have the 17th off?" and he said, "that's 2½ weeks away; I'll let you know next week."
Th: Did you tell him why you wanted the time off, and why you'd like to know as soon as possible?
P: What for? I figure that's none of his business.
Th: Maybe so. But you're asking for a favor and it might help if he knew you had a special reason. He's used to you demanding things and maybe didn't understand that this was a special request.

The therapist actively intervenes in shaping the experience, utilizing Janet's demonstrated capacity for personal perspective, to see herself in a situation from an observer's perspective. Janet doesn't yet see that asking may also entail justifying. She is already acting at a level beyond her previous modes of function. If she achieves this objective, the therapist may go on to show her how explaining herself can be a different way of showing strength. In that process, she may discover the power of language as a coping resource, thus aligning enhanced ego strength with a self-image of being strong. Reorganization is, for the moment, complete. Janet is encouraged to return to her boss and try out the new approach, or wait for a similar situation in which to try it. It is likely she will need some practical help with the social skills of negotiating—a world unknown to her. Further experimentation may be necessary before the new learning is tested and adapted to Janet's own style and readiness. This is where review and synthesis enters the process.

Review and Synthesis

The final step in the process sequence is that of review and synthesis. For lasting change to occur, patients need to discover their ability to create rewarding new ways of functioning, ways that are compatible with cherished aspects of self. Then, new skills need to be internalized and integrated with other aspects of ego and self, if change is to be more than cosmetic. These processes may not occur spontaneously, and the therapeutic gains may be transient if not thoroughly assimilated into organismic functioning. Janet reported her follow-up of the previous session:

> *P*: I figured that I could try to talk to my boss before he decided about my weekend off. The next morning at coffee break I went over to him. I could tell right away it didn't look good. So before he could say anything I told him about my sister's baby and how it was the first one. But he still didn't say okay.
>
> *Th*: What did he say? (did she give him a chance to talk?)
>
> *P*: You could tell he wasn't going to give me anything. He started telling me about how it's the busy season, and we've got to keep the lines moving, and all that shit. . . .
>
> *Th*: And what was going on inside you? (refocusing on her observing ego, from which the controls must come)
>
> *P*: I started getting that feeling in my gut . . . and I knew I'd better do something fast or I'd really blow. So before he could say anything else I said: "What if I get somebody to fill in for me, can I get the weekend off?" and he stopped a minute, and then kind of mumbled okay, and walked off.
>
> *Th*: Any luck finding somebody? (supportive comment on her effort might have been a preferable intervention before proceeding)
>
> *P*: Yeah, Annie said she'd cover for me. She needs the money.
>
> *Th*: Well, how do you feel about the way it's worked out?
>
> *P*: The miserable son of a bitch! He didn't give me shit.
>
> *Th*: Maybe that's his job. But the important thing is what you did. He didn't give you anything, but you still were able to get the weekend off. And it wouldn't have happened if you hadn't gone to him in the first place. Your talking to him made it possible.
>
> *P*: He's still the same miserable lowlife.
>
> *Th*: And you were still able to get what you wanted. If you had to do it all over again, what would you do?
>
> *P*: I don't know.
>
> *Th*: Think about it, and we'll talk it over next time.

The battle was won but the war was not over. Janet was able to inhibit her rage long enough to squeeze in a negotiating chip, and it worked. The rage and its lurking gratifications are still there, however. But a psychological wedge—her successful ego operations—is now in place. She can exercise control, and it can work to her benefit. While the objective outcome was a success, clearly the patient still has many reservations. Further review of her wishes and intentions for that incident will enable the partners to continue to enrich their understanding. Does she see it as an empty victory, too high a cost? How has the experience, and its consequence, affected her perspective? Future events, as much as conscious review, will elucidate what has been assimilated and whether further reworking is needed.

Whatever the short-term consequences of the experiment, review and synthesis are necessary ingredients of the therapeutic process. A felicitous experimental outcome benefits from reexamination of its effectiveness. The review and synthesis helps patients to internalize the experience, ultimately resulting in new mental representations. The newly internalized experience then can modify or compete with existing mental representations of self and other in the ongoing process of transformation. Where the reorganizational outcome has been unfavorable, review and synthesis will lay the ground work for more effective second efforts. In both cases, patients discover their operational capabilities in the therapeutic process of reviewing their everyday activities. Coupling this learning laboratory approach with traditional intrapsychic techniques grounds the therapy more deeply in the patients' life experience without pandering to cosmetic change or intellectualized insights.

But this procedure requires unfailing attention to the nature of the process: that it be grounded in experiential learning. To be effective, material must be based on affectively meaningful associations and experiences. Constant evocation of patients' inner awareness, and attunement to the vital issues of the person's life, keep the process of reorganization and synthesis personally and psychologically relevant. In such a climate therapeutic restructuring can have a powerful effect.

THERAPEUTIC TECHNIQUE

Technique is actually a highly idiosyncratic matter. The same word or gesture, coming from two different therapists, can have a quite different impact on patients. Conversely, entirely different words or gestures communicated by the two therapists could convey similar meanings to their patients. There is a way to circumvent the problems posed by divergent personal and linguistic styles. By describing the principles and purposes of a technical intervention—rather than its precise mechanics— therapists can adapt the concept to their own style and personality. As the chapter continues, some of the issues to be examined are better described as working principles rather than specific techniques. Nevertheless, they reflect the actual implementation of egoself psychotherapy.

Psychotherapeutic technique includes four steps: recruitment, mobilization, experimentation, and review. Technically, restructuring begins with recruiting and mobilizing resources, those aspects of healthy ego, self, and object relations operation already observed in the patient as well as those which are developmentally prepotent. Implementing the resources so that they are psychologically useful to patients is the work of experimentation and review. The structural emphasis in these four steps requires focusing the attention of the therapy dyad on close exploration of patients' experience. Involving patients in this analytic work elucidates egoself operations at the same time that it stimulates their active participation. Technically, this work is highly confrontive and therefore bears all the risks associated with the use of confrontation. For this reason, convergent focusing, confrontation, and supportive confrontation are extensively discussed and illustrated in this section on technique. The discussion and illustration of these techniques now follows.

Recruitment

Recruitment, and its counterpart mobilization, are central ingredients of egoself psychotherapy. Recruitment consists of identifying and highlighting both current resources and those potentially available to the patient. It is an approach which begins in the first sessions and continues throughout therapy. During the assessment process, which examines the content of patients' problems and pathology, ego assets, self structure, and developmental status are carefully evaluated. Thus, at the same time that patients' psychopathology is scrutinized, therapists also note the egoself assets that may be available. Psychotherapists can become so attuned to pathology that strengths are sometimes overlooked. The person who says, "I sometimes feel like I'm about to lose my mind" is describing a manifest problem, feared insanity. But the patient is also acknowledging the

importance of retaining ego control. His potentially recruitable
assets include the ego's current capacity for tolerating anxiety,
and, tacitly, a view of control as ego syntonic. The patient's
differentiation of expectation from occurrence (". . . like I'm
about to"), and relativistic thought process ("sometimes"), suggests that development has gone at least as far as adolescence.
Verbal fluency, an asset in most psychotherapies, is suggested
by the choice of language and use of nuance. These preliminary
inferences, drawn from one sentence, suggest that clues to recruitable assets can be as richly harvested as we are accustomed
to doing with evidence of psychopathology.

Upon noting a recruitable asset, the therapist may simultaneously explore and highlight it for further use simply by
reflecting the word or phrase. Just a brief focusing is usually
enough to help the partners mark that quality for the future.
Sometimes clarification or supportive confrontation is needed
in order to establish the viability of an important ego asset.

> P: I don't know if I can avoid getting into an argument with him.
> Th: Didn't you once mention a time when you were in high school. . . .
> P: The time with my friend Bobby? Is that what you mean?
> Th: Yeah. Didn't you walk away from a fight that time?
> P: That's right, I guess I did.

Recruitment identifies an actual capability from the patient's
experiential history. Developmental assessment may suggest
other recruitable assets, but these must be tested before it can
be assumed that they are available for mobilization.

Mobilization

As the supplementary process to recruitment, mobilization is
the activation of those resources which have been previously
identified. Capacities can be mobilized which have been used
before in other contexts. Other capacities can be mobilized even
though they are only developmental prepotencies. Either way,
mobilization activates specific psychological operations in the
service of the therapeutic procedures previously discussed.
Mobilization offers patients their own recruitable assets as an
alternative to their current debilitating ways of dealing with

problems. But utilizing capabilities which patients are able and willing to apply cannot deteriorate into fatuous advice, suggesting "rational" alternatives which the patient is unable to incorporate. Nor does the therapist simplistically assume that pathology is reducible to "poor learning" or "bad habits." Recruitment and mobilization are the companion techniques for intrapsychic restructuring.

Invoking psychological operations is somewhat similar to microsurgery, in that it puts in place the capacity for new or restored function. By bringing patients into proximity with small, specific, doable actions, which link motivation to capability, their pathology may seem less overwhelming. In addition, mobilization concretizes the capacity for change beyond the vague assumption that growth occurs automatically, once the pathology is resolved. The focus on tangible competence in the immediate reality is more than support, however. By setting up the behavioral mechanics of change, the stage is laid for understanding the nature and role of the pathology in the patient's current psychic operations. Identifying resources within the patient's grasp may help the therapy to move into an exploration of the patient's resistance or readiness for change. In short-term therapy changes in function can lay the groundwork for gradual spontaneous reworking of unconscious issues. With longer therapy contact one can work backward from the overt change to its impact on earlier self-definition. Recruitment and mobilization together constitute the irreducible essence of therapeutic technique in the egoself approach.

Mobilization is a direct intervention technique. Whether the problems are manifested as interpersonal, intrapsychic, philosophical, or situational, in the final analysis patients' intrapsychic experience, and reaction to that experience, are the parameters over which they can exercise some control. Consequently, therapeutic strategy concentrates on optimizing their functioning in that small sphere of control. Whether the underlying issue can be resolved by attitude restructuring, or by being able to more effectively impact on the behavior of others, or by an enriched self-understanding may not be determinable at the outset. Mobilization of resources is simply the method used for that purpose. Mobilization involves clarifying the nature and use of the resource, and then assisting patients in planning, designing, and detailing alternative experiences in their problem areas, based upon implementing the resource.

The actual process of mobilization faithfully exemplifies the principle of an egalitarian partnership in the egoself psychotherapeutic relationship. Both partners participate actively in recruiting and mobilizing patient resources. Therapists use their assessment skills to predict, identify, and sensitize patients to their resources. But patients ultimately determine which resources get mobilized. Adept therapists draw on patients' personal experience and subjective awareness to elicit those capabilities which are the most prepotent. At any given point in time, a patient may be theoretically able to apply a variety of egoself resources. The patient's specific choice may seem suitable or inappropriate to the therapist. But whether a theoretically feasible asset can be operationalized, or a pathological reaction modified, is a matter that the partnership must resolve. For both partners, the most viable criteria are: does the apparent change really work, what are its consequences, is the patient willing and able to live with them?

The mobilized resources emerge from the amalgamation of the professional's clinical knowledge with the person's storehouse of private experience. For either partner to preempt the contributions of the other could diminish the efficacy of the therapeutic work. Two common forms of mobilization will be illustrated. In the first an identified developmental prepotency is recruited to replace a chronic defensive pattern:

> Mr. P is in his early fifties. When he was nine his dying father appointed him the "man of the house." Ever since, he had rigidly controlled all emotional experience so that he never cried, rarely laughed, and responded to affective arousal by withdrawing until he felt under control. Now, on the verge of being divorced, he is confronted with the necessity of finding out what he wants. He is vaguely aware that he has been depressed for the last several years. He has no friends. The only people he sees apart from business are his wife and children. During the first two sessions his ego functioning seemed relatively intact.
>
> In the second session Mr. P became tearful when describing the accidental death of an older sister thirty years earlier. He apologized to the therapist, expressing his embarrassment and

concern over this unusual behavior. At the start of the third session Mr. P described how he isolated himself for two days after the last session, spending the time "composing myself." At this point the therapist intervened,

Th: You're so used to shutting out your feelings, it seems like something's gone wrong when you feel real emotion.

P: Yes. That's why I had to get away.

Th: That's always been your way, and perhaps that's how it has had to be, when you were a kid and having to control your fears. But it is natural for middle-aged men to be more sensitive to their feelings.

P: I don't know what to do when I feel like that. This is the second or third time that's happened to me lately, but it never happened before, for as long as I can remember.

Th: This is an important thing for you. You're trying to figure out what you really want in life, but you can't do that without knowing how you really feel. And now, for the first time, you're in a position to experience your feelings and let them help you.

The stage is set for recasting a developmental prepotency—affective sensitization in middle age—as an empowering asset, in a man who defends against emotion, whose identity is linked with being emotionally overcontrolled. A next step might be to locate an everyday incident in which he became aware of his feelings. Then the partners could explore the incident, to see if that awareness was an advantage. What did it cost, what did he gain?

The second illustration involves recruiting a known asset, such as a coping process observed in another realm of client activity, and applying it to the problem area.

Mr. G was in therapy for characterological problems of passivity and depression. His marriage, which he valued, was being put in jeopardy by his way of relating to his wife. She was a needy, impulsive person who was continually asking him to buy this, or do that for her. Mr. G would initially acquiesce to any request, then fail to make good on his promise. His wife would accuse him of being unreliable and unloving, and reject him. He would then lapse into self-accusation and depression.

While some of his derelictions were passive aggressive, often passivity and guilt prevented him from refusing her request when he knew beforehand it would be impossible to fulfill it. Mr. G was a deliberate man whose best functioning took place when he had time to plan his actions. At his therapist's suggestion, he began responding to his wife's requests with positive but noncommital statements, such as, "I'd like to; let's get back to it later this week." These comments, exploiting his ability to apply delay in behalf of judgment, had a twofold advantage: it provided Mr. G with time to analyze his own needs in the situation; it also permitted exploration and differentiation of defensive procrastination from ego-mediated planning. In the process, the patient gained in self-esteem. As he became more responsive his wife's neediness declined. Mr. G had found a way to adapt his planful skills to his marriage, but also discovered he could take selectively assertive action with his wife—a significant reversal of his characterological passivity.

Generally, successful activation of a resource depends upon honing it to situational requirements as well as intrapsychic capacity. Experimentation and review are necessary technical interventions to assure that the resource is appropriately fitted to the circumstances of the patient's intrapsychic interaction with the situation.

Experimentation

In order for recruitment and mobilization to be effectively implemented, fairly precise location and utilization of the identified resources are needed. This sort of precision depends heavily upon the quality of communication between patient and therapist. Each instance of recruitment or mobilization is a new excursion into terra incognita for the partners. Much like the dentist fitting her patient with a new tooth, the change must not only be technically correct, but must also fit and feel right. Neither the dentist nor the patient can achieve that result independent of the other's contribution. The final outcome is accomplished by successive approximation, as each responds to the finely tuned reactions of the other.

Sometimes recruitment or mobilization is successful at the first attempt. Mobilization, in particular, often is not. Consequently, experimentation will be needed to shape the resource to its most effective utilization by the patient. Conceptualizing the potential resource and identifying its general location usually comes from the therapist's earlier recruitment work. But in order for patients to participate actively in an unfamiliar procedure it is helpful to pave the way with discussion, translating the concept into a therapeutic intervention in which they can place credence. The specific intervention is a trial version of the mobilized resource, which can be developed jointly by patient and therapist. This trial version is then subject to further shaping by the partners. Therapists guide the procedure in conformity with intrapsychic objectives; patients ensure that the operations are compatible with their experiential sense of good fit. Once the principle is clear, patients can experiment on their own, using their everyday lives as a kind of living laboratory. In subsequent therapy sessions they can report on the experiences, exploring the results or considering whatever further modifications may be indicated. While the manifest technical procedure may look like classic behaviorism its therapeutic value derives from the underlying intrasystemic processes. Patients' role in this procedure embodies the most essential principles of effective learning: personal investment, active participation, pragmatic relevance, and attainable objectives. In turn these translate into assertive involvement, analysis, and confrontation of existing self–world and self representations, selective stretching of ego functions—a miniature instance of separation–individuation. By actively monitoring the quality of that experience, and by holding to the experimental format as a way of augmenting it, egoself therapy becomes a relevant approach to intrapsychic restructuring.

In the following case illustration, the patient is a woman referred to elsewhere in this book as a person obsessed with fears of hurting her child. But her fear of inflicting bodily harm on others actually dated back to childhood, before she was eight. This series of excerpts took place midway through the second year of weekly therapy sessions. Much of the work prior to this segment dealt with helping her explore and grapple with the more diffuse but acute anxieties provoked by her narcissistic self-preoccupation: anguish about psychotic members of her nuclear family; her marriage; fears of losing her job, and financial insecurity; grotesque images of social perceptions of her mild case of cerebral palsy. As these concerns were described and explored, Mrs. C began to focus on her relationship with her young daughter. She began to realize that her daughter might be suffering from an emotionally paralyzed mother as much as from potential physical harm. The clinical material has been compressed in the interest of brevity.

> *P*: I see Sara turning into an insufferable little brat, but I'm afraid to go near her for fear of what I might do to her.
>
> *Th*: What makes you think you'd do anything harmful to her?
>
> *P*: I . . . I . . . I have these thoughts I might choke her by the throat, or pick up a scissors and stab her, or grab her and throw her out of the window . . . (sobs)
>
> *Th*: Is that an idea you have, or is it like an urge?
>
> *P*: I don't understand what you mean.
>
> *Th*: That's part of my point. Is it a thought you have, or a feeling, or a tension in your body?
>
> *P*: I do feel a tension. I think, "Suppose I got so mad I just went at her," and I get tense and terrified. It's so awful. Then I start thinking about what kind of person could have thoughts like this about her own child.
>
> *Th*: I understand. Tell me about the tension you feel: where is it? Can you locate it in any part of your body?
>
> *P*: (ponders) It's mostly in my arms, I think. And my hands—my fingers. It's in my fingers and up through my forearms (flexes her fingers).
>
> *Th*: Anyplace else?
>
> *P*: I think that's where I feel it the most.
>
> *Th*: Would you be willing to try something? It might help you with that tension, and take some of the pressure off you when you're getting upset with Sara. Stand about two feet from a wall, facing it, like this (therapist demonstrates exercise, describing it simultaneously).
>
> *P*: But Sara will think I'm crazy if I start doing something like that when I'm talking to her.
>
> *Th*: Then maybe you could go into another room and do it. You can't do anything with her anyway when you're feeling like that.
>
> *P*: I need some time to think about this. Is it all right with you if we wait a while? It seems so unfamiliar.

Terrified by her fear of destructive action, it was important for the patient to experience ego mediation of motor activity. Even though her pathology was obsessional, in her own view Mrs. C was at the mercy of her impulses. The prescriptive intervention was a first try at helping her find a motor discharge which would help her to feel she could control herself. Her obsessional agitation and preoccupation left insufficient time for more traditional exploration, given weekly contact. But even that approach had its problems: the narcissistic insult Mrs. C experienced at the prospect of such unusual activity. Two weeks later, Mrs. C reported that she had decided to try out the method, and had some questions.

P: I tried clenching and unclenching my fists, but I still felt tense. I don't know why. I didn't like making a fist. It seemed to symbolize anger, and that bothered me. Then I tried pushing against the wall the way you showed me, and that felt somewhat better. But it still isn't quite right. When no one was around I went into the bedroom and pounded my arms and fists on the pillow, and screamed into the pillow. That didn't seem to work. I feel like such an idiot doing these things.

Th: I know its extreme, but you don't feel great with the way things are, do you? It sounds like you've been doing some experimenting with different methods.

P: Is that all right? I thought I could perhaps improvise on your idea, but if you don't think I should. . . .

Th: Oh, that's fine. Its got to be something that fits you, so try anything that feels right, and then we can talk about it

The following week, Mrs. C reported on her most recent experiences:

P: Sara was being such a pain, about which vegetable she would or would not eat for dinner. I told her I couldn't talk with her, and went into the bedroom. The poor kid must have been in shock, wondering what's going on with her weird mother. I tried that pushing against the wall exercise, but it didn't really help. Then I asked myself what would feel better, and it seemed I wanted to stretch out the muscles in my forearm. I looked about the room and then I got on a chair—this is going to sound really weird—and I grabbed the top of the closet door and let my feet dangle loose. And when I let go, I could really feel a difference.

Th: That's terrific. You found something that really works for you. Relieving the tension in your hands and arms may make it easier for you to deal with Sara when she upsets you. I hope you'll be able to try it one of these times when you're upset with her so that we can see what the effects are like.

With support, the patient began to work with the exercises. As she did, some things were discovered: she found the exercises compatible, perhaps because of her past history of physical activity; then, the ludicrous aspect of doing exercises in the middle of her frightening obsessions struck her. Somehow, those narcissistic preoccupations were counterbalanced by a capacity for ego distancing she had never shown before. The sheer absurdity of the contrast was a revelation, and led to the first instance of an observing ego she had ever described in these situations. That result was not predictable. But the theoretical rationale—to intercept the pathological reaction by locating and experimenting with resources which could mobilize greater ego mediation of her problems—was entirely consistent with egoself theory. The serendipitous discovery of Mrs. C's capacity for humor was the happy by-product of mobilizing adult resources, drawing on the latent strengths that people acquire over the course of their development.

With mobilization of Mrs. C's readiness to use exercise as a safe discharge modality, experimentation freed her to try out methods that fit her style. But successful experimentation only begins with client compatibility. As with any other technical intervention, its efficacy is measured by clinical outcome. This is when review becomes important.

Review

While the experimental aspects of resource mobilization can be of intrinsic therapeutic value, those experiences are theoretically and clinically incomplete. The emphasis on structural reorganization requires that experience be incorporated with ongoing egoself operations. No matter how gratifying or revealing the experimental discoveries may be, their therapeutic value must remain suspect until they are demonstrated to be both useful and durable. The review phase studies the structural impact of experimentation. Review consists of several steps: eliciting recent experiences which demonstrate operation of the new resources, verifying with patients that the resource was used, observing its consequences, evaluating the sequence and outcome with the patient.

Review technique is not simply a recounting of recent events, however. The technique entails recalling the events, focusing on the patient's active experience in those events, differentiating out the specific resources, and closely examining their manifestation, operation, and consequences. Finally, the patient's own appraisal of its impact must be incorporated and worked through. These activities are vital to internalization of the experience as a resource. Restructuring ultimately results from this synthesis of patients' phenomenological experience with the operation of their egoself functions. New self representations may be created or connection made to earlier images. Specific ego operations may be identified as demonstrable capabilities. During this review similar situations can be discussed, along with how the patient might respond in the light of these new discoveries.

Reviewing the experience includes a consideration of whether any further modifications are necessary. How successfully has a resource met patients' needs? Effectiveness of outcome is one criterion, but "fit" with patients' style and values is equally important if any improvement in functioning is to be durable. During the review patients are encouraged to explore and evaluate the experience. By this means, patients function as active partners in locating and shaping these therapeutic resources.

Returning to the case of Mrs. C, excerpts from the review will illustrate some of these points.

P: Bill, my husband, has been teasing me about these exercises. He says things like, "I always knew you were a little off the wall, but swinging from doors. . . ."

Th: What's that like for you?

P: I had a number of reactions. At first I was hurt and angry. Then I realized he wasn't saying it maliciously and I got a mental picture of what I must look like, and it must seem pretty strange (smiles).

Th: How is it working out?

P: I'm not sure. What happens now is that every time I start feeling that way with Sara I run into the bedroom and hang from the door. It relieves the tension but by the time I come back it seems too late to go back over what she did that got me upset.

Th: So you don't really get a chance this way to find out if its helping you deal with Sara any better.

P: That's right. And meanwhile, I still get these thoughts, these bad thoughts, not only with Sara but everywhere.

Th: I don't know if these exercises will help you with the thoughts, but it would be nice if you could feel more comfortable in parenting your daughter. Do you think, next time a situation comes up, that you could bring yourself to get back to Sara after you've exercised? It may seem somewhat artificial after the incident is over, but the issue is still alive—whatever she did that upset you.

P: Well, that's true. I'll see if I can do it but I'm not going to promise you.

Th: Not at all. You're not doing it for my sake. If it's not right for you, it probably won't work anyhow.

Once again, Mrs. C gives evidence of an observing ego in her reaction to her husband's comments. Prior to this time tears and anger would have resulted. During the review the therapist stays close to the experience and its immediate impact. When Mrs. C tried to relate the event to her obsessional "bad thoughts" she was brought back to the immediate experience. Only if restructuring does occur can its impact on the pathology be assessed. A couple of sessions later, after talking about job problems,

> *P*: Oh, I wanted to tell you this. Two nights ago Sara went into one of her fits, because I told her she couldn't sleep over at her friend's house this weekend since we're going away. She started screaming at me and I began to get upset. Then I found myself getting really mad and I grabbed her arm and told her to go to her room, that I was tired of her screaming at me.
> *Th*: Wait a minute. Let's do this again. Sara had a fit, you got upset, you didn't go into your bedroom to exercise, you got mad at her and told her off?
> *P*: I don't really understand it. I knew if I went into the bedroom she'd get away with it again, that screaming at me.
> *Th*: Up to now you've been getting upset, but not really mad at her?
> *P*: When she's like that I would get these awful thoughts—what if I picked up a knife and stabbed her. And I'd get so upset and frightened I just wanted to die or disappear.
> *Th*: And now, after you've been doing these crazy exercises, you felt real anger at her and you didn't let her get away with it.

Having differentiated between affects (upset and anger), and affect and impulse (fear and action), her usual reaction and this new sequence, the partners proceed to a review of the consequences:

> *Th*: Okay. Then what happened?
> *P*: What do you mean? I decided to make myself some herbal tea. . . .
> *Th*: How did you feel? What happened with Sara?
> *P*: I guess I was sort of stunned and numb, not knowing what to think. But a little while later Sara asked if she could come out of her room, and apologized for yelling at me. We hugged and I was filled with love for her.
> *Th*: So getting angry didn't result in you hurting Sara. You could be a natural parent and it brought the two of you closer together.
> *P*: That's how it seemed to me. I just hope I can do as well the next time.

Th: I think if you can remember that exercise when you get upset you may find yourself getting better at handling Sara.

A not uncommon event in therapy is that the patient may fail to recognize a more effective way of functioning. This is not surprising, since object relations theory teaches us that inner representations can be more real than actual experiences. For that reason, review technique is essential to the incorporation and ultimate internalization of experience. Without this vital step restructuring may not take place.

Mrs. C can tentatively agree that there is a difference between her observed feelings and actions and her fearful expectations. The therapist suggests that there is a functional connection between the value of the exercise and Mrs. C's improved parenting. While the exercise is cathartic, awareness of her fear now can serve as a signal function for Mrs. C. Arrayed against early intropunitive self representations are new competing images of positive self valuation and competence. This is the raw material from which restructuring can eventually emerge. The reviewed sequence of events becomes a sort of paradigm, demonstrating that Mrs. C's own actions (her capacity for ego mediation of her anxiety-ridden obsessions) can ameliorate her frightening obsessive thoughts. The review will be repeated many times in future sessions. By continuing to monitor the intrapsychic processes involved restructuring is aided, and further changes can be instituted with the same techniques of experimentation and review. This approach, building egoself resources, seems particularly suitable for long-standing, chronic problems such as the one described here. It will be noted that the therapist studiously avoided the transference material which emerged on several occasions, consistent with the position decribed in chapter 5.

A particular feature of weekly egoself therapy, noted earlier, is that of funneling observations, interventions, and patients' experiences toward a focal issue. This technique, convergent focusing, requires further elaboration.

Convergent Focusing

The assessment and extension of egoself operations is begun by centering attention on those operations as they are currently manifested. This technique, convergent focusing, subjects an area of self or ego function to close, careful study of specific operations. Patients are actively involved in this process, partners in the analysis and assessment of their functioning. Convergent focusing tests and expands patients' awareness of their egoself operations. By centering attention on patients' in vivo experience of their functioning, the therapeutic work is pragmatic rather than intellectualized, and tailored to the tolerances of each person's egoself organization.

Convergent focusing was particularly useful with Mrs. C, the woman with obsessional fears of doing harm. Terrified by what she might do to her child, she was unable to provide any discipline or limit-setting for her. The child, undoubtedly responding to her mother's anxiety, became more demanding and difficult, thus exacerbating the problem.

Th: When you say you're afraid you'll hurt Sara, what do you really mean? (narrowing and deepening experiential focus)

P: This is very hard for me to talk about. I get frightened just thinking about it.

Th: I understand. You can stop at any point you want to (respect for and empowerment of partner).

P: Something like that happened the day before yesterday . . . (goes on to describe specific incident) . . . and then I got scared and I was afraid she'd see me trembling and . . .

Th: What scared you?

P: I got this thought, . . . oh, this is so awful to talk about (stops and wipes tears).

Th: I know. Can you tell me what was going on inside you?

P: I . . . got the thought, what if I did something dreadful?

Th: Did you have a thought of something that was dreadful? (trying to specify, also checking her ability to differentiate image, affect, impulse)

P: (reluctantly) Yes . . . that maybe I could strangle her.

Th: That you could, or you wanted to—which? (bringing her closer to her experience; checking reality testing, differentiation)

P: I don't know; it was so frightening, I tried to push the idea out of my mind.

Th: You call it an idea; was it like a thought, or a mental picture or an urge . . . (noting facial and body reactions as well).

P: I remember saying to myself, "What if you wanted to strangle her?" (becomes tearful again)

Th: And then, what did you do? (what does her fantasy evoke?)

P: Do?

Th: Well, you were thinking of strangling Sara. What did you do about it—did you move toward her, warn her, how were you feeling? (by verbalizing specific options the distinction between wish/fear and action is concretized)

P: I felt so awful about myself I wanted to run out of the room, go hide or something.

Th: So how much danger was Sara in? What you're describing is the anguish you had with yourself, not how you had to prevent yourself from hurting her (confronting client with her own processes, which were consistent with observable affective and motor cues).

P: Are you saying I would never hurt her? (seeking reassurance, but also seeking external/magical controls)

Th: I'm saying that what happened was within yourself, not with Sara (the focus remains on the immediate situation, and on the client's ego and self processes).

It can be seen that the two main elements of convergent focusing are the detailed sequencing of key ego operations, and its grounding in specific real life experiences. The immediacy and relevance of the experience help to focus patients' awareness on a finely tuned exploration of the psychological events in that experience. Most elements of intrapsychic experience can be identified in this fashion: impulses, fantasies, intentions, actions, coping, defending, self representations, and their interaction and sequencing. Defensive omissions and distortions also become more apparent under this close scrutiny. Many ego operations can be observed that would otherwise have to be less precisely inferred. Therapists integrate these observations with their own clinical notations, gaining a clearer picture of patients' ego strengths and vulnerabilities in a vital area of function. By selectively sharing this information, their patients gain an expanded awareness of their own inner processes, promoting ego growth. However, convergent focusing is only one intervention technique. Its effectiveness depends upon being incorporated with the other technical interventions which are, in turn, part of the overall therapeutic procedure. A practical consequence of convergent focusing is that it readily generates supplementary interventions: confrontation and supportive confrontation.

Confrontation

Since the analysis of everday experience is so central to the egoself approach, confrontation assumes a proportionately large role in its implementation. A great part of each session is spent in examination of recent events in patients' lives. Patients are encouraged to describe these occurrences, emphasizing what they intended to do, how they experienced the episodes, and what the consequences were. Confrontation is that technique in which patients are brought face to face with the behavioral results of their psychopathological functioning (Adler and Myerson, 1973).

Among people with significant developmental deficits, structural malformation can result in impulse disorder, perceptual distortion, or other ego dysfunctions that eventuate in a variety of harmful behavior patterns. At higher levels of function when anxiety-laden intentions, ego dystonic motives, or covert gratifications are involved, defenses are likely to obscure personal responsibility for the activity. But the therapeutic task is to help shed light on what is obscure, making clear the connection between intention, action, and consequence. Because egoself therapy concentrates on contemporary experience, confronting the several aspects of that experience is a vital part of its work. Focusing on patients' everyday experience also has the distinct advantage of working in an arena which is familiar, where they can function knowledgeably and with a sense of control. For patients, describing their lives to another person helps objectify their experience and facilitates the attainment of observational perspective, so important to effective ego mediation. For therapists, patients' problems are cast within their natural habitat, providing a context for a more empathic understanding of the person's life and functioning. The images of patients' primary relationships, home environment, work milieu, and diurnal flow of activity provide a myriad of clues about the specific workings of both healthy and pathological operations.

The scope of confrontation is always a sequence of psychological events, concluding with pathological outcome or consequences. These include overt behavior but also extend into patients' affective, cognitive, somatic, and motor reactions. Patients' descriptions of wishes, fears, impulses, and expectations are a necessary complement to therapists' observations of their egoself operations. As the exploration proceeds, patients gain an understanding at the level closest to their own ability to intervene, at the point of familiar experience.

This approach is not without its problems, however. Confrontation brings special burdens to the therapy. Constant highlighting of everyday details can augment patients' feelings of living under a microscope. This is particularly true with adolescents, and others for whom self boundaries are already tenuous. When these analyses regularly yield evidence of dysfunction and failure, patients' sense of narcissistic injury may increase. In this climate of pain, therapists can be seen as the messengers who bring the bad news—agents of pain rather than providers of relief. A buildup of such feelings can undermine the therapeutic partnership, increase resistance to constructive exploration, augment negative transference reactions (Buie and Adler, 1973). In addition, there are times when confrontation may seem to have moralistic implications. Therapists are susceptible to being cast in the role of critical parent, or punitive superego, when they confront patients with their pathogenic wishes or deeds. Furthermore, countertransference reactions are more likely when therapists encounter patients' intentions, thoughts, or actions which are repugnant to them. But these problems are not eliminated because therapists circumvent directly engaging patients' behavior. Egoself emphasis on partnership does not mandate ignoring those times when the therapy requires management of transference or countertransference material.

Therapists must always be vigilant for signs of transference and countertransference, and patients' problems can be threatening whether or not they involve morality. Confrontation must be used sensitively if it is to avoid excessive abrasiveness. Being aware of the risks attendant upon its use, therapists confront judiciously, when timing and content are ripe, and the intervention is clearly relevant to patients' problems. Another safeguard is built into the role of confrontation within egoself theory. The directional trust of confrontation is baldly functional: what was achieved by the patient's reactions, and at what expense? "What did you get, and what did it cost you?" The therapeutic focus centers on self-appraisal, continually placing the confronted material within the scope of whatever ego functions and self-esteem are currently within the patient's capacity. Careful application of this technique uncovers psychological costs previously denied or not recognized by the patient. Among those patients who function at fairly primitive levels, there are often immediate consequences which have not been functionally connected to their own actions. Among higher functioning patients the longer term consequences of their actions may contain the most ego dystonic elements.

Moralizing, rarely a useful therapeutic activity, is replaced by the blunt economics of enlightened self-interest. Confrontation is particularly well suited to locating and resolving problems whose immediate manifestations are ego syntonic. In these instances there is little motivation for change, until the consequences are shown to be costly in ways that matter to the patient. With the conditions of personal cost more clearly in focus, and specific operations clearly targeted, readiness for change is sharply improved. The sheer willingness to work toward change contributes to egoself development, since it entails the activation of numerous ego functions: delay, analysis, reality testing, energy and attention focusing, and so on. Sometimes the area targeted for intervention is not where the most severe or repugnant acting out occurs. It may be necessary to begin where the likelihood of positive impact is greatest, working where the patient is most able and willing to work. Effective intervention at that point mobilizes resources for further efforts later.

Summarizing the use of confrontation, it is an intervention which focuses patient attention on a sequence of intrapsychic and behavioral experiences which eventuate in pathogenic consequences. By highlighting the sequence the partners can review its functional relevance to patients' intentions, costs, and benefits. Among people with problems of impulse control the approach is no less applicable. Confrontation addresses two key therapeutic considerations: the point at which ego controls are overwhelmed and the gratifications achieved by the impulse. The partners trace the sequence in reverse, back to a point at which ego controls still remain competent. By proceeding in reverse it is often possible to begin the sequence at the point of cost—often temporally removed from the pathogenic process—and thus functionally connect it to the gratifications. In some cases of ego syntonic acting out this confrontation is most central. In other instances, where the primary issue is the inability of ego processes to mediate impulse expression, intervention is geared to determining alternate pathways prior to the point at which the client loses control.

Mr. W, twenty-seven, had been warned by his wife that she would divorce him if he did not end his physical abusiveness. After the last incident she left him and returned to her parents' home. Mr. W was distraught. He desperately needed his wife, but periodically lost control of his temper and hit her. It soon became evident that Mr. W regularly fought with men also, and that he took some pride in being "a guy that nobody pushes around." But it was also apparent that his fighting was not always volitional, that there were times when he "got carried away, out of control," when he was violent despite intentions to the contrary.

The work with Mr. W exemplified several uses of confrontation. The first instance occurred as the patient was describing fighting with his wife:

P: She kept needling me, telling me I was stupid, and a jerk. So I told her, "Look, smartass, I'm not so stupid I don't know how to shut you up." But she kept on gabbing, and I finally just nailed her one.
Th: You nailed her?
P: Yeah, a backhander, right cross the chops (eyes glisten, faint smile).
Th: How did you feel about that?
P: She was asking for it, and she got it.
Th: But how did you feel?
P: She had it coming.
Th: Yeah, that's the sense I got. That she had it coming and that there was some pleasure in it for you. It didn't bother you to do it.
P: I don't know if you would call it pleasure, but I didn't mind it at all. I warned her.
Th: Yeah, you got some satisfaction out of it. What did it cost you? Did it cost you anything?
P: Cost? It shut her up. She stopped calling me things and cried a little, and then she shut up.
Th: That's what it got you—she shut up. But what did it cost?
P: Cost? What?
Th: She shut up, but then she left you.

The first confrontation focused on Mr. W's satisfaction in hitting his wife. His recounting disclosed the act and disavowed blame, but did not acknowledge his gratification. With another person the therapist might have pointed out the facial cues, but

Mr. W had previously been unable to accept that sort of connection. The second confrontation presented Mr. W with the
consequence of his attack, couched in cost–gain terms. Con-
trasting the cost with the gain—she shut up, but she left—
completes the psychological sequence by connecting his wife's
behavior to his assualt on her.

The value of confrontation is well illustrated here. Despite
the evidence from his wife's behavior, the patient clung to a
belief system in which his intentions and their consequences
were in synchrony, where he got what he wanted by doing what
he intended. While it may appear that the patient was invoking
denial, his overall primitivity would also be consistent with an
impulse-bound lack of time sense. Focusing his attention on the
unforeseen consequence (his wife leaving him), and connecting
it to his abusive behavior, restructured the pattern from one
which was ego syntonic to one that cost him dearly. As the
connection became clear the patient indicated a desire to change
his ways, even though he felt that the angry outbursts were
beyond his control. At this point the confrontations took the
form of focusing awareness on his internal, nonverbal cues.

Now intervention traced his reaction pattern backward,
looking for a place in that sequence where ego controls were
still operative. Confronting him with his vulnerabilities—the
limits of his controls—was also important here.

> *Th*: When did you decide to hit Vera? or did you decide?
> *P*: I can't tell. I knew I was getting good and pissed off. Then I just
> belted her.
> *Th*: Have there been other times, maybe even with somebody else, that
> you can remember knowing that you were going to hit them?
> *P*: Yeah . . . Friday night at the bar, as a matter of fact. This guy was
> downing the Celtics, saying Larry Bird was way overrated. I could
> feel my face getting red, and I knew I was gonna tell him to button
> up or I'd shut him up.
> *Th*: From your face getting red you knew you were getting ready to
> belt him. Do you ever get that feeling with Vera, that she's getting
> to you that way?
> *P*: Of course. That's when I tell her she better shut up.
> *Th*: So, at that point you're still in control. You can still decide whether
> or not you're going to hit her when you start to get that feeling.

Helping the patient to confront the connection of a particular event with his inner experience establishes the point at which ego mediation remains effective. The patient's intention to attack apparently enters consciousness with a somatic reaction. At that point he can still exercise choice, and can be confronted with his ability to choose. Putting it another way, ego mediation can be recruited, anchoring it to the patient's internal signal. As patients recognize that they can choose, their willingness to consider alternatives can be explored. At this point the cost–gain principle is often reintroduced, to involve the patient's self-interest—a more dependable incentive than morality for primitively organized people. Once the patient is ready, experimentation, which we discussed earlier, can begin.

Confrontation is not moralistic, nor is it a covert form of aversive conditioning. It involves the patient's own perception, judgment, awareness, and decision making. In short, it utilizes a range of ego functions, including consideration of consequences. However, it is essential that ego competence be established prior to confrontation. It is futile to imply that the patient has choices at a point when actions are beyond current capacity to control. In egoself therapy, neutral support for the process rather than empathic activity is preferable during this type of confrontation. The therapist's affective availability is in support of ego growth, but the specific direction it takes is for the patient to choose. Countertransference behavior is more likely when active empathy is offered during this phase of treatment. Instead, egoself therapy utilizes supportive confrontation, which we consider next. This is a specific confrontive technique whose purpose is to consolidate evidence of effective ego functioning.

Supportive Confrontation

Supportive confrontation is as important conceptually and systematically as it is in application. As applied to everyday practice, supportive confrontation is a method for focusing patients' attention on unrecognized or underutilized resources. Whatever their nature, the resources are identified because they are psychological competencies: planning ability, personal warmth, social skill. It cannot be assumed that patients always recognize or utilize their resources, particularly intrapsychic assets which are less accessible to awareness. One of the least justified assumptions made by early therapists was that patients automatically put their best psychological resources into play once their conflicts were resolved. Neither learning theory nor the dynamics of identity formation, as we now understand them, justifies the assumption of automatic activation of assets by patients. Too often patients are unaware of their specific capabilities. Helping them to understand their problems without also helping them to identify their assets can lead to equally unsatisfying alternative reactions or a regression to previous patterns.

In egoself practice supportive confrontation is a basic technique which identifies and highlights patient capabilities, using the methods of ordinary confrontation. There are several advantages to this technique. By uncovering unrecognized talents, patients are encouraged and empowered in their efforts. And seeing that the same process of therapy which challenges them can also yield supportive revelations improves their tolerance for that form of intervention. Individuation and the enhancement of self are augmented. By this means some patients learn that their defensive shutting down of awareness also deprives them of access to valuable aspects of their functioning. Finally, since the recruitment and mobilization of resources is a crucial part of egoself therapy, this use of technique is consistent with theory and precept. On the debit side, patients for whom fears of object loss predominate may be threatened by premature confrontation with evidence of their autonomy. Operationally, supportive confrontation uses the same methodology as other confrontations—progressively isolating a psychological process related to real-life activity. The prime distinguishing feature is that the effect of the process is to reveal efficacy, discover or highlight a patient asset.

> P: Well, I fucked up again.
> Th: What happened?
> P: My first week on the job and I'm in trouble with the boss. I used the wrong forms and a whole bunch of work has to be redone.
> Th: That's too bad. How do you know you're in trouble with your boss?
> P: Do you really think they appreciate having people come in and start fucking up right away? I must have wasted half a day doing all that stuff wrong.

Th: What was your boss's reaction, what happened?

P: She came over and asked how I was making out, and then she said I had used the wrong forms. I wanted to crawl under the table, I felt so stupid.

Th: Can you remember what she actually said, how she acted?

P: Well, first she looked real happy, said something like "You've gotten a lot done." Then she saw which form it was and said, "Oh, there's been a mistake; that's not the right form."

Th: Is that how she said it? That doesn't sound very angry to me.

P: Well, she didn't sound angry. She said that the other tabulator must have given me the wrong forms by mistake.

Th: It doesn't sound like she's blaming you either.

P: Well, no. She didn't act like she was blaming me. . . .

Th: All I hear so far is that an honest mistake happened during your first week on the job, that it really had nothing to do with you, and that your boss complimented you for being a fast worker. Has she given you any other clues that you're in trouble with her?

P: No. The only other thing she's said to me so far was that it was nice to see someone showing up for work five minutes early instead of five minutes late.

Th: It sounds to me like you could hear very clearly about a mistake, but didn't hear your boss telling you that she appreciates you being punctual and quick.

P: Hm.

Th: Are you punctual and quick?

P: Let me think about that. Hmm (client then recalls a number of corroborative incidents).

This chronically self-critical patient was heading toward another immersion in self-blame. Instead, the therapist chose to focus on recapturing the actual events. (Had the patient been unable to recall them, the therapist would have confronted her with her readiness to criticize herself without any realistic basis for doing so.) At the outset, the therapist only knew that the inquiry would yield material concerning such things as the patient's reality testing, and her way of perceiving and handling herself in a new situation. By differentiating between recall and meaning making, and then focusing on remembered details, the patient was confronted with the contrast between her fantasies of failure and the reality of her work skills, the expectation of criticism and the reality of compliments.

To some therapists this emphasis on reality may seem like ignoring unconscious motivation, of blaming the victim, confronting patients with their distortions as though it was something they could change at will. The paradox of therapy is that, while people cannot change themselves at will, they are still the prime architects of their own changes. Egoself therapy addresses structure before etiology. And, if restructuring is to move in beneficial directions, patients need to know their capabilities, and how to apply them. Supportive confrontation serves that purpose by identifying specific resources already at the patient's command. However, supportive confrontation is only a technique, to be applied as part of a therapeutic process which requires intensive exploration of meaning and outcome. It should not be confused with supportive therapy. By contrast, supportive therapy is intended to provide a generic type of encouragement to shore up and stabilize existing defenses. Supportive therapy is applied in the service of better adjustment, not restructuring and growth. In the worst case, nonspecific support can encourage people to attempt things which are premature or beyond their capabilities.

While this listing of therapeutic techniques is only a portion of those utilized in the ordinary course of psychotherapy, these are the ones that are more specifically emphasized in the structurally oriented approach I have been describing. Procedure and technique, in turn, are part of a larger fabric which includes the several forms of therapeutic relationship. Weekly practice of ego–self therapy is examined from that perspective as we continue.

CHAPTER 5

RELATIONSHIP ISSUES

The nature of the therapeutic relationship illustrates some of the clearest differences between weekly egoself therapy and standard psychoanalytic technique. Like psychoanalysis, traditional psychoanalytic psychotherapy is rooted in utilizing transference material as a prime therapeutic tool. Freud's design of the psychoanalytic milieu intentionally fortified both preconditions. The rules of abstinence, by frustrating various aspects of gratification, encourages regression. The ambience of the analytic setting, unobtrusive therapist, couch, subdued lighting, multiple weekly sessions, emphasis on dreams and associations, are orchestrated so as to encourage transference formation. By contrast, weekly psychotherapy is structured in ways precisely opposite to those Freud designed specifically to optimize the emergence of transference reactions. Weekly psychotherapy has special impact on the character and potency of these aspects of the therapeutic relationship. The relatively infrequent contact has the effect of diluting the intensity of transference material (Wolberg, 1954). The therapist's verbal as well as nonverbal activity level typically increases. The more realistic aspects of the interaction, including face-to-face seating, are intensified at the expense of fantasy and genetic associations. As far back as the 1953 Conference on Psychoanalysis and Psychotherapy (see chapter 2) psychoanalytic practitioners have recognized the strict limitations that psychotherapy imposes on the role of the transference, as regards both intensity and depth of regression.

VARIETIES OF RELATIONSHIP

But the issue transcends the nature and character of transference in psychotherapy, a view which is essentially subtractive. Extensive experience in recent years makes clear the variegated nature of the transactions that occur between patients and therapists during the course of psychotherapy. The therapeutic relationship is an extremely complex interpersonal situation. For one thing it is a professional relationship, unique in its exchange of intangibles. One of those intangibles is the power interaction. In the psychopolitical dynamics of any professional relationship the patient is inherently cast in the posture of being needy, deficient, a supplicant; the professional is an authority, expert, capable of providing special services. The fantasies generated by this psychopolitical imbalance endow the professional as someone having "special powers," yet also perceived like one of the capricious Greek gods: susceptible to human frailties, capable of causing great harm or good, someone to be propitiated, someone to be wary of. The mystical attributes of therapists increase in proportion to the need, primitivity, and pathology of our patients. Taken together, conditions favor an extreme misalignment of felt power and indigence among the participants. The system is, moreover, self-sustaining; the subtle gratifications available to both sets of participants are seductively attractive.

> As a predoctoral psychology intern I was careful to introduce myself to patients as "Mr. —." In addition, my age and youthful face marked me objectively as unlikely to be more than a student. Nevertheless, patients consistently addressed me as "Dr.—," even after I corrected them. My own reactions were first those of being flattered, then feeling fraudulent, and finally coming to recognize that patient need, not my personal qualities, was the determining factor. In retrospect, my inner pleasure at the "mistake" may well have contributed to that mutually gratifying interaction which seemed so irrational at the time.

Another form of relationship is the working alliance, based on the patient's capacity to perceive and respond to the therapeutic effort with an adult observing ego. Strupp and Binder (1984) also describe unconsciously provocative, self-defeating relationship patterns, carried over from everyday life, which create interpersonal problems for the patient in and out of therapy. Support as a specific intervention has long been recognized as a necessary part of therapy. But it is also an appropriate relationship pattern for many patients (Dewald, 1964; Werman, 1984). Paolino (1981) describes both a narcissistic alliance prior to formation of the transference neurosis and a "real relationship," the latter featuring the objective positive and negative personal impact of the participants. Blanck and Blanck (1979) note that some clients are incapable of transference because they cannot differentiate between past and present objects. A "real object" relationship (1979) is indicated in these situations. Finally, both the healthy, integrated aspects of the therapist's personality and the inevitable instances of countertransference provide further variations to the therapeutic interactions.

The structure and frequency of weekly therapy augments these varied relationship components. The everyday events of patients' lives compete with their intrapsychic issues for saliency. Therapists' expressions and mannerisms are much more obvious, and potentially distracting. As a result, therapists can expect to encounter relationship interactions which may have less to do with traditional transference material. The other relationship features noted above regularly occur in weekly psychotherapy, in different combinations and with differing emphases, within sessions and from one week to the next. Continuous monitoring of interpersonal material is necessary in order to determine which of these relationship features are operative at a given time. Depending upon the therapeutic approach, different therapists handle these relationships in different ways. Strupp and Binder (1984) recognize this complication by considering all interpersonal material as relevant for therapeutic exploration. Within the scope of their time-limited approach, any interpersonal issue around the identified affective theme becomes the focus of inquiry. Paolino (1981) sees psychoanalytic psychotherapy as a modification of analysis, and holds strictly to intensive contact. Thus, his approach requires fewer concessions to the features that make weekly therapy distinctive. As a result his handling of the relationship is less applicable to the demands of weekly contact. Weekly egoself therapy, since it is broader and more extensive in scope than the time-limited approach, yet much less intensive than a modified psychoanalysis, adopts a somewhat different tactic.

Regarding the role of the relationship, the potential value of transference analysis in weekly psychotherapy is not challenged. It is simply aligned alongside the other clinically demonstrated forms of therapeutic relationship. Taken together, they constitute the bedrock upon which effective psychoanalytically oriented psychotherapy must stand. Since transference is so influenced by frequency of contact, it is not a viable centerpiece in weekly psychoanalytic therapy. Consistent with this change, the therapeutic role is not as constrained by abstinence as transference elicitation requires. Instead, the therapist's activity is augmented in quantity and character, tracking development and intervening on behalf of the restructuring process. These strategies and interventions serve better the psychodynamic requirements of weekly psychotherapy. Still, the interactive process between patient and therapist continues to fuel much of the treatment effort, and where transference surfaces it must be appropriately managed. The term *relationship* remains a useful umbrella concept for the several types of interaction pattern encountered in the course of weekly psychotherapy. By referring to relationship as the generic term, and stipulating the specific character of that relationship, one retains greater precision regarding the varied forms of interaction which emerge in therapy. The important distinctions between classical transference, real object (Blanck and Blanck, 1974), therapeutic alliance, idealizing and mirroring transference (Kohut, 1971), and the reality-based features of the interaction are retained. These are further differentiated from partnership, the particular method of interaction used as a grounding point in egoself therapy. For the specific requirements of weekly frequency a partnership model of therapeutic relationship has been added to the spectrum noted above.

PARTNERSHIP IN WEEKLY PSYCHOTHERAPY

Conceiving of the therapeutic work within the context of a partnership has both practical and heuristic advantages. As the word *partnership* implies, patient and therapist are collaboratively engaged, working jointly in a common cause. While their contributions are qualitatively different, their peer status alerts the therapist to deviations from that state of equality, whether due to transference, countertransference, psychopolitics, or other distortions. Using the partnership model as a yardstick provides the therapist with a valuable clinical guide to the nature of the ongoing vicissitudes in relationship pattern and meaning. At root, partnership is an affirmative statement acknowledging that in the face-to-face therapy experience dispassionate neutrality is a myth. Successful weekly therapy requires the active participation of both parties in a shared mission. Partnership underscores the clinical truth that patients are as expert in certain areas of their psychic experience as their therapists are in other aspects of the treatment process. The patient perspective must therefore be understood along with the clinical perspective.

Egoself management of the partnership opens the door to exploring these perspectives, carefully and selectively:

Emma, just entering young adulthood, is in a period of twice-weekly sessions. She is impulsive, depressive, and accident prone. During this session she is telling me that her radical feminist friends chide her for seeing a male therapist.

Th: Why do you? (choose to see me)
P: I like you; I feel its important. It's too easy to walk around hating all men, with all the rape and oppression that's going on. My first therapist was a male, and he was bad news with all his heavy interpretations.
Th: What kinds of things did he say?
P: I don't really remember; I didn't like his way and didn't give it a lot of my energy.

Viewed transferentially, Emma's denigration of her previous therapist is consistent with earlier criticisms of her father. It may well harbinger the onset of negative transference attitudes in

our work. At the same time, as a young adult for whom ideo-
logical issues have organizational value in ego development, the
political concerns of her peers cannot be dismissed. As it happens, the sociopolitical pressure from her feminist friends col-
ludes with her own readiness to deprecate any male parental
figure. Addressing the issue as a reality invites the patient to
compare her own attitude with that of her friends, in the service
of differentiation. The therapist's second comment brings the
content back to its incipient transferential or other relational
implications.

Both the reality issue for the partnership and its dynamic
aspects in the transference are examined in this illustration,
providing different contexts in which the material can be understood. Ignoring either relationship could significantly affect the
therapy. If I had been seeing her at our more usual weekly
frequency my intervention would have been no different. The
clinical issue is to be attentive to the alternative relational aspects.

A fundamental aspect of the partnership entails clinical
and empathic recognition of each partner's status at any given
time. Partnership is thus viewed as a dynamic construct, susceptible to ongoing fluctuation over the course of therapy but
within the session as well. Changes occur as a function of the
material being handled but also as a result of stresses external
to the therapeutic moment, which impinge upon the lives of
either of the participants. Paolino (1981) gives a clear example
from his own practice, citing the effects of his newborn child
on his energy level and his patient's reaction to his fatigue. Only
when he was willing to acknowledge this realistic influence on
his behavior with the patient could she produce the associations
it evoked from her own life. This basic respect for the physical
and psychological integrity of both partners may seem obvious,
but it is easy for the transference-oriented therapist to minimize
the relevance of everyday reality considerations when primary
interest is focused on displacements from the past. If the therapist is unaccustomed to seeing patients only once a week, the
unfamiliar potency of reality factors under these conditions can
obscure their importance.

Variations due to ethnicity, culture, or gender can also
impinge upon the partnership. Apparent seductiveness when

the patient moves his or her chair closer may be due to cultural differences in what is a comfortable psychological distance. It may even be due to a patient's hearing impairment. Therapeutic attunement to such factors can enhance the working alliance by acknowledging the patient's individuality. Failure to acknowledge the realistic influences of life stage, cultural–ethnic differences, or *weltanschauung*—especially with higher functioning patients—can demean the person's sense of integrity and impede therapy. As therapists we are accustomed to offering patients our professional concern and attention. Less often do we recognize the psychopolitical effect of the patient role on their self-esteem, and the sensitivity people may feel about presenting themselves to the therapist as damaged or impaired. These self-perceptions can augment regressive and self-critical tendencies already inherent in the patient's pathology, further complicating the work of promoting growth and health.

Two principles govern the partnership approach, its developmental texture and its egalitarian stance. Each person functions within a range of developmental levels which vary subject to psychogenetic, situational, and other issues in their lives. Therapists who have undergone intensive personal therapy or analysis are likely to function in a range closer to their ontogenetic level, and tend to be more aware of their own regressive vulnerabilities. Patients tend to function over a wider developmental range, from their most mature areas of intrapsychic and social competence to their most primitive and regressed. Their awareness of, and willingness to communicate, their inner experience constitutes the most vital data available to the therapy. But that awareness rarely permits patients to understand the developmental level at which they may be operating. Thus, whether or not the patient comprehends the nature of a reaction, it remains the therapist's task to recognize whether the person is demonstrating a failure of object differentiation, adolescent separation, or an adult disagreement. If therapeutic interventions are to have optimal impact they must be compatible with the developmental level at which the patient is functioning during the experience (Gedo, 1979). Each intervention makes implicit assumptions about the developmental level of the patient. In the partnership arrangement therapists focus on the patient's current developmental range of operation during the session. What is the optimal level of intrapsychic operation of which the person is now capable? Is the partner currently able to employ her observing ego functions? Which developmental stage does the patient's regressiveness suggest? Just as one respects the adult functions of the patient in those areas in which they are operative, the vigilant therapist seeks to recognize when a therapeutic expectation may exceed the patient's capacity at the moment.

> Dr. R's chronic emotional depletion was buffered by the support of fellow residents during her training. Later, unwilling to commit herself to a medical practice, she temporized by going to work in a hospital emergency ward on a fee-for-service contract. Although technically competent, the affective demands of twelve-hour shifts with acutely ill people drained her. She became morose, withdrawn, and moody with the medical staff, distant and superficial in her patient care. As a recent arrival from another city, she was referred by her former therapist, a highly reputable psychiatrist with whom she had had five years of intensive psychoanalytic psychotherapy. Dr. R spoke despairingly of her situation, but was adamantly unwilling to continue in intensive treatment. She agreed to meet weekly, with the option of additional sessions in a crisis.
>
> Blindly critical of herself and others at one moment, Dr. R could also be empathic and tender with patients and friends. These labile shifts could occur within the same therapeutic hour in one weekly meeting while another session would be entirely occupied with primitive depression and rage. The therapist soon learned to design his interventions to harmonize with the fluctuations in Dr. R's developmental level. Any attempt to intervene, even supportively, while Dr. R raged at herself or others invariably resulted in the therapist being included in the undifferentiated hostility. As the rage abated, gradual attempts to introduce self-soothing could be made. Often no more than one or two of the therapist's comments could be heard by Dr. R during an entire session. Therapeutic strategy dictated use of a nonverbal holding environment when Dr. R's primitivity held sway, and actively mobilizing her empathic self-awareness to explore her capacity for soothing and buffering when her adult ego operations were in evidence.

A second kind of developmental tracking was reported by a colleague who was treating a woman who had had a chronic incest relationship with her alcoholic father. As the patient re-lived some of her memories, her therapist asked how she might have responded as an adult. Passively she described herself as powerless to stop him. Then the therapist recalled how the woman had described herself at age twelve as being spunky and feisty. Rephrasing his earlier question, he asked her to say how she might have dealt with her father when she was still a spunky twelve-year-old. With energy and affect the patient sponta-neously created a scenario in which she successfully repelled her father's advances.

Another application of developmental sensitivity to the partnership involves differential evaluation of similar devel-opmental levels. Two males, ages seventeen and nineteen, were arrested for similar offenses and remanded to therapy at a court clinic. Each received the same diagnosis after careful psychiatric evaluation. The two young men came from remarkably similar backgrounds, featured by a relatively benign early history ex-cept for anger at their remote, professionally successful fathers. By coincidence the boys had even been musicians in the same band, at different times. But one patient had evolved the young adult capacity for personal perspective while the other re-mained absorbed in adolescent narcissism. As a result, the first was able to utilize an exploratory therapy successfully while the second was unable to tolerate any intervention beyond sup-portive work.

Sensitivity to the patient's developmental level provides the insight to help that person participate in a working alliance, by sharpening our ability to meet them at the levels at which they are functioning. But our training in psychopathology predis-poses us to focus on the regressive aspects of patient function. The second partnership principle serves to balance this tend-ency by emphasizing the egalitarian nature of the relationship; that is, the most appropriately mature level of interaction is the preferable level for engaging the partnership. This is the de-velopmental level at which patient and therapist are functionally the most effective. When it is feasible to be treated as an adult equivalent the patient's adult ego operations are activated for optimal recruitment in the therapeutic tasks which await. By contrast with intensive psychotherapy and analysis, where regression may be encouraged, egoself mobilization in behalf of restructuring is the ruling dictum for weekly psychotherapy. Regression is difficult to monitor when there is weekly contact, and patients should not be exposed to that pain and risk without adequate therapeutic support.

But the other issue has to do with an important difference in the theory of therapeutic technique. Conscious participation of the patient as a partner mandates that person's sense of empowerment as an equal. The specific therapeutic tasks—such as confronting pathological formations, interactions, and issues; strengthening and extending ego functions; enhancing the diversity and complexity of object relations; facilitating growth and development of self—are significantly augmented by the patient's experience of being engaged and held accountable to equal adult status in the relationship.

As the previous discussion has made clear, the standards of adult partnership are not imposed as a moral imperative or in disregard of the patient's developmental impairment. Rather, partnership is a means of maximizing patient participation in the therapy. It is a mode of interaction which actively involves patients in the fullest use of their intrapsychic capabilities, and provides the therapist with a useful measure of those resources. This "stretching" of egoself resources activates function and promotes ego growth (Blanck and Blanck, 1979). As partners in the therapeutic process, patients are encouraged to go beyond exploration of their feelings, attitudes, and memories. At each significant juncture their ego functions are activated and integrated into the therapy. Some examples follow:

Integration of present–past perspective:

> P: (describes childhood relationship with older brother)
> Th: How did you feel toward Tommy then?
> P: He was the greatest; he could do anything he wanted. I worshiped him.
> Th: And as you look back now, how does he look to you?

Affect differentiation:

> Mr. B: When he said that to me I got the weirdest feeling.

Th: What was it like?

Relocating projections in object representations:

Ms. D: He's like a lot of men I meet: macho, superior, looking to put you down every chance they get.
Th: What are they saying to you with that attitude?

Soliciting the patient's perspective on intervention:

P: (describes a distressing event)
Th: What do you need at a time like that? (or)
Th: Has anything ever been helpful when you've felt like that before?

In each instance, egoself participation is invited: to reflect on early object relations with an observing ego; to differentiate affective experience; to clarify self and object representations and their boundary definitions. At one level the invitation indicates a respect for the patient's integrity as an active partner, enhancing self-esteem. At the same time it creates an opportunity for the patient to exercise ego functions. Finally, it permits a therapeutic assessment of current self structuring and ego operation as the patient engages in the organizational task. In each instance significant therapeutic material is produced, as the process itself contributes to ego assessment and growth, enhanced self-definition by the patient, and strengthening of the working alliance. Consistent with egoself thinking, this approach focuses on structural aspects of ego and self. At the more subtle experiential level of the relationship a number of therapeutic "active ingredients" are at work. Patients ultimately discover they can be safe in a close encounter with another human. They learn to recognize inner thoughts and feelings and the value of applying them to their lives. And the face-to-face availability of a caring human being provides the "nutriment" for egoself growth in areas where earlier identifications and self–objects may have been insufficient. Patients can internalize both the constancy of the therapist's acceptance and the respect for their competencies. Progress in therapy is ultimately based on improved ego effectiveness and self-acceptance. By emphasizing and utilizing an equal partnership whenever conditions permit, the relationship becomes not only the medium for therapeutic work but an important component of the treatment. As a result, the reduced role of transference in weekly therapy is compensated for by exploiting features of the relationship that are more distinctive characteristics of weekly contact.

These illustrations indicate the effectiveness of partner-oriented interventions which engage patients' adult functions, utilizing the partnership to extend the structural base of ego and self operations. Unlike simple support, these interventions take the patients' resources beyond shoring up and restitution. Their objective is to promote structural growth, beyond the limited gratification of enhanced self-esteem. But these partnership interventions must be consonant with specific therapeutic issues to be effective. Their therapeutic value does not rest with their content, but with their judicious use in the context of ongoing assessment of the patient's intrapsychic operations. Nor is it the unique personality of the therapist as an ideal object that is the therapeutic focus. On the contrary, the therapist's role as a representative of realistic human operation aids patients by countering the magical attributes usually projected or the transference aspects displaced. The partner exemplifies human commonality, tacitly encouraging patients to recognize and recruit those capacities within themselves.

In other respects, the egalitarian aspect of partnership may pose its own set of problems. As contemporary observers note, reality factors are much more a part of weekly psychotherapy than was the case traditionally. In a relationship between partners certain reality matters attain greater saliency. In the area of personal disclosure, for example, there is an obvious and necessary paradox. On the one hand, therapy is a professional relationship, designed to handle patients' pathology and distress. The ethical imperative to help patients is the therapist's first priority, and therapists' personal lives and personal needs are subordinated to the patients' during the therapeutic hour. Yet, egalitarian pressures might seem to argue for personal disclosure on the part of therapists, if only to counterbalance patients' revelations. Moreover, there are times when disclosures by the therapist seem unavoidable. In addition, countertransference reactions may necessitate certain disclosures. We return to these issues later in this chapter.

TRANSFERENCE IN WEEKLY PSYCHOTHERAPY

Despite the ubiquitous occurrence of transference material in all therapeutic relationships, there are major qualitative differences between the material produced in analysis compared to that which emerges in weekly psychotherapy. While much of the current literature examines transference in light of the patient's pathology, the special conditions of weekly therapy establish a context which often limits the effectiveness of transferential interventions.

The classical definition of transference refers to those aspects of the relationship in which experiences with primary objects form the basis for subsequent displaced reactions and attitudes. Instead of using these transference reactions as the basis of psychotherapy, the egoself approach is geared to direct ego and self restructuring. Consequently a somewhat different mode of management is applied to transference material. Unless or until it intrudes upon the egalitarian working partnership, transference material is monitored covertly. Consistent with most contemporary thought, weekly therapy is an inappropriate medium for the induction or spontaneous emergence of a regressive transference neurosis. Where transference issues relate directly to the patient's problems, particularly in short-term work (Mann, 1973; Malan, 1980; Sifneos, 1984), connecting past patterns to present interactions can be demonstrably effective. However, short-term therapists unanimously urge careful screening of candidates for this application of therapy, emphasizing qualities such as psychological mindedness, or a circumscribed problem area. More typically, only potentially disruptive transference manifestations are directly addressed in weekly psychotherapy. In these instances structuring, rather than silence or insight-oriented uncovering, is used:

P: Were you being sarcastic just then?
Th: No, that's not how I meant it.

This intervention allows the patient to test reality, at the same time that it permits the therapist to see whether the patient's functioning is adequate to that task. If a pattern of such comments develop, it may then become advantageous to explore further.

In analysis, as in intensive psychoanalytic psychotherapy, some form of transference neurosis is a natural outcome of the focus on introspection, dreams, and associations. An important function of transference in these conditions is that of eliciting in the therapeutic hour the pathological distortions involved in the etiology of the patient's disorder. The analysis of transference and resistance necessitates a level of ego strength commensurate with this level of uncovering activity. When the therapy sessions take place only once a week, even more stringent demands are placed upon the ego's integrity. Undermining of defenses leaves patients far more vulnerable when there is only weekly contact. By the same token, resistance can more readily stiffen in weekly therapy and therapists may be tempted to press more aggressively for transference material as it begins to surface, recognizing that a week later defenses may once again occlude the dynamic content. For patients who are psychologically unsophisticated, focusing on reactions to the therapist may seem irrelevant to their presenting complaints and may alienate them. Accordingly, the transference-oriented approach is best limited to psychologically aware, high-functioning patients. As a result of these factors the role of transference interpretation has been necessarily modified and constrained in weekly therapy. However, the need for therapeutic acuity in the operation of transferential patterns is in no way reduced. If anything, the task of management is both more subtle and more demanding. With less patient contact time, monitoring is made more difficult at the same time that the options for intervention are more restricted. Effective management of transference requires a combination of vigilance, empathy, tactical sensitivity, and careful ongoing assessment.

Since the constraints of weekly contact rarely permit genetic reconstruction—and even these tend to be derivatives of later etiology (Dewald, 1964; Colarusso and Nemiroff,

1981)—transference interpretation is usually subordinated to other interventions. But assessment of transference remains an integral part of the therapeutic process. Transference material is routinely evaluated against a spectrum of criteria: intensity, access to consciousness, ego-disruptive potential, relevance to other immediate clinical issues, amount of time remaining in the session. Transference management is at least as important as exploration when therapy is conducted weekly.

By contrast, weekly psychotherapy is the typical treatment for an increasingly broad spectrum of disorders, even when clinical judgment might favor more intensive work. As a result, the use of transference material must be carefully evaluated in each case. In weekly therapy many of the shortcomings of transference as a therapeutic medium come into sharper view. Since transference is imbedded in the past, patients must be capable of understanding that the roots of their present difficulties lie in early experience. This way of thinking is alien to many people, and accounts for much of the difficulty in routinely applying psychoanalytically oriented work to blue collar, minority, Third World, and indigent populations. The seeming irrationality of transference behavior is so threatening to the bulk of pragmatically oriented people that it can readily evoke fearful anger. Patients may repudiate not only their therapist but their therapy as well, if transference interpretations are not timed and communicated with great skill. Unfortunately, use of transference is greatly complicated by once weekly contact. Timing and depth of intervention is heavily dependent upon a number of considerations, such as the patient's ability to tolerate and retain material from one weekly session to the next. Infrequent contact further encumbers the task of eliciting sufficient content to make the pattern clear to the patient, yet allow sufficient time in the hour to keep the material experientially vital. Finally, it is difficult to monitor the regressive effects of genetic exploration when the client is seen infrequently. Where transference is the focus of therapy, resistance is likely to be augmented. It is noteworthy that intensive therapy is stipulated by Kohut, Kernberg, and others who work transferentially with more primitive disorders. As suggested by Blanck and Blanck (1974, 1979), moreover, working with transference is contraindicated when the problems are of developmentally early origin, such as in borderline conditions.

But although the transference is necessarily more diluted its role in weekly therapy is still valuable. Transference material is a major link to earlier object relations, as well as a barometer for gauging the therapeutic climate. A first priority is to help patients sustain a level of transference that is consonant with the limited opportunity for examination in weekly contact. To this end it is preferable simply to monitor transference, and usually counterproductive to probe for interpretable material as one would in intensive therapy. Instead transference manifestations are examined in other contemporary relationships. This aids in the assessment of present distortions and in examining the character and quality of the patient's object relations. In practice, the therapist works to sustain the partnership context while monitoring the transference.

> Ms. T was an established adult trying to preserve her second marriage. Early experience with an abusive father had led her into an impulsive marriage to an equally abusive husband. Her second husband was much more emotionally controlled, but Ms. T provoked angry battles by attacking him with sarcasm and demeaning remarks. Quite fragile herself, during each session she would fearfully check the time and express concern that she would be able to last for the entire meeting. Her anxiety about being with an older male therapist was palpable. At the content level therapeutic material dealt with her marital relations. Ms. T would begin with a description of her week with her husband, and gradually the focus would shift to her inner experiences of that interaction. Although she never spoke of it, her acute distrust of both husband and therapist mirrored her earlier life. She complained she could not rely on her husband because he was a "wimp," and at the same time she feared she would be devastated by the therapist's comments.
>
> Therapeutic strategy for the relationship took two paths, one based on partnership while the other maintained the transference at a third-party distance. In her interactions with her husband there was a close exploration of how her feelings and actions related to his behavior with her. In her reaction to the therapist she was invited to refuse to answer questions which upset her, to indicate if she was feeling frightened, and to communicate any malaise she was experiencing.

Anticipating an intense, ambivalent transference with this fragile woman, the therapist opted to structure the relationship as a safe experience with an older male. At the same time, transference derivatives would be explored as they continued to emerge in her marriage. By monitoring her partnership behavior it was possible to gauge her ability to form alternative male object representations. On the content level the patient's contemporary interactions in her marriage could be explored as they related to past and present. At the process level the goal of therapeutic restructuring was addressed by providing a relationship that contrasted with her early experiences and expectations. Self restructuring was promoted by explicitly acknowledging her right to safety, while providing her with an opportunity to experience an alternative type of relationship with a male in which her own reactions could be supportively confronted.

This means of balancing the patient's sense of safety with restructuring was compatible with once a week contact. The more primitive the transference the greater the imperative for management rather than probing and analysis. This intervention strategy can often be implemented, as above, in the interactive process, without making the content explicit.

> Mr. L, a doctoral student in sociology, was referred for depression and chronic inability to sustain an intimate relationship. At the second evaluation interview he looked beseechingly at the therapist and said, "I want to feel safe and secure; I'd like to climb into your lap and just cuddle there." The therapist maintained compassionate eye contact but made no other response. In the next interview, the following week, Mr. L mentioned that he trusted the therapist and felt his compassion. "I feel your empathic touch, like we're connected by a tube that flows from your forehead to mine." Again the therapist maintained eye contact but did not otherwise reply. As weekly therapy developed the idealizing transference continued, following the same pattern. Sometimes the therapist would break off eye contact when it was apparent that the patient was fixating on that to the exclusion of other material. Meeting the patient at his level of need had to be juxtaposed with assessing his capacity to develop further.
>
> The patient's extremely labile ego structure, with its associated problems in maintaining boundaries, militated against

moving beyond nonverbal acceptance of the primitive transference. For most of the therapy relationship interventions centered on real object and partnership issues. His early experiences with a depressively withdrawn father contrasted with the therapist's active interest, but the patient was allowed to experience this tacitly, internalizing an alternative object in the process. This allowed more time to deal with his magical thinking, depression, and thwarted love relationships. There was neither need nor purpose in discussing an important, already effective therapeutic process. Over an eight-year course of therapy, almost exclusively weekly, the transference intensity very gradually abated but was never addressed directly. The patient married, the depression lifted, and he completed the Ph.D. Four years after termination he was continuing to function at a high level. He could establish and maintain ego boundaries, had achieved greater self and object differentiation, and was thus able to engage in a permanent and intimate relationship.

By contrast, when transference material threatens to rupture or otherwise impair the therapeutic effort it may be imperative to intervene directly. The extent of overt intervention is generally proportionate to the severity of risk rather than the blatancy of the transference material.

Ms. N was referred for a variety of somatic complaints and recurring moderate depression. The mother of two young children, she was married to a devoutly religious man to whom she had been primarily attracted by his intellect and prestige. Her own career was reduced to unfulfilling part-time activity due to her parenting responsibilities. More important, her childhood role as father's favored child contrasted with her husband's devotion to their two daughters. Ms. N was an overly protective mother, deeply enmeshed in family activities, and unconsciously embittered by her husband's relative neglect.

By the twelfth session Ms. N's references to the therapist took on progressively more explicit erotic tones. She was sure that he, unlike her husband, must be a passionate lover and sexually attentive partner. Her fantasies and dreams were increasingly frequent, sexual, and centered on her therapist. At the same time she grew progressively dissatisfied with her marriage and her husband. In the fourteenth session she came in visibly agitated, and with considerable embarrassment said that she would like to have an affair with the therapist. He gently but actively explored what she knew about him, and was gradually able to draw together the connection between the relationship with her father which gratified her but did not satisfy all her yearnings, her expectations and disappointments in her marriage, and her fantasies about what an affair with her therapist would offer her. Armed with this understanding she was able to discuss her needs for personal time with her husband, but also to more fully appreciate how devoted and loving he was.

This transference reaction was less abrupt and no more blatant than the case of Mr. L above. But Ms. N's reaction prevented her from looking at the deprivations in her life and jeopardized both the therapy and her marriage. As a result active intervention into the transference was indicated. The neurotic character of the problem and Ms. N's relatively high level of ego development enabled her to tolerate both the frustration and active interpretation, and to apply these effectively to her situation. In a more primitively organized person transference wishes and impulses pose greater management problems, and are better understood in the context of real object relations, to be discussed below (p. 172).

Other complications to our understanding of transference have emerged from studies of adult development. Focusing upon early origins of transference as the primary technique can accentuate resistance with patients who are beyond young adulthood. Established adults' time orientation is embedded in the present and near-term future; past history is out of synchrony with the demands and high activity level of their everyday lives, particularly in weekly psychotherapy. Middle-aged adults tend to be more reflective and disposed to reviewing childhood, but have forty to fifty years of life history intervening. When a middle-aged adult says, "I don't remember," it may not be repression. Conversely, what is reported as early memory may have little reconstructive value as biographical material (Vaillant, 1977; Schafer, 1980). Among senescent adults, the tendency to reminisce is normative and adaptive in appropriate amounts. But the unexpected activation of parental and childhood memories is commonly associated with central nervous system deterioration, and may be particularly threatening to patients who are vulnerable to such disorders. As a separate point of caution, older patients can displace relations with their adult children onto the therapist (Colarusso and Nemiroff, 1981).

The characteristics of weekly psychotherapy thus constrain many traditional applications of transference. At the same time, other facets of the therapy relationship are more clearly brought into focus. The real object construct occupies such a position.

REAL OBJECT RELATIONSHIP

Another instance of the greater precision in elucidating facets of the therapy relationship is Blanck and Blanck's (1979) exposition of real object interactions. Blanck and Blanck take the position that pathological ego development prevents a true transference in those patients who have not evolved the capacity for displacement. In these early disorders the past is coterminous with the present, and hence the therapist and parent are interchangeable. The therapist is not *like* the father; she *is* the father. In this sense the relationship is not transference, but with a real object. By real object Blanck and Blanck refer to the therapist as an object in present time, not the realistic qualities of the therapist. The therapeutic task becomes one of ego building, rather than repair or reconstruction. Instead of permitting affect to intensify, therapists are advised to intervene. These patients lack the ability to differentiate the therapist from the early dyadic figure and have often failed to acquire appropriate buffering or self-soothing skills from parenting. The most appropriate interventions are those which enhance the patient's rudimentary organizational processes, helping the person to develop the ego operations which are lacking.

As a real object the therapeutic role is that of intervention on behalf of ego development (Blanck and Blanck, 1979, p. 123). By active empathic concern for the patient, the therapist's person becomes available as a developmental model. Interventions are guided by what is most appropriate to the specific ego developmental needs at the time. Personal disclosure is irrelevant, since the patient is unable to perceive and interact with the actual person who is the therapist. As one example of real object intervention Blanck and Blanck describe a patient who continued to apply her mother's childhood advice to watch television as a substitute for parental contact. The therapist intervened to suggest that before turning on the TV set the patient wait a few moments to note her own thoughts, as a way to enhance her capacity for self-soothing. In time the patient let go of her attachment to "the external 'soother,' " the television set, and found comfort instead in her own creative thoughts (1979, p. 114). In another example, "[the] patient is helped to correct affective distortions of the object world" (p. 123) for the purpose of expanding that object world beyond what it was in childhood experience. "The object world expands and the organizing capacity can be expected to take over and build structure with less hostile and distorted self and object images than existed before" (Blanck and Blanck, 1979, p. 123). I do not share Blanck and Blanck's conviction that "organizing capacity" (i.e., ego) develops spontaneously in the absence of pathology. As they suggest elsewhere, sensitive intervention "quickens" ego development. Lacking ego and self structuring interventions to encourage growthful exploration, the person can readily lapse into familiar early patterns with their supportive secondary gains rather than venture into new and uncertain modes of operation.

In certain respects the real object relationship is not unlike Kohut's management of mirroring and idealizing transference (Kohut and Wolf, 1978). Mirroring and idealizing transferences also originate from inadequacies in very early developmental experience. But because Blanck and Blanck are concerned with the psychopathology of ego development and Kohut's work focuses on the psychopathology of early self structuring, similarities in their respective theories may have been obscured. The common denominator to both theories is early object relations. As presented in chapter 8, self and ego can be understood as complementary intrapsychic systems which are also interdependent. This common ground is demonstrated by the similarity in clinical procedures advocated by Kohut and Blanck and Blanck. In both cases an empathic therapeutic environment aims at providing patients with a contemporary opportunity—the mature intrapsychic organization of the therapist—for structure-building experiences to fill gaps in early development. But, while empathy creates the opportunity, it is only the affective medium through which patients can gain access to those attributes of the therapist which they may internalize for their own growth; it is not of itself the therapy.

For Kohut (1977) the "experience-near" contact, building what was not originally provided, is indispensable:

> The importance of the two-step sequence—step one: empathic merger with the self-object's [therapist] mature psychic organization and participation in the self-object's experience of an affect signal instead of an affect spread; *step two: need-satisfying actions performed by the self-object—cannot be overestimated* [p. 87; emphasis added].

In a similar fashion, Blanck and Blanck (1979) see the goal of real object interactions "to promote development of ego apparatuses from the conflict-free sphere if these have been 'started up' in early life, but not encouraged to develop to the fullest extent" (p. 109).

In deference, perhaps, to Kohut's influence, Blanck and Blanck later (1986) relinquished the concept of the real object relationship and placed this interaction under an expanded definition of transference formations for the sake of "communication with the therapeutic community" (p. 77). But clinical precision legitimately differentiates between classic definitions of transference and broadly expanded versions which include everything that goes on in the therapeutic relationship. The vital function of restructuring object relations, which is the key to promoting lasting therapeutic improvement, is materially benefited by recognizing and working within the parameters of each kind of relationship encountered.

COUNTERTRANSFERENCE AND PERSONAL DISCLOSURE

The difference between psychoanalytic technique and the practice of weekly psychotherapy is further illustrated by the issues encountered when one examines countertransference and personal disclosure. Holding to the classic definition, the designation of countertransference is restricted to those instances in which the therapist's unresolved conflicts—or their derivatives—impinge upon the conduct of the therapy. "In countertransference, the analyst has displaced onto the patient attitudes and feelings derived from earlier situations in his own life" (Moore and Fine, 1967).

Since these attitudes and feelings originate outside the therapy and derive from the analyst, not the patient, they represent an intrusion into the therapeutic process. Herein lies one of the strongest arguments for therapists having a personal analysis. When reactions are evoked in the therapist which are unrecognized and/or uncontrolled there is risk of a countertherapeutic effect on the patient.

But the issue is more complex. Countertransference material rarely emerges sui generis. It is typically a reaction evoked by the patient, and in that sense a product of the therapeutic interaction. To the extent that the therapist can become aware of what features of the patient evoke these feelings, they may be helpful guides to what is going on either in the relationship or within the patient. Some traditional practitioners have cautioned in favor of minimal therapist activity as a safeguard against infusing the therapy with countertransferential material. But in recent years the trend has been to acknowledge the inevitability and utility of the therapist's active presence, more so in psychotherapy but also in analysis. Therapeutic presence assumes several forms, however, with different implications for the conduct of therapy. As caring, empathic, trained professionals the impact tends to facilitate evolution of a strong working alliance, as noted earlier. As imperfect human beings therapists are subject to the influences of their own dynamics, as seen in countertransference. As psychologically sophisticated adults therapists are unusually sensitive to the subtle meanings of their own inner experience, which can make personal disclosures therapeutically valuable. Acknowledging that therapy is mutually interactive has complicated and enriched the process. For example, Kohut (1977) argues that an emotionally distant stance may be indicative of countertransference withdrawal rather than a dispassionate professional stance. To this Blanck and Blanck (1979) add the suggestion that the therapist's self-monitoring during the hour can be a useful guide to commonly shared experiences, such as anxiety and therapist silence. But they also caution that very early experiences such as fear of object loss predate memory and should not be confused with later-occurring phenomena. Implicit to these discoveries is the mandate that self-monitoring can be as important as observing the patient's covert reactions.

While countertransference reactions are inevitable, how they are handled can be of fundamental importance. Giovacchini (1975) sees the issue as crucial: "not only characteristics of the patient but also *the assets or limitations of the analyst are important factors in deciding whether he can treat the patient and whether the patient is treatable*" (p. 445). Thus, the treatability of patients can hinge upon the capacity of their therapists to handle the limitations imposed by their own countertransference reactions. On the one hand contemporary therapy requires a more active role than the blank screen that Freud originally envisioned. On the other, Giovacchini notes that patients can elicit countertransferential reactions which occlude progress. One young man who was unable to show anger apparently discovered that his fledgling therapist would giggle nervously whenever he expected an angry display. As the patient came close to presenting a situation in which he inhibited anger he began describing it in a humorous vein. The therapist's nervous giggle seemed to be a "natural" response to the humor until he realized its inappropriateness and was able to recognize his unconscious collusion. Therapists who have completed personal therapy are better equipped to recognize their own intrapsychic vulnerabilities, so that these can signal issues being generated by their patients. Even though certain problems may be incompletely resolved in the therapist's personal life, awareness of them can reduce the risk of their intrusion upon the therapy.

But the nontreatment aspects of therapist influence do not cease at that point. Patients frequently apprehend their therapists' unspoken values and attitudes, sometimes internalizing those qualities as the therapy progresses. Whether or not this is a desirable occurrence it is a spontaneous feature of experiential learning. In similar fashion, patients often recognize whether one therapist tends to prolong therapy while another prefers shorter term contact, and may adapt to these stylistic preferences. Evidence increasingly supports the view that the here-and-now interaction is an inevitable component of therapy. Such being the case, it is most important that those therapist influences which are not germane to the patient's clinical needs be monitored and their intrusion minimized.

At the same time, recognition of the inevitability of human interaction leads to consideration of how to optimize this process for therapeutic purposes. While I concur entirely with the view that "adult pathology cannot be repaired by simple interpersonal experience" (Blanck and Blanck, 1979, p. 133) one cannot ignore or trivialize so powerful and subtle an influence. Interpersonal experience with significant figures continues throughout life as the data base from which ongoing object relations are formed or modified. Consequently, exploration of these relationships has a significant application to weekly psychotherapy. Ego and self restructuring benefits from alternative self and object representations to those which derive from the past. In addition to those qualities which are unconsciously incorporated by identification, and which one hopes are growth-enhancing, the therapeutic work can usefully address how therapists handle self-revealing material.

The use of personal material with patients is hardly new. Greenberg and Mitchell (1983) report from first-hand accounts that Freud communicated a variety of personal views to his patients. Indeed, Freud used persuasion, suggestion, and discussed his personal views to an extent that few modern practitioners would find suitable. Benefiting from almost a century of experience, and reaffirming the difference between psychoanalysis and weekly practice, factors other than precedent clarify how the therapist's side of the relationship is employed for therapeutic effect. The distinction between therapist self-awareness and activity is focal here. Whether the self-awareness is that of feeling sadness or of one's eyes moistening, what the therapist does is guided by its immediate and long-term relevance to the working partnership. One therapist, whose eyes frequently moistened around issues of reunion, commonly made no comment when this happened so long as it was congruent with the therapeutic material. Those patients who noted his eyes watering readily understood it as an indication of his warmth or sentimentality, taking it as a sign of his caring. But on one occasion, with a patient determined to divorce his spouse, it was necessary for the therapist to say: "I was affected by your wife's desire to stay married, but we have to look at what you want and feel about your marriage."

It is the nature of countertransference material to be involuntarily evoked. The therapeutic task is to recognize the source of the reaction, relate it to the current situation, assess as best one can its impact on the therapy, and respond accordingly. As always the first dictum is to avoid harming the patient. Second, how can the reaction be most usefully applied to the therapy? Is the reaction an intrusion of the therapist's own making, or was it provoked by the patient, consciously or not? From these questions emerge the specific techniques to be employed in the situation. Accustomed as we are to multiple tracks of simultaneous thought, choosing an adequate response may take less time than it has to describe the process. Often it is the subsequent interaction more than the precise phrasing of the response which has the enduring clinical significance. Consistent with the position throughout this book, a vital consideration is to couch any response so that it conforms to the ego–self status of the patient at the time. The therapeutic needs of the patient should never be subordinated to what social etiquette might prescribe in a different set of circumstances. By the same token, respect for the patient's integrity cannot be sacrificed to the therapist's holdover omnipotence needs. These principles govern therapeutic activity whether the intervention is based on countertransference or personal disclosure.

In contrast to countertransference, personal disclosure ordinarily occurs at the conscious option of the therapist. Not all therapist reactions are attributable to the inadvertent surfacing of unconscious issues. Opposing beliefs or noxious traits can, over time, provoke behavior which may be relevant to the therapy (Strupp and Binder, 1984) or can be a revealing instance of inevitable interpersonal conflict between humans in confined and extended contact.

Mr. Y's narcissistic self-protection turned every perceived slight into a diatribe on oppression, and every therapist reaction into an inadequate response to his desperate need. Session after session was filled with his pleading for help and raging attacks on the inadequacy of the therapist's response. After one such attack the therapist blurted out angrily, "it won't matter what I say!" Mr. Y's head jolted as though struck, and he cried, "I don't need your sarcasm on top of all my other problems." The therapist recovered his composure and answered by apologizing for the anger, but then went on to describe his utter frustration with being continually and angrily repudiated. When the patient peevishly responded, "that's part of my problem" the therapist acknowledged and said, "but I'm human too."

A patient who could say "that's part of my problem" was also capable of internalizing the therapist's comment. A serendipitous outcome of this exchange was the patient's dawning awareness of his aversive impact on others, with some gradual effort to modulate his behavior. His narcissistic disorder continued unabated for a considerable time longer. But his social behavior began to change and his relations with friends and coworkers improved, contributing to his eventual therapeutic progress. The interaction was unplanned, and technically was an intrusion of the therapist's needs into the relationship. Yet, as a tolerant human being abused for attempting to provide help the therapist's impulsive behavior was understandable. Perhaps because of its inherent humanness it touched that part of the patient's autonomous ego operations which had the adult capacity to attend.

Another form of personal disclosure occurs when the therapist deliberately chooses to cite personal experience in order to elucidate an issue which has emerged in the session.

Len, a chronically depressed, socially inhibited adult had just ended an unhappy fourteen-year marriage, He despaired of entering the "singles scene," yet his depression intensified when he was devoid of female company. His therapist, who had divorced and remarried several years earlier, briefly described his own felicitous experience in using a reputable dating service. Like Len, he had been unwilling to frequent bars or depend on his friends for meeting new people.

Underlying this disclosure were several considerations. The patient had extricated himself from a difficult marriage but was likely to suffer greater depression and self-recrimination as an immediate consequence of "losing" his wife. Although he was not at serious risk of suicide, further self-denigration would be countertherapeutic. By sharing a similar experience the therapist tacitly supported the "normalcy" of leaving a destructive marriage as well as the appropriateness of finding a comfortable way of meeting women. On both points the therapist's behavior challenged Len's punitive superego by providing a manifestly acceptable alternative. The intervention was a sharing of personal experience in a way which supported and empowered the patient by differentiating between existential distress and intrapsychic pathology. Unlike bland reassurance or information giving, this intervention took account of the patient's ego and self needs along with the reality factors.

> A third form of therapist disclosure was used with Mr. K, a chronically passive dependent middle-aged man enmeshed in an idealizing transference. The therapist would periodically comment on current sports events, an interest he shared with Mr. K. At times this would be followed up with a question, soliciting Mr. K's greater knowledge of some facet of sports. These interventions helped facilitate the internalization of more appropriate self representations: "Like my therapist I am someone who knows sports; and he even asks me for my opinion." Where other supportive interventions were often beyond the patient's self-comprehension, these egalitarian interactions could be tolerated. Ultimately the patient began making decisions in his personal life.

Obviously the timing and frequency of personal disclosures, as with overt countertransference reactions, is as relevant as their actual content. In any psychoanalytically oriented psychotherapy interventions of this type are predictably atypical and infrequent. The focus of therapy properly is on the patient's inner experience, not the therapist's. Nevertheless, the verities of face-to-face therapy on a weekly basis do militate in favor of a different interactive stance than that called for by intensive contact. If anything, contemporary literature suggests that numerous psychoanalytic writers find an expanding role for these nontraditional interventions (Giovacchini, 1975; Gedo, 1979; Paolino, 1981; Greenberg and Mitchell, 1983; Strupp and Binder, 1984; Blanck and Blanck, 1986).

The impetus behind personal disclosure is not to demonstrate that the therapist is "humanistic" or "authentic," or even democratic. Patients find more dependable ways of assessing their therapist's genuineness as and when they need to do so. In every instance the driving force motivating personal disclosure is to enhance structure. Personal disclosure is used when it is targeted to a specific aspect of structure-building or, as with managing countertransference, when the therapist needs to correct an inappropriate reaction. Disclosures which confuse flattery or support with structure building offer little by way of therapeutic substance. Conversely, unwillingness to employ relevant personal data at those rare but important moments may deprive the therapy of a valuable ancillary technique. There are times when nothing else is quite so compelling as a statement by someone trusted that says, "I have been in that situation too." A guide to assessing the utility of personal disclosure is to ask to what extent it helps the patient extend and employ ego resources. A disclosure which sheds light on an experience or a possible means of coping with a situation is quite different from one which may, by intervening, dilute the salutory impact of the patient's experience.

> Suddenly a single parent and faced with her daughter's resentment for ending the marriage, Ms. T was encountering an enormous affective drain. While her narcissistic disorder was much improved, she was working full time, setting up a new apartment, and living 1,250 miles away from her lover. Therapeutic strategy dictated that her self-soothing and coping tolerances be monitored. Interpretation and confrontation were counterindicated due to the regressive risk at a time when all her resources were fully taxed. Although the therapist herself had experienced a similar situation she did not reveal this. Ms. T needed to work with her own reactions first, comparing her inner feelings with how she managed her life situation. The therapist did not probe for fantasies or genetic associations, but instead monitored closely Ms. T's ego functions and self-esteem. The attacks by her daughter aroused Ms. T's guilt and self-recrimination, jeopardizing her resolve to end the unhappy marriage. But exploring her own parents' unhappy marriage as it affected her did little to relieve Ms. T's mounting anxiety. To help Ms. T better cope the therapist used a third-person form of disclosure: "Someone I know was in a similar situation; she found that her daughter's

school was helpful; it's such a frequent situation today." The tacit support of "it's . . . frequent" was intended as minor buffering; primarily the intervention sought to offer Ms. T a means of taking constructive action, seeing if she could help herself by reaching into the community for assistance. By contrast, for the therapist to have shared herself as a kindred spirit would have contributed nothing to the patient's growth and coping. At the other extreme, offering potentially valuable personally acquired experience was preferable to assuming that the patient might come upon this or some other avenue spontaneously, at a time when her own resources were being critically strained.

Used in this fashion personal disclosure can be a systematic intervention, in harmony with the overall therapeutic thrust. It is suspect only when it is uncoordinated with regard to the main therapeutic effort. In these latter instances one must be alert to the possibility of countertransference acting out; for example, a seductive offer of friendship in place of professional help, an overprotective or oversolicitous identification with the patient.

SUMMARY

By acknowledging the enormous complexity of the therapist–patient interaction we tacitly recognize that errors of omission and commission are probably unavoidable. The self-understanding acquired from personal analysis will help to reduce or mitigate some of the more damaging instances. In addition, patients are forgiving when their therapists can honestly cope with technical errors, and those instances are the exception rather than the rule. There may be no safer guide through the turbulent waters of the therapeutic relationship than therapists' own fluidity in lending their unconscious processes to that purpose.

Above all, therapy rests on a relationship of compassion. The people who seek our help are wounded and hurting, however they may behave. We offer an empathic contact between adults, no more and no less. Our patients' problems, in part, remind us of our own vulnerability and thus our shared humanness.

CHAPTER 6

EGO, SELF, AND OBJECT RELATIONS: ASSESSMENT

The psychotherapeutic community is increasingly populated by a barrage of practitioners, offering some two hundred "different" approaches to treatment. More than any other single quality, assessment skill distinguishes the psychoanalytic practitioner, whose clinical examination derives from an extensive body of systematic knowledge. In contrast to the "lets-get-acquainted" free introductory offers, in psychoanalytic psychotherapy assessment is among the most demanding tasks that the therapist performs. From the first contacts, when suitability and form of therapy is evaluated, to the continuous monitoring of patients' intrapsychic integrity and capacity, assessment is necessary for planning and managing the conduct of therapy. Progress can be impeded, and the health and safety of the patient or others jeopardized, by well-intended efforts that do not take into account the kind and quality of structuring available to the patient at any given point.

While these considerations apply to therapy in general, the approach to weekly psychotherapy described in this book is specifically predicated upon the mobilization, enhancement, and restructuring of intrapsychic operations. Inevitably, therefore, one of the most fundamental competencies necessary to implement therapy is the ability to assess which operations are deficient and pathological, which are working effectively, and which are potentially available for recruitment. In the interest of more precise analysis it is necessary to separate the components of the egoself system into their integral units.

Psychoanalytically oriented assessment requires a solid grounding in the theoretical and clinical manifestations of object relations, self, and ego, which are the framework for organizing the complex variety of observations and information generated in each therapy session. At the same time, assessment requires an attitude of professional openness—a willingness to consider alternative ways of making sense of the clinical material. And all this activity goes on while one engages the patient in establishing and maintaining a working relationship! Assessment further requires the personal fortitude to continue revising and honing earlier impressions, using new material to inform theory and experience, deepening one's understanding of the patient's vulnerabilities and strengths. As therapists, access to our own intrapsychic processes are another important source of information. As Stanton (1953) observed many years ago, we are "infinite receptors" who pick up subliminal cues from patients—and ourselves—and apply them to the therapeutic effort.

But there are important differences between assessment and therapeutic procedure. Assessment is invariably more global than therapy. It is a first mapping, a panoramic scanning to understand the patient and his or her pathology. Therapeutic work is much more finely attuned to a smaller field of activity at any given point. A rough analogy might be drawn to what happens in planning a long trip, compared with monitoring it along the way. The initial mapping cannot account for every town and every bridge, but successfully managing the voyage entails coordinating the overall planning of routes, climate, terrain, and duration with the local conditions encountered each day. The trip is more likely to be successful when there is periodic reexamination of the original plans. Assessment is that preliminary and recurrent charting of the territory which will be traversed in therapy. Initial assessment identifies significant issues that therapy will more closely investigate. As the therapy gets under way, continuing assessment clarifies and refines the earlier impressions. By comparison with intensive psychotherapy, weekly egoself therapy places relatively more emphasis on structural features, and on identifying recruitable strengths along with the extent and depth of pathology.

Consistent with the line of thought just described, this chapter presents assessment in the dual perspective of locating assets as well as pathology. To this end I draw upon the same rich sources of clinical, theoretical, and research data that are discussed in chapter 8. Readers may find much of this material familiar and some of it less so. Some unfamiliarity is to be expected because the proliferation of discoveries stimulated by ego psychology, self psychology, and object relations theory has been so great that even the most well-read practitioners are overwhelmed by the sheer volume of professional literature. The same patience and tolerance which characterizes good clinical work will aid the reader's journey here into those areas which may be less familiar. Elucidating central aspects of intrapsychic operation is the indispensable first step toward extending clinical observation from the domain of concept to the reality of practice. The focus of this chapter is on how the concepts are manifested. Recognizing vital aspects of self and ego structure lays the groundwork for egoself reorganization, which is at the heart of this object relations approach to weekly psychotherapy.

Assessment of egoself operations has dual objectives: that of locating pathological operations—the structural basis of the psychopathology—and identifying those structural assets which form the substrate upon which therapeutic intervention will be based. The chapter's organization reflects this dual purpose, with the first section devoted to normative operations and the second to pathology. For purposes of exegesis each section looks separately at ego, self, and object relations. A third section takes the analysis one step further, into a case illustration of egoself assessment. One final introductory comment is needed. Coverage of topics will be uneven, with light coverage of more familiar material such as defenses and other ego functions. Aspects more central to intensive therapy or psychoanalysis are similarly accorded less space here. In particular, extra attention is given to elucidating evidence of intrapsychic resources. Some readers may opt for a "refresher course" by reviewing the material in chapter 8 before proceeding here.

NORMATIVE EGO OPERATIONS

Various writers have undertaken to identify ego operations which constitute the basis for healthy functioning. As modern psychoanalytic psychology has gained prominence, the relevance of previously unrelated sources of information—in personality research, brain physiology, life span development, learning theory—has become clearer. Chapters 8 and 9 detail many of these contributions, a number of which originate outside traditional psychoanalytic circles. But whatever their origin, if they are solidly documented and clinically useful our work is enriched by their inclusion. Included under the heading of normative ego operations are the specific ego functions, coping processes, and the upper end of the defense hierarchy. On a broader level, it is also important to include other indices of healthy operations: ego strength; ego integration; higher levels of cognitive process; experiential regulators. These and related areas will be addressed in turn.

EGO FUNCTIONS

Among the most complete listing and description of ego functions is to be found in the research of Bellak, Hurvich, and Gediman (1973). These authors identify twelve ego functions, culled from the clinical literature in psychoanalysis yet demonstrably suitable for rating "in the course of regular psychoanalytic therapy sessions" (1973, p. 3). As universal aspects of ego operation, these functions can be observed and assessed in nonpsychotherapeutic settings also. "Ego functions are theoretical constructs based on observations of behavior and on patients' reports of their experiences. . . . [They] refer (among other things) to adaptively relevant actions and reactions of the individual person" (Bellak, Hurvich, and Gediman, 1973, p. 71). Ego functions are core operations, describing how the executive actions of organization and prioritizing take place.

1. *Reality Testing.* Accurately perceiving and interpreting the distinction between inner and outer stimuli, and recognizing

distortions. Accurately perceiving and interpreting real world events relative to time, place, and person.

2. *Judgment.* The ability to anticipate probable consequences of intended behavior, and the extent to which manifest behavior reflects that awareness. Appropriateness of emotional attunement and behavior to external reality.

3. *Sense of Reality of the World and of the Self.* The extent to which the person has a sense of identity and clearly defined ego boundaries. External events and bodily experiences are demarcated from each other. Self and object representations are distinct from each other.

4. *Regulation and Control of Drives, Affects, and Impulses.* The effectiveness of delay and control mechanisms; frustration tolerance. Ability to channel drive derivatives through ideation, affective expression, and manifest behavior.

5. *Object Relations.* Degree and kind of relatedness to others, free from patterning on early relations, and reflecting choice over closeness and distance. Capacity for object constancy; tolerance for the physical absence of the object.

6. *Thought Processes.* Ability to conceptualize at levels which are appropriate to the situation. Efficiency of memory, attention, concentration, and communication.

7. *Adaptive Regression in Service of the Ego (ARISE).* Ability to relax perceptual and conceptual acuity in order to increase ego adaptive awareness of previously unconscious or preconscious content. Controlled use of primary process content.

8. *Defensive Functioning.* Adequacy of defenses in containing disruptive affects. Extent to which defenses have maladaptively affected ideation, behavior, and other ego functions.

9. *Stimulus Barrier.* Threshold and sensitivity levels for registering sensory stimuli, internal or external. Capacity for adapting to sensory stimulation.

10. *Autonomous Functioning.* Adequacy of primary autonomy functions (attention, concentration, memory, learning, perception, motor function, intention) and secondary autonomy functions (habit patterns, work routines, hobbies and interests).

11. *Synthetic-Integrative Functioning.* Ability to tolerate and reconcile discrepant or contradictory attitudes, behavior, and

self representations. Ability to integrate intrapsychic and behavioral events.

12. *Mastery-Competence.* Subjective feeling of competence and the expectancy of success in actual performance. Actual abilities in mastering and affecting the environment.

In a listing of my own creation, functions 3 and 5 would belong under object relations, and 11 and 12 under self processes. However, Bellak, Hurvich, and Gediman reflect accurately the historic location of these functions. In truth, any such discrete listing inevitably distorts the essential interrelationship of ego, self, and object relations.

Assessment of ego functions is both extensive and intensive. A great amount of information can be revealed with very little material, to be further elaborated by other observations over the subsequent weeks or months.

Mr. D, a middle-aged man, came to therapy with a presenting complaint that he rarely experienced emotion. Owner of a machine parts business which he had started himself, married, and father of four young adult children, he thought of his life as "not bad but not satisfying." As he spoke his face was expressionless, eyes alert and appraising, voice controlled and flat but not dysphoric. He chose words carefully, frowned when the radio in the adjacent room emitted static. Mr. D wore a freshly pressed shirt without tie or jacket; his shoes and slacks had a crisp, neat look. He had come ten minutes late to the first appointment, yet walked with an unhurried but coordinated gait and sat comfortably in his chair. The evidence of competence and accomplishment in his career and personal life indicated mastery skills but his interview behavior suggested difficulty in integrating affective, intrapsychic, and behavioral events. Delay and control capacities were apparent, and thought processes appeared intact. Inhibition, repression, withdrawal, and compulsive attention to detail suggested a consistent picture of defenses which were intact. A low threshold barrier was indicated by his reaction to the radio static. Like his visual alertness, it implied a readiness to experience irritation, at variance with his bland demeanor and presenting problem. His difficulty in integrating experience with affective reactions pointed to strenuous countercathectic efforts expended to defend against emotions. Identity and self representations seemed stable, but dysphorically toned by dissatisfaction and implied self-criticism.

Ego boundaries and object representations were almost too well defined.

Ego functions thus incorporate the discrete operations which are necessary for managing the complexities of everyday life. In addition, they encompass the major subsystems which help shape personality development: object relations, the self, and the autonomous functions. Thus, the processing of experience—those interpretations of events which make meaning out of sensory data—are embedded in the ego functions.

This experiential perspective, inherent in object relations theory and self psychology, is an essential part of modern psychoanalytic theory. It underscores what Piagetians call constructionism, the position that humans play an active part in structuring their own adaptation and growth. More particularly, identification of the meaning-making processes in ego function provides a clinical grounding for the study of healthy and pathological processes. In this connection, the distinction between coping and defense enunciated by Haan (1977), referred to in chapter 8, takes on specific significance.

Coping and Defense

The traditional view of defense is of a mechanism designed to ward off anxiety triggered by intrapsychic conflict. This view, promulgated by Sigmund and Anna Freud, unmistakably ascribes purposeful intent to the operation of defenses. Ego was construed as the executive system of the person, organizing his or her experience. In the specific case of defense mechanisms that intention was for the purpose of protection. Defenses can be adaptive to the extent that they promote continued ego functioning and, in some cases, permit limited neutralization of impulses (Hoffer, 1954). Defenses can also be categorized according to their level of primitivity or pathology (Kernberg, 1967; Lowenstein, 1967; Vaillant, 1971). To the extent that defenses always result in pathological impairment of integrative functioning, Sperling (1957) concludes they are ipso facto pathological. Others have shown that there is a connection between cognitive controls and defense preference. But while defenses are activated by internal conflict, cognitive controls may reflect personality style (Bellak et al., 1973).

Haan (1977) continues in this tradition, making the point that while the person's purpose is to ward off anxiety, defense is not the only possible response. Both intention and ego efficacy determine the nature of response to anxiety. Successful activation of a defense has the ironic consequence of perpetuating the anxiety arousing conditions as an unconscious threat. By containing the anxiety, and thus supporting whatever secondary gains are unconsciously derived, the defense perpetuates the conflict by palliating it without effecting resolution. As the person continues to develop, acquiring greater ego assets, there is increased capacity to rework pathological formations and resolve ego anxiety laden conflict. If anxiety can be modulated, and healthy ego resources mobilized in the anxiety arousing conditions, the conflict can be addressed and the pathological reaction may be dissipated. The key element in identifying a coping process, then, is to determine if the ego reaction is mastery oriented rather than defensive.

What Haan asserts is that the various ego operations may function as defense or coping processes, or may fragment—depending on how they are invoked. When their operation is simply countercathectic the result is a defense. But when they focus on mastering the source of the anxiety arousing conditions the process constitutes coping. When ego operations are overwhelmed, even temporarily, the process is called fragmentation. In contrast to other approaches which distinguish between healthy and primitive or pathological defenses, Haan provides a model for assessing ego operations which goes beyond description of the form and adequacy of the defense. Like Freud, her approach to assessment includes the person's intention. Consonant with modern theory, Haan's model extends beyond defense to assess whether efforts to master the situation, coping—rather than defense or fragmentation—is being activated. The implications of this model for therapeutic intervention is profound. Traditionally the goal of weekly psychotherapy has been to shore up and support any existing defensive structure. But the coping process suggests that by helping clients to mobilize ego resources toward coping activity, weekly psychotherapy can have restructuring as well as supportive effect. Coping begins with recruiting the patient's unimpaired autonomous functions. In the example below, perception and intention are recruited.

As Mr. D's therapy continued, repressed angry feelings toward his wife emerged in the sessions. When he expressed concern that he would erupt with uncontrollable anger toward her, Mr. D was helped to recognize his ability to control or delay powerful emotions in other life situations—a coping process he had used to good advantage in his business dealings. This helped him realize he could be angry without becoming overwhelmed with rage. Gradually he became able to let his wife know when she was angering him. In turn, these expressions of controlled anger improved communication between himself and his family.

Another approach to assessment of defenses is offered by Vaillant (1977), whose research on a developmental hierarchy of defense mechanisms attempts to update the work of Anna Freud and others. Like Haan, Vaillant's work begins by looking at healthy rather than pathological functioning. By comparing the adaptation levels of Harvard alumni, Vaillant found that those whose career, social, psychological, and physical health were strongest used the defenses of altruism, suppression, humor, anticipation, and sublimation. His neurotic group used intellectualization, repression, reaction formation, displacement, and dissociation. The immature defenses are listed as fantasy, projection, passive aggression, hypochondriasis, and acting out, while the psychotic defenses are denial, delusional projection, and distortion. Vaillant's theory usefully differentiates pathogenicity of defenses, providing a readily available hierarchy for initial assessment purposes. Haan extends defense theory to provide an explanation of how patients can get beyond containing anxiety and into conflict resolution, or ego restructuring.

Ego Strength

Ego strength has enjoyed wide currency as the clinical construct describing overall efficacy of the system of ego functions. Ego strength incorporates the overall breadth and stability of defenses, adequacy of reality testing, extent of diffuse anxiety, number and severity of unresolved problems, resiliency in the face of stress, amount of secondary process functioning, and the ability to modulate anxiety. Customarily ego strength is estimated from interview behavior and the person's psychosocial competence, as evidenced by work history, intimate and social relationships, and leisure activities (Phillips, 1968).

The character of ego strength is described by its rigidity or flexibility, permeability or nonpermeability, depth or veneer, vulnerability or resilience, lability or stability, fragility or durability, differentiation or diffusion, integration or fragmentation. Ego strength is thus assessed holistically as well as by analysis of its components. What is most distinctive about the assessment of ego strength is the explicit consideration given to weighing patients' ego assets along with psychopathology. As clinical experience reveals, severe pathology can coexist with the highest levels of achievement, creativity, and interpersonal success. While pathology defines the person's level of impairment, prognosis and treatment are often most crucially affected by the ego assets which are available for recruitment. The direction in which psychotherapy proceeds is in large measure determined by the quality and character of the person's ego strength. Dewald (1964) prescribes supportive or uncovering psychotherapy based on his evaluation of ego strength. Blanck and Blanck (1979) urge major reformulations of therapeutic strategy in those cases where ego operations are severely impaired. In a similar fashion, Kohut's (1977) self psychology derives directly from his work with the primitive structuring found in narcissistically disordered personalities.

A primary factor in assessing ego strength is to evaluate ego assets independent of the evidence of pathology. While assets and pathology are to some degree interdependent, their status is not complementary; that is, the status of one is no simple index to the status of the other. We find both healthy and pathological processes in all our patients. The presence of thought disorder does not automatically preclude successful career accomplishments; and, short of intimate commitment, some people with severe early object relations impairment can enjoy satisfying interpersonal relationships. An effective assessment of ego strength covers all the ego functions previously listed.

Among the more puzzling clinical findings is the erratic nature of the relationship between early experience and ego strength. We have all worked with people who are psychologically crippled by seemingly mild pathogenic histories, while others appear to have overcome extremely adverse pathological conditions. Yet even the most complete analyses of early object relations and subsequent life history can fail to account for the variations of strength and pathology that are regularly encountered in clinical work. Whatever the ultimate determinants of ego strength, they are complex: the interweaving of experience and meaning making with an "undifferentiated matrix" of potentialities having its own complex origins.

> Betty, a college sophomore, was referred to the psychological clinic by her advisor after reporting she was depressed and having trouble sleeping. Betty was living with her maternal grandmother, who was blind, arthritic, and suffering from severe congestive heart disease. Her grandfather had died two years earlier and Betty feared that her beloved grandmother would soon follow. Although she received a tuition scholarship, Betty still had to work twenty hours weekly to supplement her grandmother's pension. Betty was concerned that she would not be able to maintain her grades—upon which her scholarship depended—while also nursing her grandmother and working. Thus she was at risk of losing her dearest relative as well as sacrificing her life dream of attending college. At the initial interview Betty was depressed, worn, and tearful. As she spoke of her situation her anxiety became acute and she looked desperate.
>
> Betty was born backstage in a burlesque theater, where her mother had been a stripper. Father, an alcoholic, deserted the family but periodically reappeared only to disappear again. Mother was addicted to drugs and alcohol, using prostitution as her primary source of income to support her addiction. From earliest childhood Betty had memories of being evicted from the bed she shared with her mother when the latter would come home with one of many "uncles." Betty had grown up functioning as parent to her mother and younger brother, living from hand to mouth and from one rooming house to another. Around age ten, her grandparents arrived and took Betty to live with

them. They were the only stable figures in her life, as mother, brother, and father irregularly floated in and out of her world. Now one grandparent was dead and the other seemed to be terminally ill. With supportive weekly psychotherapy over the academic year Betty reconstituted her ego resources. A follow-up contact two years later revealed that her grandmother had died, but that Betty had gone on to finish college, graduating with honors. She had met a young man a year earlier and was anticipating marriage in the near future.

Despite repeated early trauma and unstable primary objects this young woman somehow developed a stable self structure and degree of ego resilience that enabled her to utilize minimal therapeutic intervention and function at a level that would be compatible with the most benign of early and subsequent life experiences. While the psychological components of ego strength are well recognized, its totality sometimes appears to be more than the sum of its parts. A growing literature on people who seem to profit from early adverse experience reminds us of how much more remains to be discovered about intrapsychic origins and operation.

Autonomous Functions

While psychotherapists often evaluate the autonomous functions as part of ego strength, their importance for weekly psychotherapy justifies considering them separately. Physical activities such as posture, locomotion, and motor coordination provide cues to body armoring (Lowen, 1970), conflicts and defenses, and somatopsychic integration. Language and speech are important indicators of thought patterns, imagery, and symbolization capacity, suitability for a "talking treatment" approach. Complex autonomous functions such as learning, intention, and perception are important ingredients of every assessment.

Above all other considerations, successful psychotherapy depends upon the patients' ability to profit from interventions and experience, to learn. With the emergence of ego psychology came access to the considerable data on learning achieved by research psychologists such as Kohler (1925), Hull (1943), and

Tolman (1945). For decades the mainstream of psychoanalytic work had no systematic conception of the learning processes. Fundamental concepts such as insight, working through, secondary gain, and chronicity were presented as disparate issues rather than as instances of types of learning. On their part, learning theorists tended to emphasize the cognitive aspects of the learning process, viewing affect, motive, and drive as complicating variables rather than essential components of the process. It was John Dewey (1938), the distinguished educator, who enunciated the principle that learning rooted in experience is the most effective basis for development and growth. This linkage between educational theory and psychoanalytic practice energizes a vital aspect of intervention technique in weekly psychotherapy: the role of autonomous functions such as experiential learning in promoting psychotherapeutic change. The following case illustrates the use of an anomaly in another autonomous function, respiration, to uncover a childhood trauma.

> Although he was a college graduate and a skilled writer, Mr. V found it difficult to communicate orally. His verbalizations were usually cryptic, defensively employing sarcastic humor. His relations with others were peppered with stormy emotions and regular breakdowns of even rudimentary dialogues. As therapy labored through long silences and sarcastic accusations the therapist observed an anomaly in Mr. V's respiration. His inhalations lasted twice as long as his exhalations. After much resistance Mr. V agreed to try extending his rate of exhalation. As he did so the therapist asked him to close his eyes and report any images or ideas that occurred to him. Suddenly Mr. V gasped. He began recalling a childhood incident with his father in a swimming pool. Father prankishly dunked his young son's head under the water unexpectedly. Unable to stand up in the deep water, the boy came up choking and gasping only to have father push him under again. The incident had been repressed, but Mr. V's hostile relationship with his father was found to have dated from that time. Shortly after recalling this memory the patient decided to quit chain smoking and also began to relinquish his defensive sarcasm.

The spectrum of patients who come to the office for weekly psychotherapy is markedly broader than those encountered in intensive psychotherapy or psychoanalysis. Patients' psychological and cultural backgrounds are more diverse, and their autonomous functions are presented in a wider variety of expressive style, body language, and verbal fluency. The adaptive resources of the clinician are challenged to shape a psychoanalytically oriented practice to the needs of this clientele. To the extent that we practice in an increasingly diverse world, psychotherapists preconsciously learn an enormous amount about ways of relating to people from different stages and stations of life. Making these experiences more conscious can carry over into practice in ways which are often helpful. Closer and more systematic attention to the presentation of autonomous functions can aid the clinician in attuning psychotherapy to this expanding realm of operation. In particular, recognizing nonverbal indices of mature and pathological function may supplement other impressions.

OBJECT RELATIONS ASSESSMENT

While object relations is customarily described as an ego function, its salient influence in healthy and pathological development is well recognized (Horner, 1979; Blanck and Blanck, 1986). As Kernberg puts it, "the structural consequences of his past internalized object relationships . . . have crucial consequences for the development of all psychic structures" (1975, p. 144). The separation–individuation paradigm (Mahler, Pine, and Bergman, 1975) enunciates the exquisite interdependence of object relations with ego development and self structuring. The relevance of that interdependence does not end with successful passage through the separation–individuation subphases, however. Object relations theory accounts for the processes by which experience is internalized throughout the life span (Panel, 1973a,b). That ongoing system of organizing and making meaning from everyday activity is the foundation for the continuing evolution of self and ego.

The character of a patient's self and object representations is a useful clinical clue to the capacity for internalizing interpersonal experience. How and where has differentiation proceeded beyond me/not me or good–bad polarization? Does the

presence of projective identification suggest even more primitive levels of object relations? We are accustomed to assessing
object relations against the yardstick of Mahler's separation–
individuation subphases, consistent with estimating depth of
psychopathology. But our clinical sensitivity is also directed
usefully at the evolution of object relations across the entire life
span. The borderline condition which includes a history of
friends and lovers is quite different from one in which each
intimate encounter is a prelude to attempted suicide. Unfortunately, the object relations literature is much less attentive to
manifestations of mature development.

At more mature levels assessment seeks evidence of clear
self–other differentiation, of tolerance for interpersonal closeness and distance, of a range of significant-other representations: among peers, among authority figures, and among
figures of sexual preference. The ability to tolerate a spectrum
of emotions with the same person, to accept intimate closeness,
to reconstitute after separation or loss, these are dependable
indicators of mature object relations. Can the person structure
relationships that are not reenactments of earlier past experience, differentiate affectively between friends, lovers, coworkers? Object constancy, once considered a developmental marker,
is now viewed in a lifelong context (Lax, Bach, and Burland,
1986).

Object relations ultimately infuse experience with the impersonal world as well. Tolerance for change and diversity is
indicative of richer, more complex, further developed object
relations. Here we include tolerance for dissonant and unfamiliar experiences and people, and a readiness to incorporate
such experience into restructured internalizations, the nutrient
material for continued growth and development. In a similar
vein, the internalization of values, tastes, preferences, and individual personal style indicate the maturation of object relations beyond childhood and adolescence and into the adult
domain of identity development. Chapter 7 on developmental
assessment elaborates many of the expectable changes as the
person continues the lifelong process of "metabolizing" experience.

Assessment of Self Processes

The assessment of self processes includes an analysis of the structure of both self and narcissism. The latter is not always thought of as a structural component. But to the extent that narcissism has a regulative impact on other aspects of personality function it seems appropriate and useful to describe its operative variations in the context of clinical assessment.

Self

Where ego is an organized system of functions, self is a system of perceptions, of affectively infused images, fantasies, beliefs, and fears. The experienced, the real, the anticipated, and the idealized selves coexist in a mélange of stable and transient images and structures. In the mature self, conflicting perceptions of who one is are expectable and tolerable. Unlike ego operations, which are usually outside awareness, the content of the mature self is readily accessible to report by the patient. The capacity to describe various self-percepts and to fantasize oneself in different situations realistically is indicative of healthy structuring. The ability to report accurately on one's attributes, traits, and stylistic preferences are clues to the ability to take perspective on oneself—and particularly when dystonic aspects can be acknowledged. Studying the patient's capacity for self-delineation will reveal the level of complexity and integration attained, the ability to synthesize disparate components which is a harbinger of mature self development. Included in this assessment is the patient's value hierarchy, the relationship of wishes and needs to each other, goals and how they have been established. Here it is important to distinguish between ego and self operations. The ability to estimate how reasonable a goal might be is an aspect of reality testing, judgment, and planning—ego functions. But the willingness to consider a personal goal or fantasy, or to undertake a commitment of self, is a measure of the integrity of the self system.

In Western cultures effectiveness of the self has traditionally been indicated by people's ability to conceive of themselves as agents of their own destinies. A self-image as active, capable,

and willing to take initiative are attributes of mature self structure. Recent cross-cultural research and studies of women's
development (Chodorow, 1980; Belenky, Clinchy, Goldberger,
and Tarule, 1986) suggest that this picture is framed too nar-
rowly. Many women, and people who originate from Eastern
or Third World cultures, conventionally define themselves in
the context of their primary group affiliations, such as family
or partner/spouse. But healthy self structure nevertheless mandates a history and experience of active participation within
these interpersonal contexts. To perceive oneself as being interdependent with others is qualitatively distinct from experiencing oneself as powerless, a helpless victim, or the passive
instrument of another person.

Narcissism

Our improved understanding of the developmental importance
of normal narcissism permits its inclusion as an indicator of
powerful clinical resources. While the therapeutic value of self-
esteem was recognized by Freud, conceiving of narcissism as a
developmental line is more legitimately attributed to Kohut
(1971). Its role in the person's self-maintenance and well-being
is now widely accepted. For assessment purposes locating the
nature and extent of healthy narcissism is fundamental to key
elements of successful therapeutic intervention: restructuring
object relations and building a viable working relationship. Evidence of healthy narcissism is readily available in the clinical
interview and is routinely noted. These signs include areas and
extent of self-acceptance; a sense of competence or skill; elements of self-confidence or security. More explicit inquiry can
reveal indications that early experience included adequate
emotional caretaking, preferably with affectionate handling. It
is particularly important to assess these early salubrious influences while exploring for pathogenic history, since neither factor obviates the other. A useful clue to self-acceptance—and,
hence, a reservoir of healthy narcissism—is the person's tolerance for criticism, from self or others. There may be no better
clinical index of healthy narcissistic endowment than that as-

cribed to Gordon Allport: the ability to view oneself with complacency.

Kohut and Wolf (1978) suggest other indices that narcissistic investment contains wholesome aspects: the ability to take pleasure in one's realistic accomplishments; an empathic capacity; an appreciation of humor; sexual satisfaction; acknowledging and pursuing ambitions. The presence of these indicators does not contraindicate significant pathology of self structure. It does point to the availability of resources suitable to therapeutic utilization. As with other personality processes, pathology and health often coexist. Consistent with Kohut's belief that narcissism is part of the self system, another resource to be assessed incorporates both constructs: self-soothing.

Self-Soothing

Among the various self-protective methods people devise for themselves, self-soothing ranks among the earliest and most potent. While other procedures may eliminate pain, self-soothing has the additional virtue of providing self-administered gratification. We must presume, therefore, that it occupies a central role in normal narcissistic development. From early infancy onward the organism demonstrates built-in and acquired ways of regulating experience to provide comfort. While most psychoanalytic literature emphasizes the self-soothing techniques observed in infancy and childhood, experiential regulators for self-soothing seem to evolve across the life span. In all cases, self-soothing regulates experience by introducing a comfort level of reassurance. Unlike defenses, which block anxiety, or coping processes, which address the anxiety-provoking conditions, self-soothing sustains the person by comforting. Its significance for object relations theory extends beyond its value as an experiential regulator, however. Self-soothing is a provider of narcissistic supplies, promoting the development of positive self representations and self-esteem in healthy form and contributing to autistic withdrawal in severe pathological narcissism.

During infancy and childhood self-soothing techniques tend to focus on tactile and kinesthetic gratifiers which directly address the sensory apparatus. Rocking, sucking, hair twirling, and genital manipulation are commonly observed instances of pleasure-giving which are self-administered. While defensive operations protect the child from anxiety, they do so at the cost of altering or diminishing the scope of the child's sense of safety in the world. By contrast, self-soothing may permit the person to tolerate levels of anxiety which would otherwise overwhelm ego operations or evoke defensive withdrawal.

Self-soothing is a common but subtle part of everyday experience, manifested in psychomotor activities such as leg-rocking or in internal dialogue such as "don't give up; you can do it." Antonovsky (1979), investigating how people sustain themselves under severe stress, discovered a Weltanschauung he named "the sense of coherence." In those circumstances where people can feel that they are part of a life system which provides organization and predictability, they feel order and security in their lives. This sense of coherence acts as buffer against debilitating stresses of famine, disease, and other hardship. With more mature ego organization self-soothing is aided by the ability to modulate anxiety by applying ethical, moral, or other belief systems to threatening circumstances. A highly organized egoself system modulates intensity of experience, channels and integrates sensory and cognitive data, prioritizes and mediates among impulses, defusing and regulating inner experience so as to optimize the person's tolerances for dystonic input. In the mature ego even acutely threatening experiences, such as the impulse to kill one's infant child, can be assuaged by a complex integration of ego operations: "Wow, that's a crazy idea" (use of perspective and reality testing); "hold on a minute" (delay and modulation); "do you really hate it enough to kill it?" (affect differentiation); "the damn kid never stops crying" (self-justification). By now the sequence of intrapsychic processes has focused the person's attention long enough for restitutional controls to intervene.

Self-soothing can therefore utilize many ego and self operations, from simple sensory pleasure to complex combinations of sensory, motor, and ideational processes. Its clinical significance lies in the fact that since self-soothing can be another reasonably healthy expedient in mediating anxiety, it is an important self process to evaluate. One suspects that meditation, reciting mantras, and "positive thoughts" may be salutory in part because they are self-soothing techniques. Within the context of assessing egoself functions for weekly psychotherapy, self-soothing can be an asset to be supported and cultivated or a regressive gratifier to be confronted at an appropriate time. As an experiential regulator it can aid frustration tolerance and help modulate the impact of other stresses. As a self-controlled, self-initiated process it is recruitable for enhancing narcissistic self-esteem, and for strengthening self-structure by way of personal empowerment.

Clinical analysis of areas of egoself potential underscores the truism that assessment based only on the patient's psychopathology must necessarily be incomplete. Mobilizing patients' indigenous growth capability is indispensable to any therapeutic agenda. In weekly psychotherapy particularly, where time pressures are more acute, locating egoself assets relevant to pathology is essential. The clinical maxim that one does not deprive patients of their pathology before there is a preferable alternative further underlines the necessity for identifying egoself resources. These resources provide the options most readily accessible to the patient, options that can be brought to conscious awareness at the appropriate time. As we turn our attention now to assessment of psychopathology the same emphasis on structural aspects will be evident.

ASSESSMENT OF PSYCHOPATHOLOGY

Consistent with the approach taken to this point, the assessment of psychopathology will focus on egoself operations, rather than diagnosis per se. This approach keeps close harmony with the psychoanalytic tradition of emphasizing intrapsychic processes rather than their behavioral manifestations. The structural orientation is also in keeping with current thinking about the nature of psychopathology (Kernberg, 1975; Kohut, 1977; Horner, 1979; Blanck and Blanck, 1986). Although the literature on psychopathology is of staggering size and complexity, the task of organizing it relative to egoself operations is not insuperable. By holding to a focus on processes, operations, and organization—the way object relations structure pathology in ego and self—the assessment of pathology takes on more manageable proportions. More specifically, psychopathology will be evaluated along the dimensions of severity, chronicity, and primitivity. The goals of assessment for weekly psychotherapy are effectively served within this narrowed framework. It may be helpful to recall that, for various reasons, neither psychoanalysis nor intensive psychotherapy are options for these patients. As a result, the fine points of differential diagnosis which engender active debate between Kohut and Kernberg partisans are less urgent when transference and countertransference reactions emerge with less intensity. Instead, distinguishing the pathological features of ego, self,.and object relations formation, and their vulnerability to further decompensation, are more focal to the assessment process. I tend to agree with Blanck and Blanck (1974) that, beyond broad differentiation of neurosis, psychosis, and other primitive patterns "the purpose of treatment is to change the diagnosis" (p. 97).

As therapy proceeds other aspects of dysfunction are addressed on an as-needed basis. But the delineation of the most essential psychopathological components can be dependably subsumed under the topical headings of severity, chronicity, and primitivity. Evidence of pathology in ego, self, and object relations structuring will be examined under those headings.

Severity of Psychopathology

Naturally enough, severity of psychopathology is a prime assessment concern of the clinician. On a process level severity is indicated by the degree of psychological disruption suffered by the patient. In manifest behavior, severity of psychopathology impacts directly upon the safety and well-being of patients and/or the community. That risk is significantly enhanced in acute conditions with rapid exacerbation or decompensation. We are familiar with most obvious indices of severity such as loss or breakdown of essential ego functions: vegetative processes, ego boundaries, core defenses, reality testing. More generally, to the extent that ego operations are impaired, distorted, or inoperative, dystonic experiences can overwhelm the individual. Finally, the complex interaction between self, ego, and object relations is such that serious dysfunction of any system eventually becomes an assault upon the others.

The assessment of severity proceeds along several simultaneous lines of inquiry, sharing as their common concern the degree of egoself impairment. Psychodynamic considerations alone, such as self-hate or fear of abandonment, are unreliable indicators of degree of disruption of the organizing processes. Similarly, sheer quanta of dysphoric affect measure distress but not actual severity.

1. *Disruption of Autonomous Operations.* We have already noted the essential importance of vegetative functions such as eating and sleeping, because of their life-threatening potential. But problems with motor coordination, such as balance, motility, manipulation of objects; or sensory experiences, such as impairment of vision, hearing, touch, are also indicative. Since all these operations depend upon ego regulation, pathological dysfunction is manifested by inhibition, exaggeration, or distortion of these functions. By virtue of their centrality to the ego's life maintenance tasks, severity of disturbance in autonomous operations is a useful indicator of the severity of ego impairment. While relatively minor disruptions such as blurring of vision may be the presenting complaint of a severely disturbed person, serious disruptions are not only physically hazardous but can also reflect ego impairment of major proportion. By comparison, hysterically based sensorimotor disruptions rarely threaten the person's actual safety. Highly anxious, fearful, or narcissistic people often report their concerns about irregular functioning: loss of sleep, dizziness, lack of appetite, constipation, headache. It is important to determine whether relatively moderate autonomic dysfunction is impacting upon a hypervigilant person or whether serious autonomic disruption is involved. Evidence of conscious control over the disruption may be an unreliable index of severity. Anorectic or psychotic individuals can be at serious risk by deliberately starving themselves, while depressed patients may not notice or report their insomnia.

Severe pathology in object relations formation and in narcissistic self-regulation can be manifested by the way patients describe their autonomic distress. Distant, dissociated blandness can reflect autistic distortion of self–other representations, intellectualization, and denial, or resigned hopelessness. Ability to differentiate among these may provide directional cues to the intrapsychic system most amenable to intervention, whether self, ego, or object relations. Other hazards to safety, such as impulsively destructive acting out, are discussed below under their appropriate headings.

2. *Distortions of Reality*. The reality testing function is among the most central and fundamental of ego activities. Severe psychopathology is manifested by problems with distinguishing between internal and external experiences, and by distortions of time, place, and person. Confusing events, times, and persons represents a failure of accurate perception and interpretation (Bellak et al., 1973), whether or not these distortions reflect psychodynamically determined distortions. Reality testing impaired by substance abuse or tissue damage is still psychopathological in terms of ego functioning. Distortions of reality may permeate ego operations broadly or, as in the case of paranoid delusions, be confined to particular thematic content. The consistency and extent of impaired reality testing are dependable indices of its severity. But the degree of distortion also measures ego impairment to the extent that prior learning is sacrificed to autistic demands. Severity of self pathology can be estimated by the extent and depth of investment in either grandiosity or self-hating. The capacity to differentiate between "it is as though" and "it is" is crucial. This determination requires that the clinician peer through the veils of linguistic imprecision to specify the patient's actual experience. What is really believed and what is being glossed over with rationalization? One patient, describing his reaction to his wife leaving him, was experiencing the loss of an introjected object exactly as he presented it: "Part of my insides have been torn out." There was no "as though"; his facial grimacing and body contortions vividly conveyed his inner reality. Another patient in a similar situation, whose reaction was, "Fuck her; I'll get over it" experienced equivalent psychic pain. Yet, the ability to dif-

ferentiate self and object protected him from suffering the further decompensation affecting the first man.

Reality testing is not constant, of course. In therapy it is dependent upon the patient's structure and the therapeutic interaction. The cost of shoring up defenses, like the cost of eliciting transference material, is to strain reality testing. As Haan (1977) notes, to the extent that defenses are automatized processes for containing anxiety derived from the past, they inevitably distort current experience. When reality testing is fragile, the clinical choice between permitting pathological distortions to emerge versus intervening to strengthen ego operations is a sensitive one. The use of supportive intervention to shore up defenses can be an unfortunate compromise in this situation. An important difference between egoself therapy and supportive therapy hinges on the therapist's commitment to expanding the domain of structure rather than sustaining existing structure. When the emergence of pathological distortions can be buffered and brought under ego mediation, that approach is preferable to the dubious value of sustaining defense processes that ultimately perpetuate the pathology.

Transference material is clinically significant precisely because it is a distortion of reality. In weekly psychotherapy with severely disturbed people the strength of transference reactions must be monitored with particular care because the strain it exerts on fragile reality testing is in a context of relatively infrequent contact. Permitting the buildup of transference is subordinate to the priority of building egoself resources. The mandates of weekly therapy are clearly different from classical intensive or supportive approaches in this regard. But while the approach is qualitatively distinct from intensive therapy, it need not be any less useful. Kernberg's (1980) view that psychotherapy is the appropriate treatment for borderline states can be extended to my experience in using weekly contact.

Among narcissistically disordered patients the insidious impact of pathology invades even mature egoself operations. Whether the narcissistic distortions are grandiose or self-directed shame and hate, and even when their reality testing "tells" patients that their self-perceptions are distorted, the pathologically distorted beliefs are remarkably intractable. According to Kohut (Kohut and Wolf, 1978) psychoanalysis of the narcissistic transference is often the treatment of choice. But weekly egoself therapy, extended over many years, has also proven to be effective with these cases. In these instances abatement of the narcissistic disorder is accomplished by restructuring the self, relinquishing magical beliefs, and a qualitative improvement in reality orientation. As discussed in chapter 3, active intervention as well as empathic presence can promote the internalization and transmuting of objects into beneficial self representations.

3. *Integrity of Egoself Boundaries.* Egoself boundary refers to the differentiation and subsequent integration of self and object representations structurally and experientially. It also refers to self–other differentiation and the permeability of that distinction, including tolerance thresholds for both intimacy and loss. Self-in-relation, self–object, psyche–soma, body image, impulse–action, fantasy–reality, and idea–affect are examples of egoself boundaries. Self structure and ego organization both derive from the integrity of object relations. Numerous investigators have concluded that the various forms of intrapsychic differentiation derive from initial me/not-me distinctions, but articulation of self and object representations derives from the earlier self–other differentiation, described by Spitz (1959) and elaborated into separation–individuation theory by Mahler (1972). Body image is particularly vulnerable to distortion from infancy onward. Early sensory awareness of the body and its parts makes it accessible to narcissistic cathexis long before ego and self awareness is developmentally attained. Somatic reactions are experienced from birth, and provide a natural channel for absorbing distress. Indeed, body image distortions are so widespread that only the most extreme distortions are likely to indicate severe psychopathology. Conversely, some people subvert intimate psychological contact by substituting sexuality for intimacy. A number of boundary problems were illustrated by Ms. T:

> A single woman in her late twenties, Ms. T spent most of each session denouncing her therapist in a loud, agitated voice. She could not explain why she came for therapy or why she contin-

ued to keep her appointments. She would regularly storm out of sessions, slamming the door behind her, only to return a few moments later because she had left her car keys or wallet on the chair. She claimed to be sexually disinterested and nonorgasmic, yet soon after meeting a man she would suggest they go to bed: "That's what you want, isn't it?" she would say.

Structure formation evolves from the delicate inter-dependence between early object relations and meaning making. This is what shapes the development of ego and self. Beginning with separation–individuation—the earliest object relations—ego and self functions evolve, differentiate, and are integrated into overall personality structure. However, ongoing differentiation and integration characterizes personality development over the entire life span. So, even though early experiences are the foundation of object relations, psychopathology at any point in life is a function of the current integrity of those intrapsychic processes. Egoself boundaries thus encompass not only the earliest structuring of ego functions and self and body images, but how these regulative processes have evolved over the person's life to the present time.

4. *Pathogenicity of Defenses.* Despite the variety of opinions about defenses, concerning those which are adaptive (Freud, 1926; A. Freud, 1936; Hartmann, 1950), pathogenic (Arlow and Brenner, 1964; Kernberg, 1967; Altschul, 1968), or vary according to situation (S. Sperling, 1957; Geleerd, 1965; Lowenstein, 1967), on one point there is consensus. Defenses which hamper other egoself operations are pathogenic. Thus, a relatively adaptive defense which wards off anxiety is pathogenic to the extent that it precipitates regression, interferes with concentration, or undermines self-esteem. Similarly, when a defense impedes ego development or distorts reality it augments psychopathology. The writings of Kernberg on defensive splitting and Vaillant's research on defense hierarchies illustrate this distinction. Thus, how a defense affects overall personality functioning is a major determinant of its pathogenicity. At the same time, the strength of defenses overall, and the character of individual defenses as they function situationally, is a necessary component of any clinical assessment.

Generally speaking, involuntary erosion or decompensation of a defense indicates serious ego dysfunction, a disruption of the organizing process. Erosion, fragility, or brittleness of defenses—in the absence of therapeutic intervention—presages further ego disruption and decompensation, and a person at risk. The clinical indicators of defense vulnerability are well known, and Bellak et al. (1973) have reviewed that extensive literature. The most pervasive signs of defense vulnerability are regression and personality constriction, when intrapsychic retraction is observed in several areas of functioning. Structural evidence is revealed by recent appearance of primary process operations; eruption of previously unconscious material; exaggeration and/or disruption of previously intact defense processes. Other clinical manifestations include: evidence of confusion or cognitive dysfunction in overintellectualized patients; eruption of nightmares, phobias, or diffuse anxiety in patients who repress, avoid, and deny; eruption of intense impulses or emotions, and acting out. In situations such as these either the actual risk, or the patient's anxiety over perception of risk, can overwhelm ego operations and precipitate crisis conditions. Active psychotherapeutic management is a necessity during periods of heightened defense vulnerability.

A thirty-five-year-old man who referred himself for therapy ostensibly because of a mild drinking problem became progressively more agitated and anxious as therapy ensued. Fantasies of crashing into cars while commuting home led to fear of traveling. But staying home evoked a claustrophobic reaction, as did working in his office. He began to have fears of killing someone, and fantasies of watching old women urinate. Acute anxiety about "having a nervous breakdown" gave way to thoughts about the safety of being institutionalized. His therapist offered to admit him as a voluntary patient and the client made an appointment to enter the hospital on his own. He walked up to the admissions clerk, stopped at the desk, turned around and went back home. Seeing his therapist the next day, the patient explained that he could not walk out on his wife just as her pregnancy came to term. He felt that the opportunity afforded him to make a choice about being hospitalized clarified his thoughts and strengthened him. The patient's symptoms rapidly dissipated over the next few weeks, he returned to work, and remained free of symptoms for the next three years. In this unusual case defense decompensation was apparently arrested when the patient was helped to confront a choice between regressive yearnings, ego-ideal expectations, and guilt.

Although defense vulnerability is a warning sign at any stage of therapy, as restructuring takes place vulnerability may signal an opportunity for growth. As Blanck and Blanck (1974) observe, the emergence of repressed material during psychotherapy may indicate that some ego building has already occurred. Effective psychotherapeutic management usually entails helping patients to relinquish defenses in favor of more effective means of functioning. During this delicate period of change sensitive monitoring and guidance are essential to therapeutic restructuring and growth. Gauging defensive fragility and its relationship to other structural components of the patient's ego operations is a major aspect of ego assessment during these periods.

In egoself terms, a well-defended patient is paying dearly for the benefits of adaptation. It is a clinical commonplace to observe patients whose symptomatic discomfort is less disabling than other areas of severe defensive constriction. A combination of effective repression and displacement may jeopardize the marriage of a man who cannot acknowledge his bitterness at working for his father and attacks his wife instead. Weekly therapy could take a number of directions: counseling the patient to find another job; exploring the history of the father–son relationship to surface the source of repressed conflict; examining the patient's view of his job and marriage to identify his adult priorities for therapy. It may turn out that marital problems are also being repressed and displaced, and that eliciting anxiety rather than avoiding it is a preferable therapeutic objective. In other words, defense pathogenicity is assessed relative to vulnerability but also with regard to its role in the psychic economy of the person's overall life.

5. *Regression.* In the assessment of severity of pathology it is appropriate to follow a discussion of defense vulnerability with its most common consequence, regression. Viewed as an assessment tool, regression is a valuable index of ego pathology. However, severity of psychopathology is not a simple function

of depth of regression. Rather, it is necessary to look at regression in the context of overall ego operations, differentiating its pathognomic presentation from other clinical manifestations. Some patients regress under minimal duress, and just as readily reconstitute their defenses. Regression is itself a defense, and a source of secondary gain in many instances. Regression in the service of the ego is adaptive, not defensive. Fluidity of defensive and coping structure is an important assessment consideration therefore. Regressive functioning is more specifically pathognomic in a context of defensive fragility or brittleness, where ego strength is problematic.

The relationship between regressive triggers, depth of regression, and extent of decompensation constitutes a triadic interaction of great value for clinical assessment. Triggering events may be objectively mild or major, highly specific with regard to time–place–person or widely variable. Depth of regression can be relatively independent of degree of decompensation. Two fathers, jealous of their newborn children, each regress to orally demanding levels. One father teasingly plays with his wife's other nipple as she breast-feeds their child; the other has a raging tantrum because his own dinner is delayed. For one father the regressive trigger is the sight of his wife breast-feeding; for the other, any time his wife attends to their child jealousy overcomes him. In this example, severity of psychopathology is proportional, not to depth of regression, but to the extent to which mild triggers precipitate significant decompensation.

Another aspect of assessing regression is the syntonic–dystonic dimension. Patients vary considerably in their tolerance for their own regressive reactions. The father who teases his wife might be acutely embarrassed to confront the regressive nature of his behavior; the enraged father might feel entirely justified in his neediness. A third man might react to the confrontation with intense guilt or shame. Personal comfort with how the regression is perceived, as syntonic or dystonic, impacts upon ego organization more than the behavior itself. Underlying this reaction is the patient's narcissism, and the extent to which it is pathologically structured. But even high-functioning people can suffer psychic insult to the extent that ego ideal representations experience affront.

Finally, assessment of regression should differentiate between regressive process and regressive behavior. The fundamental tenet that process underlies behavior is nowhere better applied than in the assessment of regression. The involuntary regressive process betokens psychopathology, dysfunction in ego operations. Severity of psychopathology is directly tied to ego decompensation which affects ego organization first, then manifest behavior. By contrast, behavior which appears regressive can reflect differing constellations of ego organization, depending upon its role within the overall psychic economy at the time. We are all familiar with instances of regression in service of the ego. In addition, passage across normal stages of life-span development can evoke episodes of regressive behavior reflecting adaptation to psychophysiological change such as those occurring at puberty, or in primipartum pregnancy.

6. *Restitutional Deficiency.* An egoself system deficient in restitutional capacity is an intrapsychic system at grave risk. Restitutional deficiency is signaled by evidence of rigidity, lability, brittle defenses, personality constriction, paucity of ego resources, inability to bind or safely discharge anxiety. More serious evidence comes from a history of continued impairment resulting from earlier mild to moderate problems, such as recurrent alcoholism dating back to job loss. Conversely, resilient response to adversity is a positive indicator of ego strength. In Heath's (1969) study of mature function the ability to handle anxiety, rather than the lack of anxiety-laden issues, was a distinguishing feature of his subjects. As in so many other areas of intrapsychic operation, restitutional capacity cannot be determined simply by assessing manifest psychopathology.

Effective assessment locates restitutional features in context with the totality of the patient's egoself operations. Pathological lability is found in severe psychopathology, but also in hysterical disorders; and, phenotypically similar manifestations of lability are normally expectable during certain developmental periods as well. What is the personality structure prior and subsequent to cycles of regression and restitution? Are the person's defenses fragile or permeable, primitive or relatively mature? What is the status of object relations development, and of narcissistic organization? Fortunately, the additional information needed is usually available from clinical observation and the person's history.

The most reliable indicators come from the person's history: What was the response to earlier emotional losses or injuries? Is there evidence of recovery to premorbid levels, compared to a lower level of function or continued decline? Were the reported changes cosmetic or did they reflect reconstitution of intrapsychic capacities? How has the person responded to previous psychotherapy? What was the extent and type of therapy? How do the patients account for their recovery or inability to recover? Clinical observation during the interview would note patients' response to specific situations: How does the person react after an ego dystonic experience in everyday life? What is the response to therapeutic interventions that challenge current beliefs? Simple acquiescence does not indicate resilience. Rather, it is the ability to absorb and recover from dystonic experience that denotes restitutional capacity or deficiency.

> A middle-aged man was referred for treatment of depression and alcohol abuse. He came to the first interview with clothing disheveled and fifty pounds overweight. The patient reported that his heavy drinking had commenced when his wife indicated she wanted a divorce. Further probing revealed a history of excessive drinking since adolescence, however. As a further complication, the patient admitted harboring recent thoughts of suicide. A lifelong history of poor achievement and interpersonal difficulties further clouded the prognostic indications. The patient appeared passive, apathetic, and expressed feelings of hopelessness for himself and his future. This grim picture was mitigated when the therapist asked if he had ever felt any better in his life. The patient immediately brightened a bit, and described his period of service in the Marine Corps and a previous course of psychotherapy. Further exploration altered the assessment from one which would recommend hospitalization to accepting the patient for weekly outpatient psychotherapy by virtue of the demonstrated evidence of restitutional capacity.

The principal importance of restitutional deficiency for ego assessment is its value as an index of limitations in ego plasticity. By itself, psychopathology has little to do with areas of conflict, as Hartmann (1939) observed long ago. "Subsequently the discovery was made that conflicts such as those we had come to regard as pathogenic could be shown also to exist in healthy people" (p. 308).

Where traditional psychoanalytic theory emphasized psychodynamic content, contemporary ego and self psychology and object relations theory emphasize structure. Thus, intrapsychic organization in reaction to distress, rather than the dynamic content of the distress, indicates extent of psychopathology. Plasticity, a hallmark of healthy structure, is addressed further in assessing chronicity.

Chronicity

A regular feature of egoself assessment for weekly psychotherapy is the structural change engendered by chronically disordered processes. The issue of chronicity is a somewhat different matter than etiology. Assessment of psychogenesis provides a basis for understanding primitivity of ego organization and its implications for therapeutic intervention. But the other part of that assessment is to ask, "What have been the consequences of long-term adjustment to the pathology?" However recent the onset of symptoms, it is a rare adult patient whose problems did not originate years or decades earlier. The developmental effects of adapting to chronically impaired self and ego structuring require clinical attention.

Developmental theory teaches that constancy is an abstraction, that all things change over time. In the human life span, rate and direction of change vary as a function of facilitative or inhibitory conditions. Dystonic experience can produce premature development, regression, or other pathological disruptions of normal growth (Blanck and Blanck, 1974). In every case, however, the adaptational thrust of ego operations is to create some form of intrasystemic equilibrium (Hartmann, 1950). The long-term effect of dealing with chronic disruptions of ego development is an ongoing process of psychopathological adaptation. Pathological formations are a composite of earlier disruptions of ego development and the effects of living with impaired functioning as development continues. These effects can be grouped under four headings: encrustation, habituation, internalization, and secondary gain.

Encrustation. Encrustation is characterized by a hardening, a rigidification of reactions. Defensive splitting, dissociation, and other forms of defensive walling-off, tend to produce characterological reactions which become progressively resistant to change. Unlike the fluid, evolving structures typical of early childhood these encrusted structures tend to become embedded as simplistic and self-perpetuating defensive reactions.

Habituation. Habituation is a more experiential feature of chronicity. As encrusted processes are repeatedly employed they become a routine, familiar mode of response. Adaptation to the disrupting affect is facilitated by familiarity with a routine reaction. Like other forms of simple conditioning, the response is learned by contiguous association and repetition (Hilgard, 1948). Cognitive, somatic, and motor pathways of response become subtly ingrained aspects of the person's awareness of self, conscious and unconscious.

Internalization. Internalization assimilates learning into the egoself structure where it is cathected as one of the mental representations of self (McDevitt, 1979). With continued experience the self representation may become further elaborated as a personality trait and an aspect of the person's identity. With these modifications the internalized reaction gains increasingly powerful narcissistic cathexis.

Secondary Gain. In this context, the meaning of secondary gain is extended to include the findings of object relations theory. In its traditional usage secondary gain is an aspect of the synthetic function of the ego (Nunberg, 1930), usually associated with some partial gratification of basic drives. In the present context secondary gain serves the broader imperatives of adaptation, as ego and self processes evolve from the assimilation of early experience. Clinically, ascribing this process to secondary gain accounts for the tenacity with which even inappropriate and counterproductive reactions are retained, long after their destructive consequences are seen by patients. In spite of the objectively ego dystonic character of the pathogenic reaction, it is experienced as ego syntonic due to its powerful narcissistic cathexis as part of the self. Later attempts to relinquish it in therapy are experienced as threats to the integrity of the self, and actually giving it up can be experienced as a serious loss.

Thus, chronicity results in the embedding of impaired operations into the developmental process, adapting to the limitations imposed but also incorporating them into the ongoing evolution of ego and self. The original impairment becomes part of organizational process, part of self structure, and part of the experienced self, one's identity. Ironically, the intractibility of certain chronic problems may be attributable to their assimilation into normal developmental process.

Primitivity

In locating primitivity last in this discussion of ego assessment we have come full circle. The original importance of object relations theory derived from the urgent need to find means of working with primitive disorders, which did not respond to classical psychoanalytic theory and treatment technique. As noted in previous chapters, object relations theory cast ego psychology in developmental terms, describing how organizational structure evolves over the early years and later over the entire life span. From its first formulations object relations theory emphasized the pathological formations of primitive ego operations, enriching our understanding of psychosis, borderline conditions, and narcissistic disorders. Primitivity thus has special meaning for the psychotherapist assessing egoself operations.

Blanck and Blanck (1974, 1979, 1986) eloquently trace the contributions to this extensive literature, reported earlier in this book. For present purposes, evidence of primitivity will be described as it is manifested in clinical context. Blanck and Blanck (1974) describe various types of ego primitivity:

1. Premature ego development, a "pseudo-self-sufficiency in which part of the ego replaces the symbiotic partner [with] concomitant absence of object cathexis" (1974, p. 340). Patients

describe an inner voice which is a split-off part of the unconscious ego, not an internalized other.

2. Ego distortion, characterized by negatively cathected self and object representations prior to differentiation of self and object. As a result the therapist will also be negatively cathected, viewed as a criticizing part of the patient's self.

3. Ego deviation, resulting from fault in the developmental sequencing pattern as it converges with biological maturation.

4. Ego regression, which, as the name implies, is a loss of previously acquired function rather than developmental failure or inadequacy.

5. Ego defects, which are constitutional, result in psychosis, and are untreatable because they originate in the undifferentiated matrix. They are characterized by the inability to enter symbiotic experience.

While they acknowledge these distinctions in early ego formation, Blanck and Blanck are less optimistic about efforts to diagnose differentially between what they call "prefulcrum" disorders of organization, those originating prior to the rapprochement subphase of separation–individuation. "Kernberg and Kohut are to be credited with having made bold forays into relatively unknown territory. It is our own opinion, nevertheless, that, at our present state of knowledge, it is premature to attempt to delineate specific diagnostic entities for which specific courses of treatment may be prescribed" (1974, p. 87). Nothing in their latest writing (1986) modifies this firm statement of position. Whatever the differences of opinion may be with regard to finely tuned diagnosis, the purposes of weekly psychotherapy are best served by familiarity with the features of egoself primitivity. The general characteristics of primitive organization have been enunciated by Werner (1940), Spitz (1959), Mahler (1968), and others. Rudimentary structuring, undifferentiated functions, and diffuse experience describe the basic character of primitivity. At the earliest levels there is an inability to distinguish between raw sensory experiences, including self and object. Organismic responses are reflexive and automatic, pleasure–pain reactions independent of time, place, or person, except for the mothering figure. Somatic and motor

responses are diffuse, unmodulated by environmental variations. Experience is autistic and symbiotic. Somewhat later, but
still within the primitive period, differentiation begins, permitting self and object representation and early ego processes
such as concentration and denial. Response patterns remain
rigid, lacking option, alternative, or reserve resources. Primary
process functioning is normative; the abilities to test reality and
defer gratification are nascent. Narcissistic cathexes are diffuse,
highly vulnerable to dysphoric experience.

Nevertheless, development continues. That is the law of
living things. But from this vortex of characteristics emerge the
features associated with primitive organization in adults. The
person functioning in a primitive way is relatively insensitive
to events or objects beyond the perimeter of immediate experience. Behavior is impulse-driven, fueled by pleasure–pain,
approach–avoid regulation. Since much of primitive behavior
patterning is preverbal, motor and somatic reactions predominate, and cognitive connection to these reactions is often absent. Ideation and imagery range from autistic to magical,
emphasizing immediate gratification or fearful avoidance. Reaction patterns tend to be simplistic, automatic, and resistive to
experience. Basic needs served by unconscious processes may
reflect little evidence of socialization or ego modulation. Awareness of consequences beyond immediate narcissistic pleasure–pain
is usually absent. Reality testing is weak or distorted. With these
data as baseline, manifestations of primitivity can be evaluated
in the individual case. But primitivity alone is rarely seen in
clinical practice, even with borderline and narcissistically disordered adults. The severely disturbed adult presents with an
amalgam of primitive pathological processes, as they have
evolved over decades of life experience. Interwoven are autonomous functions and those object relations which are, to a
greater or lesser extent, free of pathological influences.

Borderline and narcissistic disorders are distortions of ego
development and self structuring, which include the residuals
of primitive organization as affected by decades of life passage.
It is useful to recall that we are referring to pathologically primitive processes and not to primitivity per se. Primitivity is a
universal experience, selectively affected by subsequent devel-

opment. Accurate assessment differentiates pathological primitivity from other ego adaptations of primitive process, such as
regression in the service of the ego. Differential assessment
must also account for naiveté, immaturity, and cultural variations, as well as neurotic incorporation of primitive proccsscs.
For example, adolescent thought and speech are often polar-
ized and simplistic, descriptively similar to defensive splitting
but quite different in etiology and dynamics. Consistent with
general principles of development, in severe pathology primitive process is more closely bound to immediate experience and
less accessible to the consequences of experience, or the reality
principle in general. As a result it is reflexive, guided by pleasure principle dynamics.

The coexistence of pathological primitivity with other indices of high level function is best illustrated by those socio-
economically successful but personally miserable people who
seek therapeutic relief. They are often highly talented, sometimes endowed with great warmth and charm, yet their lives
are tormented by shame, self-hate, grandiose expectations, and
an incapacity to sustain enduring intimate relationships. Our
understanding of the dynamics of early object relations formation and the pathological distortions of narcissism associated
with them equip psychoanalytically oriented clinicians with
unique insight into these paradoxical syndromes. If our ability
to help these deeply afflicted people has not yet caught up with
our etiological understanding, we have at least learned to respect anew the exquisite complexity, plasticity, and sensitivity
of the developmental process. From their earliest structuring
to the elaborate sophistication of adult egoself operations, the
continuous thread is the active role people take in creating
pattern and meaning in their development and in their pathology. In assessment the clinician's task is to gain access to
that internal process. Understanding how it works in each individual case is our best guide to effective intervention.

ILLUSTRATING THE ASSESSMENT PROCESS

While most patients consider weekly psychotherapy to be somehow less serious than intensive therapy or analysis, therapists

confront the paradoxical situation of knowing that weekly contact is more difficult and runs greater risks than does intensive contact. Fifty minutes after the first meeting starts the patient leaves, scheduled to return seven days later. During this limited interview time the amount and kind of material disclosed is more subject to the patient's volitional control. Thus, the extent of pathology is more readily obscured, with a week intervening to permit resistances to resurface and distorted perceptions to fulminate. At the same time, there is less opportunity for the patient to build any counterbalancing trust in the new relationship. The perception of therapy tends to be more circumscribed. Even its financial impact is more dilute, typically covered by insurance at the outset. Weekly therapy is commonly thought of as potentially valuable, but not essential. Meanwhile, therapists are left with bits and pieces of clinical impression to synthesize. Fortunately, it is not the function of assessment to blueprint the therapy. The initial task is to evaluate whether the patient is suitable: assessing egoself operations, what dangers exist, how favorable the prognosis. The primary assessment considerations are structural.

> Mr. J was referred by a colleague. He arrived ten minutes early, dressed in a business suit and tie, smoked two cigarettes while waiting, offered a firm but moist handshake. Mr. J was young-looking, overweight, visibly uncomfortable, embarrassed and anxious. His first comments were, "I don't know what to say, you'll have to tell me where to begin; I don't even know why I'm here." He chose a chair directly across from the therapist, sat stiffly upright, hands folded tightly against his chest. Yet his face was soft, the lips faintly smiling, his eyes appealing for help.

Initial impact suggested diffuse anxiety in a young executive-type man. He appeared to be quite concerned about whatever was troubling him, yet disavowed knowledge or responsibility. Mr. J's postural behavior was consistent with this: passively beseeching help and defensively inhibited, constricted, perhaps repressed.

> After several gentle exploratory inquiries Mr. J reported that while at work the previous week he had gone into his office, closed the door, and suddenly burst out sobbing. At this point

he stopped, again looking beseechingly at the therapist. Further inquiry gradually elicited the information that the outburst had terrified him: "What's happening to me? Am I having a breakdown?"

The unexpected eruption of affect confirmed earlier impressions that Mr. J relied on repression and inhibition, defenses which had now been breeched. Yet he still needed considerable help to bring out these truncated reports, indicating vulnerability rather than decompensation of defenses. His meager emissions of material also suggested an underlying anal retentive character style, which was apparently intact. Structural analysis to this point indicated an episode of ego fragmentation, resulting in serious narcissistic insult and dystonia, but not severe risk. Rather than offer reassurance at this point, therefore, the therapist decided to use Mr. J's anxiety as leverage against his character defenses in order to generate further information. Considerable caution and careful monitoring were necessary, however, since the assessment was still in very preliminary form. The therapist was ready to provide explicit support to the extent needed. Meanwhile his nonverbal expressions of interest and concern provided an atmosphere of acceptance and support.

> *Th*: What was going on at the time?
> *P*: (Mr. J shrugged) Nothing. (The therapist chose the recent time context, seeking contiguous associations, but also assessing the client's more immediate awareness.)
> *Th*: Has anything like this ever happened to you before?
> *P*: No. (Now Mr. J's eyes seemed to glint, as though he was feeling some inner pleasure! Was the client deriving some secondary gain from his repression? Was it something more bizarre? Did the therapist misperceive?)
> *Th*: Then it must have scared you to break into tears suddenly, like that.

Patient showed little awareness, indicating a pattern of defensive blanketing or, possibly, further retentive resistance. Even the probing he has requested evokes defensiveness. Silently noting the strange glint, therapist chose to address the patient's fears instead. This circumvents the resistance, helps create an alliance, and permits exploration of how Mr. J handles affect he is aware of.

Mr. J's eyes watered and his face reddened. In a soft voice he responded, "Yes, it did." "What was that like for you?" The patient was puzzled by the question, and only gradually understood he was being asked to describe his experience. Over the next twenty minutes, aided by gentle questioning and his own efforts, Mr. J produced a series of phrases which concluded with, "Last Sunday was my thirtieth birthday; my life is half gone, and where am I?"

The therapist's empathic clarification of his feelings elicited a strong affective response, but little verbal content. Mr. J's personality is organized around a repressive, retentive style. Only a combination of support and active probing yields content. Either this man will require intensive therapy–analysis to address his underlying character pathology or weekly therapy will have to design a strategy to circumvent his passivity and inhibition. At the manifest level, Mr. J is apparently confronting a developmental crisis.

With about fifteen minutes left in the session, further exploratory assessment was discontinued in order to offer some impressions to Mr. J and discuss further plans with him. "I think the last thing you said—that you've just turned thirty and where are you—really got to the heart of what you've been feeling. But it doesn't say what is so upsetting about realizing that." The therapist then went on to recommend two or three more exploratory interviews, being careful to solicit Mr. J's reactions, impressions, and thoughts. An agreement was made to meet two or three more times, at which point there would be feedback and summary and a discussion of future plans.

The therapist focused on an explanation of the presenting problem as the patient's primary concern. The developmental crisis was immediately accessible to his understanding, and Mr. J showed little likelihood of comprehending issues that more fundamentally impaired his functioning. At every opportunity the therapist emphasized Mr. J's participation: using his words, soliciting his review of the material, requiring his decision, rather than urging his acquiescence, in considering further meetings. Mr. J agreed, eagerly, to meet again and left, seeming somewhat reassured.

The next session began with a brief silence. Still physically rigid but with a more cheerful expression on his face, Mr. J took the same chair and waited for the therapist to say something. "What was your reaction to last week's meeting?"

Mr. J's nonverbal behavior spoke volumes: his overt passivity, the contradictory messages of body rigidity and facial expression. To wait out the silence would underline Mr. J's responsibility but put strain on the tenuous relationship. The therapist chose to speak first, focusing on the patient's exercise of ego functions (perception, judgment, reality testing, self–object differentiation) rather than the more primitive pleasure–pain dimension that would be suggested by "how did you feel?"

P: (smiling winningly) Much better (he was silent once more).
Th: I don't know very much about you; why don't you tell me about yourself, what you're doing, how you grew up.
P: There's not much to tell—sort of a usual, you might say a boring life.
Th: Well, you know about it but I don't. So why don't you tell me.
P: There's not much to tell, I'm afraid; where do you want me to begin?
Th: Anywhere, it's up to you.

During the first interviews assessment takes priority over therapeutic process. The therapist notes but continues to ignore Mr. J's passivity (retentiveness, hostility?) in the service of learning more about the patient. His response to the first meeting was affective rather than reflective, suggesting very early issues. At the same time, his response was comparative rather than absolute, indicating relatively high levels of ego development (see chapter 7). Mr. J's reaction to his life is not simply resistive or retentive. It is also self-demeaning, suggesting a depressive core. The therapist continues to speak to the most developed aspects presented by the patient, calling up his expertise in the area of his own personal history and empowering him to use his own judgment in organizing his life experience for the view of another person.

Consistent with intervention strategy, the assessment period undertakes the tripartite task of evaluating pathology and egoself resources while simultaneously building a working partnership and establishing the guidelines for conducting weekly psychotherapy. While it would be inappropriate to preclude analysis or intensive psychotherapy at this point, it is imperative to begin using the principles of weekly psychotherapy.

> Phrase by phrase, sentence by sentence, Mr. J limned out a description of his current situation and then his developmental history. He described himself as "shy, someone who held back," the youngest of four children raised by alcoholic parents living in a small New England town. While the family was not economically deprived, emotional turmoil was prevalent. Mr. J learned early to remain inconspicuous in order to avoid the alcoholic tirades of his parents. His emotionally withdrawn behavior carried over into his interpersonal experience and at school. He grew up with a self-image of being "barely average" and chronically dysphoric. He began drinking at fourteen and joined a small group of boys like himself, whose camaraderie was based on drinking. A relationship with the parish priest inspired him to plan for college, but also augmented the guilt he felt about drinking. He was at present a retail store manager, living at home with his widowed mother, not dating, drinking more heavily, feeling increasing social isolation as his friends married and drifted away.

Mr. J's history reflected chronic affective blunting and social reclusiveness, rigid ego boundaries, and self–object differentiation, with withdrawal and constriction as primary defenses, alcohol abuse as primary gratifier, and repression and intellectualization as ancillary defenses. Reality testing was fairly intact except for an undertone of irrational self-criticism. His worklife achievements were considerable, particularly in view of his depressive affect and underlying low self-esteem. Through the second and third interviews Mr. J kept referring to himself as "average" and "nothing special." Only after close examination could he acknowledge that he privately assessed himself as deficient, and yet—as the youngest store manager in the chain—he was proficient in certain ways. He also expressed a fear of becoming an alcoholic like his parents. Thus far there was little upon which to base a hopeful prognosis. The chief indicators pointed to underlying character pathology, with a developmental crisis as trigger for his acute anxiety and depression.

Without therapy continued decline could be expected. The final assessment question was to explore the strength of his resources.

> The therapist asked, "How do you account for the fact that you were a successful salesman and got promoted to store manager at age twenty-nine?" After some resistance to this supportive confrontation, Mr. J could acknowledge that indeed he had earned the promotion. Next he was asked what he hoped to achieve from psychotherapy. He responded, "I don't want the second half of my life to be like the first half." Pressed further, he expressed a wish to stop drinking, meet some women, and stop living "like a vegetable." The therapist indicated his willingness to work with Mr. J toward these goals and therapy was formally instituted.

By the end of the third interview Mr. J's assessment had revealed a number of potentially recruitable assets. Autonomous functions were represented by the fact that he could persevere and advance through college and work, learning psychosocial competencies and applying them effectively. He responded effectively to confrontation—at least in the short term—by seeking therapy and then by self-exploration at the end of the third interview. His goals for therapy were appropriate and tangible, indicating a self structure capable of envisioning an attainable future. He could relinquish (however briefly) his inconspicuous, average know-nothing defensive facade. Finally, the constructive outcome of his earlier relationship with the parish priest suggested some potential for profiting from professional intervention, the capacity to internalize and reconstitute from contemporary figures the deficiencies in his early object relations.

The egoself approach to weekly psychotherapy relies heavily on the recruitment of intrapsychic resources from areas of healthy functioning. Consequently, assessment of resources figure every bit as prominently as does evidence of pathology. Assessment had provided a basis for recommending psychotherapy. Still, major areas of uncertainty remained, awaiting further exploration. An endogenous depression could not yet be ruled out. The countervailing pressures to grow and the regressive urge to stay in the parental path of alcoholism would have to be fleshed out. The patient's repressive–avoidance and passivity suggested he would terminate therapy once symptomatic relief was obtained. Was it feasible to plan for more extensive goals?

The patient was seen in weekly psychotherapy for twenty-three sessions over a seven-month period, then continued for an additional eleven meetings over the next eight months. During the summer when the therapist was away the patient chose to stop drinking on his own initiative and remained sober for the next year. He arranged a shift of work assignment from management to administration and also extended his social activities, including dating. While some modest improvement in self-esteem and confidence was noted, there was little other evidence of underlying structural change. The therapist anticipated that eventually Mr. J would require more extended therapy. In retrospect, it is likely that mobilization of egoself resources enabled Mr. J to move into the "second half" of his life and make psychosocial changes consistent with his own aspirations. Sufficient early individuation had occurred to permit character development, which included some pathological distortions. Moving into intensive therapy would require the patient to confront dystonic passive and retentive wishes, threatening his tenuous accomplishments in self-esteem. In view of his significant progress, the patient's resistance to further work, and the risks attendant upon moving into earlier pathology, Mr. J's wish to terminate was supported. Subsequent follow-up would help determine whether a continuation of treatment was indicated.

CHAPTER 7

DEVELOPMENTAL ASSESSMENT

Developmental assessment is an inevitable feature of every therapeutic evaluation. Psychoanalytic psychotherapists routinely explore early etiological dynamics in formulating treatment plans. Yet developmental assessment includes so much more. As we become attuned it will also become apparent that we intuitively utilize a variety of other developmental cues as a necessary part of the sense we make of the data presented by our patients.

The application of developmental theory to psychotherapy begins with developmental assessment. As the 1974 Conference on Psychoanalytic Education urges: "The longitudinal view of the patient as still developing has a further advantage. It focuses on the formation of psychic structure in process . . ." (p. 14). Developmental assessment addresses a number of salient clinical issues: What is the patient's developmental status, from the most primitive levels to the most advanced? What are the expectable issues, problems, resources? Are there developmental lines of ongoing difficulty, or are problems clustered in particular life periods? How are the later developmental tasks being handled? What is the operational status of autonomous functions, relative to the level of structuring of self and object representations? Which stage-specific resources are evident?

Unfortunately, few psychotherapists have been exposed to life-span developmental theory, and even fewer to its application to everyday clinical practice. One reason has been the paucity of literature in the field. Until recent times psychoanalytic studies have been directed to the earliest periods of the life span. As a result, research into life-span development has lagged behind. In addition, for reasons that perhaps date back to their own professional training, therapists tend to focus on the childhood years in their assessment of patients' development. It may be helpful to list some of the ways developmental assessment benefits therapeutic planning.

Faithful to the principle that psychoanalytically oriented psychotherapy treats the whole person, it is necessary to assess the person's normative functioning in ontogenetic perspective. Stage-specific expectations and tasks provide the context for evaluating patients' current level of functioning, along with other criteria. Describing someone as unmarried takes on differing connotations, depending upon whether the person is fifteen, thirty-five, or fifty-five.

Developmental assessment highlights areas of regressive vulnerability, such as body image problems in the later adult years. Of at least equal importance, developmental assessment can alert the clinician to current and potential ego resources, many of which become salient over the adult life stages. Familiarity with life stages and the developmental pressures inherent in them also helps the practitioner to recognize signs of incipient transitional crisis, and to anticipate patients' susceptibility to emerging life-span challenges. Recognition of stage-specific potentialities, such as the impulsivity and narcissistic exacerbation of early adolescence, can be central to the short-term management of intrusive events or assessing the efficacy of different treatment modalities.

Life-span assessment is not the only dimension covered in this chapter, however. An impressive body of research is concerned with reexamining the expectable differences that occur in gender development. Gender identity interacts with fundamental aspects of intrapsychic development, affecting the psychogenesis of psychopathology, its manifestations, and access to treatment. The perceptions and needs of men and women differ as well as overlap. Furthermore, gender identity is not an all-or-none phenomenon. Gender dysphoria produces a variety of pathological reactions, which sometimes create and always complicate psychotherapeutic activity. As social mores and systems change, customary sex roles and attitudes, including object preferences, also undergo degrees of transformation. The assessment of psychopathology can depend upon the assumptions made about which definitions are sociologic and which are based on a developmental understanding of intrapsychic operations. The psychological status of homosexuality, for example, cannot be reduced to a legalistic definition any more than can the diagnosis of psychosis. Gender development and gender identity are therefore significant issues in developmental assessment procedures.

A third major parameter of developmental assessment concerns its hermeneutic status, its interpretive meaning. Development is a process in which the person's ongoing participation is a distinctive feature. In the course of living through the developmental experience, people also shape the meaning that the life course holds for them. In turn, those perceptions color the process itself, interacting with self and object representations and influencing the person's world view. This inner meaning of the developmental process is called the developmental mode (Bocknek, 1984). By understanding this inner meaning therapists gain a more empathic understanding, aiding the alliance and guiding intervention strategy. The patient who views life as a struggle for sheer survival, for example, may be unable to consider personal fulfillment. The patient who "only wants to be happy" may not have internalized mastery and competence as part of the life process.

PARAMETERS OF DEVELOPMENTAL ASSESSMENT

It is rarely necessary for practitioners to redesign their usual assessment procedures in order to include developmental material. In large measure, the therapist's perspective simply expands, like the expert photographer who routinely adjusts his camera lens to enhance the quality of his pictures. Colarusso and Nemiroff (1981) suggest a number of developmental lines for tracing major themes across the adult life stages: intimacy, love, and sex; the body (as image as well as physical capacities); time and death awareness; relationship to children; relationship to parents; mentor relationships; relationship to society; work;

play; finances. It is apparent that most of these issues would emerge spontaneously during the preliminary assessment interviews. Colarusso and Nemiroff recommend noting the chronological evolution of these developmental lines as the material emerges. They also describe an outline for developmental history which begins with pregnancy and continues through adolescence. In addition, they describe three major adult stages and "the dynamic adult developmental tasks that roughly occur within these arbitrary chronological demarcations" (1981, pp. 199–200).

As we know, simplistic indices such as chronological age or physical appearance do not adequately estimate developmental maturity. The practitioner recognizes that developmental status subsumes a number of psychodynamic and structural parameters. While these parameters are interrelated, they can function relatively independent of each other. Social development does not predict intellectual development, although both are probably related to ego development. Assessing developmental status is like assessing other multidimensional constructs. While the concept is commonly used as though it was a discrete entity, there is general recognition that is comprised of several factors with varying degrees of functional relationship to each other. In this sense, developmental status is derived as the interaction of life-span location, gender, and developmental mode.

Developmental assessment typically describes a range of functioning. The functional capacities of the individual may vary between developmental modes and across several developmental stages. The verbally articulate executive may become a juvenile stutterer whenever he tries to express tenderness. The primitive street kid may have a sophisticated adult's ability to differentiate between the stupor of an alcoholic and the lassitude of a heroin user. Both the manager and the urchin divide their lives in the service of survival, mastery, and potentiation, manifesting both early and mature developmental operations. For the clinician these variations in functional capacity are often the most significant aspect of a developmental assessment. An optimal evaluation should, therefore, include an assessment of highest, lowest, and typical developmental functioning, and of the conditions under which these variations are likely to occur.

LIFE-SPAN ASSESSMENT

Over the past few decades, a body of information pertinent to life-span assessment has begun to form. Longitudinal studies of adult development (Vaillant, 1977; Gould, 1978; Levinson, Darrow, Klein, Levinson, and McKee, 1979) demonstrate significant intrapsychic changes, consistent with Erikson's (1950) earlier position that psychological restructuring occurs throughout the life span. For clinical purposes, a graphical representation of the life span can be a convenient aid. Such a model is guided by the principles enunciated in chapter 9: ongoingness, sequentiality, stage-specific prepotencies. As Levinson (1986) notes, such models need to reflect universal patterns, and account for decline as well as growth. Colarusso and Nemiroff (1981) apply an assessment orientation to life-span analysis, focusing on several developmental lines as they are manifested in late teens and onward, over the adult life span. The developmental lines include intimacy, love, and sex; the body; time and death; relationship to children; relationship to parents; mentor relationships; relationship to society; work; play; finances. Examples of how each of these developmental lines may present across the life span is shown in Table 7.1.

While a number of life stage models already exist, for clinical purposes I have adapted an earlier schema (Bocknek, 1980) for use in egoself therapy and assessment. This model is provided in Table 7.2. Each life stage is identified by its distinctive features on each of three dimensions of psychological activity: intrapsychic issues to be encountered, key interpersonal relationship needs, and mainstream cultural expectations. These dimensions reflect central realms of developmental experience and are structured in ways that readily present in clinical material. Consistent with psychoanalytic precepts, the model depicts expectable issues, and not necessarily what is observable behavior. By virtue of focusing on psychological processes, rather than manifest behavior, the therapist is alerted to what may be avoided or repressed, latent or potential, as well as what is most apparent. While gender, culture, or class differences may well affect how an issue is engaged, this model describes what is believed to be human readiness across the successive life

TABLE 7.1

Colarusso and Nemiroff Model of Developmental Lines

DEVELOP- MENT LINE	LATE TEENS AND EARLY 20s	20s AND 30s	40s AND 50s	60s AND 70s
Intimacy, Love, and sex	Capacity for tender caring	Ability to share children	Redefinition of relationships	Tolerate loss, and death
The body	Devel. physical abilities		New body image	Phys. decline
Time and death	Awareness of personal history	Time, awareness	Death of loved ones	Prepare for own personal death
Relationship to children	Ability to care for, nurture	Love, set limits	Interact with growing children	Grandparent-hood
Relationship to parents	Forging a separate identity	Adult–adult relationship		Care for aging parents
Mentoring	Role as a mentee	Loss of mentor and passing on the torch		
Relationship to society	Change, improve society	Accept society		Adapt to social change
Work	Identify and develop skills	Work ident.	Use power, skill	Retire, transfer power
Play	Participate and enjoy	Play as release		Development as mastery
Finances	Supporting oneself	Attitudes and use of money		Plans for money

stages. In keeping with the mission of applying developmental theory to weekly therapy, the model reflects the fact that most of the life span takes place after childhood, and that most patients are past childhood.

The life stages are described by their encounter with three fundamental dimensions of psychological development, represented in the columns. The intrapsychic issue is a developmental challenge with which the organism must come to terms. As natural aspects of the person's experience with self, these issues are not necessarily problems to be solved or conflicts to be terminated. Instead, they can be thought of as facts of intrapsychic life to be lived with, assimilated, and understood. The intrapsychic issue is the least overt and most universal of the dimensions listed. Because it is generated by the person's encounter with self, the intrapsychic issue is less accessible to the influences of acculturation and is therefore the most consistent feature of developmental experience.

TABLE 7.2
Life-Span Development by Stages

STAGE	DIMENSION		
	Intrapsychic Issue	*Interpersonal Focus*	*Intracultural Expectation*
Infant	Separation–individuation	Mothering figure	Tolerance for anxiety, loss
Childhood			
Early	Mastery	Parental figures	Accommodation with authority
Late	Gender identity	Primary group	Social role
Juvenile	Competence	Community	Role exploration
Adolescent			
Early	Identity and sexuality	Peers	Heterosexual initiation
Late	Resolution of identity	Inspirational figures	Life plan experimentation
Young adult	Self-particularization and ego integration	Intimate joining and separating	Founding a family Building career
Established adult	Effectuation	Everyone	Sustaining the social unit
Middle-aged adult	Self-confrontation	Personifications of life issues	Maintaining and mentoring
Senescent adult	Death	Remembered ones	Retirement

Acknowledging that human development is inextricably embedded in interpersonal experience, the interpersonal focus defines the life-span passage by systematic alterations in the saliency of particular figures. Certain kinds of human inter-action have special relevance during particular life periods. By referring to figures I mean that the person will find or create, to the extent possible, the human equivalent needed for that developmental purpose. Thus, a sister ten years senior to a small boy may be a mothering figure during infancy, an erotic object when he is adolescent, and a peer in established adult-hood. These modifications of perceived roles reflect basic, stage-specific, developmental needs: for parenting, gender differentiation, relating to people who are older or younger, male or female. These needs are present in every epoch and culture. The process of interpersonal development is part of human natural history, vital to the fueling of object relations throughout the life span.

The intracultural expectations column is based on the mainstream expectations of our own society, recognizing that even that boundary line challenges description. Faced with seemingly limitless variations of social structure and culture content, one is hard put to generalize about universal cultural expectations. But, while the mores of societies are diverse their purposes are not. The culture that does not serve human needs does not survive; the culture that does not insure its own perpetuation either changes or disappears. In these fundamental considerations all societies share kindred expectations: organization and structure must be sustained; new generations must be produced and brought to maturity; the required social and technical skills must be replenished, by the young with the aid of the old. As a result, certain learnings must be universally expected even though others are more specific to a culture and time. Table 7.2 lists those intracultural expectations which seem most dominant in our society, some of which are undoubtedly universal.

But even the best efforts to describe universality fall short of the richness of human diversity. To meet the demands of a workable model comprehensive detailing is subordinated to organizational clarity; similarity is emphasized at the expense of uniqueness. Faithful to the belief that weekly psychotherapy is becoming more diversely accessible, the model is designed for broad applicability—across the boundaries of race, gender, culture, and geography. If theories are made to be modified, utility is the yardstick for measuring the fit between precept and practice. If clinicians are to use egoself psychotherapy in diverse settings with diverse populations, the model must be adaptable to those needs.

The depth and breadth of the life span can only be highlighted, not covered, by this model. It is intended to supply just enough material to acquaint the practitioner with the signposts for a life-span assessment. More extensive detailing of each life stage, even within the limits of present knowledge, would extend this book intolerably. Acknowledging these constraints, we continue.

Infant

Of all newborn creatures, the human neonate is the one most poorly equipped for independent survival at birth. The neonate's biological helplessness is also the determining psychological fact of its life. At whatever level of awareness it may have, contending with survival is paramount. Central to this diffuse experience is its linkage with mothering, the holistic nurturance which literally seems to shape the structure and tone of the earliest experiential representations. Inevitable ingredients of the infantile period are its experiences with whomever provides the mothering it requires, and what it learns about tolerance for the unavoidable frustrations in its nurturance. These experiences inaugurate the earliest object relations. In addition, they initiate the infant to frustration and anxiety in a world that will require their ultimate management. As Mahler points out, it is not the objective conditions alone, but how they are experienced by the infant, that ultimately determine their impact on development.

Child

The transition to mastery begins long before any awareness of it. Mastery is based on awareness of self and nonself distinctions, so that the child can learn to connect its volition with its actions and then with the consequences of its actions. The precursor to mastery, then, is the advent of motility and, probably, the beginnings of speech. Anyone who has observed small children sees the delight of the child with its newfound capacities. But these skills also enable the child to encroach on its surrounding world, risking danger to itself and provoking others to set limits. This stage is a natural setting for self–world conflict, between the demands and dangers of the environment and an exploratory child who acknowledges no limits. For the future of both the child and its culture, the optimal resolution is an accommodation in which each party recognizes the valid claims of the other. Accomplishing this difficult work falls to the child's caretakers, since this is the critical task of parenting. Setting limits without squelching initiative demands a high order of delicacy and patience. Moreover, it is an entirely different sort of role from the nurturance of mothering. In most societies the parenting function is distributed among several people, who thus participate in the child's first experiences with authority.

For most of human history the everyday work in a culture has been sex-typed. Sex roles and expectations are imparted to the child from birth on, and are eventually assimilated into awareness in late childhood. Establishing a gender identity has, at the outset, less to do with anatomy (Money and Ehrhardt, 1972) than with the personal, social, and interpersonal significance of having a defined place in one's primary group. As an intrapsychic organizer of who one is, gender identity assumes early and lifelong potency. The child's growing ability to differentiate the significant figures in its primary group enhances its own growth and sharpens its relationship to these persons. Play, which has been called the working world of children, is the natural milieu for gender and generational differentiation. Some of the first formal rules and regulations are also experienced at this time. While rules are taught as part of the socialization process, they are internalized as components of emerging self and object representations.

Juvenile

This third life stage is a period of expansion. Earlier developmental acquisitions are extended a step further. Discrete skills are now integrated into coordinated competencies. Personality traits, talents, and liabilities are more pronounced. Self-image is closely linked to one's sense of competency, but tends to be experienced in vague, general terms. But because of the linkage between competence and self-image, capabilities need to be developed and recognized. There is an expansion of interpersonal contact and awareness, beyond the home and into the local community. A wider array of adult and peer models is encountered, extending social learning significantly. With greater abilities, widened perspective, and social expansion comes the challenge to meet others on a different plane of interaction, that of cooperation. (Competition, by comparison, probably originates in the mastery strivings of childhood.) Learning to participate in sharing, to subordinate oneself in a group effort, develops relatively late in humans. Yet it is absolutely essential to social living. Juveniles who are unable to achieve a cooperative relationship with peers will often seek the experience with an accessible adult. In either case, the juvenile can be expected to encounter and explore various social roles in the local community.

Adolescent

While puberty is recognized universally, and in many cultures is attended by an initiation ritual signifying a coming of age, there are still parts of the world where adolescence is not acknowledged. As a result, behavior attributable to psychological development may be attributed to sexual development instead. Other reactions, rebellious behavior for instance, may serve the developmental needs of distancing from family, but may also be a subcultural initiation rite. Sex, drugs, or petty theft may serve this ritualistic purpose in some communities.

Whether culturally acknowledged or not, adolescence is a life stage in all cultures, whether it begins before or after puberty in the individual case. Psychologically the most dramatic features of adolescence are those which are intrapsychic: the disruptions of the identity crisis; the ongoing struggle to incorporate strong, unfamiliar impulses, including the explicitly

sexual. These pressures strain ego resources, leaving the adolescent vulnerable to affective lability and impulsivity, heightened narcissism, and withdrawal or acting out. Ideals, values,
and goals emerge. The focus of interpersonal relations now
shifts to peers. Peers provide alternative standards to those
traditionally offered by parents and other adults. Thus peer
relations facilitate development toward adult self-regulation.
Meanwhile, cultural pressures urge the individual toward preliminary exposure to heterosexuality, in preparation for later
mating and reproduction. Latent issues of sexual preference
or gender identity are likely to surface at this time, for those
young people whose inner experience is not consonant with the
dominant sociosexual ethos. Either way, compatible or not,
whether conscious or repressed, heightened sexual awareness
is a dominant theme of adolescence.

During late adolescence the person's intrapsychic issue is
the resolution of the identity crisis, reestablishing a sense of
basic psychological coherence. Adolescents frequently identify
with a person, or an attribute of a person, as an inspirational
symbol for their own lives—an organizing focus for their emerging sense of identity. Some of the stresses of adolescent development can be deferred when the young person makes an early
identification with an inspirational person or activity. But later
complications tend to result if this "identity foreclosure" (Marcia, 1967) inhibits personal exploration. In most societies, people in late adolescence are expected to be well along toward
fulfilling the expected social roles. In our culture, this period
is usually considered to be a time of trying out life roles. It can
also be a time of acute psychosocial alienation, particularly
among racial and ethnic minorities, when opportunities for role
exploration in the mainstream culture are not available. Life-
threatening and antisocial behaviors can be the consequence of
this felt exclusion.

Young Adult

Adolescence is thought to end with the emergence of a coherent
sense of identity. The intrapsychic encounter with young adulthood moves identity formation forward, to detail the ingredi-

ents of one's identity and organize them, centrally and hierarchically, into functional and structural wholeness. These are the processes of self-particularization and ego integration (Bocknek, 1980). Taken together with full physical maturation and a dawning sense of being adult, a compelling sense of personal capability is also achieved. Interpersonal relations develop toward more complex peer contact, learning to create relationships which provide gradations of intimacy yet permit the continuing development of each partner's individuality. Amid this intrapsychic and interpersonal activity, young adults move increasingly into the secular world, drawn by their energetic idealism as well as by cultural expectations. The universal cultural imperative is to create and provide for a new generation. In our culture, this imperative is translated into the mandate to found a family and build a career.

Surfacing of the capacity for personal perspective (including an observing ego) typically dates from this period. Readiness for innovation and change flourishes in young adulthood. The dualism of adolescent thought has developed into a capacity for acknowledging the plurality and relativity of ideas and opinions. The capacity for mature commitment evolves at this time (Perry, 1970). A more comprehensive understanding of the surrounding world begins to emerge. Despite being psychologically and physically adult, however, acceptance into the adult social structure tends to lag behind.

Established Adult

A period of settling into adulthood is the next stage (Super, 1957; Levinson et al., 1979). Established adults face the intrapsychic challenge of implementing their acquired competencies, across the full range of personal and cultural expectations. Now fully accepted as adults, they also shoulder much of the burden for making the social system work, functioning as its experienced front line officers. Idealism erodes under the pressures of everyday pragmatism; the perceptual lens is narrowed and focuses on the tasks of providing for a stable, dependable life. Established adults deal with everyone: children, parents, partners, competitors, males, females. While they are not the major decision makers of their society, their close contact with its daily operation enables them to make small changes as part of maintaining it. Internalization of social norms and standards as necessary and useful commonly occurs during this stage, and qualities such as commitment, responsibility, and practicality are highly valued. The day-to-day running of a culture's social and economic subsystems is largely dependent on the competence of its established adult cohort. Sociocultural demands upon the adult are greatest at this time. During this period people are vulnerable to the "midlife crisis," when everyday reality falls short of their expectations.

Middle-Aged Adult

The self-confrontation of middle age is distinctive because of its retrospective casting—"What have I done with my life?" rather than "What am I doing?" or "What will I do?" The confrontation acknowledges that youth is gone and aging has begun. One witnesses dying parents, and children becoming adult. The stage-specific facet of interpersonal relations is its symbolic quality; people represent personally meaningful issues and principles: "Sue was so popular—is she happy now?"; "If Jan is so successful, how have I been different?"; "Was I a good parent? Was it worth it?" Confrontation successfully addressed frees the person to continue or redirect life, often with new enthusiasm. Conversely, denial or flight may put the person at risk for physical or emotional breakdown. Cultural demands slacken at this stage of life; maintaining oneself, economically and physically, is the primary expectation. Age and experience may reap a certain respect and status. Cross-culturally, people in middle age gravitate toward advisory activities, applying what they have learned to the task of "passing the torch" (Vaillant, 1977). Middle-aged people are inclined to take on a tutorial role, acting as mentors to younger adults who are entering situations in which the older person has had long experience. In this way the work of cultural maintenance and continuity is accomplished between adults, similar to the way that parents are the mediators of culture for their children. As middle-aged people become aware of time's passage, quality of life issues may become more salient for them.

Senescent Adult

As one's peers die and disappear, and as one's own body gives unmistakable signs of erosion, people come to face the imminence of their mortality. The psychological fact of one's dying and death is compelling, and working it through is the intrapsychic issue of the last stage of life. Death strikes at the core of narcissistic self-esteem, each person's need to feel significance. By facing biological finality, senescent adults engage in a review of their lives. People are remembered as they were, and reminiscence becomes an important developmental tool. As the life-span attenuates, confronting the meaning of death assumes greater significance. The cultural and personal freedom potentially available through retirement can only be impeded when death remains a fearsome specter. Continued development in senescence is contingent upon coming to terms with the naturalness of dying. Unlike abstract reasoning, which seems to decline over the lifetime, reflective judgment and acquired knowledge can continue to expand as a result of extended life experience. Moreover, these cognitive skills harmonize well with developmental proclivity. The historic traditions which associate aging with wisdom find application in the overview on human affairs that senescent adults can provide.

Senescent adults must contend with the loneliness that often accompanies the loss of friends, relatives, and partners. As they confront personal death they also experience a psychological distancing from the everyday patterns around them, as though conserving their energies for more selective investment. Continued activity—cognitive, social, sexual—is essential to further development. When retirement, the cultural expectation, means enforced passivity, it accelerates deterioration and death.

APPLYING LIFE-SPAN ASSESSMENT

This synopsis of the life stages is a grounding point for life-span assessment. More detailed understanding of specific life stages will vary according to the specialty needs of each therapist. But this synoptic view can be fruitful for purposes of preliminary assessment. Sensitivity to stage-specific expectations provides the clinician with material for appraising patients' range of developmental activity, and overall maturity. We become so accustomed to looking for the signs of early pathology that the variability of functioning across the life span can sometimes be neglected. In therapeutic planning for weekly psychotherapy, it is often necessary to target those issues which are accessible to intervention within time and money constraints. Assessment of the patient's developmental *potentialities* becomes particularly important under these conditions.

> Ms. L was referred for treatment of agoraphobia. She was a black woman of twenty-three, married and the mother of two preschool children. She was living in the same neighborhood where she grew up, went to school, and was gang raped at age sixteen. After that trauma she remained housebound for about six months, in terror. She eventually returned to high school, graduated, met her husband, and married. The husband, a TV repairman, insisted that she be subservient to his wishes. Onset of symptoms was traced to her discovery that her husband's depleted paycheck was due to heavy use of "reefers." She had a horror of marijuana use, associating it with degeneration and depravity. Despite her pleas, her husband refused to give up smoking. Of late he had become less attentive to the children and generally erratic in his hours. Ms. L was becoming increasingly anxious, waiting for him to come home, and looking for telltale red eyes when he walked in. She was afraid to leave the house because she didn't know what he might do if he returned to find the apartment empty. She was also afraid to leave the children with a baby-sitter, fearing he might abduct them. She also feared meeting her neighbors, who were sure to have recognized the telltale signs of his drug use. Finally, she was afraid to run into her father, who lived nearby, fearing he might do something violent to her husband for upsetting his daughter.
>
> Life-span assessment revealed a woman centered in the young adult stage. Despite her experiences with violence from men she had been able to meet and marry a man, and build a stable family life for several years—significant accomplishments. While her thinking reflected the absolutist dualism of adolescence, resolution of her identity had been achieved by choosing among options. As further evidence of her adulthood, she also had fairly keen awareness of her priorities in a number of key areas, indicating ego integration. She could examine her feelings about men, and how her relationship with her husband had

evolved, reflecting a good sense of personal perspective. With supportive attention focused on her wants and priorities, her sense of enforced passivity gave way to an active examination of her situation, and what avenues were available to her. She began to assess her marriage, and to confront her husband with her concerns for their future—her first priority. She gave thought to her own work options and reactivated her longstanding interest in clothing design. She renewed her determination to move out of the ghetto, away from the city, and to an area where she could find work in the leisure clothing field. Ultimately she arranged to place her children with her mother, while she moved to a section of California which was a center for leisure clothing design. Her husband agreed to join her with their children after she got settled.

By traditional standards the developmental assessment was incomplete. An appraisal of her current developmental functioning received as much attention as exploration of early history. On the other hand, the patient's current egoself structure seemed reasonably intact. Egoself operations, the healthy and the pathological, were assessed using indices described in chapter 6. The connection between current symptoms and her agoraphobia following the adolescent trauma was acknowledged but not explored.

Descriptively, the therapeutic strategy with this woman reads like typical supportive intervention. But the approach utilized, to begin therapy by recruiting her developmental strengths, is consistent with weekly egoself psychotherapy. Perhaps a number of strategies would have been equally effective with her agoraphobia. But the egoself approach worked by helping the patient to grow, not simply reconstitute defenses, in her marital relationship, with her talents, in her life-style. Building upon her resources—well-delineated self structure, fairly intact ego operations, young adult status—rather than addressing the psychopathology or its etiology, proved to be effective. Her decision to relocate was neither flight nor simple environmental manipulation, but the outcome of close elucidation of the meaning of her marriage, her aspirations for herself and her children, her feelings of being hopelessly caught in the cobwebs of her childhood. For assessment purposes, examining this material revealed much about her intrapsychic function. The design and enactment of her plans were far more bold than any therapist would venture to suggest, but not unlike those observed in other young adults. As impressive as the symptom remission in evaluating outcome of therapy was the intrapsychic mobilization necessary to enact these changes.

But using the same basic approach could equally well have revealed grandiosity and the structural inability to conceive or implement options in someone with more pervasive pathology. The advantage of developmental assessment is that potentialities as well as pathology are surveyed.

Life Stage and Psychopathology

Just as weekly contact dilutes the intensity of therapy for patients, its effect on assessment must also be acknowledged. Weekly contact also means that therapists see more patients, and have proportionately less opportunity to reflect on each one. More time in each session is spent on "settling in" and on reporting manifest material, such as events and experiences of the week just past. These factors have an adverse effect on assessment, which must probe to understand the underlying processes. One common risk is that in gathering material for the assessment therapists may have insufficient data for differentiating between genuine psychopathology and other behavioral manifestations.

We have come to recognize that cultural or personal styles may mimic pathology, as when patients are not verbally oriented, or are emotional and voluble. Sloppy, mismatched clothing can be a current fad rather than a sign of inner chaos. But stage-specific attributes can also mimic pathology, or otherwise interact with pathological manifestations. In adolescence, for example, the presence of apparent mental confusion, affective lability, and a tendency to think in polar extremes may be developmentally normative if it is transient or situational. The meandering and ruminative thought process of a senescent adult may seem pathologically resistive to therapeutic intervention if one fails to recognize that reminiscence and the remembered past are part of the adaptive development of older people.

Pathology can interact with life stage to affect therapy in other interesting ways. Therapeutic efforts can be impeded or augmented as a function of the patient's pathological processes interacting with prepotent life-stage features.

> Mr. K was a single man just entering his thirties. His idealistic aspirations were consistent with someone still lodged in young adulthood. But it soon became clear that Mr. K's idealism also masked grandiose fantasies, so that he was caught between imperatives to act and being immobilized by the impossible extremes his pathology created. Whenever his idealistic fantasies were explored he would resort to the angry accusation that the therapist was trying to make him compromise his ideals. With the passage of time, established adult pressures to concretize and implement his aspirations increased, among his friends and within himself. Using a combination of self-soothing and coping developed in therapy, Mr. K became more willing to risk the terrors of narcissistic humiliation by finding small-sized, practical ways to take action in the everyday world. The subsequent reduction in his grandiosity was in part attributable to a shift in this man's developmental readiness, as a function of life-stage transition. Undoubtedly the therapeutic work helped to move that necessary transition ahead. In this instance, therapy and developmental growth enhanced each other's progress.

Insight into the resources and risks inherent in each life stage becomes yet another tool in the therapist's armamentarium.

GENDER ASSESSMENT

What was virtually unthinkable a generation ago is now becoming a psychological commonplace: exploration of the person's gender status. As noted previously, gender development covers identity, sex role, and sexual preference. Helping people to come to terms with their sexuality, heterosexual, homosexual, bisexual, transexual, has become a part of everyday clinical practice in weekly psychotherapy. Gender and sex-role related issues range from frank psychopathology to problems of developmental adaptation and actualization. Pathology may occur etiologically, concomitant with, or as a consequence of, coping with gender and sex-role factors. Specific sexual perversions such as pedophilia, sadomasochism, and voyeurism are excluded from this discussion.

Gender assessment is premised on the recognition that roles, preferences, and identity are much more complex than was previously believed. The awareness of other than heterosexual commitments can occur throughout the life span, and shifting from one status to another may be developmental or exploratory, transitory or permanent. Unlike other developmental phenomena, however, gender development seems not to follow predictable sequencing. For instance, a person presenting as transvestite may be permanently committed, en route to transexualism, or exploring a homosexual preference. Finally, the distinction between pathological and healthy seems to become less clear as more is learned about human sexuality. Excepting those activities which are patently abusive or exploitative, or where the psychopathology seems evident, the scope of gender development may be much wider than has heretofore been acknowledged.

With the realization that gender status is a developmental matter comes the expectation that it can undergo change. However, fear of social disapproval encourages people to disguise anything that is not traditionally heterosexual. Sex role stereotypes are zealously maintained in most societies. The following short histories may suggest something of the evolving character of gender problems as well as their range and profundity.

Mr. B was an obese forty-six-year-old, bald and homely. Twice married, he was depressed, alcoholic, and threatening suicide. Previous psychotherapy had brought some symptomatic relief, and he was accepted for treatment. Gradually Mr. B revealed that he had nourished since childhood the wish to be female. Eventually he stated that he believed he was female "inside," even though he was anatomically male and had fathered two children. At home he often wore women's clothing, and experienced a great "inner peace" whenever he did so. Two years of weekly psychoanalytically oriented psychotherapy revealed much of the early etiology of his status, identification with women, and fear of becoming a man. His depression improved but his gender dysphoria and alcoholism remained the same. He lost jobs and his drunken driving cost him his license and a brief term in jail.

Mr. B. found a physician who agreed to give him female hormones if he lost weight, since the hormones elevate blood pressure and his was already high. He lost fifteen pounds, began taking the hormones; instead of rising, his blood pressure dropped further. Mr. B bought a blonde wig, trained himself to speak in a soft voice, outfitted himself in female clothing, and began living as a woman. He stopped drinking and found steady work. Therapy terminated after four years, with now-Ms. B settled into a community, stably employed, and an active church member. Egoself function retained underlying self-recriminatory aspects, sporadic impulsivity, and residual problems with self–other distancing. Repression, rationalization, denial and withdrawal were prominent.

Two years later I was contacted by Ms. B. She had arranged for transexual surgery, with a reputable physician. There would be full castration, plus the creation of a functional vagina. She wanted to see me for a few months in preparation for the surgery. I agreed, suspecting that the impending surgery might free some still unresolved issues and negate the need for surgery. Instead, Ms.B began reporting what turned out to be a series of dreams. Over the next three months Ms. B used her dreams to reconstruct her life. In reverse chronology she relived a number of significant events: her most recent job, interacting with her children, college, the Marine Corps, back to a childhood event we traced to age two. In each dream, her associations led to an autobiographical event or person. In each dream Ms. B was, or became, female. Ms. B seemed to be reconstructing her autobiography in her dreamwork, to correspond to her new identity. The dreams associated with surgery reflected a level of anticipatory fear which seemed consistent with the seriousness of the procedure: being on a landing craft with other Marines during World War II, as they were storming an enemy stronghold: fearful of what might happen, yet determined to go ahead.

She went through the technically difficult operation and recovery without complication. Five years postsurgery Ms. B was still gainfully employed, living alone, celibate, and sober, still active in church work, still obese, rarely depressed. She occasionally sees one of her two children, now adult. She is content, as never before.

The next case balances the spectrum:

Ms. G is nineteen, with the rich black hair and eyes of her Latin heritage. She was referred by her college counselor because of episodes of blackout and fainting. Following a neurological review with negative findings, Ms. G was evaluated for weekly psychotherapy. Raised in a strict, ethnic, Roman Catholic home, the patient was a model of goodness who attempted to tailor her behavior after her chosen saint. In college, her behavior earned derision rather than approval, and she found herself progressively more socially isolated. Even her roommates began to avoid her. At first she could tell herself to be tolerant of their lack of understanding. Then she grew dismayed and depressed, all the while maintaining her outward pose of saintly good humor. The incidents of fainting and fugues began around this time, with no earlier history. Ms. G rarely dated, admitting to being wary of boys: "They only want one thing." Other girls' descriptions of sexual involvement further confirmed her sense of being odd. Her primary ties to family, sexual naiveté, and preference for group social activities suggested a preadolescent developmental status. Evidence of early pathology was negative. Gender identity and sex characteristics were clearly feminine.

Therapy was geared to helping Ms. G to relax her repressive defenses and to encourage exploration of her underlying feelings and fantasies. Her problems seemed to be of classical hysterical origin, although supported by an ethnic family infrastructure. As the patient became more expressive and self-aware, she reported having intense erotic feelings toward one of her roommates. This woman, slightly older and more sophisticated, never dated. Thus the two roommates were often alone in the dorm on weekends. As Ms. G haltingly began to show her affection, the other woman allowed her to become close. Emboldened by her efforts, Ms. G arranged for them to sleep together one night, and initiated sexual activity. In therapy we talked about the explosive release of her sexual feelings, which she came to recognize as orgasmic. Shortly after the discovery of her orgasmic potency, Ms. G reported her surprise and pleasure at meeting and conversing with a young man from a nearby college. She and her roommate gradually pulled back from their sexual contact and the relationship with the male student grew. He eventually broke off with her, but not before a sexual experience in which she was once again passionately aroused and orgasmic. Shortly afterward she terminated therapy, confident and eager about pursuing a traditional heterosexual life. Her lesbian love affair seemed to have served a developmental function, providing what was for her a safer way of exploring her emerging sexuality, and moving from child to adult. It is reminiscent of what Symons (1979) describes as normative homosexuality for juvenile boys in one Polynesian culture.

There has been an increase of interest amongst clinicians in the role gender plays in developmental health and growth. The relationship is complex, and it is not always clear how cultural, historic, and psychological imperatives enhance or confound that relationship. How does one differentiate female need for connection from symbiotic fusion, or healthy from pathological dependency? How does the therapist working with a gay man differentiate pathological promiscuity from behavior prejudicially denigrated by a homophobic culture? Fortunately, the tools of intrapsychic assessment are more free from bias than is the labeling of manifest behavior. The entire psychic economy must be included in the assessment to determine whether the reaction is disruptive, reflective of structural distortion, or developmentally appropriate.

> A sheltered workshop offered physically disabled adolescents an opportunity for their first paid employment, doing various low skill jobs. Within three weeks the adolescents had labeled each job as either "men's" or "girl's" work, independent of skill or difficulty level and despite the fact that older workers of both sexes worked on all the jobs. Sex-role typing of jobs seemed to be in the service of these adolescents' needs to affirm their own gender identity status, necessitated by their impaired body image.

Thus, a program designed to provide a career-orienting experience was preempted by more basic needs for gender role differentiation in this group of body-impaired adolescents. Another factor that may well have contributed to this narrower view was their way of viewing their own development, that self-in-world perspective referred to as developmental mode.

Developmental Mode

Assessment and interpretation of developmental status depends upon the recognition that there are distinctively different ways of conceptualizing development, based on how the person conceives his or her own place in the world. I shall describe three of these modes: *adjustment, adaptation,* and *actualization,* showing how they differ experientially and in their practical implications. Their essential features are also presented in Table 7.3.

The three modes of developmental orientation share the constructionist assumption that people are the producers of their own development (Lerner and Busch-Rossnagel, 1981). Development is therefore conceived as an ongoing process of engagement between organism and environment. The three modes have as their primary point of differentiation a teleological distinction. The adjustment mode is oriented to survival; the adaptation mode is in the service of mastery; the actualization mode is in the interest of personal potentiation. Each mode will be described by its distinguishing method of operating, the self–society relationship it implies, the goal(s) it seeks, the psychological gains provided by those goals, and the psychopathology risks most commonly associated with them.

Key to the adjustment mode is that development is geared to adapting oneself to environmental demands. The person feels unequal to the task of surviving alone in a powerful world. The method characteristic of adjustment is that of conforming to the expectations and requirements of the social, cultural, and physical environment. The relationship between self and society is dominated by the ethos of socialization to the culture's roles and customs. The goal of developmental adjustment is social acceptance of the individual. With this acceptance the person

TABLE 7.3
Three Developmental Modes

	ADJUSTMENT	ADAPTATION	ACTUALIZATION
Teleology	Survival	Mastery	Potentiation
Method	Conformity	Encounter	Exploration
Self–Society relationship	Socialized	Challenged	Self-directed
Goals	Acceptance	Competence	Fulfillment
Gains	Security	Confidence	Peaks
Risks	Anomie	Psychopathy	"Madness"

gains security—the protection of group membership and a sense of belonging and place. But by immersing oneself in the larger entity and merging with it one risks isolation from oneself, the loss of personal identity, anomie. Apathy, depression, and suicide are possible pathological consequences. The example of the handicapped adolescents cited above illustrates the adjustment orientation to development.

The adaptation mode can be described as a striving to balance or overcome environmental obstacles and pressures relative to personal wants. The individual pursues personal development, ready to modify both self and world in the service of these objectives. Environmental demands evoke assertive reactions. Hence, the method used in adaptation is one of encounter: what am I trying to achieve? What can be done about it? In the relationship between self and society, challenge rather than submission or withdrawal is characteristic. The individual strives for parity or ascendance in the social structure, a common feature of modern industrial societies. The goal achieved in successful adaptation is that of competence, being capable of having an impact on the world in one's own behalf. The single most powerful psychological gain is that of confidence: in oneself, one's place in the world, in one's developmental directions. Carried to a pathological extreme, the developmental risk is to be able to manipulate the environment without scruples or regard for the consequences, psychopathy and the grandiosity that may be associated with chronic abuse of power.

The actualization mode is characterized by seeking maximum realization of potential capacities. The method employed is to explore, probing at the frontiers of whatever seems possible. In relationship to society the person is self-directed, and, therefore, somewhat distanced from social standards. The goal of actualization is the fulfillment of one's potentialities, an unending process of discovery and disappointment. Consequently the rewards are less stable than in the other modes. Typically they take the form of the "peak experiences" which Maslow (1954, 1962) described as characteristic of self-actualizing people. But the chronic dissonance between the achieved and the perceived, between social expectations and personal directives, can put the person at psychological risk. *Madness* is a literary term which describes an existential state of anguish, one which may be psychotic, but which more often reflects the acute disharmony felt with self-in-the-world. As a clinical manifestation it is most frequently presented by adolescents and young adults. Narcissistic grandiosity can also blend with or be masked by the actualization mode.

By now it will be apparent that this tripartite classification describes developmental patterns only, and is not intended as a personality typology. The assessment and interpretation of any individual's behavior is likely to reveal all these developmental patterns at one time or another, in one area of function or another. These developmental modes provide a basis for understanding a patient's self–world orientation as it relates to motivations and perceptions. It can help account for why one person cannot say what is expected from therapy while another seems to ignore obvious pathology and focuses on high-flown aspirations. Construed as a set of working hypotheses, the chart can be used as a template for assessment in the planning and timing of treatment interventions.

Teleological models are vulnerable to criticism on grounds of reification and/or anthropomorphism. However, the constructionist view of development is founded on the premise that ontogeny is neither a biological unfolding nor the social conditioning of a passive organism. Rather, constructionism takes the position that development is patterned and purposeful. Behavior is conceived as intentional and not simply reflexive. Human function is internally organized and directed, initiating activity as well as responding to stimulation. The developmental modes proposed here are, therefore, appropriately teleological. Human behavior, except for brief periods, is rarely without purpose. The interpretation of human behavior must, therefore, acknowledge and incorporate its intentionality. Adjustment, adaptation, and actualization fit within those guidelines.

Applications

Faced with complex and sometimes imponderable issues in conducting a developmental assessment on the one side, and pressure to reduce therapeutic time and cost on the other, the practical demands of weekly psychotherapy would seem to weigh against any further investment of interview time. Developmental assessment, however desirable, may seem too time-consuming. In actual practice, the psychoanalytically trained therapist may find that time is saved by a developmental assessment. The observations and information needed for egoself assessment, including developmental assessment, tend to be less obscure to the patient and thus more spontaneously produced than the genetic dynamics traditionally probed for. And, when egoself intervention can focus on contemporary events and processes, as described in chapter 4, therapeutic time may be reduced as well.

METHODS OF DEVELOPMENTAL ASSESSMENT

Most assessment interviews provide inherent opportunities for the assessment of developmental status, including mode, life stage, and sex role. Some aspects of gender status require more extensive information. In general, the knowledge and orientation of the interviewer can be as important as the interview content. Consequently, developmental assessment often entails little more than an expansion of focus, as the clinician integrates a developmental perspective with the familiar evaluation of the material presented. Interview data can be categorized under four headings, each of which contributes to the assessment of developmental mode, stage, and gender/role.

Physical Presentation

While chronological age can be a significant developmental marker in childhood, it becomes progressively less accurate thereafter. Physical presentation, however, is a viable indicator of many facets of developmental attainment. The patient's physical appearance is accessible to observation throughout the interview. It provides the therapist with data about the intersection of physiological development with clothing style, cultural norms, and life-span location. Physiological development can be inferred from unobtrusive visual inspection: body contour, proportion, and musculature; skin texture; posture; hairiness; voice quality; facial expression. In most societies clothing style is linked to gender and cohort grouping: garments and ornamentation may indicate the wearer's personal preferences and/or socialization to local customs. Social status exercises as powerful a force as cohort membership. But cultural expectations also sanction what is appropriate dress for young and old, male and female. Finally, life-stage issues can be inferred from comparing dress and grooming with physiological indices, and estimated age.

Initial impressions of developmental mode obtain from comparing the patient's dress and styling with reigning cultural patterns for that person's gender, age range, and social position. Does the attire suggest conformity, innovation, or indifference? The prepubertal sixteen-year-old who looks like his mother dressed him provides a wealth of developmental data in a glance. Within the cultural context, what messages does the person's physical presentation convey?

Role Activities

The patient's psychosocial role activities provide a wealth of developmental data. This information usually emerges as a part of the self-descriptive statements provided in any standard assessment: marital–parental status; educational and occupational history; family history; sexual and social history; leisure activities; attitudes and beliefs. An important item is habitation style: With whom does the client live? What is the history and durability of these relationships? These data have the advantage of being readily available, and of relatively low threat value to the patient. Indications of mode derive from the picture that emerges: Are the patient's activities dominated by response to the imperatives of others? How compatible are the roles with expressed desires? Do they comply with, exceed, or ignore current role proscriptions? Important clues to patients' developmental status can be drawn from the person's work history. Comparing expectable levels of experience in the world of work with patients' attainments and aspirations can indicate how they construe the world and their place within it.

Competencies

The patient's acquired competencies are an important indicator of developmental status. The skills that are learned or not learned during the life course are a rich source of information about the texturing of the person's developmental experience: gaps as well as acquisitions. This information is revealed by attending to ongoing behavior as well as past history. The acquisition of competencies is presumably a joint function of developmental readiness, the expectations of significant others, and personal proclivity. Patients are often unaware of some of the most important psychological competencies they have acquired. Inadvertently acquired skills often go unrecognized or underappreciated. Thus, patients are less likely to report the ability to work cooperatively and also less likely to be aware of its relevance to their self-appraisal.

The assessment of developmentally appropriate skills often entails sensitive observation and probing by the practitioner. This is one of those areas where the patient's self-knowledge can be significantly augmented by the astute clinician. Thus the distinctive feature of developmental assessment is not its data base but the therapist's readiness to interpret that material in developmental terms along with its usual clinical meaning. The same assessment and uncovering skills used in revealing pathology are applied with equal effectiveness to the assessment of developmental status and its component resources.

As a final issue, with specific pertinence to weekly psychotherapy, developmental crises are an important source of clinical problems. Attunement to the nature of these forms of crisis is another benefit of a developmental orientation.

DEVELOPMENTAL CRISES

Throughout the life span, developmental crises generate clinical disorders. There are several kinds of developmental crisis:
1. *Reaction to an Impending Life Stage.* The person antici-

pates a forthcoming stage, fearful of what it will bring. Examples include death anxiety as one enters senescent adulthood, aware of one's infirmity and the deaths of one's peers.

2. *Reluctance to Leave a Gratifying Stage.* Loss, depression, and anxiety may be precipitated by an awareness that one can no longer continue as one has, that a secure and satisfying period has passed. Birthdays, anniversaries, and holidays can evoke memories, real or idealized, of earlier, more gratifying periods.

3. *Trauma of Unanticipated Developmental Change.* The advent of an awaited developmental phenomenon can bring with it unexpected and disturbing side effects. The homemaker's anticipated liberation from the demands of parenting are deadened by loneliness and the sounds of an empty house. As a general feature of development, an increase in freedom and autonomy is often accompanied by a dystonic sense of personal isolation and responsibility.

4. *Unresolved Earlier Issues.* To the extent that one meets sociocultural expectations of appropriate role behavior it is possible to obscure intrapsychic developmental issues which have been incompletely addressed. Assuming the roles of spouse and parent may present the appearance but lack the substance of intimacy, loving, sharing. Earlier developmental issues, such as self differentiation, trust, and cooperation, may not be tested until adult tasks confront the person. The discrepancy revealed, between manifest behavior and psychological deficiency, is one of the prime sources of self-referral for psychotherapy.

5. *Cumulative Erosion of Energies.* The sheer energy requirements of a new developmental demand may precipitate a breakdown of function when previous life experiences have depleted the person's psychological resources. Further strain on an ego-self system already extended to its limits can trigger a dramatic developmental crisis. In these instances, the specifics of the precipitating circumstances or the developmental vulnerability may be irrelevant. Any new developmental demand would exceed the person's tolerance level.

6. *Positive Growth Experience.* Sometimes adults discover satisfactions in a new period of life that alerts them to chronic characteristics or conditions which have been impeding their

lives. The impediment may be an endogenous characteristic such as passivity or an exogenous condition such as a denigrating job. In either case, the salutory impact of new developmental experience contrasts with chronic conflicts, earlier unresolved issues, or old dissatisfactions, challenging the person to confront what had been previously accepted.

Developmental crises can precipitate reactions as mild as situational anxiety or as severe as psychosis, depending upon the underlying intrapsychic structure, among other things. In many cases, the problem is contemporary rather than of early origin, and amenable to intervention which focuses on the current situation. This application of the developmental perspective to patients' presenting problems is consonant with the recommendation of Colarusso and Nemiroff (1981) that: "diagnosis and treatment focus on the current, phase-specific, adult developmental tasks as well as the residue from earlier experiences" (p. 217). In weekly psychotherapy developmental crises can be an opportunity for decisive short-term intervention which is rarely encountered by those who practice intensive therapy or analysis. Incorporating the skills of developmental and egoself assessment can make the difference between appropriate therapeutic work, which promotes structural change, versus palliative support which may only defer the need for restructuring therapy.

CHAPTER 8

EGO, SELF, AND OBJECT RELATIONS: THEORY

The next step is to separate clinical theory from the more general psychoanalytic theory of personality and pathology. It has been observed (Greenberg and Mitchell, 1983; Eagle, 1984) that similar patients are identified as schizoid, borderline, or narcissistic depending on the theoretical orientation of the clinical investigator. These distinctions are rooted in observations of psychopathology, usually among patients who are analysands. Often the issues under dispute are linked to clinical application: analyzability, the role of insight, the use of interpretation, empathic contact. But while clinical theory has direct relevance to psychoanalytic practice, the same issues may be inappropriate or peripheral to the mandates of weekly therapy based on psychoanalytic personality theory. Conversely, the richness and comprehensiveness of psychoanalytic personality theory has wide application to the diversity of problems reflected in the people who request weekly psychotherapy. The interfusion of ego, self, and object relations becomes even more important at the point we meet our patients, as adults. To fully understand the operation of their pathology, and how to effect restructuring, it is necessary to trace the postchildhood development of these systems. The latter section of the chapter examines that evolution.

The problems of creating a theoretical synthesis which includes drive and object relations theories, and ego and self psychologies, are enormous, perhaps insuperable. In the light of current knowledge, some aspects, such as the origin and nature of psychic energy, may truly belong in the realm of metapsychology. But by detaching the clinical issues of psychoanalysis from those of weekly psychotherapy based on psychoanalytic theory, a functional synthesis seems approachable. As I have already indicated, object relations, ego, and self are concepts whose origin and usage suggest clinical and theoretical congruence. To take the matter one step further, such a synthesis harmonizes well with the role of teleology in contemporary psychoanalytic thought. From its origins as a drive theory powered by the pleasure principle, the consistent historical task of understanding how structure and meaning are created seem to describe current thinking as well.

EGO PSYCHOLOGY

The shift in psychoanalytic theory, from a psychosexual focus to ego psychology, was a major step in Freud's dream of creating a general theory of human development. In addition to the internal modifications of theory this shift entailed, modifications which are extensively discussed elsewhere (Hartmann, 1958; Rapaport, 1967; Blanck and Blanck, 1974), the advent of ego psychology established a common vehicle of understanding which linked psychoanalytic thought with the broad data base of mainstream scientific psychology. Personality theory, developmental and social psychology, learning and perception theories, could now be applied to psychoanalytic thought and vice versa. The explanatory constructs of psychoanalysis vitalized many dormant areas of experimental psychology, which were bodies of data unconnected to other constructs. The concepts of repression and defense mechanism gave new direction and meaning to the laboratory study of retroactive inhibition and perceptual vigilance, for example. At the same time, experimental research on cognitive function, problem solving, and early development elucidated gaps in psychoanalytic understanding of normal development and learning.

The effect of this impact on the psychoanalytic schools and on scientific psychology has been to permanently affect the shape and direction of both. A thorough tracing of the history of ego psychology would overreach the purposes of this book. Instead, I will note the more significant modifications, and how they have influenced contemporary theory. The work of Anna Freud (1936) made clear that the role of ego operations was broader than that of satellite to libidinal vicissitudes. With the historic discovery of spheres of conflict-free ego function (Hartmann, Kris, and Lowenstein, 1946) the staging was put in place to conceptualize ego as a system of functions which organizes and regulates major personality functions. The hydraulic grounding of Freud's dualistic drive theory required an energy source for ego operations. But reconceptualizing ego as a predominant force in the personality was inconsistent with viewing its energy as derivative from id sources—whether directly or from the neutralization of decathected libidinal objects. Neither of these explanations could account for the sheer quantity of effort expended by the functions now ascribed to ego activity.

Three alternatives were proposed as systematic explanations. Hendrick (1943) and White (1963) have suggested that there are drives toward mastery, or effectance, drives which are pleasure-generating but which seem to be in the service of ego activity. While these concepts have clinical utility, they appear to complicate still further the place of drive theory by suggesting the necessity for modifying the existing dualistic theory or creating additional drives. In turn, these issues raised further questions about the supposed nature of the energy system, by altering existing drives and their relationship to personality development. A second alternative, suggested by Hartmann, is that the autonomous ego functions develop from an "undifferentiated matrix" of instinctual energy, a reservoir with the prepotent capacity to shape maturation of personality structures. The concept of an undifferentiated matrix provided a parsimonious explanation for the sources of psychic energy, a construct which simplified rather than complicated that aspect of psychoanalytic theory. In addition to clarifying the source of ego energy it freed theorists from the necessity of reducing all other observable events to either libidinal or aggressive origins. It had the further virtue of moving psychoanalytic theory from its biocentric base toward a posture which could more readily accommodate the data of human interaction as they influence early development. While psychosexual theory embodies the dynamics of human interaction, its toning fails to erase the impression that life experience is subordinate to the vicissitudes of biological maturation. The third alternative was the most radical. This is the approach taken by object relations theorists, who subordinate both drive and ego autonomy to the role of early experience in the formation of personality (Horner, 1979).

OBJECT RELATIONS THEORY

Object relations theorists hold the view that the primary mother–child dyad forms the base upon which subsequent psychological development is built. The infant's early mothering experiences evoke images which become internalized as mental representations (Sandler and Rosenblatt, 1962), and become the organizational framework for the evolving ego system. While they originate in the infant's earliest interpersonal experiences, object relations are separate from the actual experiences. Object relations are the mental representations of those experiences, processed by the organism's rudimentary organizing capacity and then becoming part of that processing capacity. The progressive accumulation and patterning of object relations form the child's earliest and most enduring images of self and others. Early ego development is predicated upon the efficacy of these organizing experiences.

Freud's initial use of the term *object* referred to whatever in the environment was targeted for instinctual discharge, the cathected object. Thus, object meant, and continues to mean, not just anything but that which the organism invests with value. The primacy of psychosexual stages in determining the course of development is muted or bypassed in object relations theory, although most theorists avoid direct confrontation with this issue. As knowledge unfolds in this area, the genesis of the interaction between psychobiological determinacy, ego development, and dyadic experience will undoubtedly be amplified.

Object relations theorists currently derive from two major

camps, sometimes referred to as the English and Middle European schools. The English school incorporates writers such as Klein (1948), Fairbairn (1955), Winnicott (1958), and Guntrip (1961), and is reflected in the writings of Sullivan (1953). The influence of Klein is also seen in the writings of Kohut (1977). This group describes the human organism as innately "object-seeking," and locates the roots of health and pathology in the quality of the infant's experience with mothering. Psychosexual theory is recast as libidinal urgings shaped by the mental representations of self and other derived from early mothering. Within the English school, the role of psychodynamics (such as oedipal conflict) is emphasized in explaining the etiology of psychopathology. In this regard it remains closer to earlier Freudian psychosexual formulations, whereas it is schismatic in its rejection of the primacy of instinct theory. Klein theorizes that the ego is formed and functioning at birth, reacting to reality and creating an inner world of fantasy based on its earliest object relations. She writes: "In my judgment, reality and real objects affect the child's anxiety-situations from the earliest stages of its existence" (1932, p. 302).

Fairbairn extended further the primacy of object seeking relative to psychosexual development:

> According to the conception of erotogenic zones the object is regarded as a signpost to libidinal pleasure; and the cart is thus placed before the horse. Such a reversal of the real position must be attributed to the fact that in the earlier stages of psychoanalytical thought, the paramount importance of the object-relationship had not yet been sufficiently recognized [1952, p. 33].

As this line of thinking is developed further by Guntrip, early object relations become the formative basis for personality and psychopathology. The psychosexual stages virtually disappear as crucibles of experience, and personality formation is linked with eight "minimum irreducible types of object-relationship," of which the last "is the goal towards which the psyche is growing through all the earlier forms, and it implies a full capacity to live in creative and loving ways with one's fellows" (1961, p. 375).

In comparison with separation–individuation, the English

school also emphasizes the centrality of the child's dependence upon the mother, but describes an ideal outcome which focuses on "mutuality, spontaneity, co-operation, preservation of individuality and valuable differences, and by stability" (p. 377). The basic similarity between schools of object relations is seen in Guntrip's summary statement that "the root cause of all pathological developments . . . is a fundamental ego-weakness, established as a persisting structural phenomenon in the earliest stages" (p. 418).

The Middle European school is associated with the works of Jacobson (1954), Spitz (1959), Mahler, Pine, and Bergman (1975), and Kernberg (1975), and reflected in the writings of Blanck and Blanck (1974, 1979). In these formulations, early dyadic experience provides the base upon which the structure of ego development is formed. Emphasis is upon ego as an organizing system, a system which may become distorted or incomplete depending upon the child's experiences in the first months prior to its "psychological birth" (Mahler et al., 1975). Psychosexual development, which emphasizes psychodynamics, is not rejected, but attention is focused on the importance of ego structure for theory and therapy. But the object relations thinking of the Middle European school tends to locate personality development and psychopathology more vividly around the "fulcrum" of the third year. As presented by various authors (Masterson, 1972; Blanck and Blanck, 1974; Horner, 1979) the most severe forms of psychopathology originate from disturbances during the subphases of separation–individuation, while neurotic problems occur with people who have achieved "psychological birth," the establishment of the ego's organizing processes. Developmental diagnosis is centered on efforts to locate the early origins of pathological ego development with particular attention to the status of object relations. According to Kernberg:

> [P]sychotic patients have a severe lack of ego development, with mostly undifferentiated self and object images and concomitant lack of development of ego boundaries . . . borderline patients have . . . differentiation between self and object images to a major extent and with the development of firm ego boundaries in all but the areas of close interpersonal involvement . . . and

neurotic patients present a strong ego, with complete separation between self and object images and concomitant delimitation of ego boundaries [1975, p. 39].

Kernberg's position is extended by Horner, who provides a charting of diagnostic syndromes which are directly traceable to specific processes of subphase development. The position of Blanck and Blanck is more conservative on this point; however, "one can no longer treat the adult as though development stopped at a certain point early in life and can now be resumed with the therapist. . . . It is usually impossible to designate exactly where subphase problems originated. To try to pick up and repair there is equally impossible and is likely to be simplistic" (1979, p. 123).

Object relations theory is further bolstered by Piaget's research in the cognitive development of children, which comes to similar conclusions about the role of early mental representations but from an entirely different methodological base. But clinical practitioners require that a theory have practical application, however solid its conceptual base. By demonstrating the interaction between experience and organizing structure, object relations theory offers a prime rationale for the technique and efficacy of a psychotherapy rooted in the dynamics of human experience. More specifically, object relations theory targets ego operations as a major area of emphasis for intervention strategy. The complex relationship between ego operations and object relations becomes clearer as investigation proceeds. It will become apparent that ego operations and object relations are interdependent throughout life. The basic principle, that intrapsychic development is shaped by the interaction of organizing processes with ongoing experience, is a clinical truth for adults as well as for children (Colarusso and Nemiroff, 1981).

EGO PSYCHOLOGY AND OBJECT RELATIONS THEORY

From even this abbreviated review it becomes apparent that the advent of ego psychology virtually coincides with the emergence of object relations theory. This historical convergence was not coincidental, however, since both trends evolved from the continuing development of psychoanalytic theory. With this evolutionary step, one which places experience ahead of innate forces, it became necessary to consider the nature of the relationship between ego and object relations. What is their genesis, and how do they influence each other? A further complication is due to the growing attention given to the concept self. Ongoing study of narcissistic disorders, and the paradoxical relevance of narcissism for self-esteem in healthy development, drew writers such as Kohut (1977) to argue for the centrality of self as a determining influence in growth and pathology. Kohut's self psychology reactivates the relevance of earlier self psychologists such as Murphy (1947), Rogers (1951), and Sullivan (1953).

Previous discussions described object relations as an ego function, implying the primacy of ego organization in personality development. But this view was discrete from both the Kleinian view of an innately formed ego and the undifferentiated matrix posited by Hartmann, fitting neither exactly. The primacy of ego seems more logical than empirical, particularly when contrasted with the data base of object relations theory, which derives from the child development research of Piaget and Mahler. These observations led to the position that ego organization was the result, not the cause, of object relations. As Horner puts it, "This shift from an ego psychology to an object relations theory reflects the emphasis on the central role of object relations in the overall structuring of the ego" (1979, p. 6).

Controversies over the primacy of ego or object relations will remain metapsychological or speculative until those processes can be better observed and studied. For present purposes, however, one need not pursue this path further. The convergence of data and theory points to interdependence in the development of ego, self, and the evolution of object relations. From the recognition of this functional interdependence comes a far-reaching understanding of the nature of ego operations.

The intimate, evolving interconnection between ego operations and object relations, beginning in the earliest life stages, explains why each human's intrapsychic organization is so privately individual, and so vulnerable to the viscissitudes of individual experience. The general form and content of early experience can be estimated by the skilled observer, but its unique inner impact is even more obscure. To confound matters further, this microcosmic interdependence evolves in a macrocosmic life space of nutrition, biophysiology, culture, and random chance. Structuring the meaning making, in this expectable context, can only be understood post facto, as the organizational consequence of interactions beyond calculation. Yet, these consequences are the evolving systems by which people operate. For the psychotherapist, therefore, these organizational consequences are the appropriate subject of study and object of intervention.

The emerging system ego imposes pattern on the raw data of sensorimotor stimuli, creating as well as discovering order; in part producing its own development. As Piaget describes it, the child's earliest activities create sensorimotor schemas, internalized mental representations which shape and pattern subsequent experiences. Each schema is composed of affective as well as intellectual components (Flavell, 1977). This description accounts for differentiation in object relations theory, as the earliest self and object images are distinguished and organized (Jacobson, 1954). As patterns are organized, ego operations assume form and function. The character of its experiences, and its excitation thresholds, influence the child's structuring of its experience. In the ongoing flow of Werner's (1940) orthogenetic development, differentiation is followed by integration: the hierarchical organization of structurally and functionally interrelated components under centralized regulation. This corresponds to what Hartmann describes as fitting together; assimilation and accommodation in Piaget's terms. Patterned organization becomes meaning making, which is further integrated into the organism's evolving conceptions of self, other, self-in-the-world. In its dual thrusts, ego as organizing process and ego as meaning maker, contemporary ego psychology becomes a major partner in the enterprise of tracking the human life span.

SELF PSYCHOLOGY

Psychoanalytic self psychology grounds early development in the interaction between child and parenting figures. The self which emerges is created by the child's "transmuting internalization" of the parents as selfobjects. By means of this empathic communication the child progresses through the grandiose and idealizing stages of development. Healthy development through grandiosity (primarily in relation to mother) evolves into self-esteem, ambition, and assertiveness. A healthy interaction with idealization (primarily in relation to father) is conducive to strong ideals and values. A cohesive, stable self core can emerge from either of these polarities. Disorders of the self (Kohut and Wolf, 1978) are attributable to developmental deficiencies in parenting during these stages, resulting in narcissistic behavior and personality disorders. Kohut and his adherents believe that psychoanalytic treatment based on empathic interaction with patients permits the evolution of mirroring or idealizing transference, and the "empathic clarification [which] promotes differentiation and structuralization" of the self (Stolorow and Lachman, 1980, p. 170).

Self theory offers an accounting of how the organism is organized, how it comes to know itself, regulate itself, and develop into the future. Structurally self has come to assume a superordinate role within the personality, according to Kohut and his followers. Like ego, self is defined by those agenting functions involved in directing and organizing behavior. Self theory departs from drive theory by laying primary emphasis upon relational experience in the genesis of personality and psychopathology. But Kohut stops short of disavowing drive theory. He leaves moot the relationship between narcissism and basic drives, while highlighting the developmental role of narcissism. His impact on psychoanalytic practice has been dramatic. He has asserted that primitive disorders are treatable with psychoanalysis, but that successful treatment requires analysts to build structure through empathic contact rather than through affectively detached "hovering" and insight, through interactive experience rather than interpretation. Kohut's exegesis of self is clearly differentiated from classical drive theory.

Kohut is entirely correct, moreover, in his criticism that ortho-dox theory does not adequately account for the "self-expressive or creative man"—for ambition, ideals, values, and interests. Comparisons with ego psychology and object relations theory distinctions are more vague, however. When these ideas were surfacing Kohut was most deeply immersed in the clinical in-cubation of his own theory, and his references to object relations tend to focus on his disagreements with Kernberg over clinical issues. While he acknowledges ego psychology, he disparagingly describes its termination criterion as "the degree of accretion of knowledge" (1977, p. 131). Substantive references to Hart-mann, Mahler, and kindred theoreticians are notably sparse in Kohut's writings. As subsequent authors have observed, self psychology and object relations theory have close linkage.

One encounters few references to self in Freud's translated works, and the attention given it from writers prior to Kohut has been scanty. Eagle (1984) observes that other translators of *das Ich*, notably Brandt (1966) and Bettleheim (1982), feel that "self" is a more faithful rendition of Ich. In its common defi-nition as "the person as seen [by self]," the concept self would appear to fit better than does "ego-ideal" (Freud, 1914), or "observing ego" (Freud, 1933). While there are innumerable references to the perceptual and experiential aspects of intra-psychic operation, structural theory did not locate those func-tions. Later critics also confounded experiential descriptions with Freud's tendency to reify constructs, further clouding the issue. But it is clear that Freud's major efforts were in the direction of a drive psychology, and subsequent study followed his leadership.

Hartmann (1950) makes only passing reference to the self, as the subjective center of the personality. Much that Erikson (1968) describes as identity also falls under the aegis of self, evolving over the life span. But his conception of identity, which originates in ego identity (1950) is later (1968) embellished with self identity, historical identity, and group identity, further complicating comparison. Continuing the procedure of incor-porating findings from general psychology into this inquiry, another contrast soon surfaces. The powerful clinical contri-butions of self psychology have made little impact in general psychology. Yet, the concept of self has been extensively studied and described by a number of personality theorists (Lewin, 1935; Allport, 1937; Lecky, 1945; Murphy, 1947; Rogers, 1951; Kelly, 1955; Haan, 1977; Kegan, 1979). These theories share a common treatment of *self* as the central organizing structure of the personality, and sometimes use the term as a synonym for ego. Consistent features of these descriptions include inner awareness, consistency, organization, and direction of the personality.

Lacking a coherent concept of self has forced psychoanalytic writers since Freud to blur the distinction between the operational–executive and perceptual–experiential aspects of personality regulation. Ego as executive, as coordinating system of functions, does not account well for the person as seen and experienced internally. Concepts such as ego ideal describe but do not explain the effect of interpersonal relations on the formation of a motivating image of who one is, in health or pathology. And superego does not account for the hypothetical extension of oneself into novel or unfamiliar scenarios. A sense of being, of continuity in time and space, of intention and purpose, of possibility, are lodged in the meaning of self. As pathological manifestations, grandiosity, humiliation, and identity diffusion are most clearly recognized as disorders of self.

For Kohut self is a developmental construct, powered by narcissism, organizing personality around the two primitive poles of grandiosity and idealization (1971). Functions of synthesis and organization, of initiative and motivation derive from the self's origins in the beginning of life: "the infant's primal, rudimentary self [begins when] the baby's innate potentialities and the self-object's expectations with regard to the baby converge" (1977, p. 99). In this manner Kohut postulates for the etiology of self a history which is remarkably parallel to Hartmann's notion of ego, evolving from the interaction of primary objects and an undifferentiated matrix. In a more general way it is also consistent with Freud's description of the origins of self-regard: "Part of the self-regard is primary—the residue of childish narcissism; another part arises out of such omnipotence as experience corroborates . . . while a third part proceeds from gratification of object-libido" (1914, p. 58).

These parallels are, of course, not coincidental. It is known that Kohut wanted to avert confrontation with classical theory. Perhaps for the same reasons, he takes little note of object relations theory, preferring his own terminology. In the end, however, Kohut and his followers appear to have fallen victim to an irresistible urge to assert the primacy and uniqueness of his position (Greenberg and Mitchell, 1983; Eagle, 1984), protestations to the contrary notwithstanding (Goldberg, 1983). But, in common with most good clinicians in the field, Kohut's efforts originate from and are dedicated to his psychoanalytic work with patients. While legitimate comparisons have been made between his approach and that of Carl Rogers (Stolorow, 1976; Kahn, 1985), his formulation of introspection and empathy in psychoanalysis is unquestionably historic.

It has been clinically useful to draw a distinction in the psychic economy, placing major responsibility for the organizing processes of personality within the aegis of ego operations and locating the self system as the prime repository for its experiential components. Together, ego and self account for the organization, content, and purposefulness of the personality. In no case can either entity alone account for healthy or pathological functioning. Moreover, the two systems are interconnected etiologically as well as functionally. As Kohut describes it, the origins of self are to be found in earliest object relations. It has been a short step from this conceptual posture to one which views the self as the primary organizational construct, since the self is derived from those mental representations which are the root data of object relations. Considering the close connection between the self construct and object relations theory, it is tempting to focus theory on these and to downgrade the relative importance of ego processes. But, while the construct self has inherent structural as well as content features, it is predominantly identified by those qualities which describe its content and dynamics. Kohut defines the self experientially, as "introspective-empathic." Secondarily, "in the narrower sense . . . the self is seen as a content of a mental apparatus" (1977, p. xv).

However, in later writings Kohut appears to view the self as the superordinate construct of the personality. His thesis

seems to transcend ego psychology and "theoretical formulation," to be directed at the goals of psychotherapy. Nevertheless,
he has been criticized (Eagle, 1984) for too literal an emphasis
upon repairing developmental deficits, and for failing to distinguish between patients' reports of "falling apart" and assuming structural breakdown from these reports. Kohut's emphasis
upon understanding the self shapes therapy to that view of the
person's functioning, rather than to more traditional objectives
of resolving psychopathology by attending to drive fixations or
ego defects. Thus, Kohut appears to be more concerned with
reformulating a theory of therapy than with reshaping ego
psychology or object relations theory. As viewed by Greenberg
and Mitchell (1983) self psychology attempts to provide a
"mixed model" which combines drive and relational features.

Self and Object Relations

On several points the object relations perspective of the English
school, referred to earlier, differs from the relational view of
self theory. Kohut is unwilling to describe the human being as
"object-seeking," as did Fairbairn. For Kohut, the child's inherent narcissism brings it into contact with its human environment. The object relations orientation of the English school
tends to be closer to Sullivan's (1953) interpersonal relations
theory in its emphasis on social interaction. By contrast, Kohut
emphasizes the intrapsychic aspects of experience and structure, the self as "introspective-empathic," and as a "mental apparatus" (1977, p. xv) whose structure derives from the
internalization of experience with significant figures, the selfobjects. In this regard Kohut's position closely resembles the
sensorimotor period described by Piaget (1951) and Sandler
and Rosenblatt's (1962) "representational world." In addition,
the role of object relations in shaping ego development, as described by Jacobson (1964), seems strikingly similar. Jacobson
refers to self and object *representations* to differentiate those
internal experiences from reality events.

    Self psychology places the origins of self in that represen-
tational context, developing from selfobject internalizations.
The first developmental "work" is to form some rudimentary

sense of self—experiencing real world objects as part of the self, so as to acquire intrapsychic representational forms as "stimulus nutriment," internalizing these within the empathic–affective context of experience, and gradually moving from self and object representations to some cohesion of self representations into a rudimentary self. Clearly, there must exist innate capacities to organize and perform even these primitive functions. To that extent at least, self psychology must acknowledge a biological substrate for neonatal interaction to draw upon. But acknowledging such a substrate cannot deflect from the intimate interdependence between self and object relations regarding etiology and structure. Indeed, it is its relational origin that constitutes the major dispute between self theorists and drive theorists. While Kohut attempted to sustain both conceptual and clinical adherence to classical drive theory, a genuine schism may prove unavoidable (Greenberg and Mitchell, 1983; Masek, 1986). In part the source of disagreement may be due to Kohut's absorption with his own research at a time when ego psychology and object relations theory were more visibly grappling with similar risks of fractionating the psychoanalytic movement. Later on I will propose a "solution," building upon the rationale which has apparently been taken by these earlier groups.

Kohut further elaborates the relationship between self and selfobjects as a central aspect of his thinking. The two developmental stages of infancy, omnipotence and idealization, typically involve additional differentiation between selfobjects. Omnipotence and grandiosity–exhibitionism is primarily experienced in connection with mother. Idealization typically occurs in the child's experience with father. From these interactions, internalization creates the basis of the nuclear bipolar self, which is the foundation for later growth or pathology. Absence of adequate parental mirroring, idealizing, or hopes and dreams for the developing child leads to early pathological formations: psychoses, borderline states, narcissistic behavior, and personality disorders.

Phenomenology in Ego Psychology

The phenomenological view, as originally presented by Snygg and Combs (1949), laid the groundwork for studying the perceiver's world. Perceptual and experiential aspects of function are, of course, intimately connected with the psychodynamic content of psychopathology and with such classical treatment issues as transference and countertransference. But the traditional view has been that perceptual experience is the consequence, not the determinant, of psychopathology. Self psychologists have tended to place more emphasis on the role of experience, as such, in the etiology of psychopathology.

Another position is concerned with personal experience and intention from a perspective closer to ego operations. Erikson (1950, 1982) describes identity in a context of ego psychology. Holding to Freud's original usage of the German *Ich*, literally, "I," as the designation of ego, Erikson refers to ego-identity throughout his writings: "But it is apparently one of the functions of the ego's unconscious work to integrate experience in such a way that the I is assured a certain centrality in the dimensions of being . . . like an effective *doer* . . . *Active* and *originating* . . . *centered* and *inclusive* . . . *selective* . . . *aware* . . ." (1982, p. 89).

For Erikson, experiencing the content of ego functions and processes is part of ego identity. This theoretical position holds moot the role of a superordinate self by assigning experience and agency to the ego system. In kindred fashion, Schafer (1977, 1980) applies phenomenology to the executive and synthetic functions of the ego. Schafer describes analysands' use of language to disown their active role in the conduct of their lives, saying "it gets me angry" defensively, rather than "I get angry" or "my stomach is upset" rather than "I am upset in my stomach." Schafer contends that this is a defensive disowning of "agency," or intention. Similarly, Schafer suggests that amanuensis materials be viewed, in structure and meaning, as a narrative created to conform with patients' perceptions. Although he focuses on the implications for treatment, it is clear that Schafer is describing an ego system which, like Erikson's, incorporates awareness of its own operations within its functioning. Viewed against a backdrop of the history of psychoanalysis, one sees an evolution in the conception of the role of purpose.

The experiential view is as important in understanding ego

development as it is in self theory. By virtue of its experiential role the ego system creates patterns, and then meaning, out of its sensory data. In their seminal work on language development, Werner and Kaplan (1963) state that contemplation of one's own processes represents the highest level of cognitive function. Inherent in the conception of ego as a self-regulating, organizing process is a necessary component of self-monitoring. An observing ego is one of the essential requisites for most psychoanalytic therapies. Thus it seems entirely consistent with historic definitions of ego to include within its province of operations the qualities of experiencing and oversight. But a fine distinction must be drawn between metaphoric and literal denotations of self-observation with reference to ego operations. Highlighting these qualities clarifies the nature of the ego's role in structuring experience. Ego operations, we have seen, are neither instinctual nor mechanistic. Cognitive functions, generally acknowledged to be at the heart of ego operations, denote that these activities entail *knowing*. That is, the ego system structures experience by creating (organizing) patterns. Pattern making, in the light of ego as an experiencing, knowing, intentional system, is best understood as meaning making. Thus, structure and meaning are intimately interconnected organizing principles. Each fundamentally influences ego operation. Each is grounded in, and builds upon, the organization of experience. Still, knowing the self and awareness of self as an identity may also require a perceptual–experiential perspective which transcends ego competency.

The capacity to make meaning develops as the egoself system develops, using the capacities it activates. Effective psychotherapeutic intervention is attuned to patients' experiential meaning making, just as it is to the structural processes of organization. Both components are essential to effective therapy.

EGOSELF

For forty-odd years I have studied and worked with basic drives, ego, object relations, and self—each in its turn having been presented as the centerpiece on the psychoanalytic mantle. Yet I keep returning to an association long ago evoked: the parable of the four blind men and the elephant. If those forty years have taught me anything, it is the futility of asserting that any single part of the elephant *is* the elephant.

This welter of assertions is the backdrop for much of the controversy in contemporary psychoanalysis. While much of the explicit debate occurs around clinical issues, underlying that dispute are divergent perceptions of the central issues. Ego psychologists, whether or not committed to drive theory, tend to place emphasis upon pathological dysfunction in ego operations, and are inclined to diagnose primitive pathology as borderline. Object relations therapists look for evidence of disruption in early developmental structuring, and are likely to diagnose early pathology as schizoid. Self psychologists focus on distortions of early self structure, which results in a predilection for finding narcissistic disorders (Greenberg and Mitchell, 1983). More important than diagnosis are the differences in treatment, centering around the respective roles assigned to empathy and experiential interaction on the one hand or interpretation and affective hovering on the other. Questions of analyzability figure prominently in these debates. Where the bulk of clinicians locate themselves with regard to these positions, and how firmly they align themselves with any single position, is unclear.

Unfortunately, the heat of controversy often obscures important similarities which may also characterize the several points of view. A number of clinical assumptions are tacit to all three perspectives, such as: an abiding concern for patient welfare and optimum benefit from treatment; a conviction of the saliency of the therapeutic relationship in any effective treatment; sensitive attunement to transference and countertransference reactions; an intense appreciation for the intrapsychic etiology of pathology; belief that restructuring is essential to permanent therapeutic benefit. Building upon this consensus, I would like now to address the debate by challenging the theoretical necessity for it and by suggesting immediate clinical alternatives.

Since psychoanalysis is first and foremost a theory (or set of theories) it is appropriate to begin here. Ego, self, and object relations theories have in common a grounding which emphasizes the role of human interaction as the basis for structuring personality organization, both healthy and pathological. Each of the theories acknowledges that structure develops, and is not innate, evolving from the child's biophysiological capacity to internalize significant experience from its unique interactions with others. Thus, structuring is dependent upon experiential and developmental components in order to shape the individual contours of its heritage. It seems apparent that ego and self originate in object relations, but it is also evident that growth and development over the life span affect all three. In addition, the motive power which energizes psychic activity must be acknowledged. Whether it originates in specific drive clusters, as Freud first insisted, or emerges from an undifferentiated matrix, is moot at this time. Finally, ego, self, and object relations each emphasize different aspects of personality operation, but none alone adequately accounts for it. In essence, the term *object relations* describes one of the most central facts of human functioning: the intimate and irreducible connection between human interaction and the development of personality structure. But if energy and interaction form the basis of human activity, execution and identity form its essential character. For these tasks the concepts of ego and self are imperative. One of the hallmarks of psychoanalysis in its aspiration to being a science is its unique explanation for the organization and management of innumerable psychological activities of living by a small, finite set of ego functions. But the most uniquely human of our qualities is that of reflexive awareness and contemplation—how we know ourselves and experience the world in the light of that awareness. To that vital capacity we give the name *self*.

If we are to continue the tradition we have inherited from Freud we will incorporate from the past that which we can test in the present, checking and modifying as we go. In our clinical work we know better than to urge patients to repudiate parts of themselves simply because they are dystonic. Growth more often comes from successful resolution of dissonance. That same wisdom can apply to ourselves. The synthesis of theory which I have found useful is reflected in the term *egoself*. What this term conveys is the interconnection and interdependence of ego and self, both of which originate in object relations. Egoself represents a functional integration of intrapsychic systems sharing a common heritage and overlapping, interlaced properties.

Ego and self represent complementary and necessary aspects of personality. As commonly found in the literature, neither construct effectively incorporates essential components of the other. Ego is that system of identified functions which organizes, regulates, and prioritizes the organism's interface with ongoing and impending real world events. While the ego functions are varied and complex, their operation is known, studied, documented (Fenichel, 1945; Bellak, Hurvich, and Gediman, 1973). Psychoanalytic research on ego operations is amply supplemented by a vast literature in experimental psychology, reported throughout this book. Self is a construct which is both reflexive, as in self-regard (Freud, 1914), and prospective, as regards ambitions, values, and ideals. The perceptual– experiential aspects of self functioning, including mediation of narcissism, is in counterpoint to the cognitive and spatiotemporal reality gearing of ego operations. Most distinctively, as a phenomenological function, the organizing and regulative qualities of self interface with ego operations to form the totality of personality. If we examine either system by itself, neither ego nor self adequately account for the phenomena regularly observed in pathology or health. The term *egoself* covers both the generic and interactive processes denoted by ego and self. Personality function and organization is best understood as intrapsychic interaction between ego and self and their constituent operations. A person does not defend simply because anxiety threatens; narcissistic risk and reality factors are likely to be equally important determinants of the person's reaction. Humiliation can be as crippling as ego breakdown, and either one can precipitate the other. The same object relations which lay the groundwork for ego development are the raw materials from which self structure evolves. In all instances the organism engages in experience: analyzing, synthesizing, mediating, deflecting, making meaning for itself and about itself.

Most important, in clinical work an egoself perspective avoids the confusion of bouncing between theoretical approaches and allows for more fluid assessment and intervention. The therapist can attend to the actual clinical data, using the insights which best fit the material, unimpeded by partisan allegiances. The following case illustrates psychopathology of ego, self, and object relations.

> Mr. H directed most of his rage at himself and his personal possessions—pulling his hair, smashing a chair, bingeing on food. He was chronically bitter, depressed, frustrated, sarcastic, moody, hypersensitive. His self-image was both hateful and grandiose. Situations requiring self-assertion immobilized him with panic, then despair and impotent rage. When there were no pressures in his life he vegetated at home, feeling empty, useless, a failure. He was unable to sustain intimate relationships, and had few friends. During any week his symptoms met the criteria for several narcissistic behavior and personality disorders described by Kohut and Wolf (1978), but also presented features characteristic of a borderline condition: affective instability, poor frustration tolerance and impulse control, and generally intact ego functions (Goldstein, 1985; Kernberg, 1980).

Patients today present with varied symptomatology and variable levels of function, depending upon the area of psychological activity affected. In weekly therapy this fluidity is even more pronounced, and therapists do not have the analyst's leisure in attending to the material presented. As we have seen an egoself perspective enables therapists to adapt interpretive lens and intervention techniques more readily to the changing flow of material: from fantasy to reality, and from dynamics to structure. Ego, self, and object relations share a common heritage in the structuring of personality and psychopathology. This common source is also the guiding principle underlying much of the intervention strategy in egoself therapy. Restructuring—whether by transmuting internalizations, ego building, or promoting intrapsychic differentiation and integration—is the preferred area of impact in weekly psychotherapy.

The egoself approach is also well suited to the growing recognition that effective therapy takes account of the patient's current developmental level, as Gedo puts it: "new functions learned in the context of a satisfying and age-appropriate human relationship" (1980, p. 378). Accompanying this outlook is an expanding literature on postchildhood object relations, along with life-span data on the development of ego and self. The psychoanalytic tradition is moving away from an exclusive preoccupation with the events of the earliest years, toward an acknowledgment that adult psychopathology cannot be optimally engaged without understanding the structure and nature of adult processes. As Blanck and Blanck put it: "The point we wish to emphasize is that the adult who arrives for consultation differs from the developing child in that [ego] organization, with the flaws and malformations that derive from early life, has proceeded through later developmental phases" (1979, p. 86). Egoself processes are not static. They continue to change over the entire life span, affecting and being affected by the life process. The structure and meaning of life events is inseparable from the developing intrapsychic processes of the experiencing organism. Since its inception psychoanalysis has held to this approach, in contrast with those behavioral scientists who insist that the observable event, not its organismic impact, is the appropriate object of study. We turn now to examining postchildhood development of ego, self, and object relations. Consistent with developmental theory, the generic features of increasing complexity in differentiation and organization are found in each instance. In addition, greater awareness of the world and oneself in relation to the world are basic ingredients. What follows is a discussion of how this overall pattern of experience is reflected in each of the component aspects of intrapsychic organization.

The Natural History of Object Relations

Object relations theory describes as it explains the development of ego and self. It provides an accounting which is incomplete, but it is a necessary part of the bridgework connecting clinical theory with scientific psychology. Inherent in object relations theory is its dynamic character, a phenomenon of ongoing change. Object relations describes the experiential content out of which developmental restructuring is formed. From the first internalized images of infancy to the complex constructions of adulthood, object relations shape the structure and meaning of human experience. At the same time, object relations theory explains how the events of daily living are transformed into the fueling of egoself development.

From the earliest experiences onward, the prepotencies for ego operation interact with sensory data, forming and being formed by the organizing principles of egoself development. Contemporary psychoanalytic writers describe the evolution of object relations in life-span terms. When this perspective is linked with findings in personality and developmental psychology the result is an emerging natural history of object relations over the course of the entire life span.

Sources for a model are the extensions of separation– individuation to adolescence (Blos, 1981) and beyond (Panel, 1973a,b) and other psychoanalytic perspectives on parenthood (Anthony and Benedek, 1970) and adult development (Colarusso and Nemiroff, 1981). Postadolescent cognitive development theories of Perry (1970) and Schaie (1978), the personality development theory of Lewin (1935), and the influences of stage, gender, and identity development discussed in the next chapter further substantiate this presentation. Schafer (1977) sets the tone for a life-span developmental perspective, based on a synthesis of ego psychology with object relations theory:

> Ego psychology has established as a proper subject a psychoanalytic study the whole person developing and living in a complex world. . . . We see all aspects of development as being profoundly influenced by learning in a context of object relations that are, on the one hand biologically essential and biologically directed and on the other hand, culturally molded and historically conditioned [Schafer, 1977, p. 331].

This view points to the role of learning, including the processes of socialization and acculturation, in shaping the formation of object relations and, consequently, of ego development. Most important, the process is ongoing throughout the entire life span. The separation–individuation paradigm suggests that each new phase of development engenders growth by incorporating new object relations. In part this is achieved by letting go of (separation from) existing precepts of egoself organization and restructuring (individuating), based upon newer roles, challenges, expectations, and opportunities.

From the formation of the most simple self and object images and their subsequent internalization, the joint processes of differentiation and integration are lifelong. As the child grows, its world expands. Motility and speech provide exposure to the countless interactions that build an experiential base. But this is no simple additive process; humans create pattern and meaning out of their experience, within the limits of their capacity to do so. In turn, the patterns and meanings help shape the evolving structure. While earlier patterns set the stage for interpreting current experience, each new stage of growth also entails some reorganization of structure. Consequently, each period of developmental transition enhances vulnerability at the same time that it can be catalytic to a spontaneous reworking of earlier issues.

> Mr. E was sexually inhibited throughout adolescence, in part as a function of his unresolved oedipal attachment to mother. As a result he was unable to approach females. A year after graduation from high school he had never dated. Sexual fantasy and masturbation alternately relieved and frustrated him. Five years later, with no intervening psychotherapy, he was sexually active and experiencing intense gratification. During that time he was drafted and sent overseas, creating a physical separation from mother that facilitated development into young adulthood. He subsequently married and fathered two children. Only then, seeing himself as a father, did his oedipal issues resurface.

Inherent in object relations development is the internalization of diversity. As the person develops, not only does exposure to the world expand but the functional capacity to apprehend that world also becomes more sophisticated. Progressive awareness of diversity is due to increasing organismic acuity as well as to an increasingly diverse world stage. As object relations continues to organize experience, it is also fueling egoself growth. Attunement to diversity is thus a prime feature of object relations, the way that environmental distinctions large and small are made personally meaningful.

Blos (1981) describes adolescence as a second phase of separation–individuation, in which the consolidation of an identity separate from parents is the major feature. Solnit (1972, cited in Panel, 1973b) notes that the pacing of individuation changes from rapid to slow over the life span, whereas time sense changes from slow to rapid. Thus, separation experiences are felt more acutely in childhood, when object constancy is less well established. In adulthood, slower rates of change may contribute to a more secure sense of self and object constancy. Colarusso and Nemiroff (1981) suggest that time awareness and bodily changes are "major psychic organizer[s] of the adult" (p. 96). Another central determinant of adult object relations is the effect of parenting. In a comprehensive anthology, Anthony and Benedek (1970) cover the multiple meanings that parenthood assumes in its evolving phases, from the first pregnancy to the advent of grandparenthood. Parenthood extends one's separateness from one's family of origin in the role of child, yet provides an opportunity for continuity and contrast with family roles and traditions. Benedek (1970) cites male productivity, female nurturing, and mutuality among the developmentally enriching experiences of parenthood.

Vocational activity is another developmental stimulant to object relations, and to adult development in general. Work engenders ego growth, and competence enhances self-esteem (Super, 1957). The experience of self-utilization and the role of producer–provider (Panel, 1973b) extend ego functioning and expand self-identifications and group membership. Changes in time awareness also contribute to the morphology of object relations, a topic discussed in the next chapter. These reports share a common grounding—that the nature and content of mental representations have a natural history which includes major restructuring of their content and organization over time. Moreover, that restructuring conforms to basic developmental principles, tying maturation to a centralized, hierarchically prioritized integration of structures and functions.

Adult Object Relations

This overview of the natural history of object relations indicates the strength of evidence that object relations conform to the general principles of life-span development: they reflect the effects of lifelong learning; they reflect both conservation and change; they reflect the influences of experience and bodily change; they are affected by the influences of time and culture; they evolve in the general direction of increased complexity and oganization; and some changes are qualitatively different from those of childhood structure. In young adulthood intrapsychic structure undergoes expanded breadth (Lowenthal, Thurnher, and Chiriboga, 1975) and complexity (Perry, 1970; Robbins, 1981), permitting differentiation to become more individualized. Gender differences, heightened in adolescence, are consolidated in young adulthood. According to Chodorow (1978), women clarify self-definition through relationships with female peers and in mothering. Contemporary women are likely to be assailed by inner conflict over their role priorities, particularly between achievement and affiliation (Sheehy, 1981). Nevertheless, for both sexes, self representations are better articulated (White, 1963; Bocknek, 1980) and personal priorities are internalized as part of the ego ideal (Wittenberg, 1968). Clearer ego boundaries and more textured self–other representations enhance the person's capacity for intimacy (Erikson, 1979; Bocknek, 1980).

With established adulthood comes an expansion of roles and an increased cultural embeddedness, as people apply the skills they have acquired in adult activities. This is a period in which self representations are structured around intensive narcissistic investment in everyday accomplishments (Vaillant, 1977; Bocknek, 1980; Scarf, 1980). Prioritizing and self definition by roles—partner, producer, parent—tends to shape both object relations and ego operations during this life stage. With the advent of middle age, numerous investigators report a period of ego constriction, which corresponds to the self-confrontation described in chapter 7. Object relations for men and women must incorporate the finitude of life, now that youth is past (Colarusso and Nemiroff, 1981). At the same time, middle age provides relief from earlier responsibilities and wider latitudes for new self identifications (Panel, 1973b). Observing the next generation enter adulthood, and becoming a grandparent, adds to the reshaping of self and object representations. In middle age, intrapsychic gender differences tend to lessen as women tend to become more assertive and men more emotionally expressive (Gutmann, 1975).

Object relations in senescent adulthood are influenced by death awareness and progressive disengagement (Cumming and Henry, 1961), as the imminence of mortality impinges on consciousness. The alternative structuring of object relations around ego transcendance or cathectic impoverishment is suggested by Peck's (1975) research. Acknowledging one's physical decline entails letting go of aspects of body ego as core ingredients of self representation. It may be that wisdom, as defined by Erikson (1982), is functionally connected to those ego operations described above, in which a larger cognitive perspective is incorporated by seemingly simpler cognitive structures.

This necessarily abbreviated version of adult object relations suggests the extent to which adult egoself development surpasses the primitivity of childhood object relations. From the time of the psychological birth of the infant around age three until its maturation around young adulthood, enormous changes continue to take place. But object relations continue their growth and development throughout the life span.

Postchildhood Self Development

According to Kohut, as the self continues normative development, omnipotence gives way to ambition and self-assertion, and idealization to the formation of ideals and values. A "tension arc" between the two poles leads to the development of interests and goals, so that present and future become important motivators of the person's continuing activity. By integrating the cohesive self with developmental continuity Kohut casts self psychology into life-span perspective, in consonance with contemporary psychoanalytic thought (Conference on Psychoanalytic Education and Research, 1974; Collarusso and Nemiroff, 1981). Developmental continuity of the self has specific implications. Continuity of the self includes its content and activity, but goes beyond that: "the sense of the continuity of the self, the sense of our being the same person throughout life—despite the changes in our body and mind, in our personality makeup, in the surroundings in which we live . . . emanate[s] . . . also from the abiding specific *relationship* in which the constituents of the self stand to each other" (Kohut, 1977, pp. 179–180).

This description matches closely the language of Erikson in his depiction of "identity." Essential to Erikson's concept of identity is the "samenesses and continuities," but also "an integration now taking place" (1950, p. 261) as he describes the end of childhood with entry into youth and adolescence. This similarity gains importance when one considers that Erikson was writing about "ego identity" in a context of libido theory. So, even though Kohut's thinking is lodged in object relations theory it may not be incompatible with aspects of ego and drive theory.

The further one traces the developmental course along the life span, noting the role played by the self in various theories of adult personality, the more apparent it is that ego operations and object relations are immersed in the self system. Most of adult process and behavior, in pathology and health, is mediated by aspects of self function. The interdependent connection between narcissism and self-esteem, between self–other boundaries and the capacity for intimacy or assertion, between self-percept and depression, between the internalized self and "possible selves" (Markus and Nurius, 1986) suggest that self becomes an increasingly more powerful determinant of conscious functioning after the adolescent years. More and more of the autonomous ego functions—perception, judgment, planning—are infused with the internalized experiences of succeeding years, so that who one is and how one functions become heavily dependent upon how the self has continued to develop. One's sense of capacity or liability is constrained more by self-image than by objective limits. Conversely, self-image can be powerfully affected by meaningful confrontation with personal capacity. Throughout adult development the self system remains powerfully cathected. Activities, competencies, relationships, and roles provide an ongoing source of nutriment for internalization. The self system continues to develop through the adult stages. I have previously (1980) described this evolution through young adult, established adult, and middle-age stages. In young adulthood, self-particularization involves differentiating internalized components, those which contribute to cohesiveness as well as those which are dystonic. Two qualities of young adulthood—self-particularization and the capacity for personal perspective—help explain why they, rather than adolescents, tend to refer themselves for therapy. In established adults the self structure is further elaborated and consolidated by fuller participation in adult roles. Internalization of self representations as an effective person may conflict with archaic expectations during this period. Conversely, grandiose expectations may confront the realities of adult achievement, precipitating the "midlife crisis." The severity of these disturbances is usually a function of earlier structuring. In middle age self-confrontation is normative. Matured self representations account for the accomplishments of a lifetime. When these self representations are discrepant from cherished idealizations the reaction may be a sense of catastrophic loss, resulting in severe emotional or physiological disorders.

Understanding the stage-specific evolution of self representations and structure offers access to poorly apprehended aspects of patients' experience. The expanding role of self representations during the adult years necessarily intersects the evolution of ego and object relations also. Insight into the interplay between self, ego, and object relations has particular impact on the conduct of egoself psychotherapy, due to the close interdependence between intrapsychic structure and inner experience. Meaning making is at once an ego operation, a self function, and a derivative of existing self and object representations.

Conceptualizing the self apart from the ego complicates the meaning of terms such as *ego ideal* and *observing ego*. Here are clinically meaningful terms which are predicated upon the person's introspective and self-distancing capabilities. Clearly they are functions which exceed the operational competencies usually ascribed to either ego or self alone. Meissner (1986) raises a similar issue, posing a discrepancy between describing self as representational, as an introspective object, versus self as structure, having functions such as integration and agency. Meissner wisely concludes: "I would regard the self as having no independent origin exclusive of its emergence as part of the developmental process that gives rise to the structural entities" (1986, p. 396). Of necessity this view links self with object relations and ego, as distinct from an alternative developmental line such as narcissism. From that perspective, parsimony would favor a conception such as egoself. The literature on postchildhood ego development provides more substantial support for this position.

Postchildhood Ego Development

Inasmuch as ego is generally defined by its organizing processes, it may be fruitful to examine those processes which characterize ontogenetically later and/or more mature organizational structure. What is known about the natural history of ego functions? How do early adverse experiences affect the development of those processes?

Most writers agree that there is increasing self-regulation, self-direction, and self-organized activity in the adult years. Ego organization is more complex, more centralized, and hierarchically integrated. A second point is that these functions operate in a context of organism–environment interactive experience, and are best understood in this perspective. This framework is, of course, entirely consistent with basic tenets of object relations theory, which lodges the development of psychic structure in an experiential context deriving from an undifferentiated matrix (Hartmann, 1950). Furthermore, increased self-regulation would appear to describe the continuing of separation–individuation as an intrapsychic process (Panel, 1973a; Colarusso and Nemiroff, 1981). Further data underlying this position come from a multidisciplinary knowledge base which includes anthropology, history, psychiatry, education, human ecology, and several subdisciplines of psychology. Many of these writings are to be found in an impressive anthology edited by Lerner and Busch-Rossnagel (1981). The findings are consonant with a heritage which predates Piaget and Werner, yet is resonant with other contemporary thought in psychology and psychoanalysis.

In other words, the regulative processes of system ego are

not random but systematic, not trial and error but orderly and predictable. Synthesizing a half-century of research, Bronfenbrenner (1951) concludes: "Personality development is a function of progressive expansion, differentiation, and integration of self–other relationships which is paralleled by like processes within the intrapsychic self–other system" (p. 255). Bronfenbrenner is describing a life-span object relations theory, one that is consonant with organismic traditions of scientific psychology. This tradition has already found significant application in the clinical use of Rorschach testing, where the structural organization of percepts provides primary data for interpreting the level of ego functions (Exner and Weiner, 1982; Friedman, 1952). Structural analysis of Rorschach percepts differentiates normal from psychopathological subjects. It also differentiates children from adults, and even adolescents from young adults (Hemmendinger, 1951; Robbins, 1981).

Theory, research, and practice support the constructivist view of development, that intrapsychic processes transform the data of experience, using combinations of retained information (memory), patterning (anticipation), and proactive interaction (self-initiated activity) (Labouvie-Vief, 1982). As people develop they use more information about the past, clearer expectations of the future, and greater capacity to organize their resources on behalf of their objectives. Structural change occurs throughout life, in nonlinear fashion. Patterns from the past influence current perception, but the past is continuously being reprocessed and updated by the impact of present and anticipated experience. Clinical and research data are consistent with this formulation. Vaillant (1977) reports on a thirty-year follow-up of Harvard students that "memory undergoes a metamorphosis." Schafer (1977), in a similar vein, suggests that the autobiographical associations of analysands be interpreted as ego efforts to achieve a consistent scenario, rather than as factual reconstructions of early experience. These findings accord well with the literature from the experimental psychology of learning, which demonstrates structural as well as dynamic patterns in adult recall. The ego functions to regularize experience into pattern and meaning, not to retain literal content for its own sake. At all levels of awareness, time and content are restructured to conform to current or anticipated needs. But time and content are also restructured inadvertently, as organismic processes regulate perceptions according to principles of context and pattern. Ambiguous, vaguely apprehended material, is reshaped to form more vivid patterning. Memories blur, sharpen, or condense, depending upon what they are associated with. Beliefs are regularized to conform to expectations.

Early experiences, and their internalized mental representations, are therefore subject to lifelong restructuring. It may be presumed that some of these representations become more deeply ingrained through this process, when new experiences recapitulate earlier ones. Other representations dissipate or become transformed, due to corrective experiences, alternative experiences, or the dynamics of memory and disuse. Postadolescent ego organization, at whatever state of pathology, tends to regulate personal experience in favor of internal consistency. With severe psychopathology self-regulation may take place at serious cost to reality testing, as in delusional systems.

In short, postchildhood ego development continues the unending course of change. As life continues, ego development becomes more intricately organized. This pattern is true whether development is healthy or pathologically distorted. Whatever else, the system continues to develop. The pattern of conservation and change, discussed in the next chapter, really describes rates of change. Conservation urges toward the stabilization of structure and meaning; change moves to restructure and redefine; nowhere is there permanence. Dysfunctional ego organization may have originated in the person's past, but it is the current ego system which gets overwhelmed, or distorts, or defends. It is the current ego system which has evolved capabilities and potentialities, and levels of organization, which were not available in the past. Both the structure and the meaning of early events evolve, changing as they are reprocessed by an organizing system which is itself changing. The direction and shape of the changes are influenced by the nature of system ego, as organizer and meaning maker.

These findings have important implications for psychotherapy. First, neither the patients' problems nor their ego organization remain as they were in childhood. Thus, psychotherapeutic intervention must be directed at representations of the past as they have been transformed into present functioning. Second, current ego resources can be mobilized in support of that effort. This view is consistent with the position of Blanck and Blanck (1979):

> [T]he adult patient is not at the same developmental position as he was in early childhood— . . . the interaction, or object relationship, produces a resultant within the individual, [so] that even that resultant of experience becomes organized, first at its own developmental level and then at later levels. Therefore, the adult patient we see before us presents far more than the original subphase experience . . . [p. 24].

The structural changes in ego development, which we have been discussing, are not simple mechanical adjustments triggered by some developmental clock. Nor are they cosmetic alterations of the surface appearance of ego operations. These changes are profound, and inevitable. They affect how the ego organizes experience and the meaning given to that experience. Events in present time trigger associations to past experiences. Ego reactions to those associations reflect aspects of their early impact, but are also determined by the structural and meaning-making processes which have evolved since those early years.

Continuing research provides further data on changes in ego function after adolescence. Perry's (1970) studies of cognitive processes, including their moral–affective components, suggest something of the complexity of postchildhood object relations, which links patterns of representations and interlaces them with affective, moral, and cognitive meanings. This process becomes progressively more intricate as it becomes prioritized according to internalized values and tied to belief and action systems involving one's identity. As noted earlier, identity and self are used synonymously after childhood.

Framing our understanding of egoself in terms of structure and meaning reveals the wisdom of those who have guided psychoanalysis over the past decades. The common view acknowledges the organization and intentionality of the person's entire psychological functioning. From this contemporary perspective psychopathology is recognized by its processes, which are in turn seen as part of the purposive functioning of the person. Organizing experience in order to make meaning of it is the irreducible method people have for conducting their lives. The developmental context of human behavior further informs our understanding, bringing the inevitability of change and transformation to any interpretation of psychological activity. We have seen that modern psychoanalytic theory, incorporating ego psychology, self psychology, and object relations theory, provides a bridge between the insights of clinical psychopathology and psychotherapy and those of scientific psychology. As these findings indicate, the nature of postchildhood ego development is vitally important to the planning of psychotherapeutic intervention. Since change is a universal occurrence, its effects also occur universally. More particularly, we see the progressive integration of object relations with ego and self as the irresistible consequence of organismic development. Indeed, pathology is recognized by the distortions and limitations of that natural developmental trajectory.

CHAPTER 9

DEVELOPMENTAL PSYCHOLOGY

This chapter explores those aspects of developmental psychology that have greatest impact on weekly egoself psychotherapy, and which undergird much of what has been discussed under assessment, management, and therapy. Developmental theory alerts the clinician to the evolving character of the human condition: change, not stasis, is the law of life. In psychoanalysis the role of developmental theory is of long standing. Developmental principles figure prominently in the psychoanalytic theory of neurosis (Fenichel, 1945) and character formation (Abraham, 1921; Lowen, 1970) which was predicated upon Freud's theory of psychosexual development, first promulgated in 1905. As we know, Freud's continuing work convinced him that psychopathology is rooted in the developmental experiences of infancy and childhood.

The data base of developmental psychology is obviously germane to the conceptual foundations of psychotherapeutic practice. In macrocosm, developmental psychology addresses the nature and character of the human life course. It is concerned with identifying and understanding what is expectable in the natural evolution of psychological function, structure, and experience—the life process. In microcosm, specific developmental processes are inferred from behavioral observations. By assuming that behavior is purposive and intentional, one is capable of tapping into those intrapsychic operations from which structure and meaning evolve, however their expression may be influenced by cultural constraints.

It is now clear that development continues beyond childhood and over the entire life span. As a result, psychoanalytic psychotherapy is even more deeply intertwined with the psychology of human development. The enormous literature of developmental psychology has yielded a number of basic tenets, three of which are central to egoself therapy. These three tenets are the conservation–change paradigm, constructionism, and sequentiality. Because each is fundamental to human development, each provides powerful insight as to how therapeutic intervention influences human change. Sequentiality addresses the emerging susceptibilities—both resources and vulnerabilities—which are characteristic of the life passage. Constructionism explores the way humans create pattern and meaning out of the raw data of sensorimotor experience. The conservation–change paradigm describes the ongoing tension between the inevitability of change over the life span and the organismic need for stability.

SEQUENTIALITY

The concept of sequencing connotes both order and emerging function in life-span development. Most noticeably during the childhood years but continuing throughout life, psychological development is related to the evolving capacity and experience of the organism as a whole. Much of child development theory is geared to the pacing of a biological clock. The advent of symbol-formation, locomotion, and speech depend upon the maturation of physiological readiness to grapple with experience.

But sequentiality is not limited by biological change. Erikson (1950) points out that development is literally psychosocial, that history, social recognition, and expectation play formative roles in the emergence of the crises which identify new life stages. Gutmann's (1975) research in four cultures highlights parenthood as the developmental crossroads of the life span. He contends that personality development and change is marked once people have passed through the "parental imperative" period of their lives. Levinson et al. (1979)

describe a sequence of developmental "seasons," paced by a "dream" and a "life structure," images structuring the content and organization of one's life.

Sequentiality is a central aspect of development, linked to ontogenetic experience and cultural rites of passage as well as physiological morphology. It pervades the entire life course and, by virtue of these linkages, establishes a predictable order of emergence of psychological prepotencies. Sequentiality accounts for progressive developmental change, both qualitative and quantitative. Some changes are incremental, continuations of earlier developmental acquisitions. Other changes are qualitatively discontinuous from earlier acquisitions, although built upon them. Many stage-specific qualities such as the observing ego are of this type. Developmental evolution is predicated upon prior sequential experience.

At the same time, developmental acquisitions are not, in the individual case, automatically predictable. Certain earlier formative sequences may be necessary for the fullest subsequent development to occur but they are not of themselves determinative. Sequentiality is not synonymous with actualization. Developmental sequencing describes what can occur, what is likely to occur, and the expectable order of occurrence. But the realization of developmental potential requires more than organismic readiness. Some quantum of what Rapaport (1967) calls "environmental stimuli" must be available to the person in digestible form. Even so, the deterministic implications inherent in sequentiality provoke considerable disagreement in the field, particularly among those workers who feel that non-normative and fortuitous events make the life course unpredictable (Gergen, 1980; Danish, 1981).

I share with Erikson (1950), Mahler (1972), Levinson (1986), and others, the conviction that certain developmental sequences are fundamental and widespread. These sequences are the result of the confluence of social, psychological, and biophysiological factors which are omnipresent across time and culture. Infants everywhere must contend with their psychobiological helplessness, and learn to negotiate the psychosocial resources available in and around themselves. The combination of peer acknowledgment, physical development, and identity formation augment entry into young adulthood in any culture. The sequential order and the approximate timing of these evolutionary predispositions is knowable and predictable. Yet, for each person, the life course is unique and different, due to variability of experience and how it is processed by the person.

If sequence is knowable and predictable, it follows that development is not reversible. The child who unconsciously regresses to bed-wetting has already mastered urinary continence. Sequentiality denotes that regression to an earlier period never duplicates that earlier period. Indeed, the dynamic significance of regression is based on the premise that later developmental levels have been internalized. The powerful therapeutic implications of that principle are noted at several points in this book.

Once attained, some part of development is always retained. Sequencing continues to build upon whatever is available to the organism: prior attainments, emerging tendencies, environmental facilitants, and impediments. Sequencing urges the person forward, even while other influences inhibit or pull the person backward. The past influences the present but does not determine it. Development brings with it the ongoing capacity to modify and even overturn the consequences of previous experiences. Reporting on the forty-five-year longitudinal study at the Berkeley Institute for Human Development, Macfarlane (1975) concludes:

> We have found that much of personality theory based on pathological samples is not useful for prediction for the large number of persons. Many of our most mature and competent adults had troubled and confused childhoods and adolescences. . . . They include one full-blown adolescent schizophrenic, who, without benefit of psychotherapy, now functions perceptively, creatively, and competently as a wife, mother, home builder, gardener, and community participant [p. 222].

In its most explicit form sequencing denotes stage-specific prepotency, the readiness or susceptibility of certain properties for activation at certain predictable points. Separation–individuation theory is a prominent example of prepotency. Erikson's epigenetic theory is another: "[L]aws of development . . . create a succession of potentialities for significant interaction [which] . . . must remain within 'the proper rate and proper sequence' which governs all epigenesis" (1968, pp. 92–93).

The lifelong passivity of the immature twenty-five-year-old will encounter urgings for intimacy and capability as the person inevitably is confronted with these stage-specific prepotencies of young adulthood. And even the most regressed schizophrenics will have some experience of young adulthood, established adulthood, and middle age as they go through those segments of the life span.

Development unleashes potential resources. Of all the insights provided by the developmental approach, none is more significant to the work of the professional practitioner than this. Subtle increments in functional competence lead to qualitatively new capabilities. A principle learned in one area of activity (such as therapy) abruptly finds application in a different life situation. Yesterday's novelty is routine today. The vexations of adolescence are often resolved with the tools of young adulthood.

But potential does not only refer to resources. Each new life stage also conveys new hazards, susceptibility to vulnerabilities which may not have been inherent to the previous period. Difficulty in forming relationships may be vexing in adolescence; in established adulthood it betokens psychopathology. Middle-aged adults are particularly vulnerable to stage-specific self-confrontation, now that their earlier aspirations for personal accomplishments should be coming to fruition.

Life Stages

Life stage denotes a relationship between a matrix of psychological processes and ontogenetic location. The determination of a life stage, in egoself theory and practice, is contingent upon the identification of intrapsychic and psychosocial interactions distinctive to that life period. The psychological features of a developmental life stage are clearly distinguishable from those in the immediately preceding and subsequent stages. Life stages are therefore predictable regarding both content and location.

While there is ongoing discussion about the number and location of life stages, the construct itself has long enjoyed active usage and de facto acceptance. Conversely, the absence of life-stage information is a significant handicap to professional intervention. How does one evaluate comments such as, "people don't matter to me as much as they used to"; "I don't know what kind of work I like"; "I cry when my mother isn't home"; without some estimate of the speaker's developmental status? It is obvious that therapists automatically make some developmental assessment of clients, estimating maturity against some tacit developmental standard. But when "automatic" is not necessarily conscious and "tacit" is not necessarily explicit, the risk of inadvertent error is magnified. The delineation of life stages by their psychological properties provides a consensual standard for developmental assessment. In the study of life stages, investigators identify those issues and predispositions commonly associated with particular periods of the life span. Sources of strength and risks of vulnerability can therefore be anticipated from an assessment of the person's developmental status.

From a developmental perspective, one possible assessment of such a situation is that the resources of the past are insufficient for the task at present. In this light, are there unutilized resources which are now available to significant figures in the problem situation?

> A twenty-two-year-old woman was still caught up in an adolescent autonomy struggle with her mother. The counselor determined that the woman had potentiated one of the attributes of young adulthood, a capacity for personal perspective. To mobilize this resource he adopted the role of consultant with his client, exploring with her the fears of her middle-aged mother: about aging, and losing her beloved daughter. In turn, the patient was able to recast her perception of her parent from focusing on mother's attempts to dominate her to a compassionate awareness of her mother's pain. This awareness enabled her to assume the developmentally more appropriate role of adult daughter, and resulted in a dramatic reduction in conflict between the two. At the same time, it aided the young woman's transition from adolescence into young adulthood.

Recognition of the potentialities inherent in each developmental advance equips the therapist to design interventions which optimize patients' growth directly, while simultaneously addressing the presenting problem. This tactical precept is fundamental to egoself intervention strategy.

Some investigators of women's development (Bryce, 1985) criticize stage theory for failing to account for the discontinuity of women's roles. These investigators incline toward longitudinal, life-span models. However, this creates other difficulties. One of the problems posed by life-span research is the tendency to select dimensions observed in childhood for life-span study. Of necessity, this method biases the investigation toward demonstrations of the long term continuity of development. Clayton and Birren (1980) observe: "Research in the field of life span developmental psychology has tended to neglect those qualities that might be unique to, and representative of, development in . . . adulthood" (p. 129).

By the same token, developmental life stages do not suddenly appear in whole cloth. The antecedents of growth are usually discernible in some form, but the core issue is the arena of study. By studying intrapsychic process, rather than social role behavior, the weight of evidence supports the validity and utility of conceptualizing the life span as a sequence of stages—for women as well as for men. Recent years have witnessed important contributions to the differences between later stages. One such example is the Belenky, Clinchy, Goldberger, and Tarule (1986) data on the stages in cognitive development of postadolescent women. Another body of research compares adolescents and young adults. Theoretical distinctions between these two stages have been buttressed by empirical support. Robbins (1981) compared college-bound high school students with graduate students, using projective test measures of ego function and structure derived from Blos (1962), Werner (1957), and Loevinger (1976). Consistent significant differences indicated that the older group was developmentally more advanced, corresponding to their preclassification as adolescents and young adults. Allem (1981) found that value preferences distinguished between four groups of males in the military, mean ages fifteen, twenty-five, thirty-five, forty-five. Freeman-Young and Bocknek (1982) report numerous intergender and intercohort differences in self-image representation among male and female adolescents, young adults, and established adults.

CONSTRUCTIONISM

Constructionism is aptly described by the title of a fascinating book, *Individuals as Producers of Their Own Development* (Lerner and Busch-Rossnagel, 1981). As Langer (1969) puts it, "Humans . . . are actors . . . conserving their own organization at the same time as they transform it" (p. 87). The constructionist view, of people from birth onward taking an active role in shaping their experience, underlies object relations theory. Fairbairn (1955) suggested that, from infancy on, humans are object-seeking. To that observation we can add the finding that living things are attracted to configurations—those which are familiar, such as mother's voice, or those which possess regular form. Where form is ambiguous we create pattern, using previous experience (as in the case of Rohrschach ink blots) or the structural principles enunciated by Gestalt psychology (Koffka, 1935). The fundamental rule affecting organism-environment relationships is that they are interactive. Human beings actively create pattern and meaning of their experience. Piaget, who is credited as the originator of constructionism, viewed development as serving the needs of adaptation. In Piaget's system, adaptation involves the complementary processes of assimilation and accommodation. Flavell, whose translation of Piaget's work is considered the standard reference, says:

> Assimilation essentially means interpreting or construing external objects and events in terms of one's own presently available and favored ways of thinking about things. . . .
> Accommodation . . . means noticing and taking cognitive account of the various real properties and real relationships among properties that external objects and events possess.
> Assimilation refers to the process of adapting external stimuli to one's own internal mental structures where accommodation refers to the converse or complementary process of adapting these mental structures to the structure of these same stimuli [1977, p. 7].

As noted in earlier chapters, modern psychoanalytic thought is entirely consistent with this interactive view of development. In scientific psychology the research of Grossberg (1986) and Langer (1989) provides a solid base of support for understanding human function as a process of creating structure and meaning. We differentiate by creating configurations, and ascribe meaning based on specific configuration. The differences implied by the meaning of Porsche and Chevy may be greater than their structural similarity as motor vehicles. That process of creating meaning and structure reflects also the time dimension in which we develop our lives.

Time Sense

Embedded in constructionism is more than the experience of change and its inevitability. The companion motif to the dynamism of conservation–change is the dimension of time. The power of time sense for the life span is well illustrated by Neugarten's (1969) aphorism for the advent of middle age. She describes it as that period when time is no longer measured by how many years one has lived but by how many years remain. The structure and meaning ascribed to time's passage surrounds us. The beginning and ending of life is ritualized in every culture and every era. From the most primitive times, the gods have been distinguished by their capacity to transcend mortal life. And, for about as long, humankind has struggled with the enigma of its mortality. Lifton (1976) describes the psychological conception of death as a lifelong grappling with symbolic immortality.

Sense of time is a construct whose complexity matches development. A conception of present time—now—seems to emerge in the second year of life. Only gradually does time sense expand to include past and future. By the middle of the second decade adolescents still live in an extended-now time frame, but have seemingly acquired a sense of temporal directionality. The future is understood to be less definite than the past, yet more real than it is for the child (Kastenbaum, 1973). Career planning in young adulthood typically covers a span of time including a decade or more of past history and twenty-five years into the future. By the time the person enters old age, futurity is much more restricted. The past is viewed with greater clarity, and it is more positively valued (Stevens-Long, 1984).

It may be that an abstract time sense—of seconds, minutes, and hours—is a historically recent arrival, propelled by the mechanization of life wrought by the Industrial Revolution. Rural and preindustrial societies seem much less cognizant of small time intervals and more geared to natural time clocks: tidal, diurnal, menstrual, seasonal. Much of time awareness seems geared to its rhythms and cycles, its predictability. Humans seem much less comfortable with the linear aspects of time. Interestingly, it is in the later stages of life that time appears to take on its widest salience. Senescent adults, contending with the psychological imminence of death, are the stage cohort most inclined to consider eternity. At the same time, a heightened interest in past persons and events has been frequently noted. Brennan (1981) found that elderly people use reminiscence as an adaptive device, suggesting that focusing on the past among the elderly is not simply stylistic or defensive but has a significant coping function.

Awareness of time evolves with the life span. Present, past, and future time assumes gradual meaning. The relationship between events and their life history timing is important. When people marry can be almost as important as whether they do so. But if past awareness influences the present it is equally true that the person's present life experience influences what is recalled from the past. Vaillant's (1977) follow-up of men twenty to thirty years after attending Harvard reveals that: "the metamorphosis of aging alters belief systems, instinctual expression, memory . . ." (p. 195). His subjects' recall of their college years was often at variance with their reports at the time.

Similarly, future expectations interact with past and present in an interdependent fashion. In a study of attitudes toward menopause Neugarten, Wood, Kraines, and Loomis (1975) divided 267 women into age groups twenty-one to thirty, thirty-one to forty-four, forty-five to fifty-five, and fifty-six to sixty-five. Marked intergroup differences were found, which Neugarten attributes to differing expectations and experience. The younger women assigned much greater significance to future menopause, compared to the older women, for whom it was a current or past experience.

Transitions

The study of adult development has drawn attention to periods of transition, and their clinical significance (Levinson et al., 1979; Schlossberg, 1981). Developmental transition refers to the reactions associated with significant life experiences. These experiences may be due to circumstance (physical injury, getting married) or to the developmental process itself (entry and exit from one life stage to another). In either case, the emphasis is on the meaning making/structure building interrelationship that characterizes human development.

While there is no question that some events have a transformational impact on the life course, clinical experience teaches that the event alone rarely accounts for its effects. Losing a parent can evoke sadness or grief, mourning or catastrophic loss, reflection or psychosis. The inner meaning of the event, and the role it plays in the organizational structuring of intrapsychic processes, will have major influence on its impact. From that perspective, the problematic aspect of any transition is its ego-dystonic quality. An ostensibly happy and planned-for event, like the birth of a child, can usher in the warded-off awareness of one's adulthood. In life-span development, the transition from young adult to established adult can evoke a dysphoric reaction by threatening the person's wish to conserve a familiar self-image.

Psychoanalytically oriented psychotherapists are accustomed to probing for the dynamic significance of life events, as they relate to the patient's reactions. Personal associations to the perceived event, including earlier memories and fantasies, create a shape and tone which may bear little resemblance to the objective circumstances. The developmental life-span perspective expands that understanding to include the effects of expectable life-span passage for that person. An essential feature of life-stage transitions is that there is a heightened experience of change. This can evoke adverse reactions to the extent that the imperative to change threatens to dislodge ego-syntonic self or self–world representations, or simply seems too abrupt a change in the existing conservation–change equilibrium. The ability to adapt to rapid change varies across the life span. Children can generally tolerate change well as long as they have the protection of a secure adult. Young adults generally adapt best to change, in my experience. Readiness for innovation and change seems to be a stage-specific resource of young adulthood (Bocknek, 1980). As aging continues, adults seem progressively less well equipped to handle unexpected change, whether it originates internally or from life circumstances. Therapeutic intervention in mediating change can have important beneficial effects.

The various forms of developmental crisis were outlined above on pages 255-257. At a minimum, moving from one stage to another, or from one life circumstance to another, requires the expenditure of extra energy. Even when the attractions of such a transition outweigh other factors for the person, the energy drain on an overextended intrapsychic system may require therapeutic monitoring and assistance. Growth, whether in therapy or not, can also precipitate disruption when new opportunities bring unexpected side effects. A patient who had successfully walled off feelings for years was badly frightened by his new ability to experience joy and sadness. Learning to mediate unfamiliar affect seemed more threatening than retreating to his previous state of isolation.

Transition theory provides a base from which therapists can attune to the possible effects of change on patients. Monitoring the patient's developmental status, as the obverse side of monitoring the pathology, is characteristic of egoself therapy. By remaining alert to developmental change the therapist can prepare for reactions which may be forthcoming. An advantage of weekly therapy is that the less frequent contact makes it easier to pick up changes that occur so gradually over time. A young woman whose identity was fused with her mother came in with her first report of change, a makeup preference she didn't know if her mother would approve of. Along with this step came a tinge of anxiety: was she wrong, that is, would mother disapprove? Rather than await mother's reaction, the therapist began to explore the meaning of the patient's behavior with her, so that it could ultimately be understood as growth (differentiation) on her part. Recognition of developmentally based problems often provides an opportunity for effective short-term intervention. As this is under way, continuing assessment of the patient's functioning will make clear whether more extensive treatment is necessary.

The Constructionist Self

Emerging from the constructionist school of developmental psychology is a renaissance of interest in the self. In an earlier period, Super (1957) constructed a theory of career development based on progressive vocationally oriented modifications of the self-concept. More recently, Haan (1977) and Kegan (1979) have described self operations from a perspective that is rooted in meaning making. Haan's distinction between coping and defending processes (explored in chapter 5) depends on whether a set of ego operations is applied in the service of problem-solving or to ward off anxiety; the person's intention, rather than the manifest behavior, determines its meaning and function. Kegan has developed an "evolving self" model consisting of four stages and derived from Piagetian theory.

The constructionist view of self figures prominently in current theories of women's development. A consistent feature of these theories is the central role of the self as an essential part of construing the context of moral judgment (Gilligan, 1982), cognitive development (Belenky et al., 1986), and self in relation to others in overall personality development (Miller, 1976; Chodorow, 1980). In reviewing several decades of cross-cultural research, Mead (1955) and Symons (1979) concur that gender also plays a powerful role as an organizer of personality development, a further indication that the biological clock provides only one source of intraorganismic influence in life-span human development. Clearly we as patients and therapists are active agents in producing our own development.

CONSERVATION–CHANGE

Development is ongoing. The span from birth to death is inexorable, temporal, and finite. Change, and the personal encounter of change, is an inevitable, profound ingredient of life experience. Yet one of the great paradoxes of the human condition is that the inexorable nature of change is in direct counterpoint with a pervasive resistance to change, a holding to constancy. Philosophers have observed that humans exercise a preference to conserve what is known and familiar to them. Within perception theory, it has been recognized since the time of Helmholtz (1866) that objects are seen not as they appear on the retina but as they are retained in memory. Thus, a sheet of writing paper is seen as white whether viewed in bright sunlight or at dusk. This principle of perceptual constancy has been demonstrated in experiments with color, size, shape, and brightness (Woodworth, 1938). Despite major variations of the visual field, and optical response to those changes, perception remains centered around the familiar properties of the object under study. These properties are experienced as relatively constant, despite the evidence of one's own sensory data, because the person organizes perceptual process to conserve constancy.

As a paradigm, conservation–change is found in four of the most prominent developmental theories: Erikson's epigenesis, Mahler's separation–individuation, Piaget's equilibration, and Werner's orthogenesis. Erikson (1950, 1982) counterposes the stability of identity with the urged change of new life stages coming to ascendance. Mahler (1968, 1972) contends that people cling to infantile imagery when they encounter new issues in their lives. Piaget (1951) speaks of the equilibration between assimilation (conservation) which locates new experience in earlier cognitive schemas and accommodation (change), when the organism adapts to unfamiliar experience by restructuring those schemas. Werner (1957) acknowledges an oscillation between maintaining organismic integrity and developing toward more mature forms.

The conservation–change paradigm is not an either-or condition of choice but an amalgam of opposed and coexisting tensions. Conservation and change refer to two dynamic and interacting tendencies of organisms. Change is inevitable, and yet people strive to retain what is familiar. The implications of the conservation–change paradigm have far-reaching consequences, for understanding and working with people across the life span and in a variety of contexts.

CONSERVATION TENDENCIES

Conservation speaks to continuity, stability, constancy. According to Piaget (1951), early experiences are organized into schemas, which are then used to interpret subsequent experience—the process of assimilation. Conservation is sustained by selective attention to features indicative of sameness or stability over time; by preferring existing systems and patterns over innovation and novelty; by holding to the familiar and devaluing the strange or unknown; by trusting the past more than the future.

The conservation tendency organizes the emerging skills of adaptive mastery to define one's actions in keeping with culturally based norms. Conservation is maintained by recognizing cultural patterns and role expectations, internalizing them, and adapting inner needs in conformity with them. An affinity for tradition, and ongoing customs and mores, would also be consistent with a constancy orientation. Associated with the conservation tendency is a time perspective which views the present in light of the past, an attunement to history that is both personal and cultural. Conservation represents a preference for continuity and a tendency to evaluate decisions and options in the light of their outcome as these relate to the preservation of stability and sameness.

Conservation is, literally and figuratively, self-preserving. The tendency to resist change preserves that precious sense of personal sameness which Erikson calls identity. The personality dynamics of identity foreclosure (Marcia, 1967) in adolescents and young adults and adaptive armoring (Reichard, Livson, and Petterson, 1962) in senescent adults would seem consonant with a conservation orientation. Both identity foreclosure and adaptive armoring describe personality functioning in which socially approved role performance predominates over behavior more influenced by personal motives and goals. To this extent conservation may be aligned with the adjustment mode of development, discussed previously. In more extreme form, the conservation orientation can suggest distrust or discomfort with the unfamiliar and unconventional. Psychopathological manifestations would include xenophobia, rigidity, perseveration, stereotypic thought, and compulsive ritual.

The theories of Mahler and Piaget seem weighted toward the conservation tendencies in life-span development. Both theories emphasize early experience as a predominant influence in interpreting present day life events. In Mahler's thinking, contemporary challenges evoke separation–individuation associations of loss and regressive symbiotic yearnings for mother. Piaget's theory suggests that life-span experience is progressively schematized and patterned into previously acquired classifications. Both theories, therefore, give priority to describing the stable, prestructured modes that the organism employs for the interpretation of new events. Both Mahler and Piaget can be described as constructionist in their theories; each ascribes to people an active meaning-making role in the processing of new experience. The lens through which experience is filtered, however, is in both theories a preexistent structure. Thus, the conservation of ongoing patterns of interpreting experience is the predominant motif in these two theories. In clinical work, what is seen as resistance may sometimes have this important function of sustaining a shaky identity.

CHANGE TENDENCIES

The content of change tendencies is itself bifurcated over the life span. An emphasis upon change must acknowledge its bidirectionality, including both growth and decline. While biological life curves usually portray a cycle of growth–maturation–decline, psychological development may be more faithfully described as concomitant and multilinear: growth-with-maturation-with-decline (Baltes, 1979; Bocknek, 1980). At every stage of the life span, some processes are just emerging, others attain full maturity, and some are waning. The research of Horn and Cattell (1967) on intelligence function, for instance, reports a decline in "fluid" (abstract) intelligence from the teen years onward but an increase in "crystallized" (practical) intelligence that continues well into the seventh decade.

Kagan (1980) describes four kinds of developmental change, a listing he modified from Flavell (1972):

1. Enhancement. A structure or process is better articulated or the process is more efficient, but the "essential nature of the psychological quality remains unchanged" (p. 38).
2. Derivation. A structure or process is transformed from an earlier one, which is/was a requisite for the transformation to occur. Aspects of the earlier structure or process are incorporated into the later one.
3. Replacement. An earlier structure or process gives way to a later one; the later structure or process is not determined by or contingent upon the earlier one, although it may have functions similar to the earlier one.
4. Disappearance. A structure or process vanishes and is not followed or replaced by a functionally related one. In and of itself, change need not imply either benefit or decrement. More precisely, it does imply both.

The change orientation bifurcates functioning around growth-actualization and/or regression-decline. Growth-focused change is generally manifested by increased articulation and centralization of structure, and movement in the direction of flexibility, durability, purposive choice, and hierarchical integration of functions. Time sense relates present activities to future plans. Unlike growth, actualization also denotes increment in skill and breadth of operation. By contrast, growth-oriented change may necessitate dissolution of earlier gains, dynamic reorganization, and "irregulation of systems" (Labouvie-Vief, 1982) as well. Growth, whether of individuals or of organizations, is rarely linear. It is characteristic of developmental growth to occur along qualitative more than quantitative dimensions, and to encounter learning plateaus, phases of retrenchment, transient cycles of return to earlier levels of operation. Sheer increase in size, in organizations as much as individuals, may be contraindicative of growth. Brent (1981) reports that beyond critical points, increase in size requires increased efforts for internal maintenance and coordination, resulting in "degradation of functional efficiency" relative to intended functions.

The theories of Erikson and Werner seem to account best for the growth-actualization aspects of developmental change. In Erikson's theory each new life stage includes a psychosocial crisis, an expanding radius of social interaction, and a new source of potential strength. Werner's orthogenetic principle details growth "from a state of relative globality and lack of differentiation to a state of increased differentiation, articulation, and hierarchical integration" (1957, p. 126). More specific evidence of continuing growth actualization in adults can be derived from maturational indices such as Loevinger's (1976) ego development scale, Maslow's (1954) qualities of self-actualization, or Peck's (1975) description of develomental paths in the later years. The developmental modes of adaptation and actualization tend to be associated with growth-actualization orientation. While therapists customarily ascribe positive meaning to growth-actualization, change also mandates psychic reorganization and hence the potential for new problems. The pursuit of growth-actualization, rather than relief from psychopathology, seems to motivate some of the people who come for therapy.

Change tendencies oriented to regression–decline are expectable in the natural course of life-span development. Indications of regression–decline are manifested structurally by decrement or deterioration of the organizational integrity of the person or intrapsychic system. Disruption or distortion in the functional connections within the system—slowing, erratic function, or operating in ways reminiscent of earlier levels of development—also suggest change toward regression–decline. Narrowing and personalizing of scope of attention, withdrawal and constriction of personality, arbitrary focusing on parts of the whole, and the inability to distinguish parts from the whole are further indications of regression–decline patterning. Regression in the service of the ego is an adaptive process which typically adheres to the structural properties noted above, but without the affective or chronic aspects which are now described.

Regression–decline changes may feature retrenchment, a

loss of zest, a sense of retreat. This is aptly reflected in Mahler's thinking, where development entails "a lifelong mourning [for symbiosis] process . . . from the cradle to the grave" (1968, p. 416). Particular indices include impairment or loss of cognitive and social skills or the somatic and self-preoccupation which McLeish (1976) attributes to unfulfilled lives. The phenomenology of regression–decline change is of particular significance. A dysphoric affective toning is often characteristic of this orientation. Feelings range from apathy and bewilderment through discouragement, demoralization, and depression to hostility and terror. Conscious awareness can include bewilderment, sense of loss, inadequacy, incompetence, fear of the future. Regression–decline can be transient and situational as well as chronic or pathological. Temporary regression in the service of growth—during life transitions, for example—may mimic psychopathology. These circumstances may require psychotherapeutic attention nevertheless.

In general, preoccupation with security, health, and death in the absence of realistic imminent threat is likely to betoken a tendency toward regression–decline. When accompanied by continued impairment it is often indicative of frank psychopathology.

Werner's orthogenetic principle vividly depicts the range from primitivity to maturity, providing the clearest contrast of basic developmental structure and function. Syncretic fusion, for example, refers to the undifferentiated, fused experience of sensory stimuli, at one end of the spectrum. Hierarchical integration, at the other end, is reflected in a person's selective response to simultaneous stimuli. Developmental change is routinely bidirectional in Werner's thinking. Even when the predominant influences are in the direction of maturation, they are affected by the genetic principle of oscillation which states that forward progress typically begins with a step backward. Werner's holistic emphasis further informs the analysis by pointing to the Umwelt, the vital field in which the organism is embedded, as the appropriate unit of study (Barten and Franklin, 1978). A set of perceptions are studied most meaningfully in context with the emotional climate in which they occur; a patient's tirade against his boss may have to be arrayed with workplace conditions as well as his developmental history.

The epigenetic principle (Erikson, 1950) makes change imperative, whereas the orthogenetic principle does not convey the same sense of urgency. Erikson's application of epigenesis to a psychosocial perspective implicates society—its institutions, customs, and roles—in developmental change. The "ground plan" of development *is* change; Erikson's eight stages of life are traversed universally, by whatever paths the confluence of person, culture, and history create. With or without significant regression, each person encounters the critical issues of childhood, adulthood, old age. Where Mahler and Piaget locate the fundamental elements of development in the childhood years, Erikson and Werner indicate that maturity brings distinctive growth, that development is lifelong. Erikson's (1982) theory seems to detail the life course more completely, to blueprint the predictable events and experiences. But it bears the brunt of the unknowable factors coded into its structure. The psychosocial perspective attributes significant power to social and historic influences. How have urbanization and technology affected the frontier tradition that Erikson felt was so central to the American life-span experience? What is the impact of sexual liberation on Erikson's assertions that intimacy requires "mutuality of orgasm with . . . the other sex" (1950, p. 266), or that female identity development is necessarily incomplete without an intimate male relationship? Can an epigenetic theory retain its predictive consistency and still concede a major determining role to sociohistorical trends, which sometimes reverse themselves?

Life-span research is itself in an early stage of development. Yet the conservation–change paradigm provides a theoretical foundation of demonstrable utility in accounting for a wide array of clinical observations and empirical data. If each of the theories: epigenesis, separation–individuation, equilibration, orthogenesis, is incomplete, it is equally true that each is grounded in compelling evidence. Separation–individuation describes earliest development and its regressive pull; equilibration explains developmental dynamics, the how of the process; orthogenesis speaks to the direction and structure of development; epigenesis accounts for the nature and thrust of the life span.

In the aggregate, these theories document the meanings of conservation–change. They pose a powerful response to the argument represented by Gergen (1980) that "the life course seems fundamentally open-ended" (p. 35), unpredictable and unknowable.

Clearly, there are significant implications to be derived from the conservation–change paradigm. But care must be exercised in its application. It may be tempting to infer a personality typology of people who resist change versus those who seek it, of regression–decliners versus growth–actualizers. Similarly, value implications or health–pathology implications can be attributed to one or another of these developmental tendencies. Careful reading of the theorists responsible for these versions of the basic paradigm indicates other than a typological perspective. Each theorist presents a generic view of development. What they describe is intended to portray what is common to humankind, rather than a system for classifying alternatives. Conservation–change, in all its forms, is a general characteristic of life-span development.

To the extent that these developmental findings seem redundant and self-evident from a clinical perspective, it is reassuring that independently derived information substantiates practice. It has not always been thus in the relationship between clinicians and researchers. And, to the extent that this material broadens the conception of some therapists, its value will be even more apparent.

CHAPTER 10

SUMMATION AND SYNTHESIS

In overview, weekly egoself psychotherapy is an adaptation of modern psychoanalytic thought to the constraints of weekly contact, retaining the traditional therapeutic objective of restructuring. More specifically, the integrity and organization of internal object relations, ego functions, and self operations are addressed in the context of life-span development. Therapeutic outcome is measured against the dual criteria of internalization of the restructuring efforts and patients' ability to utilize these resources. Contemporary psychoanalytic theory is the essential data base for understanding the pathology patients bring to therapy. Equally important, this background is necessary for the most effective mobilization of patients' inherent resources. Consistent with its structural emphasis, egoself therapeutic technique is a product of the evolution of psychoanalytic psychotherapy, including its integration with the applied psychology of learning and development. Intervention focuses on helping patients reorganize experience so that internalization can occur. Therapy thus targets basic intrapsychic structure in its varied contemporary manifestations, including the pathological and the healthy, what is present and what is potential.

Another way of looking at egoself psychotherapy is operationally: there are two levels of approach which must be worked with concomitantly. At the descriptive level is the interaction between intention and consequence, including both the patient's reported experience and the therapist's observations. At the process level is the interaction between ego and self with development, filtering the effects of life history, gender, race, ethnicity, situation, family. For patients, on whom the burden of enacting change devolves, the issues must be as clear and uncomplicated as possible. For this reason, the descriptive level of intention and consequence is usually the most suitable arena for patient–therapist interaction. But to help manage the therapeutic work the process level must be constantly monitored by the practitioner.

Some psychotherapists proceed on the tacit assumption that an environment congenial to self-exploration is sufficient for successful weekly therapy. Often, that appraisal may be correct. Counselors and intuitively good listeners can offer significant help in this way, as the professional literature attests. But for people whose problems are more complex, empathic concern is not enough. Good intentions and intuitive skills do not substitute for extensive training and supervised experience. The task for the psychoanalytic psychotherapist is to help patients reduce to workable form issues and processes that are really enormously complex—indeed more complex than either party can fully grasp. In this context self understanding relative to the dynamic content of problems can divert patients from the more therapeutically beneficial task of understanding and managing the how of their dynamics: becoming aware of affective variations, differentiating aspects of self and other, distinguishing between expectation and outcome, learning when and how to soothe themselves, and developing other intrapsychic mediators.

For these reasons, it is in no sense paternalistic to insist that patients have enough to do effecting change in their lives; the intricacies of psychodynamics may be intriguing, but are rarely as instrumental to patients in effecting those changes. The clinician's understanding of intrapsychic process will provide the most essential therapeutic information. But at best, our psychological understanding is always incomplete. Even the most empathic therapist cannot have the patient's interior experience of self. Consequently, both parties meet with a potential for making distinctive but difficult contributions to a task-oriented partnership. Each has more than enough to do, in working toward a successful outcome.

Interpretations which produce insight into psychodynamic

conflict and content are an important component of psychoanalytic practice. In weekly therapy genetic interpretation may
enlighten the patient, but rarely does it produce structural
change by itself. I support that view of interpretation shared
by Blanck and Blanck (1986) and Strupp and Binder (1984),
that insights often come after the problem has been resolved.
I view genetic interpretation as an intervention which often
deflects from rather than enhances the work of weekly therapy.
Interpretation proposes a causal relationship between past and
present events. But the therapeutic task is to find new ways to
function, to replace that which is painfully ineffective. Yet, people cling to the past, holding to what is part of their identity,
in spite of the pain. The risk of any interpretation (and especially the accurate one) is that it emphasizes what the patient
must give up rather than what is to be gained. Insight into why
or how Al's mother punished him may have the unintended
effect of reinforcing his infantile connection to her, rather than
helping him let go of a destructive relational pattern. The way
Al provokes his wife's anger today causes him problems, irrespective of how or why he does it. Independent of its origin,
he needs experientially to "see" that his current provocative
behavior results in problems with his wife. His readiness for
change will benefit from that understanding, of what is going
on now that he helps to create. The therapeutic task is to help
him appreciate the costs and gains of what he does now, in
current relationships. He cannot change the past, but he can
discover better ways of relating to a woman in his present life.
To disconnect wife from mother, me-now from me-then, will
be a secondary benefit and not the time-consuming focus of
therapy. To reaffirm old connections by stressing their continuation into the present may only emphasize what is lost by
giving them up. Learning how to enhance his marriage in adult
ways helps weight cost–benefit away from distorted childhood
gratification-with-pain. Exploring a new way of relating may
help internalize the experience, affording the patient a broader
range of mental representations and relationships, and discovering how to exercise ego option. Granted, it may be helpful
for the patient to understand that he justifies his destructive
actions by falsely ascribing to his wife what his mother used to

do. But even that interpretation may be of limited value, since it does not confront whether he really feels that changing would be worthwhile, or how to go about doing so. Conversely, by working on resolving his destructive interaction with his wife—invoking his adult resources—he also gains ego distance from his early maternal interaction. This modifies its insidious effects and ultimately aids in the restructuring of those early object relations.

Reconstruction of early experience undoubtedly has its place, particularly for the therapist's own assessment of the basic pathology and its origins. As an intervention technique, however, its role may be most valuable in orthodox psychoanalysis rather than weekly psychotherapy.

Keep in mind that these premises are concerned with weekly psychotherapy. Unlike psychoanalysis, where self understanding is valued for its own sake, weekly psychotherapy has more restricted objectives. Egoself theory extends the path taken by contemporary psychoanalytic writers such as Blanck and Blanck (1974, 1979) and Masterson (1976). Their position is that the therapist's role is catalytic, but that in order to promote individuation patients must learn. They believe that natural growth processes will guide patients toward health-producing discoveries. Nevertheless, for Masterson, "the act of learning . . . is as important as the insights" (1976, p. 91). Blanck and Blanck advocate "ego-building" interventions to facilitate therapeutic ego development. Both approaches emphasize the importance of a real object function for therapists, one in which real life experience is made available to their patients. By contrast with intensive therapy the weekly egoself therapeutic role may be more interactive, sometimes prescriptive but always in a context of empathic attunement.

A significant portion of people's self-esteem is attributable to competence, the discovery of personal effectiveness. Empowerment of patients is one of the foundational precepts of egoself psychotherapy. These objectives are best achieved when patients are actively involved in the design and experience of their own learning. A vital therapeutic activity is to assist patients in discovering their own learning. At the same time, therapy is more than the identification of pathological distortion. Egoself therapy does not infantilize patients, but neither does it leave them entirely to their own devices, to scratch around on a hit-or-miss basis, or in the blind faith that mature restructuring will automatically and inevitably ensue. Much unnecessary pain and frustration can be avoided, especially in weekly therapy, when therapists actively help their patients to identify, locate, and incorporate meaningful, growthful experiences. Encountering those experiences is an irreducible necessity for patients, in any therapeutic approach. Then, afterward, reviewing the impact of those events is part of the work of therapy. But this experimental part of the process is too crucial to be left at the whim of chance happenings or to the uninformed trial-and-error approach of people trying to find their way through uncharted territories.

At times, psychotherapists seem to ascribe both too little and too much to the egoself resources of their patients. By devoting their attention to the early origins of psychopathology, they may neglect to review the healthy developmental attainments of the patient. How is it that the person with ego defects seemingly dating from the rapprochement subphase of separation–individuation is a successful businessman, or a loving parent? How do the intrapsychic resources needed for those attainments affect the prognosis and conduct of therapy? Conversely, some psychoanalytic writers limit their role as growth facilitators to suggesting that "natural growth processes" are sufficient to guide effective new learning, as the psychopathological influences are reduced. If the person's early development has been severely handicapped, it seems more reasonable to assume that therapy should include the active promulgation of new learning, lest the patient slip back into the old familiar, habitual, counterproductive ways of functioning. The activation of ego resources does not, of itself, assure that they will be automatically used to best effect.

In the approach taken here, assessment of egoself operations and life-span developmental status supersedes diagnostic classification. Intervention strategy is keyed to the active recruitment and mobilization of identified resources, and focused on those intrapsychic processes which underlie the client's dysfunction. The therapeutic work concentrates on present time, intention and consequence, gain and cost. Anamnestic material informs clinical understanding of the problem and aids in assessment; it is not the focus for the therapeutic work itself. The therapist's role ranges from empathic listening and traditional uses of reflection and clarification to active recruitment of resources and prescriptive intervention. Eclecticism of technique is encouraged to the extent that it is consistent with the precepts of egoself theory.

Anyone walking regularly on Commonwealth Avenue in Boston comes to recognize another denizen of that street. He is a middle-aged man with straggly hair and beard, his clothing shabby and worn. Regardless of the season he strides along, mumbling to himself in autistic dialogue and avoiding the gaze of other pedestrians. There is little that is remarkable about this man; he is of a familiar genre, formerly a mental hospital resident and now a deinstitutionalized schizophrenic. The interested observer soon notes other features of this man's regimen as well. His faded wardrobe varies with the weather; sometimes he wears a Walkman, which seems not to interfere with his habitual hallucinating. As preoccupied as he seems, this man's journey is not aimless. He carries with him a little metal pick, which he uses to extricate coins lodged in traffic meter coin slots. He also checks each coin return of the many public telephones on his route. It seems he makes his living that way.

My point is this: human perception patterns are based on noticing familiar contours. As therapists we automatically attune ourselves to those manifestations identifiable as pathology. But to really understand the man described above, his competence is just as important as his pathology. So much of our discourse and our literature is devoted to our patients' pathological processes, and so little to their resources, upon which we depend if therapy is to be effective. Yet, in the office, with the patient, our most successful interventions are those which intersect with or stretch intrapsychic resources: the patient's capacity for reorganization, upon which change is built. Indeed, this skill has been listed among the "arts" of doing therapy. I have no wish to deprecate the exquisite aesthetic sensitivity one finds in the best therapists. What I have attempted to demonstrate throughout this volume is that substantive knowledge can now supplement those other skills. We now have the means for conducting a more explicit assessment of egoself resources, and a clearer notion of how they can be applied in therapy. As one immediate benefit, therapists who have felt constrained by the unique demands of weekly therapy on psychoanalytic practice have an approach specifically tailored to their sophisticated background.

The continued advancement of psychoanalytic psychotherapy is best served by ongoing critical analysis from its adherents. What are the "active ingredients," those which are irreplaceable and those which are more suitable for one or another modification of therapeutic practice? In that spirit of inquiry it is timely to consider the elements which together comprise weekly egoself therapy. In its broader form the theory and its application have been laid out in the preceding chapters. Now I will present the distillate, those premises which undergird the thinking and shape the practice. By making these points explicit, the fit between egoself and other variations may be clearer, furthering future discussion and study.

For the present it will be useful to organize this list of premises in several groupings: egoself operations, developmental processes, the relationship, conditions of change.

EGO OPERATIONS

The data and principles of ego psychology are essential ingredients of weekly psychotherapy. A knowledge of ego function, organization, and development is necessary for the assessment of patients and design of therapeutic strategy. Object relations theory helps to account for the process of ego development. In addition, it lays the groundwork for understanding the dynamics of psychotherapeutic change.

Weekly psychotherapy produces structural change because it is targeted at the structural system, primarily ego. Ultimately, change can be defined as ego development, since personality functioning requires the integrity and adequacy of ego oper-

ations. The egoself approach recruits and mobilizes ego resources to implement change.

Most of the known "active ingredients" of therapy, including insight, working through, and other corrective experiences,
can be subsumed under the ego function of learning. This is
because learning affects so many other ego functions: perception, memory, judgment, reasoning, analysis, synthesis, selective
attention, reality testing, delay. The effects of new learning,
therefore, always reverberate into other aspects of ego activity.

Ego operations are organizing processes, creating patterns
which take on meaning in whatever way and to whatever extent
the organism is capable. Consequently, both prior and current
experience, learning, and object relations are constantly being
modified in conformity with the ego system's developing capacities for meaning making.

SELF ORGANIZATION

At the core of meaning making are the images and narcissistic
representations that form the self. The ways by which one comes
to know oneself, whether by boundary demarcation, affective
investment, or the nature of one's object relations, organize life
by interfacing with ego operations. The patterning of information derives its fullest meaning from its relevance for the
self (Belenky, Clinchy, Goldberger, and Tarule, 1986).

From the onset of awareness, the processing of experience
to make personally relevant meaning is incorporated into self
structure. As Schafer (1977) suggests, language, like memory,
is in the service of making personal experience more coherent.
At all levels of interaction, therapeutic activity engages an organizing process geared to meaning making. The meanings
derived in the past evolve into the present, barely modified in
one instance and transformed in another. In particular those
affective images which lack adequate verbal representation can
pathologically distort self structure. Disorders of early identity,
including gender identity, are among the most intractable therapeutic challenges.

The centrality of self to human functioning assures that

later-evolving problems will also impact disproportionately on other aspects of development. Therapeutic assessment and intervention must account for how the patient structures events in the light of self-experience. Early narcissistic components of self, in particular, are least accessible to the patient's conscious report. By virtue of its highly invested, nonverbal character the most central aspects of self—those which infuse experience with its most personal meaning—are often the most obscured. Thus, pathological narcissism seriously impairs function even when there is apparent coherence of the dynamic content of self.

Weekly therapy, especially with self disorders, monitors closely the transference and countertransference, consistent with the work of the therapeutic partnership.

THERAPEUTIC RELATIONSHIP

The patient–therapist relationship has several facets, which vary across time and circumstance. The reduced frequency of weekly egoself therapy tends to mute the intensity of transference and countertransference reactions. Conversely, face-to-face contact may enhance reactions to therapists and their personal style. The real object relationship involves actual qualities of the therapist which the patient can incorporate. Finally, the ongoing context of weekly therapy is sustained by the partnership.

Successful psychotherapy sustains an environment which nourishes growthful change. The character of this environment is defined by the therapeutic partnership. This relationship mobilizes patients' capacity to explore the unfamiliar, risk narcissistic insult, and relinquish cathectic ties to dysfunctional processes. The therapeutic partnership is valuable to the extent that it supports experiential learning appropriate to the patient's treatment needs. An affectively modulated relationship is optimal for weekly psychotherapy. The therapeutic partnership features: equal members, mutually respected, each providing areas of expertise, each acknowledging their reliance upon the contribution of the other.

The principles of empowerment, accountability, and compassion for self guide the therapeutic partnership. They are selectively introduced to the patient's approach to problems whenever developmentally feasible. Supportive confrontation is a particularly useful intervention in this regard.

Intense transference reactions, positive or negative, inform but are not essential to the therapeutic work. While the frequency of weekly psychotherapy meetings helps to limit intense transference reactions, this material may surface spontaneously with certain patients. The deliberate elicitation and analysis of transference material in weekly egoself psychotherapy is discouraged. When intense transference reactions block the main therapeutic work, intervention strategy is directed at helping patients moderate and deflect the affective intensity, rather than probe to its source as a therapeutic goal.

DEVELOPMENTAL PROCESSES

Life-span development is characterized by both conservation and change. Change refers to growth and regression, while conservation is resistance to change, holding onto sameness. Development is an ongoing, sequential process, from birth to death, involving the interaction between conservation and change. The relationship between conservation and change varies over the life span, although conservation trends are usually stronger. Under optimal conditions change is associated with growth and conservation with stability. Both are necessary; growth leads to actualization of potential, and stability reinforces a sense of identity.

Gender developmental issues significantly inform attitudes, perceptions, and interpersonal expectations, even in weekly psychotherapy. The interaction of life stage with gender, as well as the empathic understanding of gender differences, constitute an important, complex aspect of therapeutic work.

Each stage of life evokes universally experienced intrapsychic susceptibilities, capacities as well as demands. In addition, the person's development at any given time is shaped by his or her world view, their developmental mode. Growth, maturation, and decline occur naturally and concomitantly across the entire life span, as various psychological susceptibilities wax and wane. Those susceptibilities which are stage specific may provide unique opportunities for intervention or portend a period of heightened vulnerability. Preexisting psychopathological processes are subject to the influence of these developmental variations. The patient's developmental status is measured by the range from the highest to the most primitive–regressed levels of function indicated. Developmental assessment and monitoring is, therefore, an essential part of each weekly session. Developmental assessment also serves the therapeutic task of recruiting and mobilizing the developmental potentialities inherent in each life stage. These potentialities represent untapped resources heretofore unavailable to the patient. In the last analysis, patients' psychological resources are the alternatives to the pathological processes currently being utilized. Psychopathology is, in part, the result of having had insufficient resources at the time for the stresses the patient previously encountered.

The egoself view is that people are participants in their own development. The evolution of their intentions and their perceptions reflects the development of the self and object representations that constitute the psychological self. As a consequence, experiential and volitional material are significant data in weekly psychotherapy. Self, like identity, develops from an accretion of attitudes and experiences which are felt and perceived. Self-image, and its developmental course, can exercise a crucial influence on patients' lives.

PRINCIPLES OF CHANGE

Since change is the law of all living things, it is inexorable and spontaneous as well as planned and induced. Egoself theory locates change as an outcome of the interaction between intention, process, and experience. Intention is an attitude expressing purpose; process refers here to intrapsychic systems of function; experience is the impact of events on awareness. Weekly egoself therapy emphasizes experience and its attendant processes, viewing intention in the light of these vectors. Patients' attentions tend to focus on intentions and outcomes.

Therapists focus more on the processing of experience as it relates to intentions and outcomes.

Ultimately, therapeutic change entails growth, by developmental expansion of function or improvement in egoself operations. In addition, patients must be willing to relinquish those partial gratifications which sustain the pathology. The cost–benefit ratio must favor change for there to be motivation to grow. Consequently, elucidating psychological costs and benefits—current and prospective—is a valuable part of the therapeutic process.

Every gain carries a cost. Every change has consequences, both benefits and costs, whether they are anticipated or are adventitious. Pathological adjustments usually include some partial gratification and/or patients' belief that there is no option. Cost–benefit analysis examines functional consequences and their attendant egoself processes. The assessment of experience, from intention to outcome, includes affective, motoric, physiological, and cognitive aspects. The immediate goal of cost–benefit analysis is to help patients to recognize the actual consequences of their intentions. The preconditions for therapeutic change often derive from this recognition.

Egoself growth is fundamental to therapeutic change. Intervention strategy is geared to ego and self structure, their constituent processes, and the self-esteem derived from the therapeutic work and relationship. Egoself restructuring is accomplished by reorganizing ego operations, aiding modification of self and object representations, and mobilizing developmental resources. The primary medium for ego restructuring is corrective experiential learning. In this sense, the weekly therapy sessions can be considered an egoself oriented learning laboratory.

Weekly egoself therapy inquires into *how* the person functions in psychopathological or destructive fashion more than *why* the person functions that way. Change is not automatically beneficial and must be adapted to patients' intentions. Learning how the person functions permits the creation of options, within the scope of the person's egoself and developmental capabilities. Assessing and restructuring intrapsychic processes from the perspective of ego psychology, self psychology, and object relations theory is the thrust of the psychotherapeutic work. Enabling patients to apply new resources to old problems is the result, optimizing the prospects for a favorable therapeutic outcome.

Therapeutic intervention operates most effectively in a present–future time orientation. Patients' problems are current, in the present; they have consequences and implications for the near and long-term future. Due to the ongoing nature of psychological development, early experiences are continuously reorganized over the life course. The past informs, but does not automatically determine the present. Past history provides clues and a baseline for an understanding of current functioning. But patients' insight into their past experiences is neither necessary nor sufficient for therapeutic change.

Egoself therapy also takes account of the effects of contemporary morality on psychopathology. Victorian codes of morality underlay the power of interpretation during the period of Freud's early discoveries. But in most of the Western world today "I want to" rivals "I ought to," without risking superego sanctions or ego dystonia as it once did. The cost–benefit model is based on enlightened self-interest, not morality. Confronting the costs of one's actions and intentions, while discovering one's own capacities for more effective function, can have powerful consequences for therapeutic change.

The facilitation of growthful change is at the heart of every theory of psychotherapy. It is anomalous, therefore, that so few theories explore in detail the process by which change is promulgated. Perhaps the underlying reason is that most theorists lack formal training in the processes by which growthful change takes place. Exposure to learning theory, developmental theory, or planned change is not a usual part of the preparation of most psychotherapists. As a result, some of our most advanced theories of therapy are seriously deficient in their exposition of the processes by which change is implemented. Some theories assume that growth occurs spontaneously and optimally, as soon as psychopathological impediments are removed from its path. Other theories use methods derived from training laboratory birds and rats. One of the distinguishing strengths of the egoself approach is that change theory is built into its perspective, since change depends upon specific egoself functions and concurrent developmental prepotencies. The operative principles in promoting change, discussed more thoroughly under technique and procedure (chapter 4), are learning and attention focusing.

Learning

Every system of psychotherapy tacitly engages its consumers in training and learning. Both therapists and patients are indoctrinated with the tools and ways of thinking that characterize training and learning in the particular system. The skills of attentive listening, reporting "random" thoughts, or ascribing words to a part of one's body are indispensable to the practice of their respective therapies. Gaining confidence in the therapeutic system and its practitioners also entails training and learning. It is, therefore, ironic that so little attention is given to the learning and training processes of the various psychotherapies.

The conception of how humans learn is fundamental to the egoself approach. As noted earlier, perception and learning are founded in pattern creation and then in meaning making. The overriding principle of egoself function is the organization of experience, utilizing the cognitive processes of perceiving, learning, remembering, and reasoning. In egoself psychotherapy therapists and patients are both adult learners, each teaching and learning from the other. But, while behavior modification techniques can be adapted to the egoself approach, the stimulus–response model of learning is contrary to the style and philosophy of egoself psychotherapy. Adult learning, and growth-oriented learning in particular, is based on using the most advanced capabilities of the person relative to the task to be addressed. The egoself approach is therefore geared to the organismic learning of its clients. Organismic learning includes the intellect but covers all other aspects of human experience as well—affective, motoric, somatic. Learning is a cognitive process in that it involves levels of knowing. As Lazarus (1984) suggests, however, cognition subsumes motivation and emotion as interdependent ingredients—"a relational and meaning-centered view" (p. 128).

Patients are helped to recognize their own patterns of experience and response, physical, emotional, imaginal, the growthful and the pathological. Egoself psychotherapy addresses the patterning of intrapsychic processes, not its etiology, as the intervention strategy of choice. Patients learn to recognize the current reaction patterns that yield them ego dystonic consequences, and then go on to explore alternatives which are personally feasible and effective. Successful intervention involves the therapeutic partnership in learning how the patient's intrapsychic processes operate—with which consequences and at what cost. Magical beliefs, secondary gains, and gratifications of acting out are arrayed against humiliation, lost lovers, failed jobs, and somatic disorders. New learning is defined, not by insight, but by practiced experience and close examination of its consequences.

Let us return to an illustration described earlier:

P: Well, I had a chance to try out that idea this week.

Th: Which idea?

P: You know, when Susie gets me mad . . . to release the muscle tension first so I won't be so terrified of doing some damage to her.

Th: What did you do?

P: Well, I tried that exercise you showed me, pushing against the wall? But that didn't seem to help. So then I experimented with grabbing the top of the door and suspending myself off the floor that way. It seemed to work much better; the tension drained from my hands and forearms. But I felt like an idiot, hanging like that from the door.

Th: Sure, but how did your arms and hands feel?

P: The tension was gone, and I felt more in control of myself.

Th: Great. Then what?

P: Well, I went back in to Susie, but by then the situation was past.

Th: Okay. But now you know how to bring that tension under control when the situation arises again, and you won't have to be afraid of what you'll do to Susie in the process.

The patient was soon able to discipline her daughter, appropriately and with increasing confidence. She gradually found less need to use the exercise when she got angry at the child. The interactive nature of the learning is interesting. While the exercise idea proved useful, the patient had to improvise a method better suited to her in order for it to work. Consistent with egoself precepts, the therapist opted not to explore the transference and control implications of choosing an alternative exercise instead of the one suggested.

Learning and preparing to learn—potentiating egoself operations—is central to egoself intervention strategy. Patients are the hands-on agents of their own problem solving. Therapy sessions are occupied with identifying pathological processes in their everyday behavioral manifestations. Therapists use standard therapy interview procedure. In addition they enhance patients' active participation by focusing attention on the cost–gain outcomes of their psychological patterns; adapt patient readiness to the recruitment of resources, guided by previous achievements and current developmental status; collaborate on the design and implementation of exploratory interventions; review and retune earlier efforts in subsequent sessions, with particular attention paid to an empathic exploration of client experiences in these ventures.

Learning is, therefore, appropriately adult in tenor and form. It incorporates contemporary tenets of adult learning: active participation, experience based, task oriented, involving as many aspects of the person and milieu as are relevant and manageable. Learning occurs inadvertently as well as intentionally. As an autonomous ego function, it occurs spontaneously and fortuitously, with or without conscious awareness. Learned patterns are conserved, internalized, and become part of the patient's identity as self representations. Egoself structuring in weekly psychotherapy is, therefore, intimately involved with experiential learning.

Attention Focusing

In the broad analysis of theory and practice it is easy to overlook a vital aspect of weekly egoself therapy. In fifty minutes a week such a tiny part of the patient's life is given to treatment that the intrapsychic realities have difficulty competing with the saliency of everyday pressures. One of the key ways that therapy is kept intensive is by selective use of attention focusing. Whenever feasible, therapeutic effort and attention is narrowed, so that the specific intrapsychic processes involved can be brought into sharply etched focus.

As is customary, during initial assessment past history is collated from the patient's imagery and recall. However, it is also useful to confront patients with past–present comparisons where these serve the work in present time. By virtue of the role of intention and consequence in egoself psychotherapy, present–future time sequences are also inherent areas of focus. But rarely are future events considered in the long term, since that sort of discussion readily becomes intellectualized, and remote from personally involved experience. Both past and future are managed therapeutically in terms of their relevance for the present.

> *P*: The way things are going, there will be a nuclear war in another five years. There's no way in hell I'm going to survive something like that.
> *Th*: How does that affect the way you think about what you're doing now?
>
> *P*: We used to go on hikes every Sunday, Dad and I.
> *Th*: What was that like for you?
> *P*: It was good, a lot of fun, except that he and Mom would fight all the time because she said he was leaving her at home while he went off to have a good time.
> *Th*: Does that remind you of anything that goes on in your life now?

But more than temporal attention focusing, egoself psychotherapy concentrates on pathological distortions of intrapsychic process, through whatever mode of expression is utilized. Attention focuses on the patient's experience, which is analyzed and explored as it is being presented. What is being reported? What does it reveal about level and adequacy of egoself development: coping and defense processes, self structure, affect differentiation and integration? What does it reveal about other developmental aspects: Is the patient's functioning stage-appropriate, oriented to survival or mastery? As problem functioning is identified, the focus across processes shifts to an intensified study of specific subsystems, directing the attention of both partners toward the area of pathology. According to Sabetti (1976) psychoanalytic focusing is general and peripheral, pulling seemingly extraneous observations into a more specific context.

The incident which follows details an illustration used earlier, on page 195. My attention focusing picked up a somatic reaction. Pinpointing the behavior produced a peripheral association from the past, which could then be refocused on the current problem:

> *Th*: As you were talking about that, I noticed something about your breathing.
> *P*: What's that?
> *Th*: Your inhaling changed; you seem to be taking short, quick breaths.
> *P*: I didn't notice anything.
> *Th*: Try this: try inhaling to a slow count of eight and exhaling to a slow count of eight.
> *P*: (tries, but soon gasps for air) I couldn't do it.
> *Th*: Try again . . . how do you feel?
> *P*: A little scared. I just remembered something that happened when I was a kid—I almost drowned one time (patient goes on to describe the incident, which sheds light on the current situation he had been talking about).

During the course of any session, attention may shift across time, situations, or persons, from imagery to emotions, from broad scanning to narrow focusing. At the critical choice points, however, therapeutic strategy focuses attention on the near term, where intrapsychic processes and their consequences can be closely examined. Narrowing the focus in order to monitor egoself or developmental functioning is a frequent occurrence in therapy sessions.

Peter is a twenty-two-year-old college dropout, arrested after trying to rob a service station. He is an angry young man who is at war with the world, including his father, a well-known scholar. As he describes an altercation with his father, I want to determine if he is capable of an observing ego perspective, a developmental acquisition of young adulthood:

> *P*: So right then, in the middle of everything else that's going on, the old man finally decides he's gonna open his mouth. And what does this great intellect come out with—"Do you need any money?" I'm talking about what this cop did and he's asking me about money.
> *Th*: Why do you suppose he said a thing like that?
> *P*: Who cares? He was just shooting off his mouth, trying to sound important.
> *Th*: Is that what he does?

P: Who knows? what difference does it make? It's probably the only thing he could think to offer.

While he prefers to think of his father in simplistic terms, closer attention to his last sentence reveals that Peter is capable of acknowledging greater complexity, of standing back and observing his father–son relationship from the vantage point of personal perspective. This ego asset was revealed by focusing attention on intrapsychic process ["Why do you suppose . . ."] rather than on the history of their interaction. The same technique is helpful in assessing self and object representations, for more precise insight into the patient's development. Continuing the session above,

Th: Do you know what you would have wanted from him?
P: What difference does it make? That's how he is.
Th: But what did you want?

The patient's level of self differentiation—addressed by the last intervention—will cue the level at which the therapist can look for structural pathology. At the same time, the therapy assumes a vitality and immediacy which patients from widely different backgrounds can understand and respect. As a final point, attention focusing is increasingly specific: progressively honing in on a particular intrapsychic process in each specific situation; examining in detail the operations in their immediate context; then designing an intervention to test, enhance, or apply that process to treatment goals.

P: Just once I'd like him to see me, to talk to me like his son, not like another problem to solve. I want him to see that I have ideas too, that I think, that I'm not some dumb yoyo.
Th: That you're really his son.
P: Yeah (eyes tearful).

Now it is clear that the relational issue is not adolescent rebellion or separation–individuation, but seeking connection. As the focus becomes more precise the structure and dynamics are made more explicit. The therapy has advanced one more step.

Developmental Resources for Restructuring

Exploring the nature of adult egoself development requires that one account for the entire panoply of life-span observations: When is early experience so overwhelming that its effects are irreversible? What distinguishes those circumstances from others in which significant later transformations can occur? Or, do factors other than early severity enter the picture?

Actually, the questions are rhetorical, and misleading. They fly in the face of all the evidence demonstrating that some transformation always occurs, that literal stasis is unknown to the human condition. Restating the questions in light of this evidence leads to an assessment of which processes or conditions favor transformations leading to healthy growth, and which favor changes which conserve or extend developmental disturbance. The literature offers a number of cues which speak to this question: the availability of new figures with whom to identify in stage-specific roles; the later emergence of qualitatively different ego resources for reprocessing early experiences; expanding opportunities for learning alternative reactions to earlier internalized experiences; later developmental and psychosocial prepotencies for restructuring personal activities and interactions. Each of these merits closer attention. Each gives indication of occurring spontaneously, or as a result of professional intervention.

1. *The Availability of New Figures with Whom to Identify in Stage-Specific Roles.* Over the life course numerous figures take on particular importance. At each stage the developmental imperative to change endows surrounding figures with saliency appropriate to that stage. As the child acquires speech and motility, members of its community beyond the primary group become available as identification figures. With adolescence comes a shifting of emphasis from parents to peers as the child seeks primary identification with its own generation. Prior to young adulthood, late adolescents seek "inspirational figures" (Bocknek, 1980) as models in the reorganizational work of identity formation. The Levinson research team (Levinson et al., 1979) described the developmental importance of finding a mentor during the young adult years. Unlike a parent or

parent-surrogate: "Mentoring is defined not in terms of formal roles but in terms of the character of the relationship and the functions it serves" (p. 98). "The mentor is *not* a parent or crypto-parent. . . . The mentor represents a mixture of parent and peer; he must be both and not purely either one" (1979, p. 99).

Gutmann's cross-cultural studies (1975) suggest that in middle age people may identify with their spouses in "sex-role reversals . . . each sex becomes to some degree what the other used to be" (p. 181). Colarusso and Nemiroff (1981) suggest that the transition to adulthood includes "the *transformation* of an infantile theme into an adult one" (p. 67) as people "redefine" themselves and their relationships. Thus, throughout adolescence and adulthood there are opportunities to reexamine earlier object relations in the light of emerging developmental prepotencies for new identifications.

2. *The Emergence of Qualitatively Different Ego Resources for Reprocessing Early Experiences.* Ego development is an ongoing organismic process throughout the life span. Vaillant (1977), building on the work of earlier psychoanalytic writers, describes a developmental hierarchy of defenses which ranges from denial and distortion in childhood to the "mature mechanisms" of anticipation, altruism, and humor. Over the twenty- to thirty-year period of the Grant Study, subjects shifted from earlier to more mature defenses as they grew into adulthood.

Other ego operations also change over the life span. The capacity for social perspective has its origins in childhood (Selman, 1980) but does not mature into personal perspective until young adulthood (Bocknek, 1980). Erikson (1982) proposes that there are specific "ego strengths" which are epigenetically linked to each life stage, building upon earlier foundations and influencing what is to come. A perceptual restructuring of time sense recurs throughout life, shifting from exclusive preoccupation with the immediate here-and-now to an awareness of future time, and then reversing around middle age (Neugarten, 1969). Cognitive functions undergo qualitative change—from "fluid" to "crystallized" intellectual processing—during the adult years (Schaie and Gewirtz, 1982).

Consequently, the natural life course equips all people at

each successive stage with egoself resources never before available to them.

3. *Expanding Opportunities for Learning Alternative Reactions to Earlier Internalized Experiences.* A dominant feature of life-span development is the expansion of the person's "social radius" (Erikson, 1950). Although object relations originate in experiences with parenting figures, from the earliest months human experience typically incorporates psychological contact with a proliferating variety of experiences and relationships. Along with evolving patterns of anxiety-laden object relations, people encounter other experiences which may be important but lack the expectable consistency of the internalized patterns. Even though these experiences may be dissonant with primary self and object representations, they are retained as valued images, internalized, and go through the transformations natural to the developmental process.

Every life history contains these discrete subclusters, counterpoints to the major themes of personality development. In structure and content they are part of ego, self, and identity development. The child scapegoated at home can be a bully at school. The aggressive bullying may later become socialized in competitive sports, where impulse control and modulated aggression are vital to successful performance. Alongside early images of "bad me" there develop integrated images of "angry me," "good me," "hero me." Even if "bad me" has the priority of primacy, and comes endowed with such anxiety that it is dissociated "especially are we to be guided by Mahler's discovery that inadequacy in a single subphase [of separation–individuation] may sometimes be subsumed normally in the long pull of development" (Blanck and Blanck, 1979, p. 25).

Another opportunity for alternative experience is provided by what Antonovsky (1979) calls "sense of coherence," "a global orientation that . . . one's internal and external environments are predictable and that there is a high probability that things will work out as well as can reasonably be expected" (p. 123) ". . . a generalized, long-lasting way of seeing the world and one's life in it" (p.124).

Antonovsky's work as a medical sociologist with an interdisciplinary team including a psychiatrist and psychologist, led him to study health, stress, and coping in cultures and people around the globe. This research culminated in identifying general resistance resources to stress, an active faith that sustains people in the face of pain and calamity. The sense of coherence seems to be a belief system which is often neither conscious nor articulated, but is found ubiquitously in Trobriander fishermen and Czarist aristocrats as well as citizens of Western cultures. It would appear that people who experience some larger order in their lives, and who have a sense of participation in that social order, may be fortified in dealing with otherwise debilitating stressors. These two features of coherence—making meaning and active participation—are also prominent ingredients of the egoself system. Having a sense of coherence may account for the resiliency found in those people who overcome seemingly intolerable life circumstances. As Antonovsky describes it, sense of coherence is learned, a view which one brings to situations and can be modified by the situation. It is a joint function of cultural context and one's role within it, and is closely tied to the belief that one has a part to play in that system.

The analogy to the patient's role in psychotherapy is too obvious to be ignored. The implications for involving patients as participant meaning makers speaks clearly to the place of ego building in the structure and process of psychotherapy. It is important to note that there is a body of empirical studies supporting Antonovsky's contention of a relationship between measures of general health and indices of sense of coherence.

Another feature of the sense of coherence relevant to this discussion is the importance of predictability, knowing what is probably to be expected. One is reminded of Hartmann's (1958) emphasis on the expectable early environment necessary for healthy ego development. In this context expectability refers to the child's realization that its wants are taken care of. And, much later in the life span, Neugarten and her associates (Neugarten, Wood, Kraines, and Loomis, 1975) find that one of the prime factors in women's response to menopause is the expectation of what it means for them. These are some of the opportunities for confronting with alternative experience the meaning ascribed to earlier egoself development.

4. *Later Developmental and Psychosocial Prepotencies for Re-*

structuring Personal Activities and Interactions. Murphy (1947) accounts for the continuity of early childhood reactions in three ways: biological continuities; early "canalizations," specific urgings which predispose the person to seek out compatible environmental components in its psychological field; ongoing frequent and consistent environmental reinforcement of early experiences.

Countering these patterns are the developmental prepotencies to restructure self and object images, which surface with each life stage. These prepotencies are capable of reorganizing earlier images and modes of meaning making, in the service of developmental needs. The child's developmental need to form an ego ideal affects its perceptual structuring of memories as well as current experiences. The capacity for object constancy is present even when its operation is not evident. Urgings for intimacy arise in young adults who are still struggling with fusion and separation issues. For some of these people, partial resolution of the later developmental issue enables them to confront the earlier one more effectively. For others, dealing with the later developmental issue with modest success enables them to move on to further developmental issues and further restructuring.

> Mr. Q was the youngest of five children, and the only son. His father died when he was ten, after years of invalidism. His mother, a volatile and demanding woman, had little energy for Mr. Q and he was raised by his sisters in an environment bare of material necessities or male models. Mr. Q finished high school, dated rarely, served in the armed forces, met a woman after being discharged from the Army, and married her two years later. Despite almost thirty years of marriage and fathering three children, Mr. Q manifests a tenuous male identity. He has never had more than mild sexual feelings, and has been passive or passive–aggressive in relations with women: mother, sisters, wife. Coitus has been experienced as obligatory more than satisfying. Yet he has been an attentive and considerate husband, the parent his children confide in, a popular member of his community, and a successful businessman. This man bears the scars of chronic, early, psychological adversity. Still, he feels an affectionate attachment for his wife and has been a loving and involved father. It would appear that his minimally adequate ability to engage the developmental demands of adolescence and

young adulthood allowed him to marry and parent children. From the subsequent experiences of maintaining a committed close relationship he was able to become an actively participating parent. A psychologically impoverished early childhood was partially compensated for by later restructuring in adulthood.

The richness and complexity of developmental experience does not lend itself to easy understanding. Its potential as a therapeutic resource is unmistakable, however. What I have tried to do is indicate some of the directions already available for recruitment in the therapeutic enterprise.

At some point, and rarely with a sense of closure, the writer brings his work to an end. Like therapy, no termination is ever completed to full satisfaction. And as is so often the case in therapy, one trusts that both the loose ends and what has been gained become a stimulus for further growth at a later time.

REFERENCES

Abraham, K. (1921), Contributions to the theory of the anal character. In: *Selected Papers on Psychoanalysis*. New York: Basic Books, 1957, pp. 370–392.

——— (1927), *Selected Papers of Karl Abraham*. London: Hogarth Press.

Adler, G., & Myerson, P. G., eds. (1973), *Confrontation in Psychotherapy*. New York: Science House.

Alexander, F., & French, T. M. (1946), *Psychoanalytic Therapy: Principles and Application*. New York: Ronald Press.

Allem, H. (1981), *Value Differences Among Four Male Age Cohorts*. Unpublished doctoral dissertation. Boston University.

Allport, G. W. (1937), *Personality: A Psychological Interpretation*. New York: Harper Bros.

Altschul, S. (1968), Denial and ego arrest. *J. Amer. Psychoanal. Assn.*, 16:301–318.

American Psychiatric Association (1980), *The Diagnostic and Statistical Manual of Mental Disorders*, 3rd ed. Washington, DC: American Psychiatric Press.

Anthony, E. J., & Benedek, T., eds. (1970), *Parenthood—Its Psychology and Psychopathology*. Boston: Little, Brown.

Antonovsky, A. (1979), *Health, Stress and Coping*. San Francisco: Jossey Bass.

Arlow, J., & Brenner, C. (1964), *Psychoanalytic Concepts and the Structural Theory*. New York: International Universities Press.

Baltes, P. B. (1979), Life-span developmental psychology: Some converging observations on history and theory. In: *Life-Span Development and Behavior*, ed. P. B. Baltes & O. G. Brim, Jr. New York: Academic Press.

Bandura, A. (1971), *Social Learning Theory*. New York: General Learning Press.

Banta, H. D., & Saxe, L. (1983), Reimbursement for psychotherapy: Linking efficiency research and public policymaking. *Amer. Psychol.*, 38:918–923.

Barten, S. S., & Franklin, M. B., eds. (1978), *Developmental Processes: Heinz Werner's Selected Writings*, Vols. 1 & 2. New York: International Universities Press.

Beck, A. T. (1967), *Depression: Clinical, Experimental, and Theoretical Aspects*. New York: Harper & Row.

Belenky, M. F., Clinchy, B. M., Goldberger, N. R., & Tarule, J. M. (1986), *Women's Ways of Knowing*. New York: Basic Books.

Bellak, L., Hurvich, M., & Gediman, H. K. (1973), *Ego Functions in Schizophrenics, Neurotics, and Normals*. New York: Wiley-Interscience.

Benedek, T. (1970), The family as a psychologic field. In: *Parenthood*, ed. E. J. Anthony & T. Benedek. Boston: Little, Brown.

Bettelheim, B. (1982), Reflections: Freud and the soul. *New Yorker*, March: 52–93.

341

Bibring, E. (1954), Psychoanalysis and the dynamic psychotherapies. *J. Amer. Psychoanal. Assn.*, 2:745–770.

Blanck, G., & Blanck, R. (1974), *Ego Psychology: Theory and Practice.* New York: Columbia University Press.

———— ———— (1979), *Ego Psychology*, Vol. 2. New York: Columbia University Press.

———— ———— (1986), *Beyond Ego Psychology.* New York: Columbia University Press.

Blos, P. (1962), *On Adolescence.* New York: Free Press.

———— (1981), *The Adolescent Passage: Developmental Issues.* New York: Academic Press.

Bocknek, G. (1980), *The Young Adult: Development After Adolescence*, rev. ed. New York: Gardner, 1986.

———— (1984), A hermeneutic analysis of three developmental modes. Paper presented at the Annual Meeting of the American Psychological Association, Toronto.

Brandt, L. W. (1966), Process or structure? *Psychoanal. Rev.*, 53:50–54.

Brennan, P. (1981), Reminiscence as adaptation. Paper presented at the Annual Meetings of the American Psychological Association, Los Angeles.

Brent, S. B. (1981), Changes in structural size and changes in organizational form. Symposium "The Contributions of Heinz Werner to Developmental Psychology." Worcester, MA: Clark University.

Brim, O. G., Jr., & Kagan, J. (1980), *Constancy and Change in Human Development.* Cambridge, MA: Harvard University Press.

Bronfenbrenner, U. (1951), Toward an integrated theory of personality. In: *Perception: An Approach to Personality*, ed. R. R. Blake & G. V. Ramsey. New York: Ronald Press.

Bryce, M. E. (1985), Female psychosocial development. *Counsel. & Hum. Develop.*, 17:1–12.

Bryer, J. B. (1981), *The Experience of Time's Passage as an Indicator of Depression.* Unpublished doctoral dissertation. Boston University.

Buie, D. H., Jr., & Adler, G. (1973), The uses of confrontation in the psychotherapy of borderline patients. In: *Confrontation in Psychotherapy*, ed. G. Adler & P. G. Myerson. New York: Science House.

Chodorow, N. (1978), *The Reproduction of Mothering.* Berkeley: University of California Press.

———— (1980), Feminism and difference: Gender, relation, and difference in psychoanalytic perspective. *Socialist Rev.*, 46:51–69.

Clayton, V. P., & Birren, J. E. (1980), Wisdom across the life span. In: *Life-Span Development and Behavior*, Vol. 3, ed. P. B. Baltes & O. G. Brim, Jr. New York: Academic Press.

Colarusso, C. A., & Nemiroff, R. A. (1981), *Adult Development.* New York: Plenum.

Conference on Psychoanalytic Education and Research (1974), *Commission IX, "Child Analysis."* New York: American Psychoanalytic Association.

Cumming, E., & Henry, W. E. (1961), *Growing Old.* New York: Basic Books.

Danish, S. J. (1981), Life span human development and intervention. *Counsel. Psychol.*, 9:40–43.

Deutsch, F., & Murphy, W. F. (1955a), *The Clinical Interview*, Vol. 1. New York: International Universities Press.

————— ————— (1955b), *The Clinical Interview*, Vol. 2. New York: International Universities Press.

Dewald, P. A. (1964), *Psychotherapy: A Dynamic Approach*. New York: Basic Books.

Dewey, J. (1938), *Experience and Education*. New York: Collier Books.

Dollard, J., & Miller, N. E. (1950), *Personality and Psychotherapy*. New York: McGraw-Hill.

Eagle, M. (1984), *Recent Developments in Psychoanalysis*. New York: McGraw-Hill.

Erikson, E. H. (1950), *Childhood and Society*. New York: W. W. Norton, 1963.

————— (1968), *Identity: Youth and Crisis*. New York: W. W. Norton.

————— (1979), Once more the inner space. In: *Psychology of Women: Selected Readings*, ed. J. H. Williams. New York: W. W. Norton.

————— (1982), *The Life Cycle Completed*. New York: W. W. Norton.

Exner, J. E., & Weiner, I. (1982), *The Rorschach: A Comprehensive System*, Vols. 1, 2, & 3. New York: John Wiley.

Fairbairn, W. R. D. (1952), *Psychoanalytic Studies of the Personality*. New York: Basic Books.

————— (1955), Observations in defence of the object-relations theory of the personality. *Brit. J. Med. Psychol.*, 28:144–156.

Fenichel, O. (1941), *Problems of Psychoanalytic Technique*. New York: Psychoanalytic Quarterly.

————— (1945), *The Psychoanalytic Theory of Neurosis*. New York: W. W. Norton.

Flavell, J. (1972), An analysis of cognitive development sequences. *Genet. Psychol. Monogr.*, 86:279–350.

————— (1977), Basic properties of cognitive functioning. In: *Human Life Cycle*, ed. W. C. Sze. New York: Jason Aronson.

Frankl, V. (1963), *Man's Search for Meaning: An Introduction to Logotherapy*. New York: Pocket Books.

Freeman-Young, E., & Bocknek, G. (1982), Self-image representation in three male and female cohorts. Poster session, Annual Meeting of the Massachusetts Psychological Association.

Freud, A. (1936), *The Ego and the Mechanisms of Defense*. New York: International Universities Press, 1946.

Freud, S. (1914), On narcissism. *Standard Edition*, 14:67–102. London: Hogarth Press, 1957.

————— (1926), Inhibitions, symptoms, and anxiety. *Standard Edition*, 20:77–178. London: Hogarth Press, 1959.

————— (1933), New Introductory Lectures on Psychoanalysis. *Standard Edition*, 22:3–182 London: Hogarth Press, 1964.

————— (1940), An outline of psychoanalysis. *Standard Edition*, 23:141–208. London: Hogarth Press, 1964.

————— (1949), *An Outline of Psychoanalysis*. London: Hogarth Press.

Friedman, H. (1952), A comparison of a group of hebephrenic and catatonic schizophrenics with two groups of normal adults by means of certain variables of the Rorschach Test. *J. Project. Techniques*, 16:352–360.

Gedo, J. (1979), *Beyond Interpretation*. New York: International Universities Press.

————— (1980), Reflections on some current controversies in psychoanalysis. *J. Amer. Psychoanal. Assn.*, 28:363–383.

Geleerd, E. (1965), Two kinds of denial. In: *Drives, Affects, Behavior*, ed. R. Loewenstein. New York: International Universities Press.

Gergen, K. J. (1980), The emerging crisis in life-span developmental theory. In: *Life-Span Development and Behavior*, Vol. 3, ed. P. B. Baltes & O. G. Brim, Jr. New York: Academic Press.

Gill, M. M., & Hoffman, I. (1982), A method for studying the analysis of aspects of the patient's experience of the relationship in psychoanalysis and psychotherapy. *J. Amer. Psychoanal. Assn.*, 30:137–167.

Gilligan, C. (1982), *In a Different Voice*. Cambridge, MA: Harvard University Press.

Giovacchini, P. L., ed. (1975), *Tactics and Techniques in Psychoanalytic Therapy*, Vol. 2. New York: Jason Aronson.

Glasser, W., & Zunin, L. M. (1979), Reality therapy. In: *Current Psychotherapies*, 2nd ed., ed. R. J. Corsini. Itasca, IL: F. E. Peacock.

Glover, E. (1958), Ego distortions. *Internat. J. Psycho-Anal.*, 39:260–264.

Goldberg, A., ed. (1983), *The Future of Psychoanalysis: Essays in Honor of Heinz Kohut*. New York: International Universities Press.

Goldstein, W. N. (1985), DSM-III and the narcissistic personality. *Amer. J. Psychother.*, 39:4–16.

Gould, R. (1978), *Transformations: Growth and Change in Adult Life*. New York: Simon & Schuster.

Greenberg, J. R., & Mitchell, S. A. (1983), *Object Relations in Psychoanalytic Theory*. Cambridge, MA: Harvard University Press.

Grossberg, S. (1986), *Neural Dynamics of Adaptive Sensory-Motor Control*. New York: Elsevier Science.

Guntrip, H. (1961), *Personality Structure and Human Interaction*. New York: International Universities Press.

Gutmann, D. (1975), Parenthood: A key to the comparative study of the life cycle. In: *Life-Span Developmental Psychology: Normative Life Crises*, ed. N. Datan & L. H. Ginsberg. New York: Academic Press.

Haan, N. (1963), Proposed model of ego functioning: Coping and defense mechanisms in relationship to IQ change. *Psycholog. Monogr.*, 77 (Whole No. 571). Washington, DC: American Psychological Association.

——— (1977), *Coping and Defending*. New York: Academic Press.

Hartmann, H. (1939), Psychoanalysis and the concept of health. *Internat. J. Psycho-Anal.*, 20:308–321.

——— (1950), Comments on the psychoanalytic theory of the ego. *The Psychoanalytic Study of the Child*, 5:74–96. New York: International Universities Press.

——— (1950), *Essays on Ego Psychology*. New York: International Universities Press, 1964.

——— (1958), *Ego Psychology and the Problem of Adaptation*. New York: International Universities Press.

——— Kris, E., & Loewenstein, R. M. (1946), Comments on the formation of psychic structure. *The Psychoanalytic Study of the Child*, 2:11–38. New York: International Universities Press.

Heath, D. (1969), *Explorations on Maturity*. New York: Appleton-Century-Crofts.

Helmholtz, H. v. (1866), *Archives of Anatomy and Physiology*.

Hemmindinger, L. (1951), Perceptual organization and development as reflected in the structure of Rorschach test responses. Paper presented at the annual convention of the American Psychological Association, Chicago.

Hendrick, I. (1943), Work and the pleasure principle. *Psychoanal. Quart.*, 12:311–329.

Hilgard, E. R. (1948), *Theories of Learning*. New York: Appleton-Century-Crofts.

Hoffer, W. (1954), Defensive process and defensive organization. *Internat. J. Psycho-Anal.*, 35:194–198.

Holt, R. R., ed. (1971), *New Horizons for Psychotherapy*. New York: International Universities Press.

Horn, J. L., & Cattell, R. B. (1967), Age differences in fluid and crystallized intelligence. *Acta Psycholog.*, 26:107–129.

Horner, A. J. (1979), *Object Relations and the Developing Ego in Therapy*. New York: Jason Aronson.

Hull, C. L. (1943), *Principles of Behavior*. New York: Appleton-Century.

Jacobson, E. (1954), The self and the object world: Vicissitudes of their infantile cathexes. *The Psychoanalytic Study of the Child*, 9:75–127. New York: International Universities Press.

——— (1964), *The Self and the Object World*. New York: International Universities Press.

Joseph, E. D., & Wallerstein, R. S., eds. (1982), *Psychotherapy: Impact on Psychoanalytic Training*. New York: International Universities Press.

Jung, C. G. (1933), The stages of life. In: *The Portable Jung*, ed. J. Campbell. New York: Viking, 1971.

Kagan, J. (1980), Perspectives on continuity. In: *Constancy and Change*, ed. O. G. Brim, Jr. & J. Kagan. Cambridge, MA: Harvard University Press.

Kahn, E. (1985), Heinz Kohut and Carl Rogers: A timely comparison. *Amer. Psychol.*, 40:893–904.

Kastenbaum, R. (1973), On the meaning of time in later life. In: *Readings in Psychological Development Through Life*, ed. D. C. Charles & W. R. Looft. New York: Holt, Rinehart & Winston.

Kegan, R. G. (1979), The evolving self: A process conception for ego psychology. *Counsel. Psychol.*, 8:5–35.

Kelly, G. A. (1955), *The Psychology of Personal Constructs*. New York: W. W. Norton.

Kernberg, O. F. (1967), Borderline personality organization. *J. Amer. Psychoanal. Assn.*, 15:641–685.

——— (1975), *Borderline Conditions and Pathological Narcissism*. New York: Jason Aronson.

——— (1980), Neurosis, psychosis, and the borderline states. In: *Comprehensive Textbook of Psychiatry*, Vol. 3, 3rd ed., ed. A. Freedman, H. Kaplan, & B. Sadock. Baltimore: Williams & Wilkins.

Klein, M. (1932), *The Psychoanalysis of Children*. London: Hogarth Press.

——— (1948), *Contributions to Psychoanalysis*. London: Hogarth Press.

Koffka, K. (1935), *Principles of Gestalt Psychology*. New York: Harcourt, Brace.

Kohler, W. (1925), *The Mentality of Apes*, trans. E. Winter. New York: Harcourt-Brace.

——— (1929), *Gestalt Psychology*. New York: Liveright.

Kohut, H. (1971), *The Analysis of the Self*. New York: International Universities Press.

———— (1977), *The Restoration of the Self*. New York: International Universities Press.

———— Wolf, E. S. (1978), The disorders of the self and their treatment: An outline. *Internat. J. Psycho-Anal.*, 59:413–425.

Kuhn, M. H., & McPartland, T. S. (1954), An empirical investigation of self-attitudes. *Amer. Sociol. Rev.*, 19:68–76.

Labouvie-Vief, G. (1982), Growth and aging in life span perspective. *Hum. Develop.*, 25:65–79.

Langer, E. (1989), Mindfulness: The roots of mindlessness. *New Age J.*, (July/August):14, 47.

Langer, J. (1969), *Theories of Development*. New York: Holt, Rinehart & Winston.

Lax, R. L., Bach, S., & Burland, J. A. (1986), *Self and Object Constancy*. New York: Guilford Press.

Lazarus, R. S. (1984), On the primacy of cognition. *Amer. Psychol.*, 39:124–129.

Lecky, P. (1945), *Self-Consistency*. New York: Island Press.

Lerner, R. M., & Busch-Rossnagel, N. A. (1981), *Individuals as Producers of Their Own Development*. New York: Academic Press.

Levinson, D. J. (1986), A conception of adult development. *Amer. Psychol.*, 41:3–13.

———— Darrow, C. N., Klein, E. B., Levinson, M. H., & McKee, B. (1979), *The Seasons of a Man's Life*. New York: Alfred A. Knopf.

Lewin, K. (1935), *A dynamic Theory of Personality*. New York: McGraw-Hill.

Lifton, R. (1976), *The Life of the Self*. New York: Simon & Schuster.

Loevinger, J. (1976), *Ego Development*. San Francisco: Jossey-Bass.

Lowen, A. (1970), *The Betrayal of the Body*. New York: Macmillan.

Lowenstein, R. (1967), Defensive organization and autonomous ego functions. *J. Amer. Psychoanal. Assn.*, 15:795–809.

Lowenthal, M. F., Thurnher, M., & Chiriboga, D. (1977), *Four Stages of Life*. San Francisco: Jossey-Bass.

Luborsky, L. (1984), *Principles of Psychoanalytic Psychotherapy*. New York: Basic Books.

Lynn, D. B. (1966), The process of learning parental and sex-role identification. *J. Marr. & Fam.*, 28:466–470.

Maccoby, E. E., & Jacklin, C. N. (1975), *The Psychology of Sex Differences*. Palo Alto: Stanford University.

Macfarlane, J. W. (1975), Perspectives on personality consistency and change. In: *Life: The Continuous Process*, ed. F. Rebelsky. New York: Alfred A. Knopf.

MacIver, R. M. (1937), *Society*. New York: Farrar & Rinehart.

McLeish, J. (1976), *The Ulyssean Adult*. Toronto: McGraw-Hill Ryerson.

Magana, H., Whiteley, J. M., & Nelson, K. H. (1980), Sequencing of experiences in psychological interventions: Relationships among locus of control, moral reasoning, and ego development. In: *Developmental Counseling and Teaching*, ed. V. L. Erikson & J. M. Whiteley. Monterey, CA: Brooks/Cole.

Mahler, M. S. (1963), Thoughts about development and individuation. *The Psychoanalytic Study of the Child*, 18:307–324. New York: International Universities Press.

——— (1968), *On Human Symbiosis and the Vicissitudes of Individuation*. New York: International Universities Press.

——— (1972), On the first three phases of the separation–individuation process. *Internat. J. Psycho-Anal.*, 53:333–338.

——— Pine, F., & Bergman, A. (1975), *The Psychological Birth of the Human Infant*. New York: Basic Books.

Malan, D. H. (1980), *Toward the Validation of Dynamic Psychotherapy*. New York: Plenum.

Manicas, P. T., & Secord, P. F. (1983), Implications for psychology of the new philosophy of science. *Amer. Psychol.*, 38:399–414.

Mann, J. (1973), *Time-Limited Psychotherapy*. Cambridge, MA: Harvard University Press.

Marcia, J. (1967), Ego-identity status: Relationship to change in self-esteem, "general maladjustment," and authoritarianism. *J. Personal.*, 35: 118–133.

Markus, H., & Nurius, P. (1986), Possible selves. *Amer. Psychol.*, 41:954–969.

Masek, R. J. (1986), Self-psychology as psychology: The revision of Heinz Kohut. *Theoret. & Philosoph. Psychol.*, 6:22–30.

Maslow, A. H. (1954), *Motivation and Personality*. New York: Harper.

——— (1962), Some basic propositions of a growth and self-actualization psychology. In: *Perceiving, Behaving, Becoming: A New Focus for Education*. Washington, DC: Yearbook of the Association for Supervision and Curriculum Development.

Masterson, J. F. (1972), *Treatment of the Borderline Adolescent*. New York: Wiley-Interscience.

——— (1976), *Psychotherapy of the Borderline Adult—A Developmental Approach*. New York: Brunner/Mazel.

McDevitt, J. B. (1979), The role of internalization in the development of object relations during the separation-individuation phase. *J. Amer. Psychoanal. Assn.*, 27:327–343.

McLeish, J. (1976), *The Ulyssean Adult*. Toronto: McGraw-Hill Ryerson.

McMackin, R. A. (1982), *The Ego-Ideal and Its Relationship to Loevinger's Stages of Ego Development*. Unpublished doctoral dissertation. Boston University.

Mead, M. (1955), *Male and Female: A Study of the Sexes in a Changing World*. New York: Mentor.

Meissner, W. W. (1986), Can psychoanalysis find its self? *J. Amer. Psychoanal. Assn.*, 34:379–401.

Menninger, K. (1958), *The Theory of Psychoanalytic Technique*. New York: Basic Books.

Miller, J. B. (1976), *Toward a New Psychology of Women*. Boston: Beacon Press.

Millon, T. (1983), The DSM-III: An insider's perspective. *Amer. Psychol.*, 38:804–814.

Money, J., & Ehrhardt, A. (1972), *Man and Woman, Boy and Girl*. Baltimore: Johns Hopkins University Press.

Moore, B. E., & Fine, B. D. (1967), *A Glossary of Psychoanalytic Terms and Concepts*. New York: American Psychoanalytic Association.

Mosher, R. L., ed. (1979), *Adolescence, Development and Education: A Janus Knot*. Berkeley, CA: McCutcheon.

Murphy, G. (1947), *Personality: A Biosocial Approach to Origins and Structure*. New York: Harper & Bros.

Murphy, W. F. (1965), *The Tactics of Psychotherapy*. New York: International Universities Press.

Nagge, J. W. (1935), Effects of hypnosis on retroactive inhibition. *J. Experiment. Psychol.*, 18:663–682.

Nemiah, J. C. (1967), *Foundations of Psychopathology*. New York: Oxford University Press.

Neugarten, B. N. (1969), Continuities and discontinuities of psychological issues into adult life. *Hum. Develop.*, 12:121–130.

―― Wood, V., Kraines, R. J., & Loomis, B. (1975), Women's attitudes toward the menopause. In: *Life: The Continuous Process*, ed. F. Rebelsky. New York: Alfred A. Knopf.

Nunberg, H. (1930), The synthetic function of the ego. In: *The Practice and Theory of Psychoanalysis*, Vol. 1. New York: International Universities Press, 1960.

Panel (1953), The essentials of psychotherapy as viewed by the psychoanalyst. *J. Amer. Psychoanal. Assn.*, 1:550–561. English, O. S., Reporter.

―― (1954), Psychoanalysis and dynamic psychotherapy—Similarities and differences. *J. Amer. Psychoanal. Assn.*, 2:152–166. Rangell, L., Reporter.

―― (1973a), The experience of separation–individuation and its reverberations through the course of life. Adolescence and maturity. *J. Amer. Psychoanal. Assn.*, 21:155. Marcus, J., Reporter.

―― (1973b), The experience of separation–individuation and its reverberations through the course of life: Maturity, senescence, and sociological implications. *J. Amer. Psychoanal. Assn.*, 21:633–645. Steinschein, I., Reporter.

―― (1979), Conceptualizing the nature of the therapeutic action of psychoanalytic psychotherapy. Annual Meeting of the American Psychoanalytic Association, Atlanta. *J. Amer. Psychoanal. Assn.*, 27:147–195. Nemetz, S. J., Reporter.

―― (1980), Construction and reconstruction: Clinical aspects. Annual Meeting of the American Psychoanalytic Association. *J. Amer. Psychoanal. Assn.*, 28:213–233. Malin, A., Reporter.

Paolino, T. J., Jr. (1981), *Psychoanalytic Psychotherapy*. New York: Brunner/Mazel.

Peck, R. (1975), Psychological developments in the second half of life. In: *Human Life Cycle*, ed. W. Sze. New York: Jason Aronson.

Perls, F., Hefferline, R. F., & Goodman, P. (1951), *Gestalt Therapy*. New York: Julian Press.

Perry, W. G. (1970), *Forms of Intellectual and Ethical Development in the College Years*. New York: Holt, Rinehart & Winston.

Phillips, L. (1968), *Human Adaptation and Its Failures*. New York: Appleton-Century-Crofts.

Piaget, J. (1951), *Play, Dreams and Imitation in Childhood*. New York: W. W. Norton.

―― (1972), Intellectual evolution from adolescence to adulthood. *Hum. Develop.*, 15:1–12.

Pine, F. (1987a), The four psychologies of psychoanalysis and their place in clinical work. Invited address, Annual Convention of the American Psychological Association, New York.

―― (1987b), Theoretical and philosophical issues in psychoanalysis. *Theoret. & Philosoph. Psychol.*, 7:48–49.

Rapaport, D. (1967), The theory of ego autonomy. In: *The Collected Papers of David Rapaport*, ed. M. Gill. New York: Basic Books.

Reichard, S., Livson, F., & Petterson, P. G. (1962), *Aging and Personality*. New York: John Wiley.

Robbins, P. (1981), *Object Relations and Ego Development in Adolescence and Young Adulthood*. Unpublished doctoral dissertation, Boston University.

Rogers, C. R. (1951), *Client-Centered Therapy*. Boston: Houghton.

——— (1954), *Psychotherapy and Personality Change*. Chicago: University of Chicago Press.

Rosenbaum, M., & Muroff, M. eds. (1984), *Anna O: Fourteen Contemporary Reinterpretations*. New York: Free Press.

Rutan, J. S. (1978), Some thoughts on endings. Commencement Address, Boston Institute for Psychotherapies. Boston, MA.

Sabetti, S. (1976), *Attention Focussing in Psychotherapy*. Unpublished doctoral dissertation. Boston University.

Sandler, J. (1986), Comments on the self and its objects. In: *Self and Object Constancy*, ed. R. L. Lax, S. Bach, & J. A. Burland. New York: Guilford Press.

——— Rosenblatt, B. (1962), The concept of a representational world. *The Psychoanalytic Study of the Child*, 17:128–145. New York: International Universities Press.

——— Sandler, A. (1978), On the development of object relations and affects. In: *Essential Papers on Object Relations*, ed. P. Buckley. New York: New York University Press, 1986.

Saul, L. J. (1972), *Psychodynamically Based Psychotherapy*. New York: Science House.

Scarf, M. (1980), *Unfinished Business: Pressure Points in the Lives of Women*. Garden City: Doubleday.

Schafer, R. (1977), *Language and Insight*. New Haven, CT: Yale University Press.

——— (1980), Human agency and the psychoanalytic process. Invited address, Annual Convention, Massachusetts Psychological Association, Boston.

Schaie, K. W. (1978), Toward a stage theory of adult cognitive development. *J. Aging & Hum. Develop.*, 8:129–138.

——— Gewirtz, J., eds. (1982), *Adult Development and Aging*. Boston: Little, Brown.

Schlossberg, N. K. (1981), A model for analyzing human adaptation to transition. *Counsel. Psychol.*, 9:2–19.

Schwaber, E. (1979), On the "self" within the matrix of analytic theory. *Internat. J. Psycho-Anal.*, 60:467–479.

Selman, R. L. (1980), A structural–developmental model of social cognition. In: *Developmental Counseling and Teaching*, ed. V. L. Erickson & J. M. Whiteley. Monterey, CA: Brooks/Cole.

Sheehy, G. (1981), *Pathfinders*. New York: William Morrow.

Sifneos, P. (1984), The current status of individual short-term dynamic psychotherapy and its future: An overview. *Amer. J. Psychother.*, 37:472–483.

Singer, J. L. (1987), Psychoanalysis and contemporary psychology. Invited address, Annual Convention of American Psychological Association, New York.

Skinner, B. F. (1953), *Science and Human Behavior*. New York: Macmillan.

Smith, D., & Kraft, W. A. (1983), DSM-III: Do psychologists really want an alternative? *Amer. Psychol.*, 38:769–776.

Snygg, D., & Combs, A. W. (1949), *Individual Behavior*. New York: Harper Bros.

Solnit, J. (1972), Life span pacing of individuation. Paper presented at the Meetings of the American Psychoanalytic Association.

Sperling, S. (1957), On denial and the essential nature of defense. *Internat. J. Psycho-Anal.*, 39:25–38.

Spitz, R. A. (1959), *A Genetic Field Theory of Ego Formation*. New York: International Universities Press.

Stanton, A. (1953), Assessment in psychotherapy. In: *Seminars in Psychotherapy*. Boston: Veterans Administration Hospital.

Stevens-Long, J. (1984), *Adult Life*, 2nd ed. Palo Alto, CA: Mayfield.

Stolorow, R. (1976), Psychoanalytic reflections on client-centered therapy in the light of modern conceptions of narcissism. *Psychother.: Theory, Res. & Pract.*, 13:26–29.

—— Lachman, F. M. (1980), *Psychoanalysis of Developmental Arrests*. New York: International Universities Press.

Strupp, H. S., & Binder, J. L. (1984), *Psychotherapy in a New Key*. New York: Basic Books.

Sullivan, H. S. (1953), *The Interpersonal Theory of Psychiatry*. New York: W. W. Norton.

Super, D. E. (1957), *The Psychology of Careers*. New York: Harper & Row.

Symons, D. (1979), *The Evolution of Human Sexuality*. New York: Oxford University Press.

Tolman, E. C. (1945), A stimulus-expectancy need-cathexis psychology. *Science*, 101:160–166.

Tuttman, S., Kaye, C., & Zimmerman, M., eds. (1981), *Object and Self: A Developmental Approach*. New York: International Universities Press.

Vaillant, G. E. (1971), Theoretical hierarchy of adaptive ego mechanisms. *Arch. Gen. Psychiat.*, 24:107–118.

—— (1977), *Adaptation to Life*. Boston: Little, Brown.

Werman, D. S. (1984), *The Practice of Supportive Psychotherapy*. New York: Brunner/Mazel.

Werner, H. (1940), *Comparative Psychology of Mental Development*. New York: International Universities Press.

—— (1957), The concept of development from a comparative and organismic point of view. In: *The Concept of Development*, ed. D. B. Harris. Minneapolis: University of Minnesota.

—— Kaplan, B. (1963), *Symbol Formation*. New York: John Wiley.

White, R. W. (1963), Ego and Reality in Psychoanalytic Theory. *Psychological Issues*, Monograph 11, Vol. 3, No. 3. New York: International Universities Press.

Winnicott, D. W. (1958), *Collected Papers*. New York: Basic Books.

Wittenberg, R. (1968), *Postadolescence*. New York: Grune & Stratton.

Wolberg, L. R. (1954), *The Technique of Psychotherapy*. New York: Grune & Stratton.

—— (1968), *The Technique of Psychotherapy*, Vols. 1 & 2, 2nd ed. New York: Grune & Stratton.

———— (1977), *The Technique of Psychotherapy*, 3rd ed. New York: Grune & Stratton.

Wolpe, J. (1958), *Psychotherapy by Reciprocal Inhibition*. Palo Alto: Stanford University Press.

Woodworth, R. S. (1938), *Experimental Psychology*. New York: Henry Holt.

Zimmerman, D. (1982), A view from South America. In: *Psychotherapy: Impact on Psychoanalytic Training*, ed. E. D. Joseph & R. S. Wallerstein. New York: International Universities Press.

NAME INDEX

Abraham, K., 293
Adler, G., 33, 84, 144, 145
Alexander, F., 17-22, 27-28, 34
Allem, H., 299
Allport, G., 200, 270
Altschul, S., 208
Anthony, E. J., 281, 283
Antonovsky, A., 201, 336, 337
Arlow, J., 208

Bach, S., 197
Baltes, P. B., 308
Bandura, A., 40
Banta, H. D., 83
Barten, S. S., 311
Belenky, M. F., 199, 299, 305, 322
Bellak, L., 84, 186-188, 190, 205,
  209, 278
Benedek, T., 17, 281, 283
Bergman, A., 196, 264
Bettleheim, B., 269
Bibring, E., 21-22
Binder, J. L., 8, 10-11, 41-42, 47, 60,
  155, 178, 180, 317
Birren, J. E., 299
Blanck, G., 8, 10, 28-36, 40, 43, 47,
  60, 77-78, 104, 112, 155-156,
  162, 167, 172-175, 177, 180,
  192, 196, 203, 210, 214, 217,
  260, 264, 280, 291, 317-318,
  336
Blanck, R., 8, 10, 28-36, 40, 43, 47,

60, 77-78, 104, 112, 155-156,
162, 167, 172-175, 177, 180,
192, 196, 203, 210, 214, 217,
260, 264, 280, 291, 317-318,
336
Blos, P., 281, 282, 299
Bocknek, G., 229, 231, 239, 284, 286-
  287, 299, 304, 308, 334, 335
Brandt, L. W., 269
Brennan, P., 302
Brenner, C., 208
Brent, S. B., 309
Bronfenbrenner, U., 289
Bryce, M. E., 299
Buie, D. H., Jr., 145
Burland, J. A., 197
Busch-Rossnagel, N. A., 250, 288,
  300

Cattell, R. B., 308
Chassel, 20
Chiriboga, D., 284
Chodorow, N., 199, 284, 305
Clayton, V. P., 299
Clinchy, B. M., 199, 299, 305, 322
Colarusso, C. A., 36-41, 43, 76, 166,
  172, 229-231, 257, 265, 281,
  283-285, 288, 335
Combs, A. W., 273
Cumming, E., 285

Danish, S. J., 295

353

SUBJECT INDEX

357